FAIRY TAIL

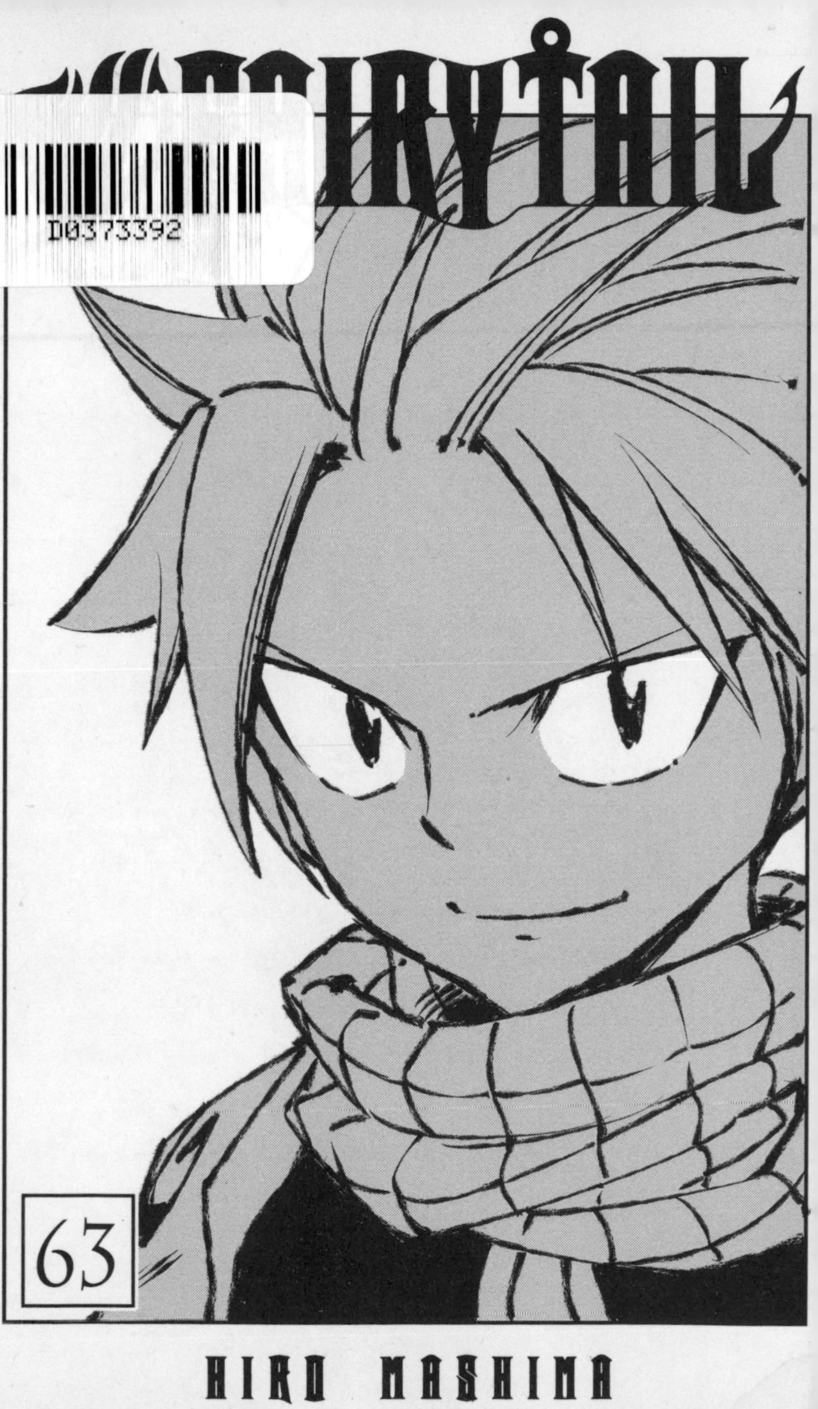

63

HIRO MASHIMA

FAIRY TAIL 63 CONTENTS

FAIRY TAIL

フェアリーテイル

Chapter 537: The Power of Life

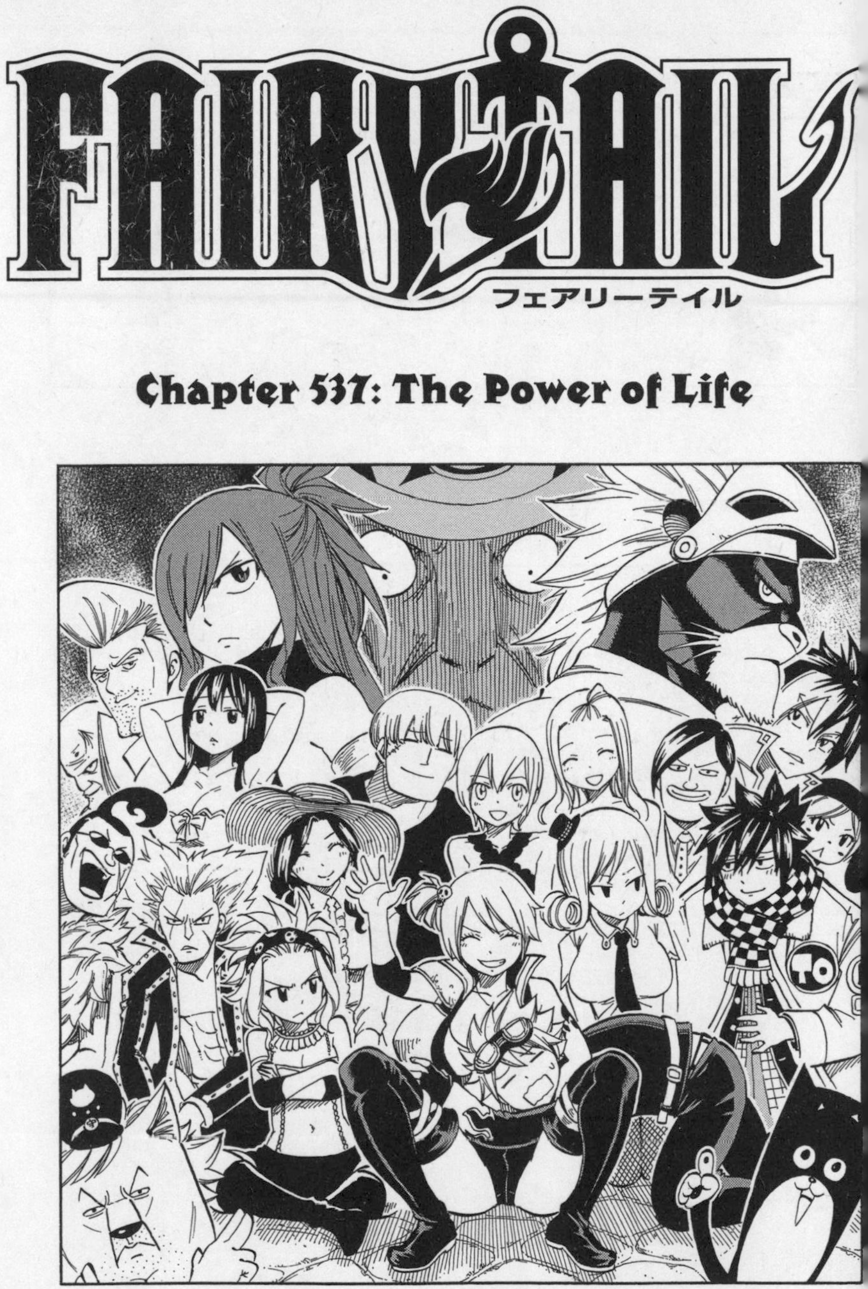
TO

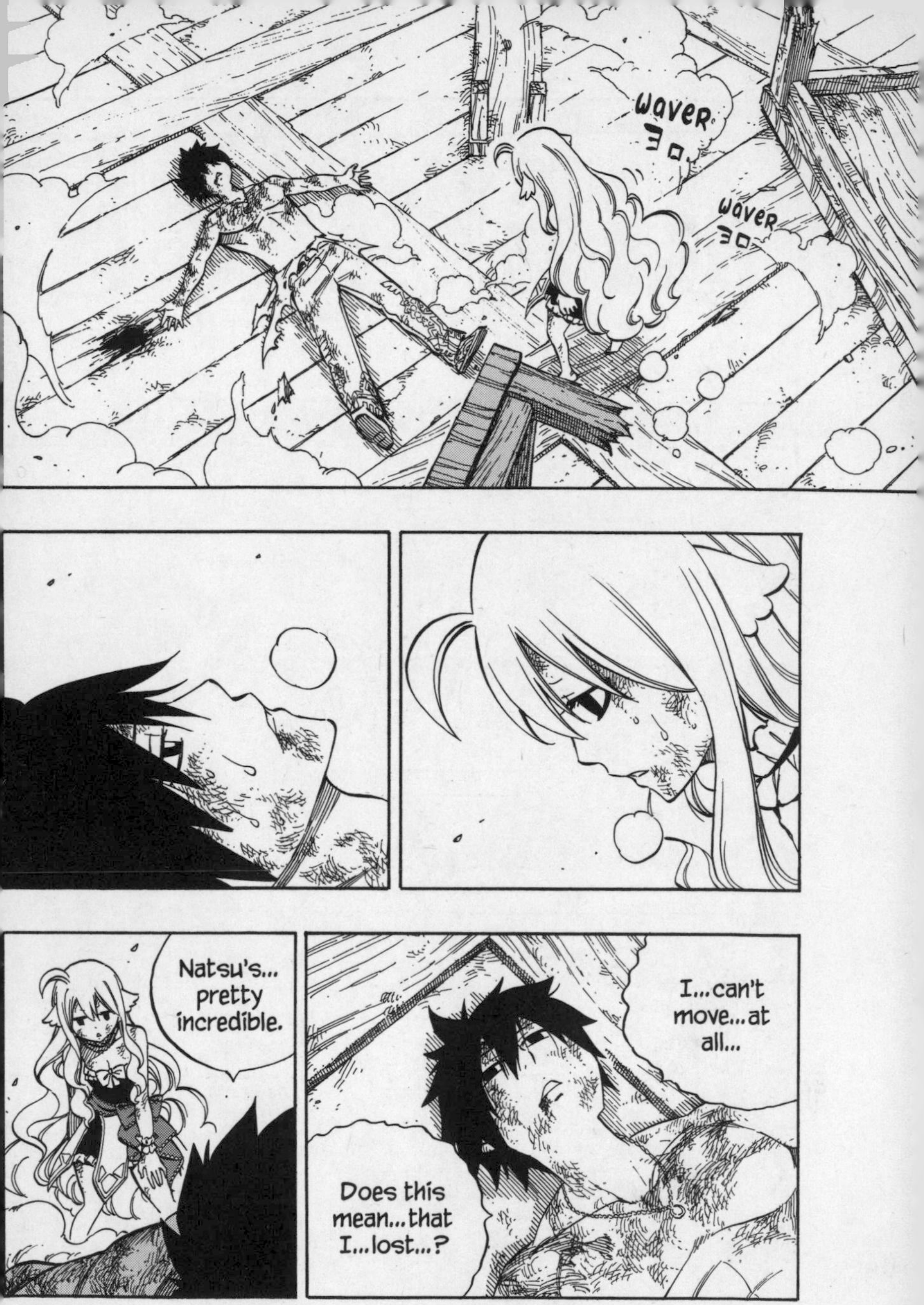
waver
ヨロ
waver
ヨロ
I...can't move...at all...
Does this mean...that I...lost...?
Natsu's... pretty incredible.

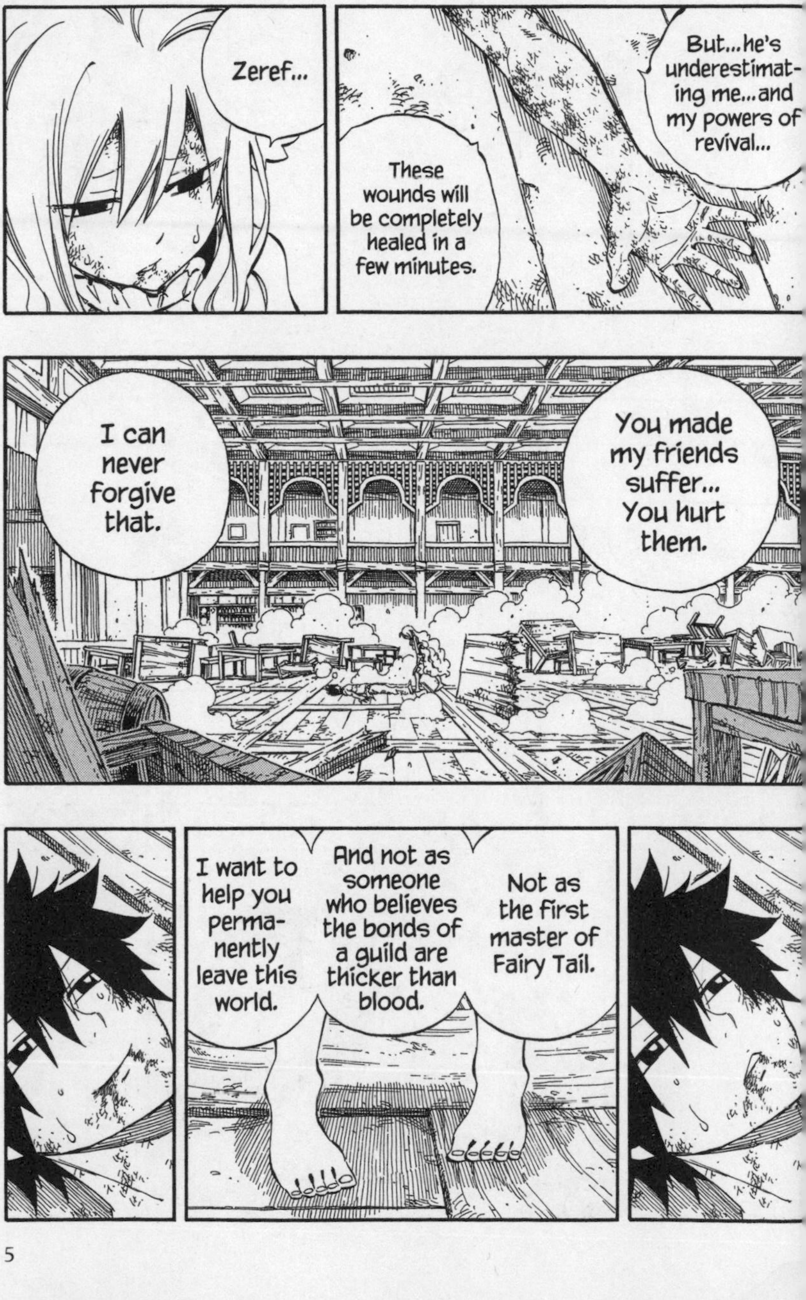
But...he's underestimating me...and my powers of revival...
These wounds will be completely healed in a few minutes.
Zeref...
You made my friends suffer... You hurt them.
I can never forgive that.
Not as the first master of Fairy Tail.
And not as someone who believes the bonds of a guild are thicker than blood.
I want to help you permanently leave this world.

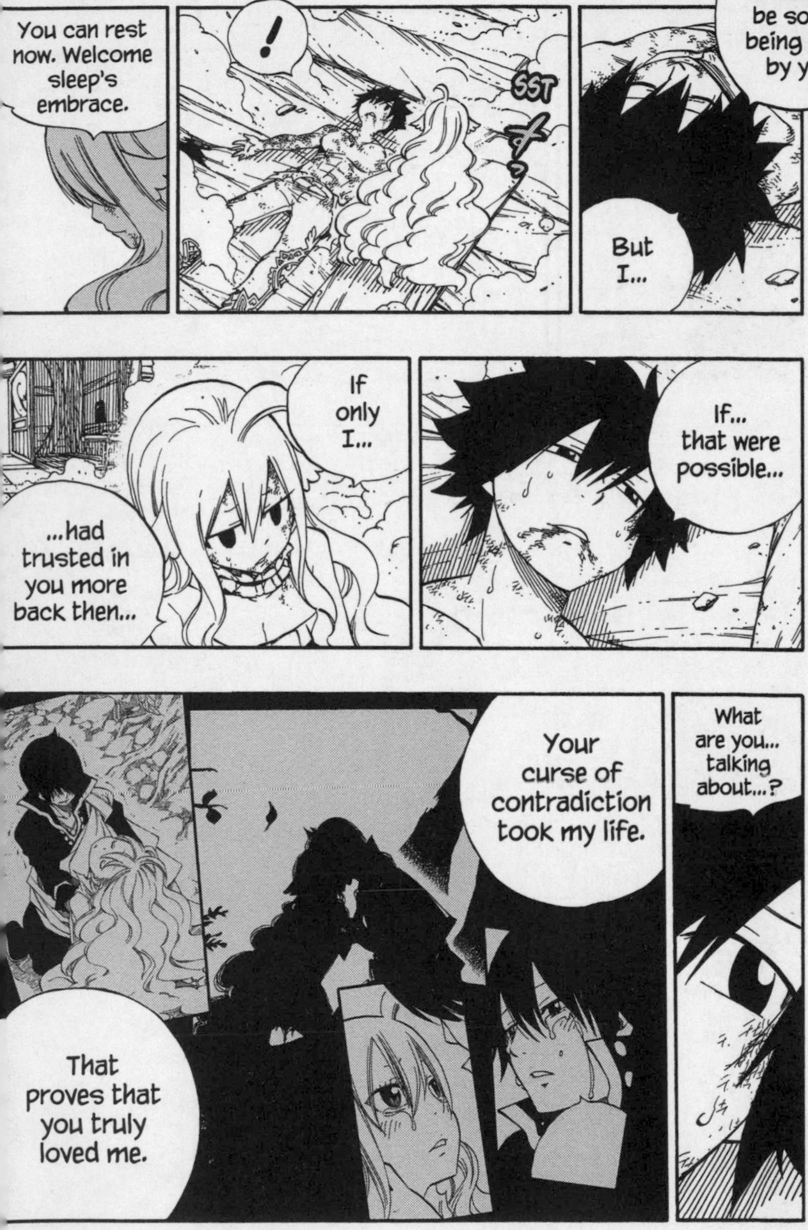
You know, it wouldn't be so bad being killed by you.
But I...
!
SST
You can rest now. Welcome sleep's embrace.
If... that were possible...
If only I...
...had trusted in you more back then...
What are you... talking about...?
Your curse of contradiction took my life.
That proves that you truly loved me.

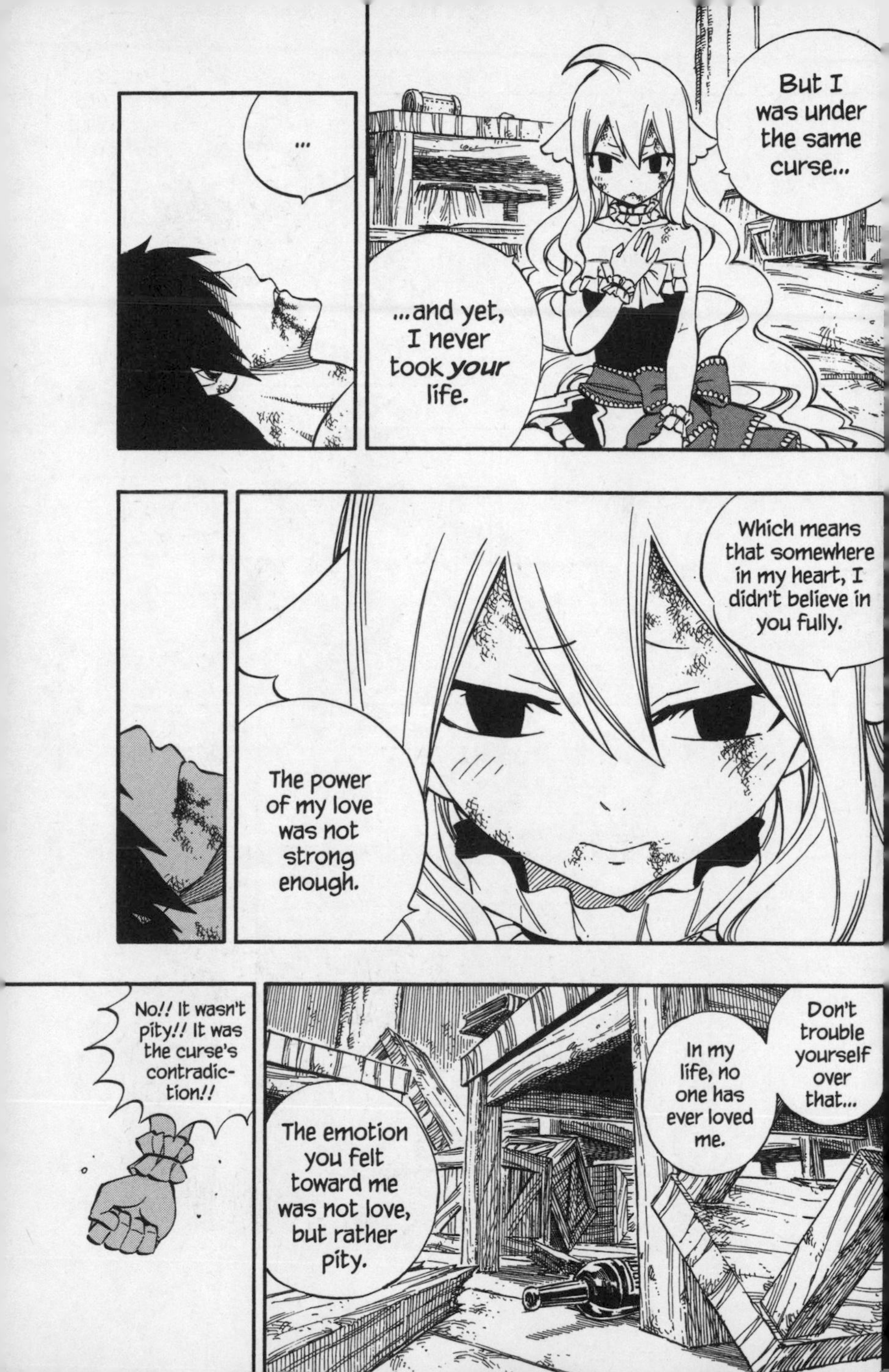
But I was under the same curse...
...and yet, I never took *your* life.
...
Which means that somewhere in my heart, I didn't believe in you fully.
The power of my love was not strong enough.
Don't trouble yourself over that...
In my life, no one has ever loved me.
The emotion you felt toward me was not love, but rather pity.
No!! It wasn't pity!! It was the curse's contradiction!!

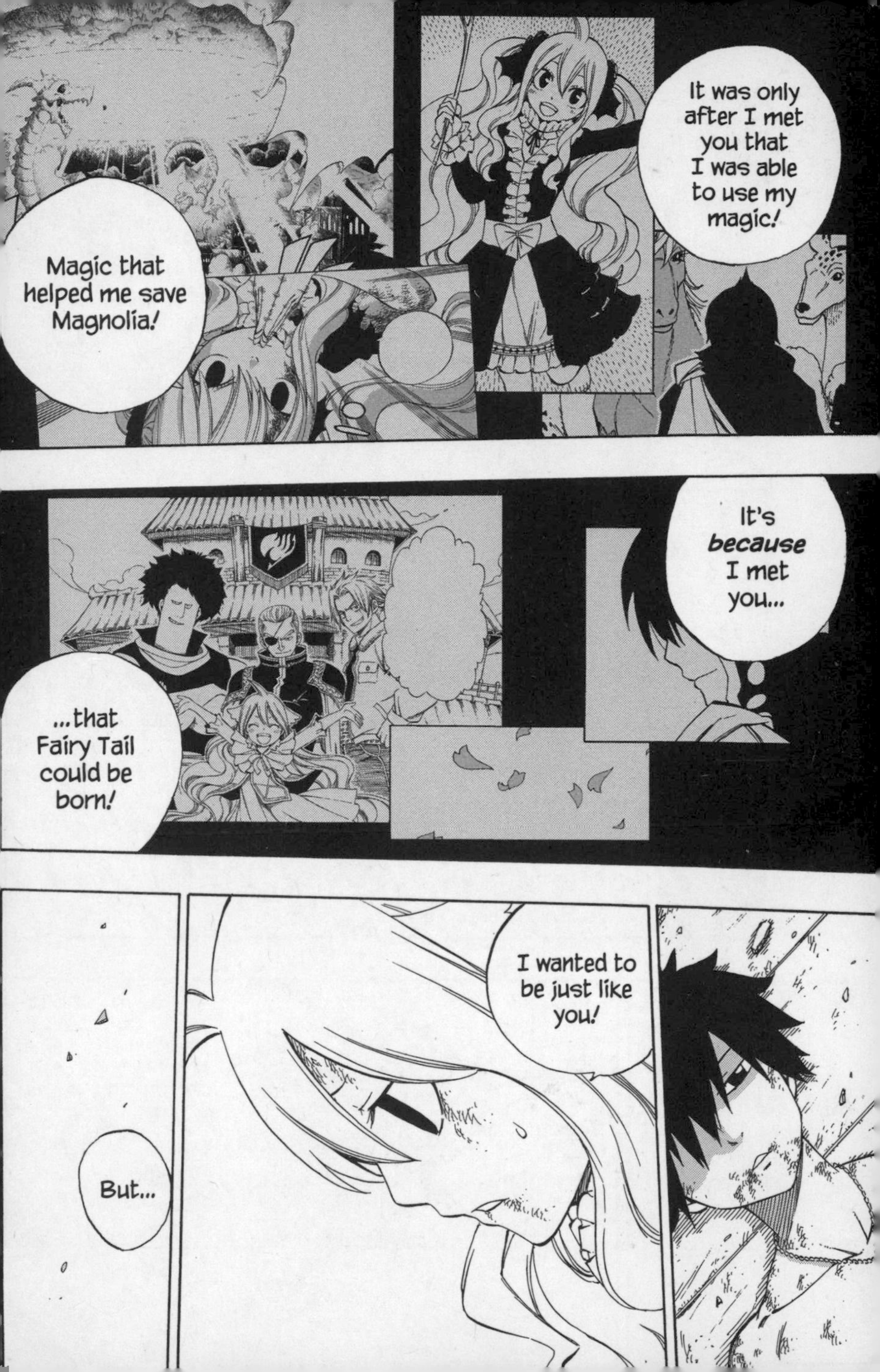
It was only after I met you that I was able to use my magic!
Magic that helped me save Magnolia!
It's *because* I met you...
...that Fairy Tail could be born!
I wanted to be just like you!
But...

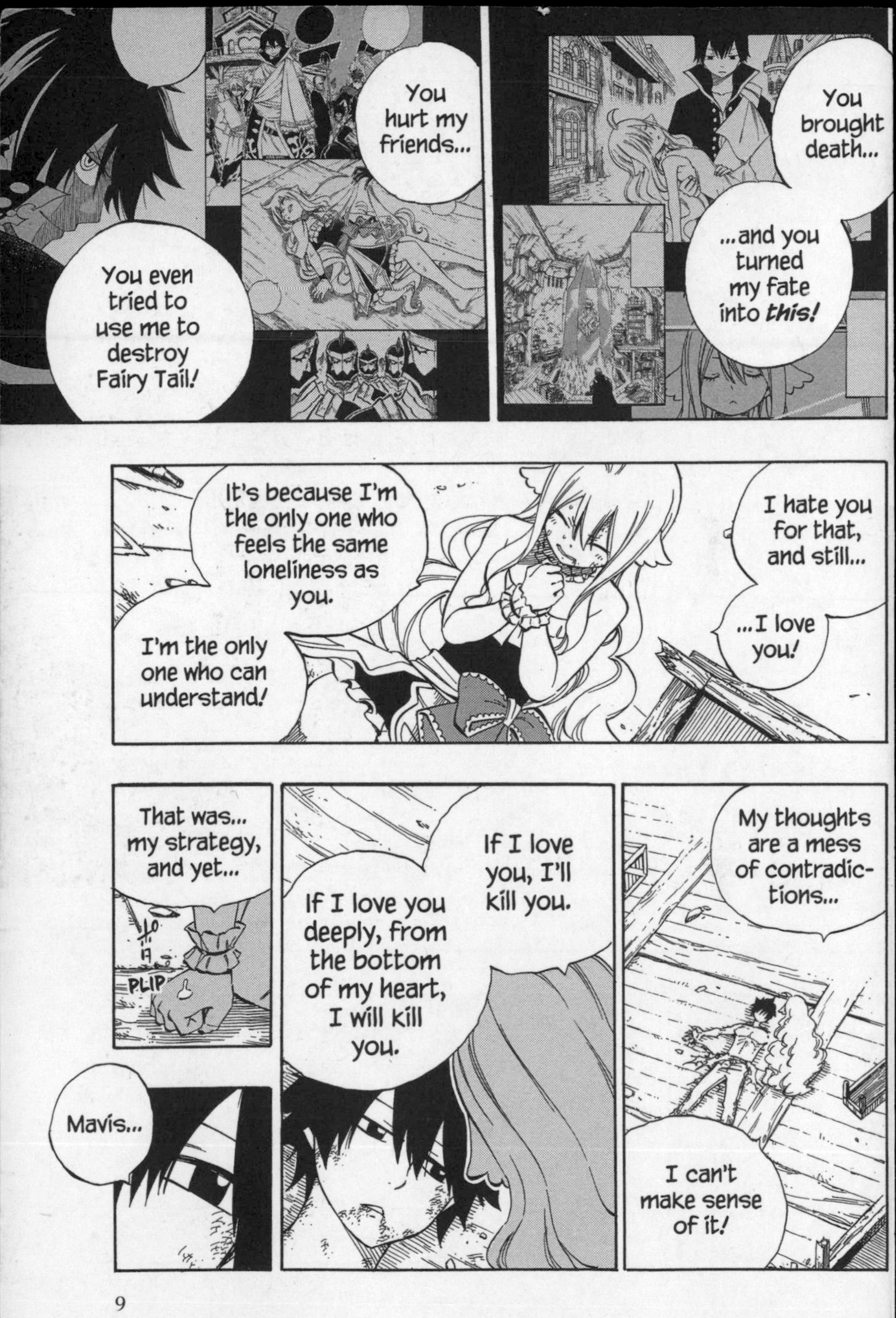
You brought death...
...and you turned my fate into ***this!***
You hurt my friends...
You even tried to use me to destroy Fairy Tail!
I hate you for that, and still...
...I love you!
It's because I'm the only one who feels the same loneliness as you.
I'm the only one who can understand!
My thoughts are a mess of contradic-tions...
I can't make sense of it!
If I love you, I'll kill you.
If I love you deeply, from the bottom of my heart, I will kill you.
That was... my strategy, and yet...
PLIP
Mavis...

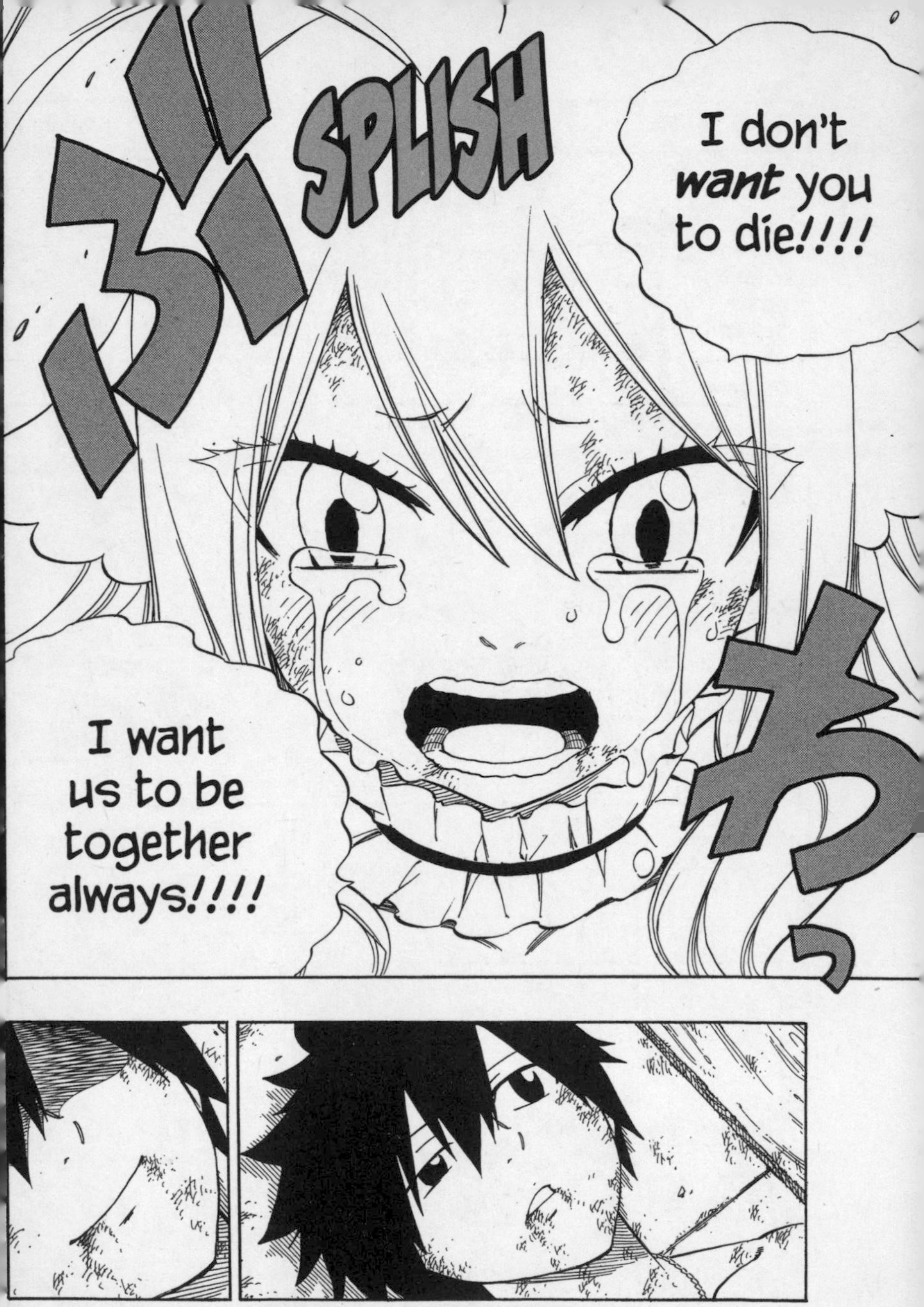
I don't *want* you to die!!!!
SPLISH
I want us to be together always!!!!

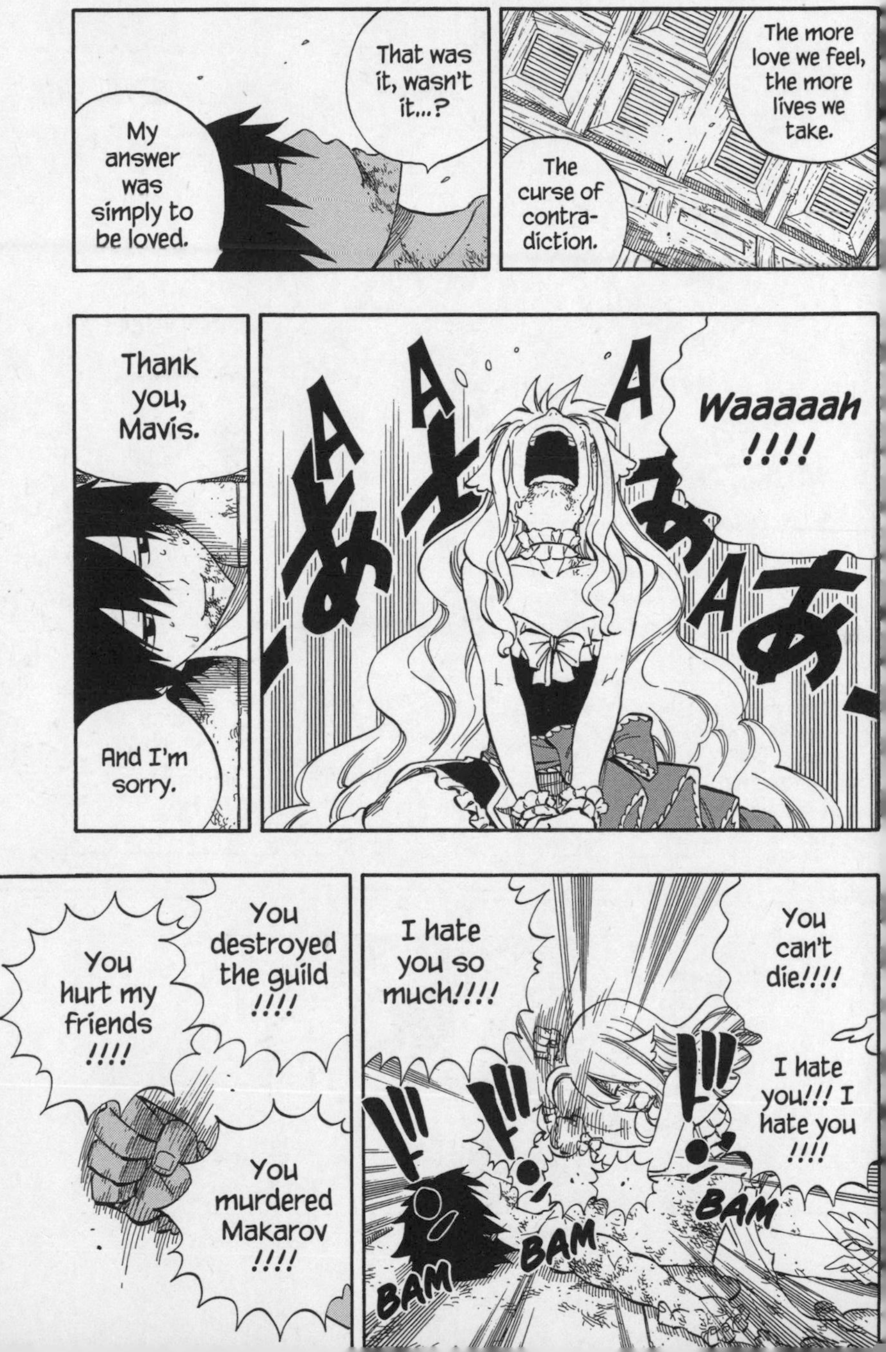
The more love we feel, the more lives we take.
The curse of contradiction.
That was it, wasn't it...?
My answer was simply to be loved.
Waaaaah!!!!
Thank you, Mavis.
And I'm sorry.
You can't die!!!!
I hate you!!! I hate you!!!!
I hate you so much!!!!
BAM
BAM
BAM
You destroyed the guild!!!!
You hurt my friends!!!!
You murdered Makarov!!!!

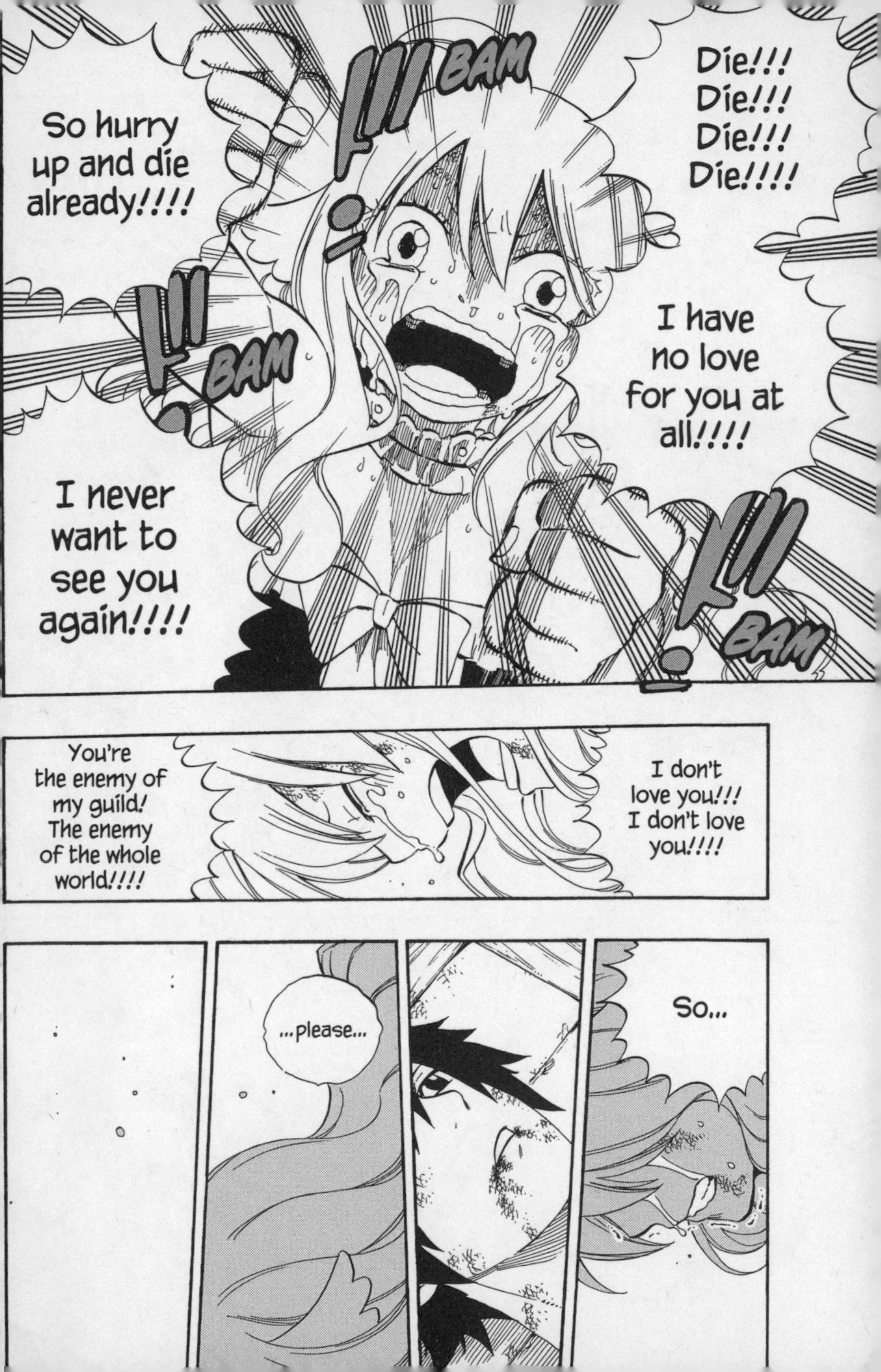
Die!!!
Die!!!
Die!!!
Die!!!!
BAM
So hurry up and die already!!!!
BAM
I have no love for you at all!!!!
BAM
I never want to see you again!!!!
I don't love you!!! I don't love you!!!!
You're the enemy of my guild! The enemy of the whole world!!!!
So...
...please...

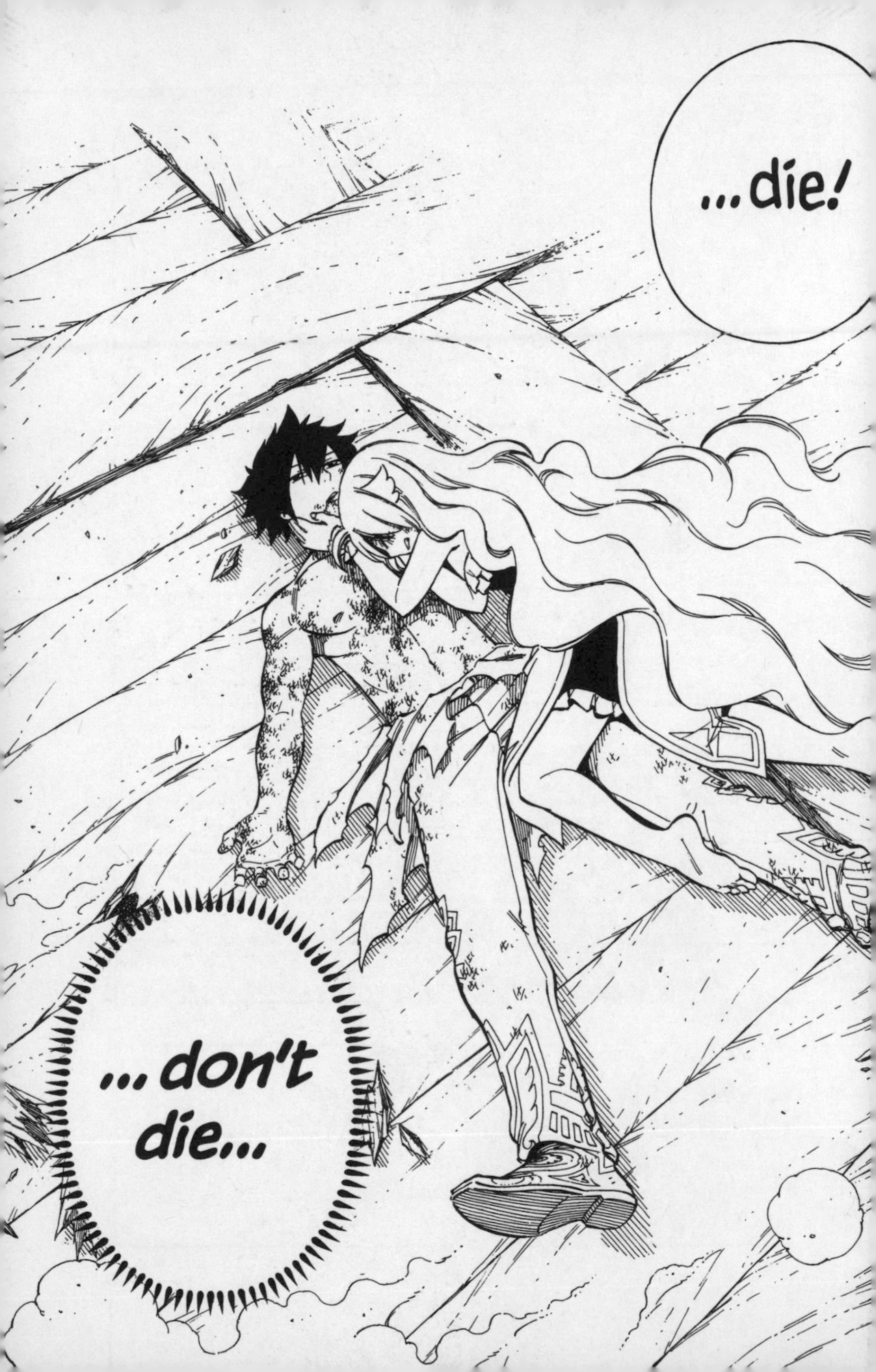
...die!
...don't die...

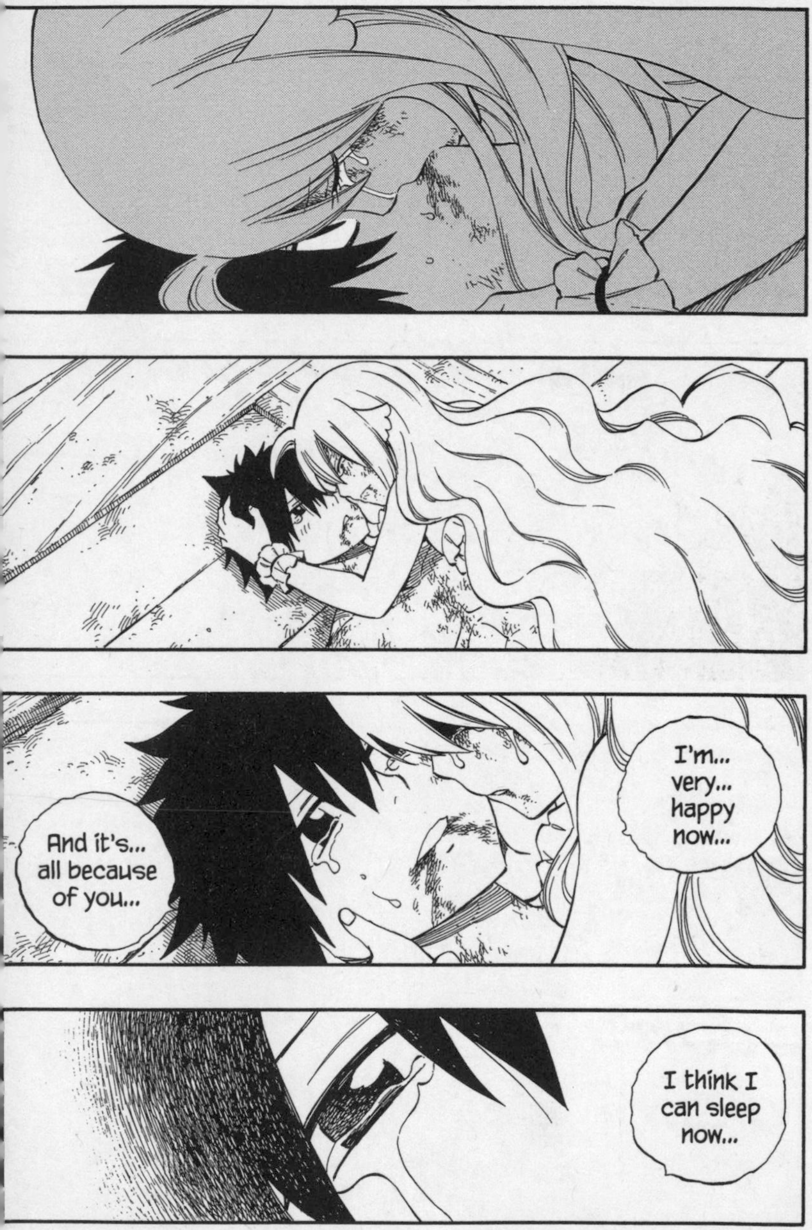
I'm... very... happy now...
And it's... all because of you...
I think I can sleep now...

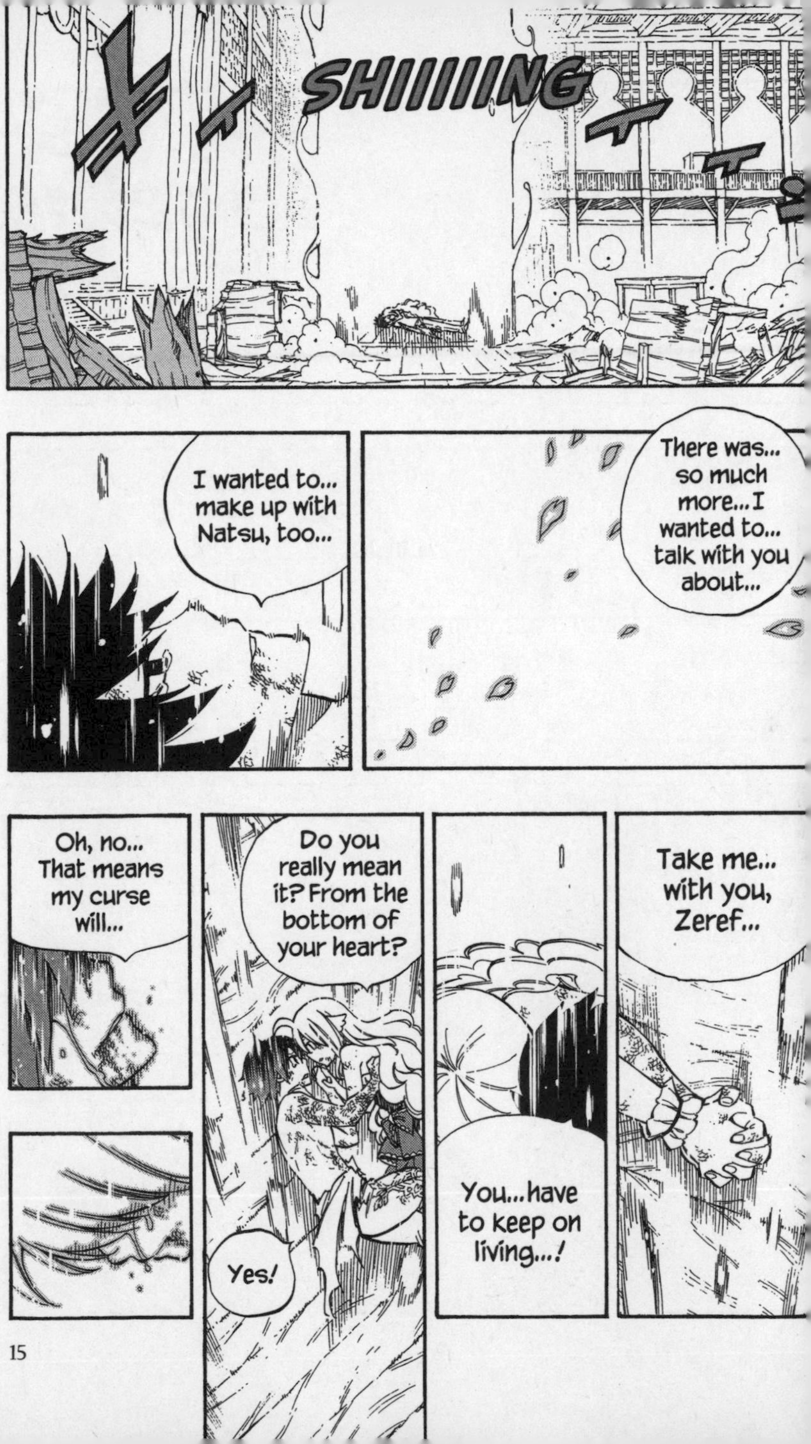
SHIIIIING
There was... so much more... I wanted to... talk with you about...
I wanted to... make up with Natsu, too...
Take me... with you, Zeref...
You...have to keep on living...!
Do you really mean it? From the bottom of your heart?
Yes!
Oh, no... That means my curse will...

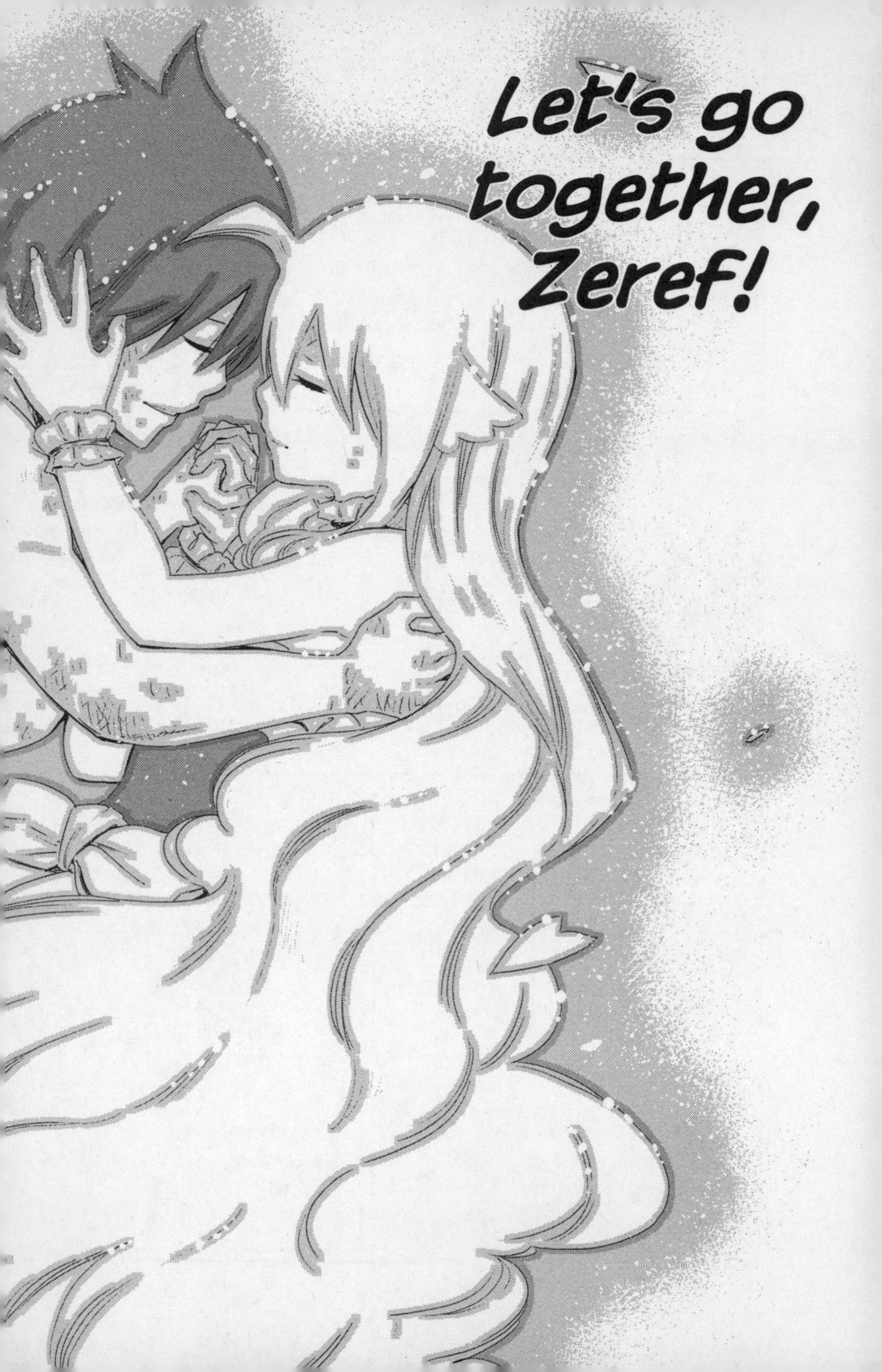
Let's go together, Zeref!

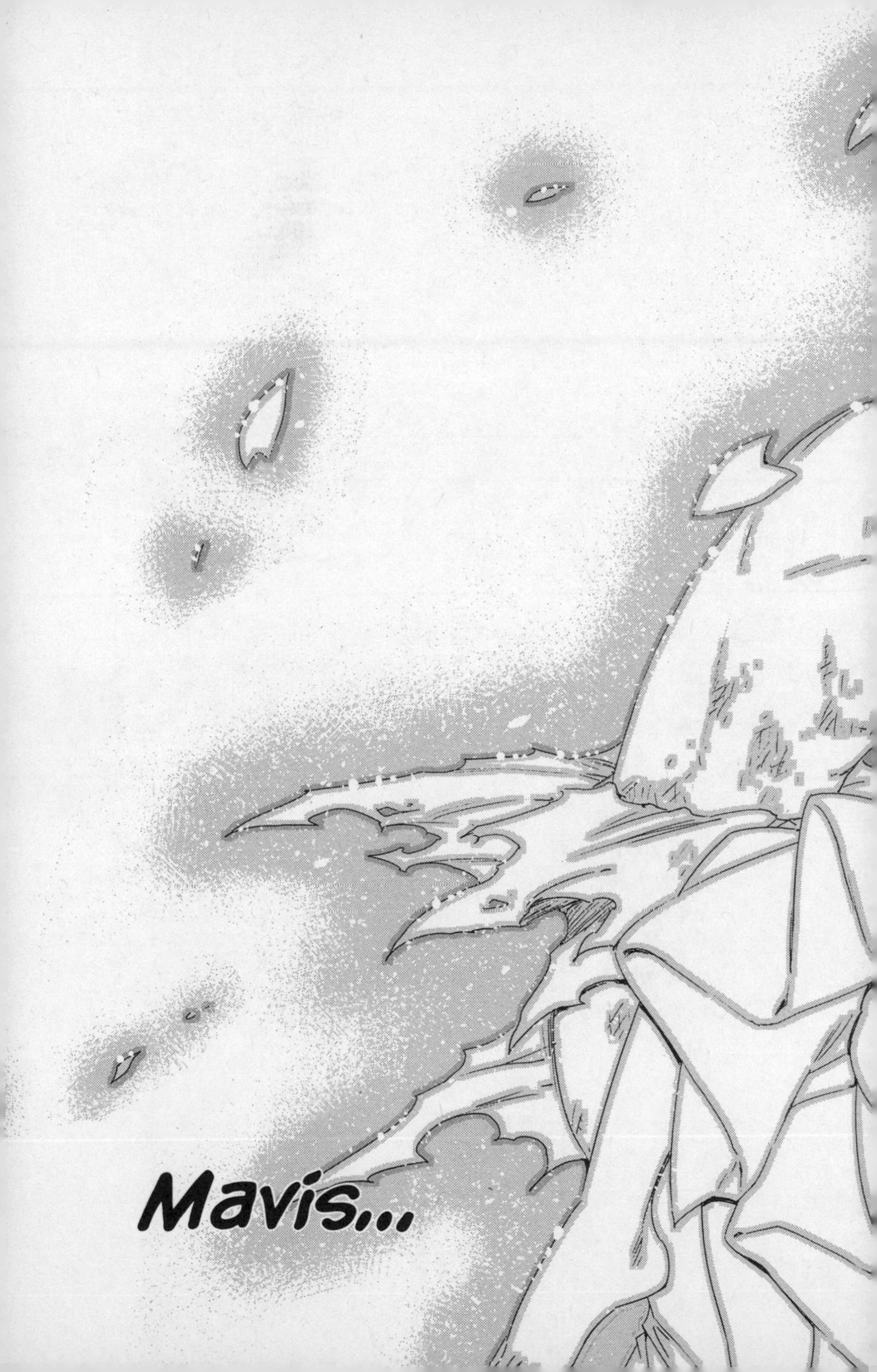
Mavis...

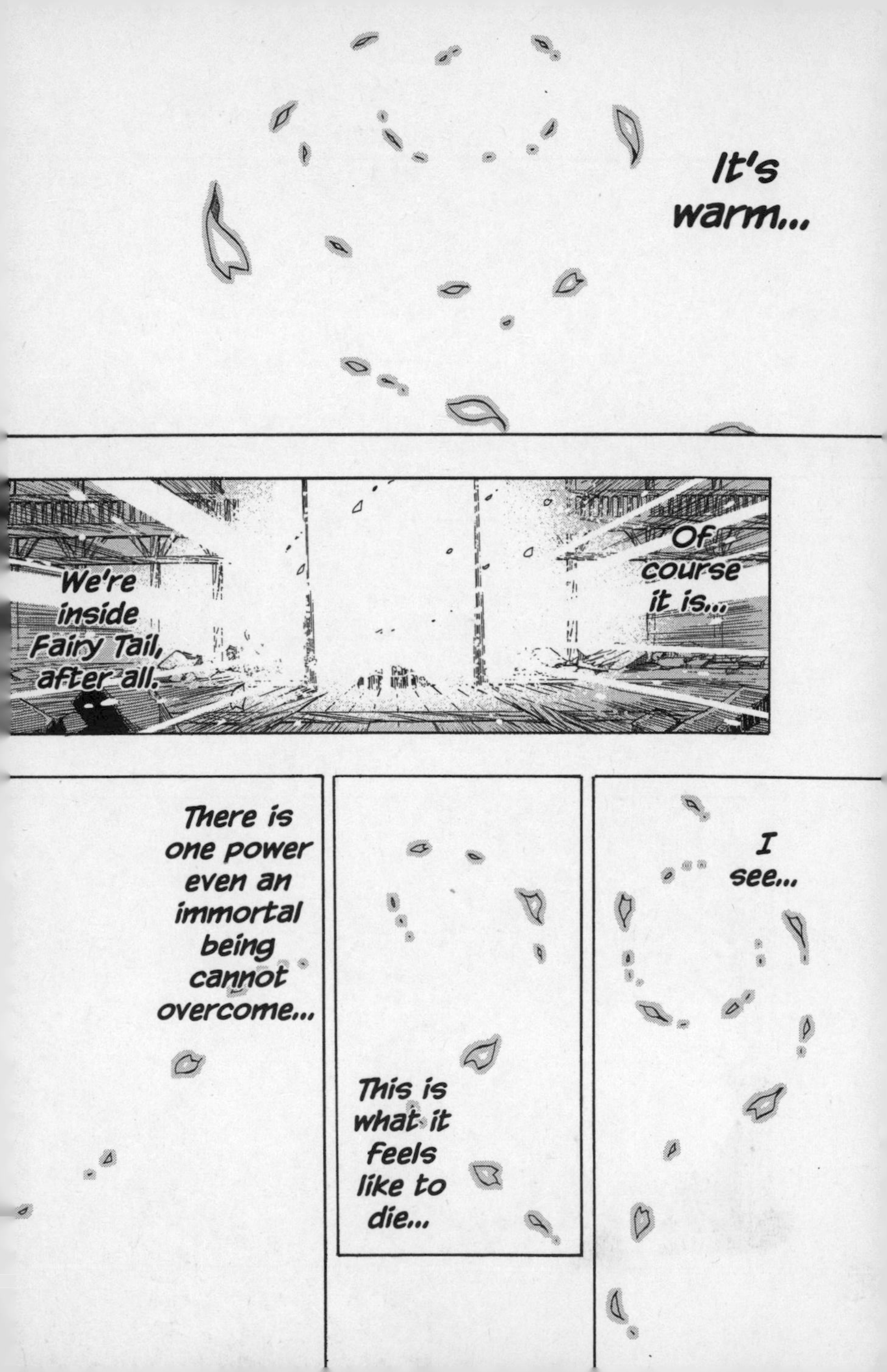
It's warm...
Of course it is...
We're inside Fairy Tail, after all.
I see...
This is what it feels like to die...
There is one power even an immortal being cannot overcome...

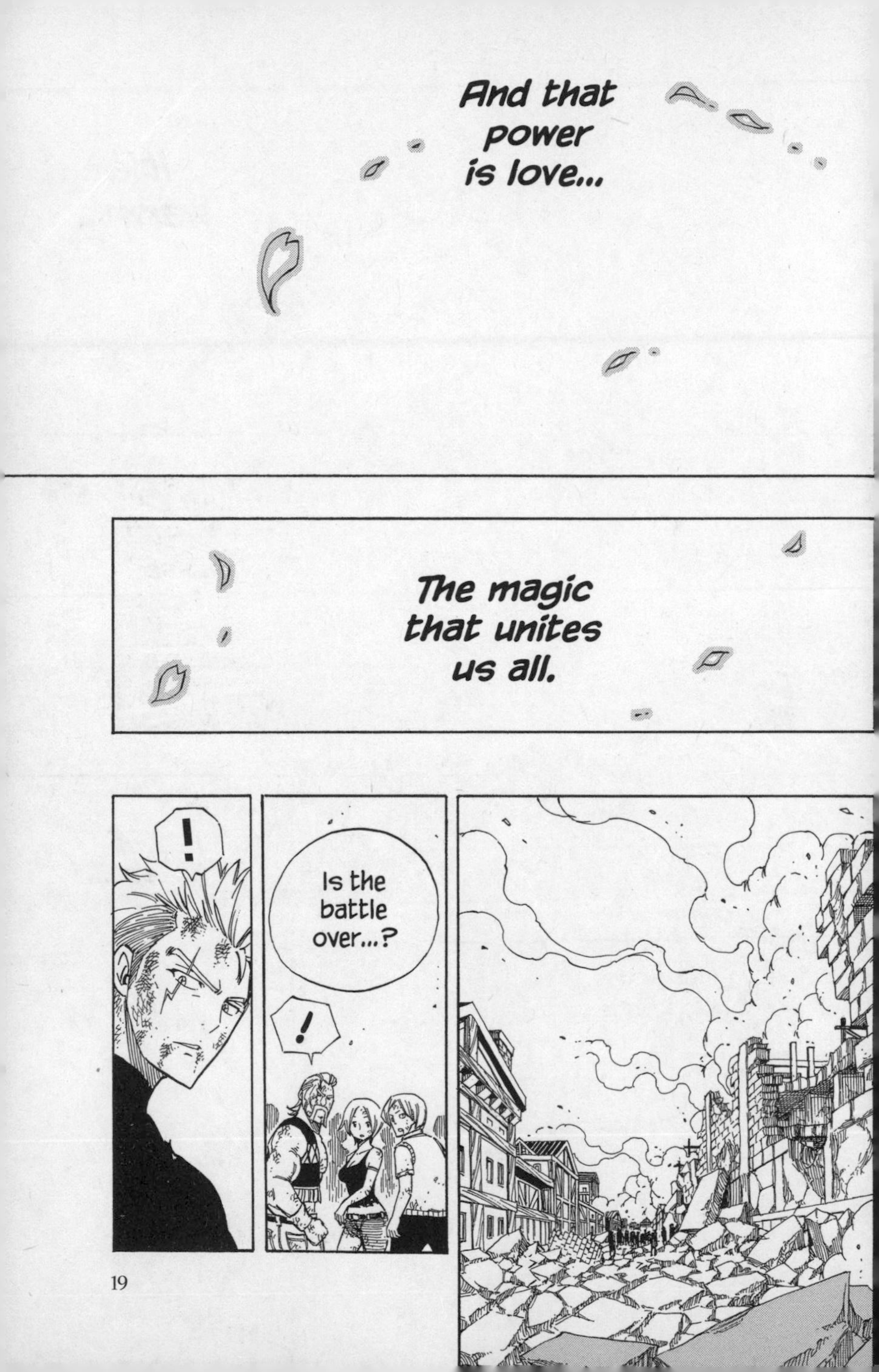
And that power is love...
The magic that unites us all.
Is the battle over...?
!
!

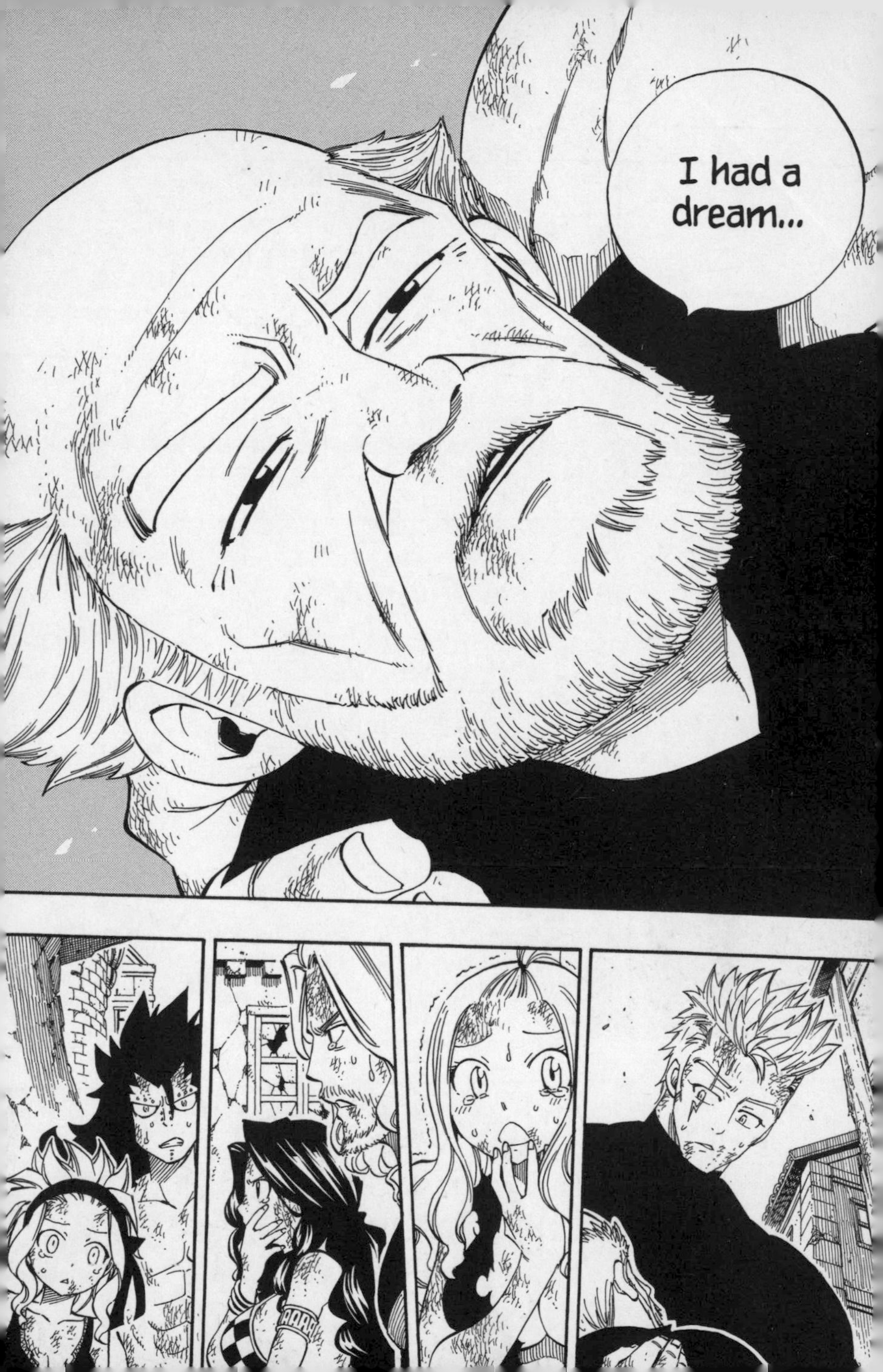
I had a dream...

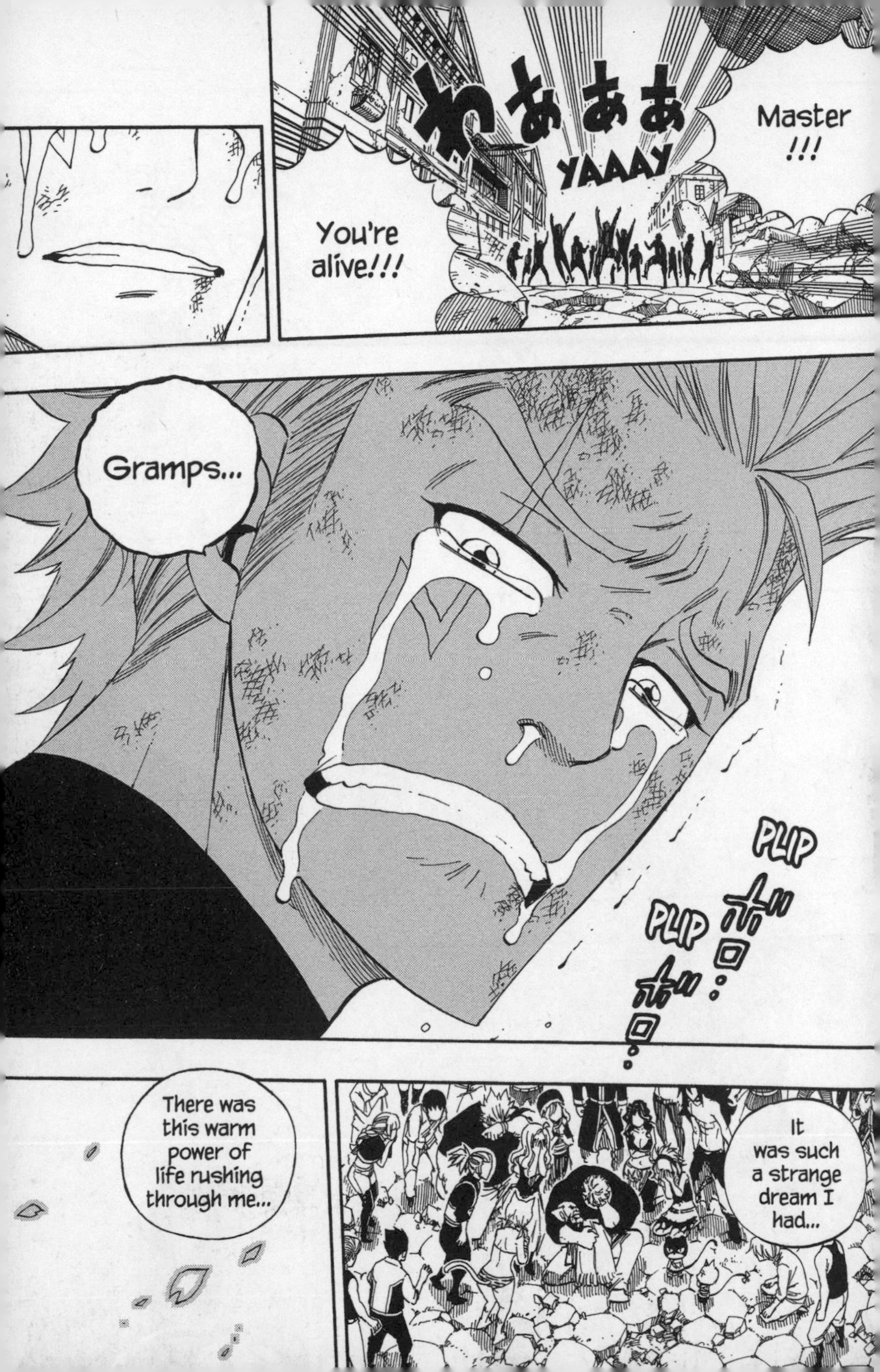

Master!!!
わあああ
YAAAY
You're alive!!!
Gramps...
PLIP
PLIP
It was such a strange dream I had...
There was this warm power of life rushing through me...

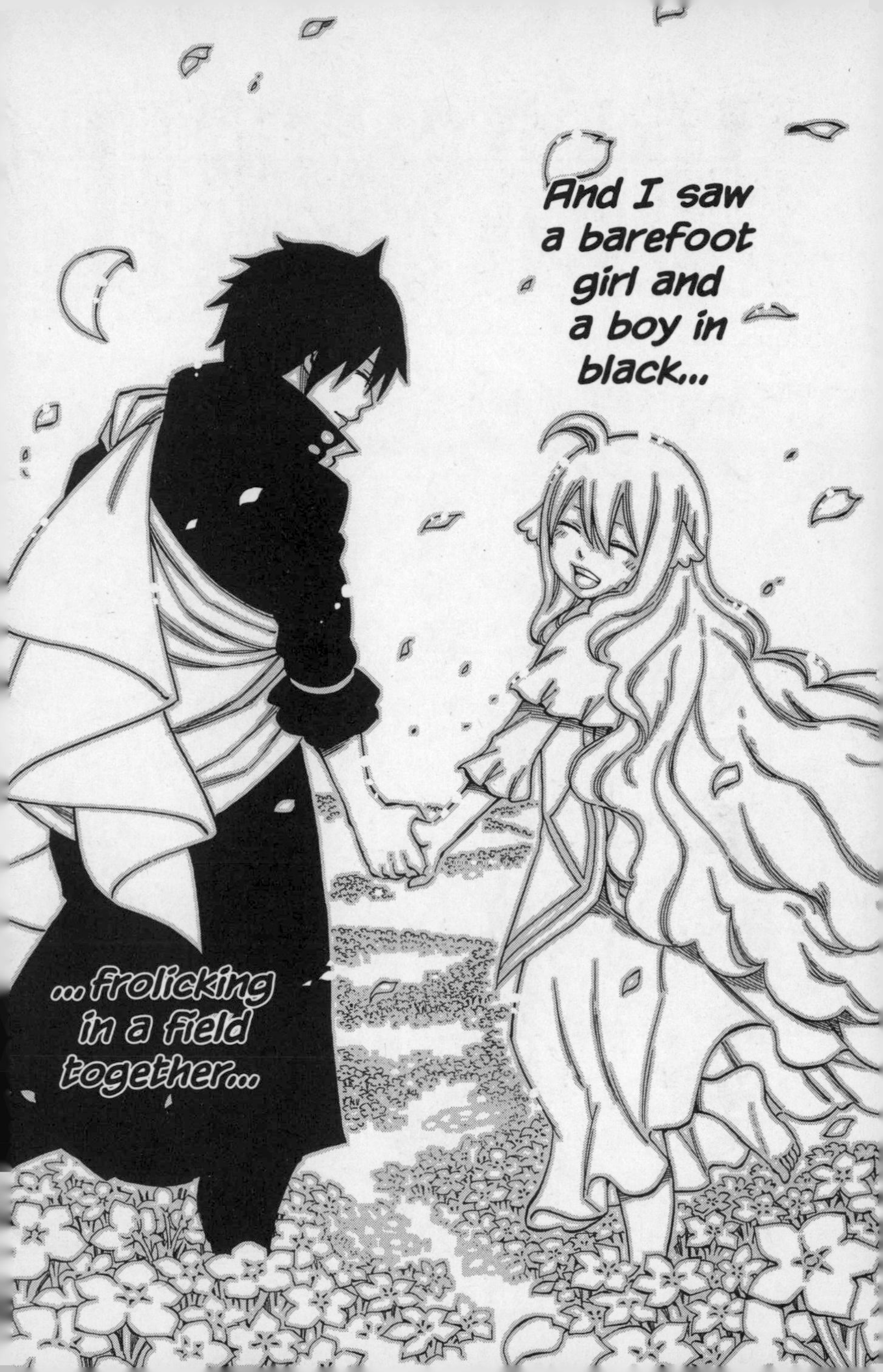
And I saw a barefoot girl and a boy in black...
...frolicking in a field together...

Chapter 538: When the Flame Goes Out

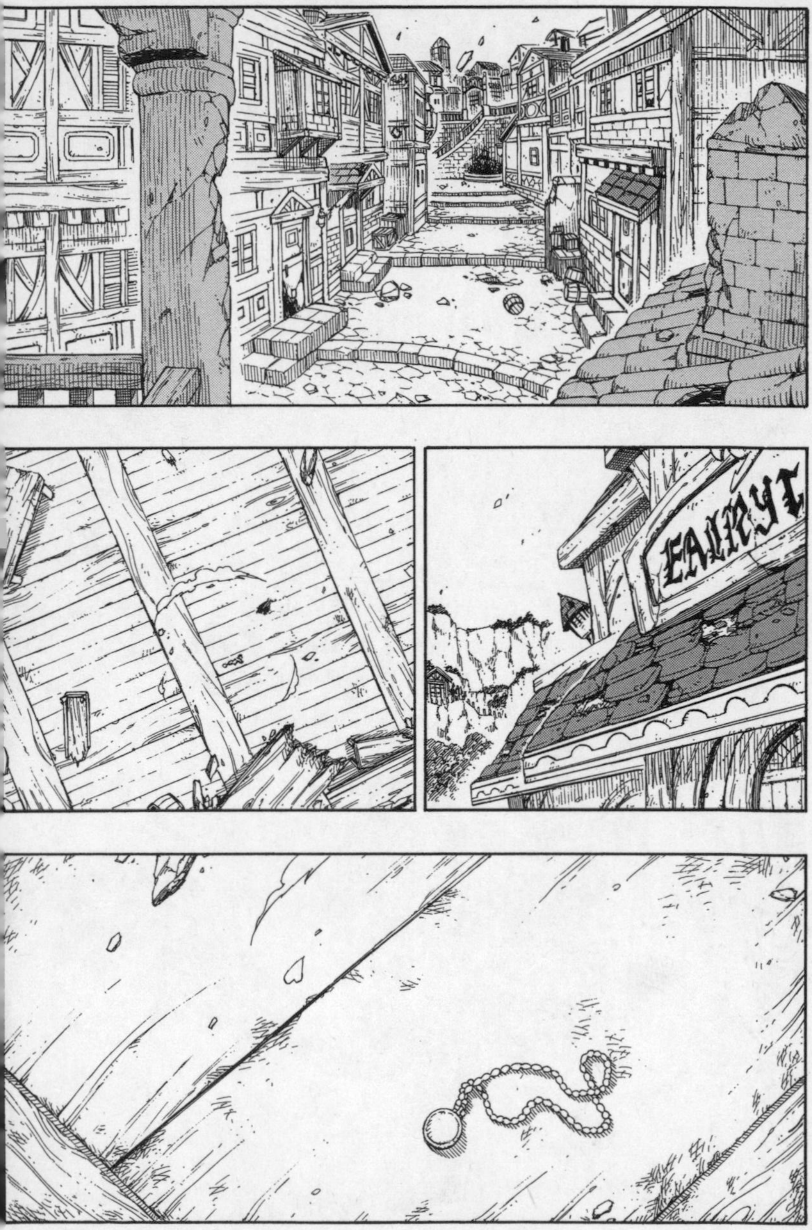

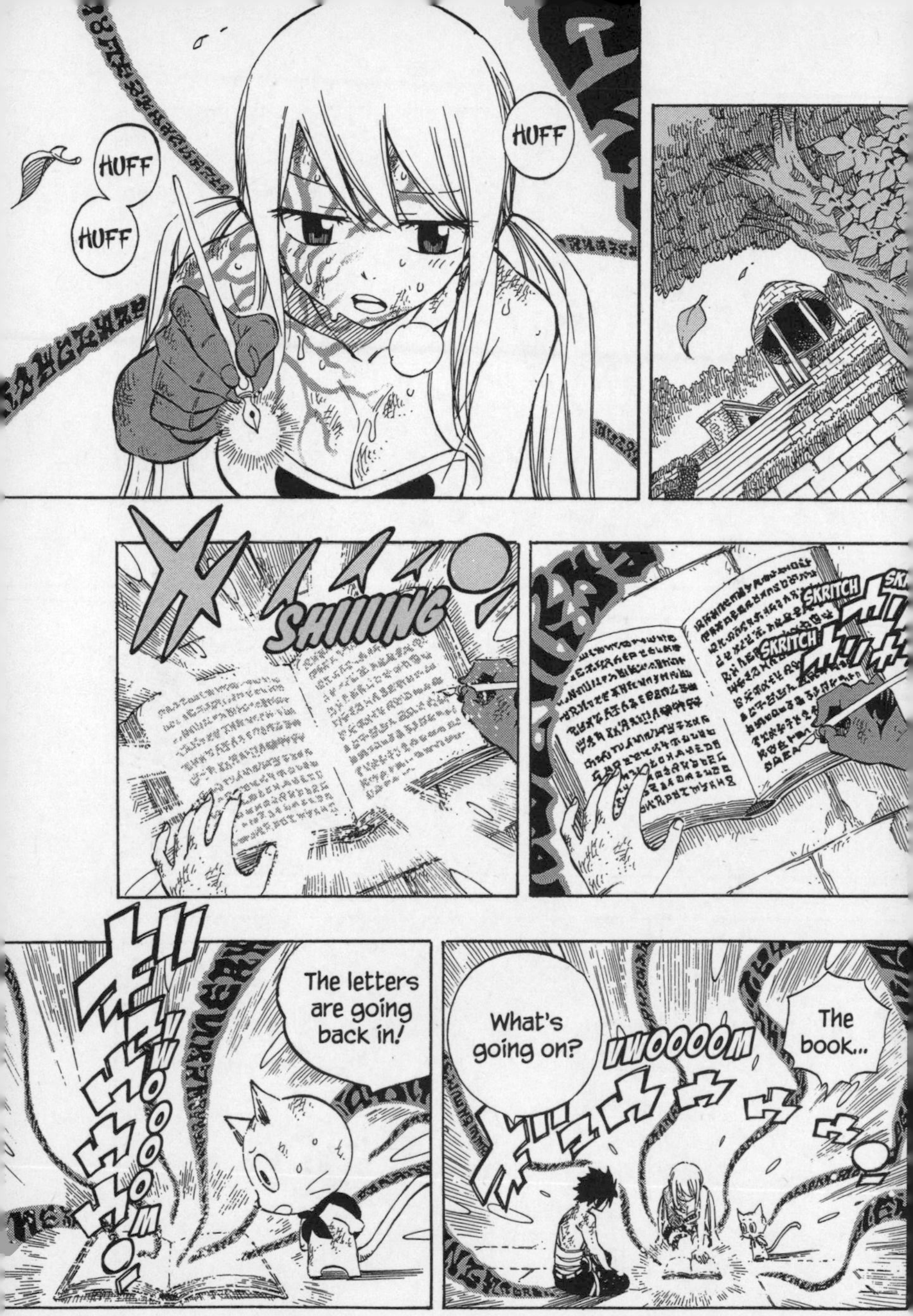
HUFF
HUFF
HUFF
SKRITCH
SKRITCH
SHIIIING
The book...
VWOOOOM
What's going on?
The letters are going back in!
WOOOOOM

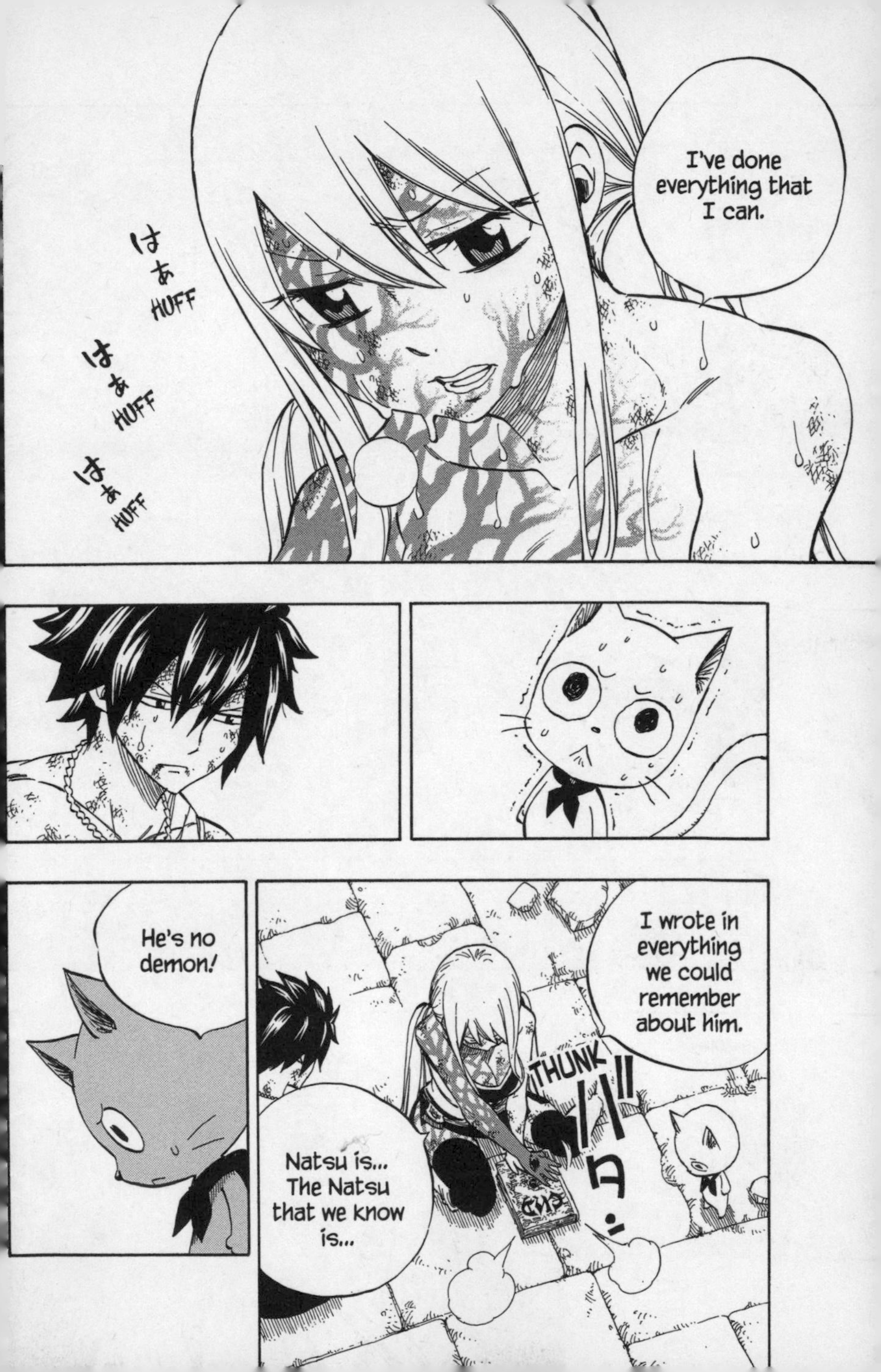
I've done everything that I can.
はぁ HUFF
はぁ HUFF
はぁ HUFF
I wrote in everything we could remember about him.
THUNK
Natsu is... The Natsu that we know is...
He's no demon!

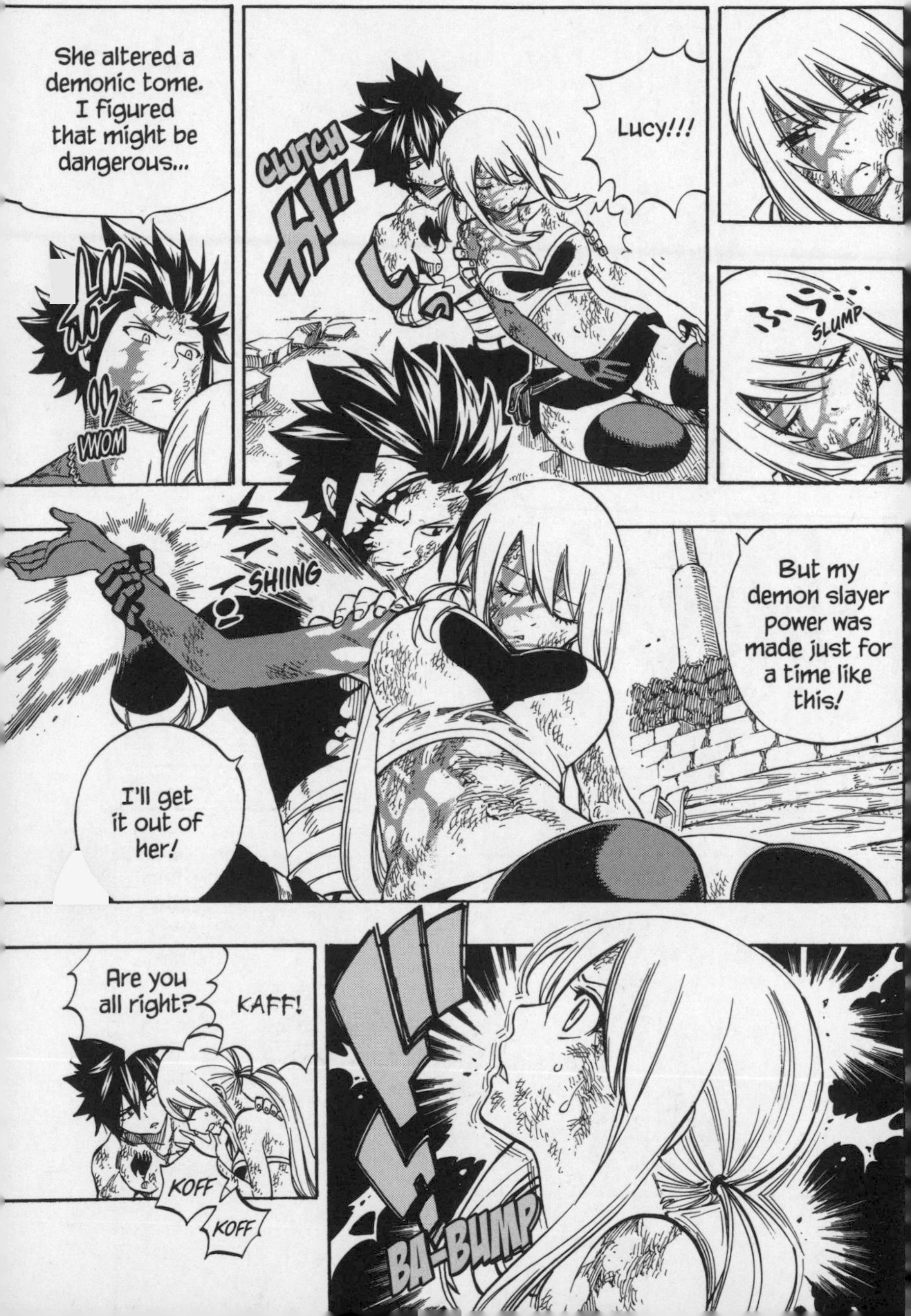
SLUMP
Lucy!!!
CLUTCH
She altered a demonic tome. I figured that might be dangerous...
VWOM
But my demon slayer power was made just for a time like this!
SHIING
I'll get it out of her!
BA-BUMP
KAFF!
Are you all right?
KOFF
KOFF

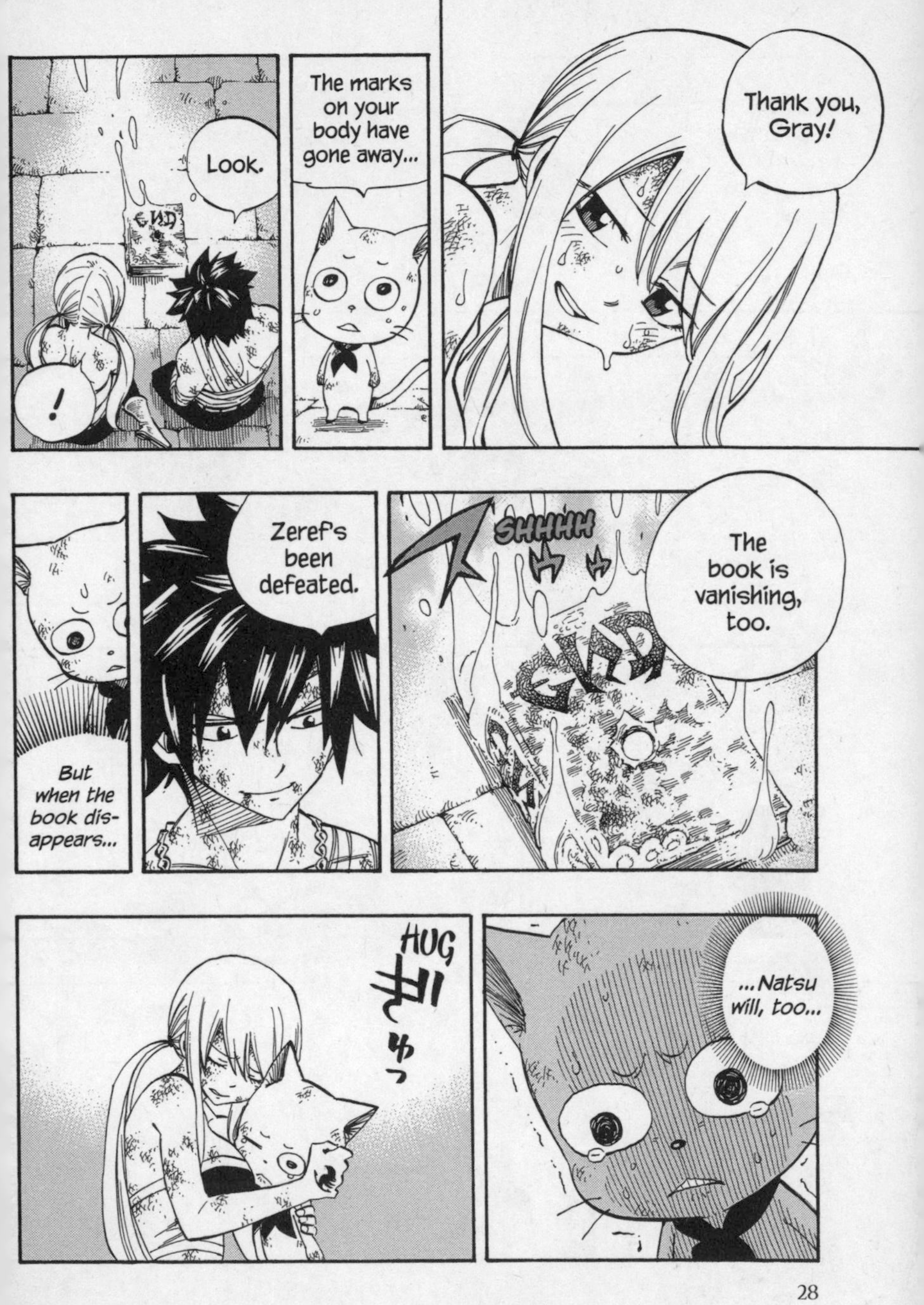
Thank you, Gray!
The marks on your body have gone away...
Look.
!
The book is vanishing, too.
SHHHH
Zeref's been defeated.
But when the book dis-appears...
...Natsu will, too...
HUG

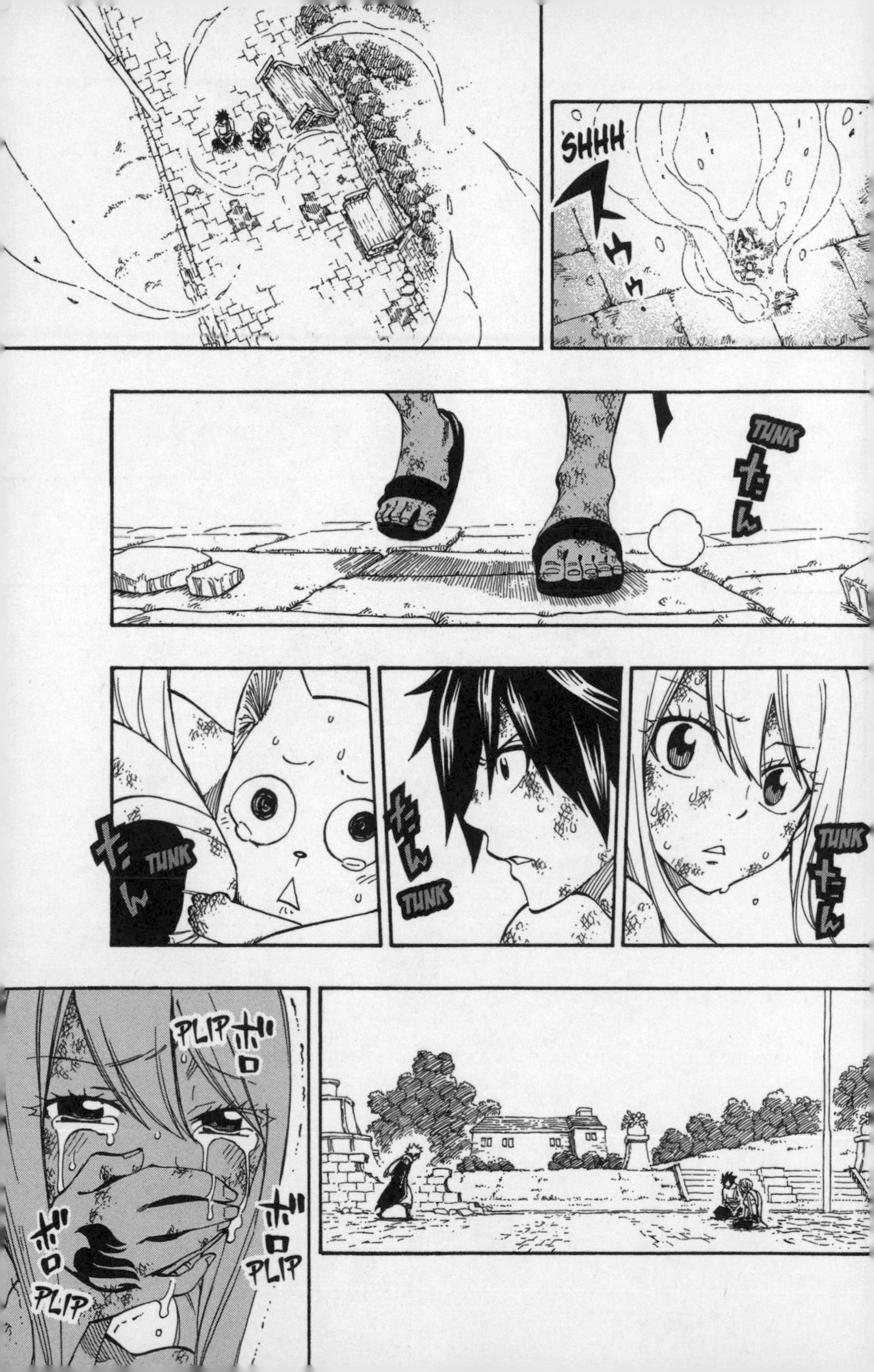
SHHH
スゥゥ
TUNK
たん
TUNK
たん
TUNK
たん
TUNK
たん
PLIP
ボロ
PLIP
ボロ
PLIP
ボロ

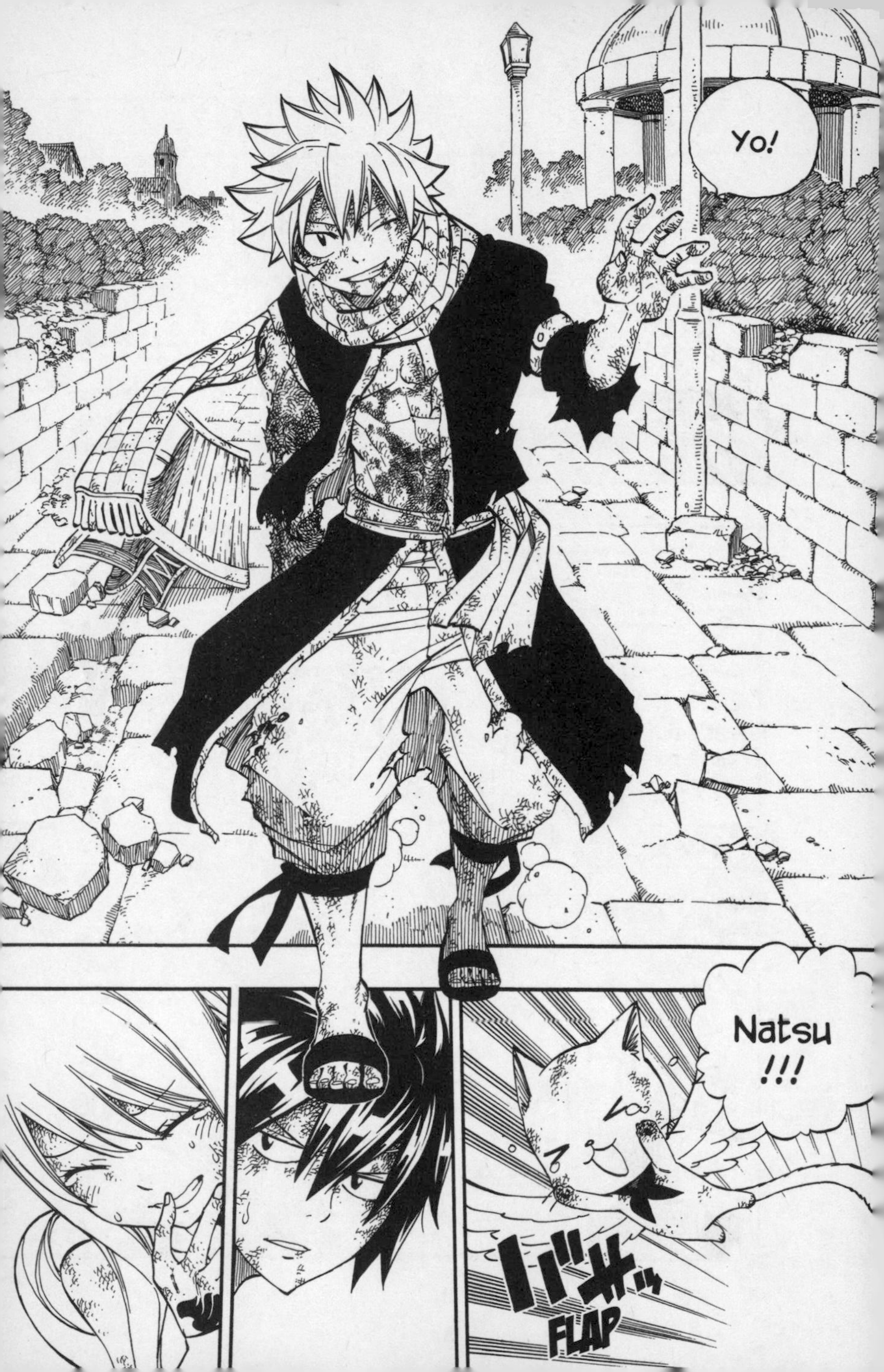
Yo!
Natsu !!!
FLAP

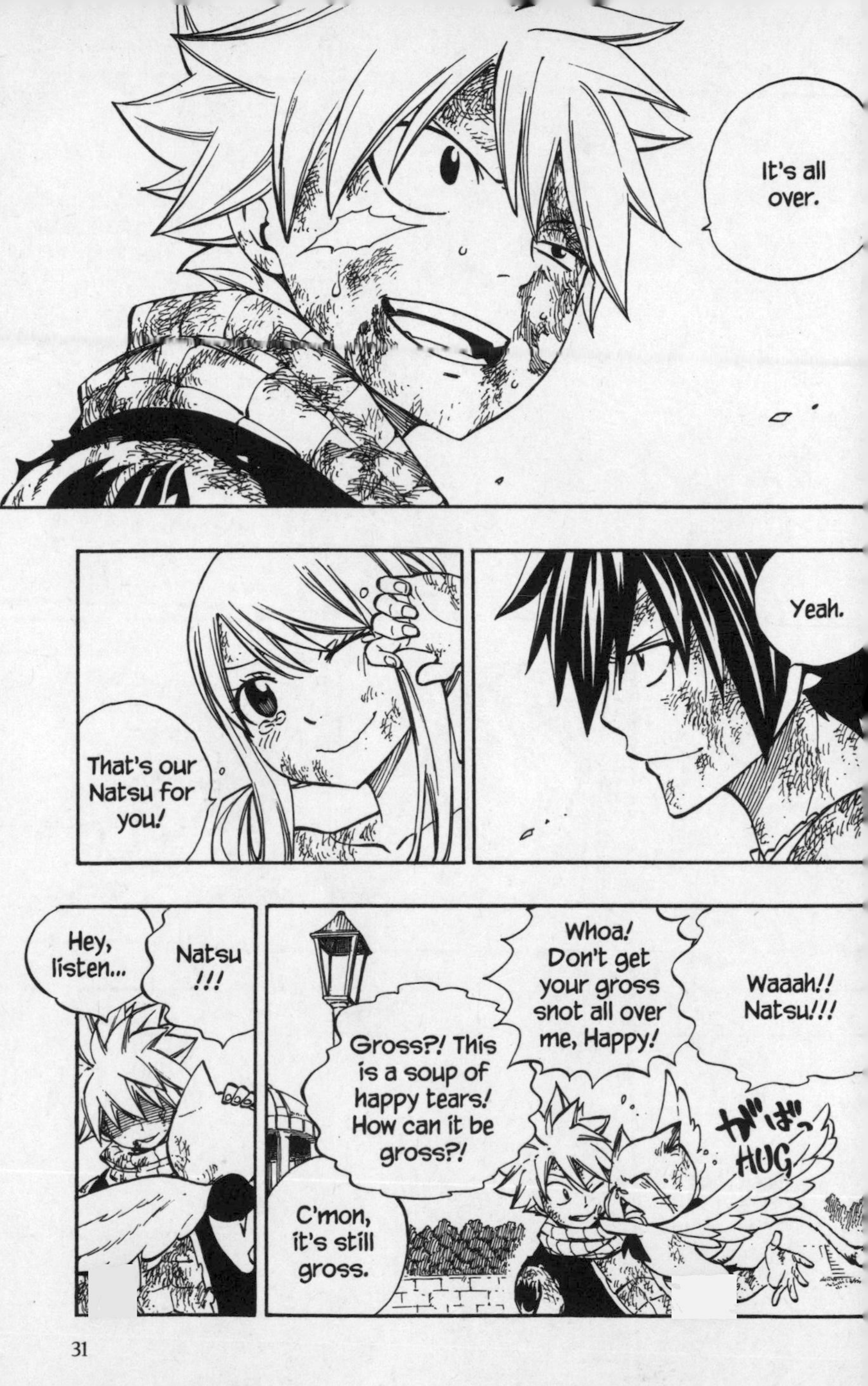
It's all over.
Yeah.
That's our Natsu for you!
Waaah!! Natsu!!!
がばっ
HUG
Whoa! Don't get your gross snot all over me, Happy!
Gross?! This is a soup of happy tears! How can it be gross?!
C'mon, it's still gross.
Natsu!!!
Hey, listen...

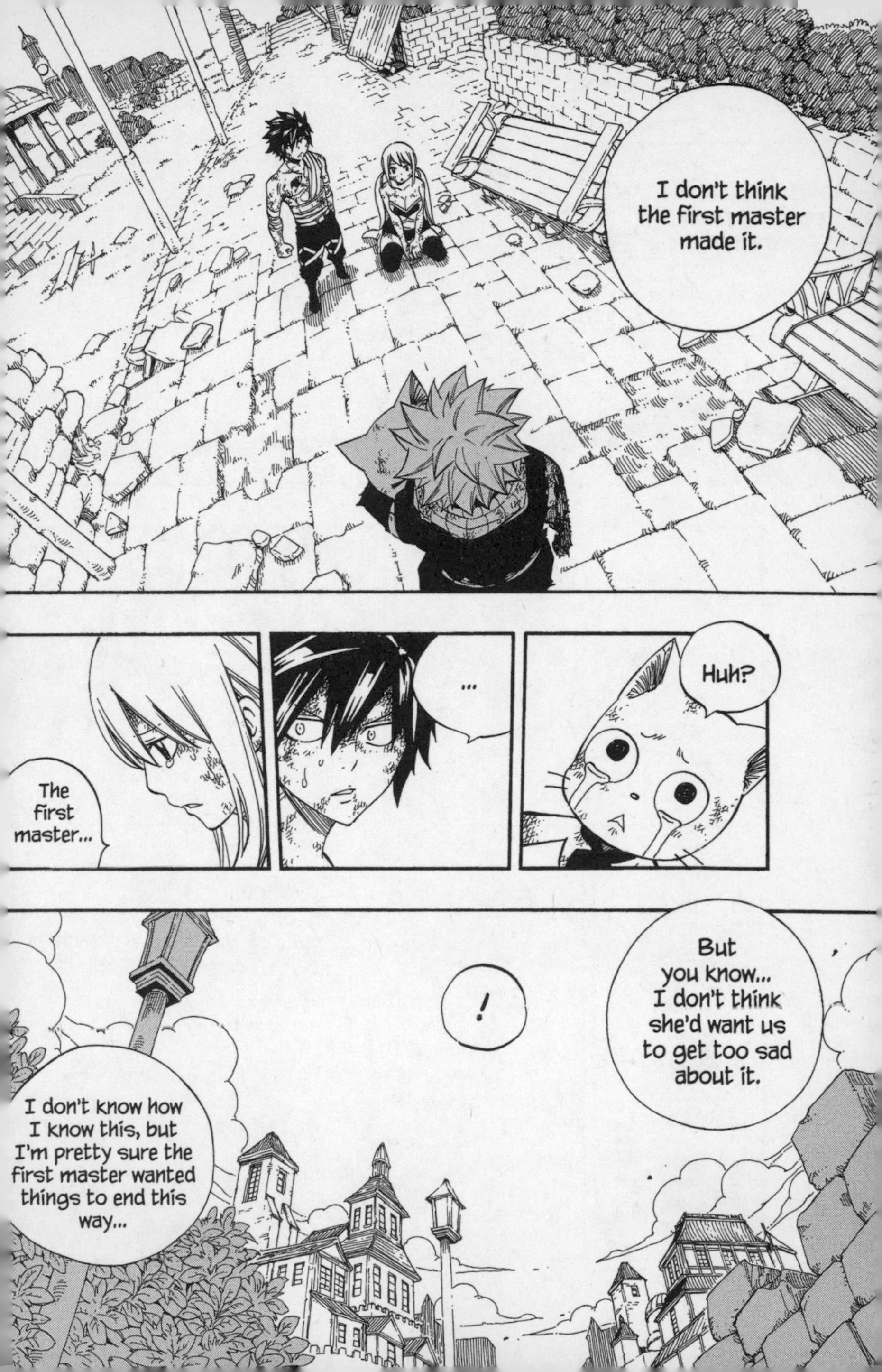
I don't think the first master made it.
Huh?
...
The first master...
But you know... I don't think she'd want us to get too sad about it.
!
I don't know how I know this, but I'm pretty sure the first master wanted things to end this way...

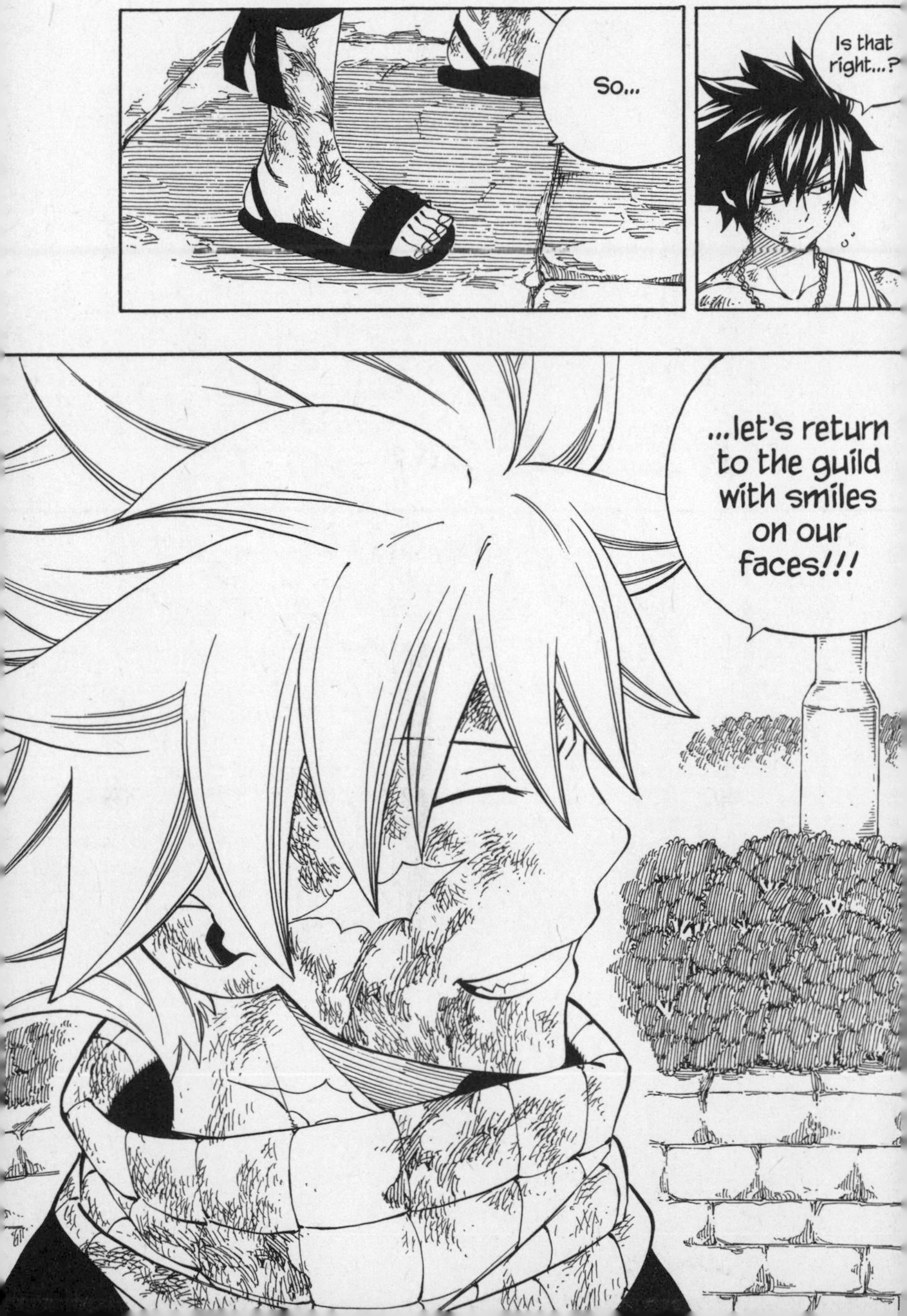
Is that right...?
So...
...let's return to the guild with smiles on our faces!!!

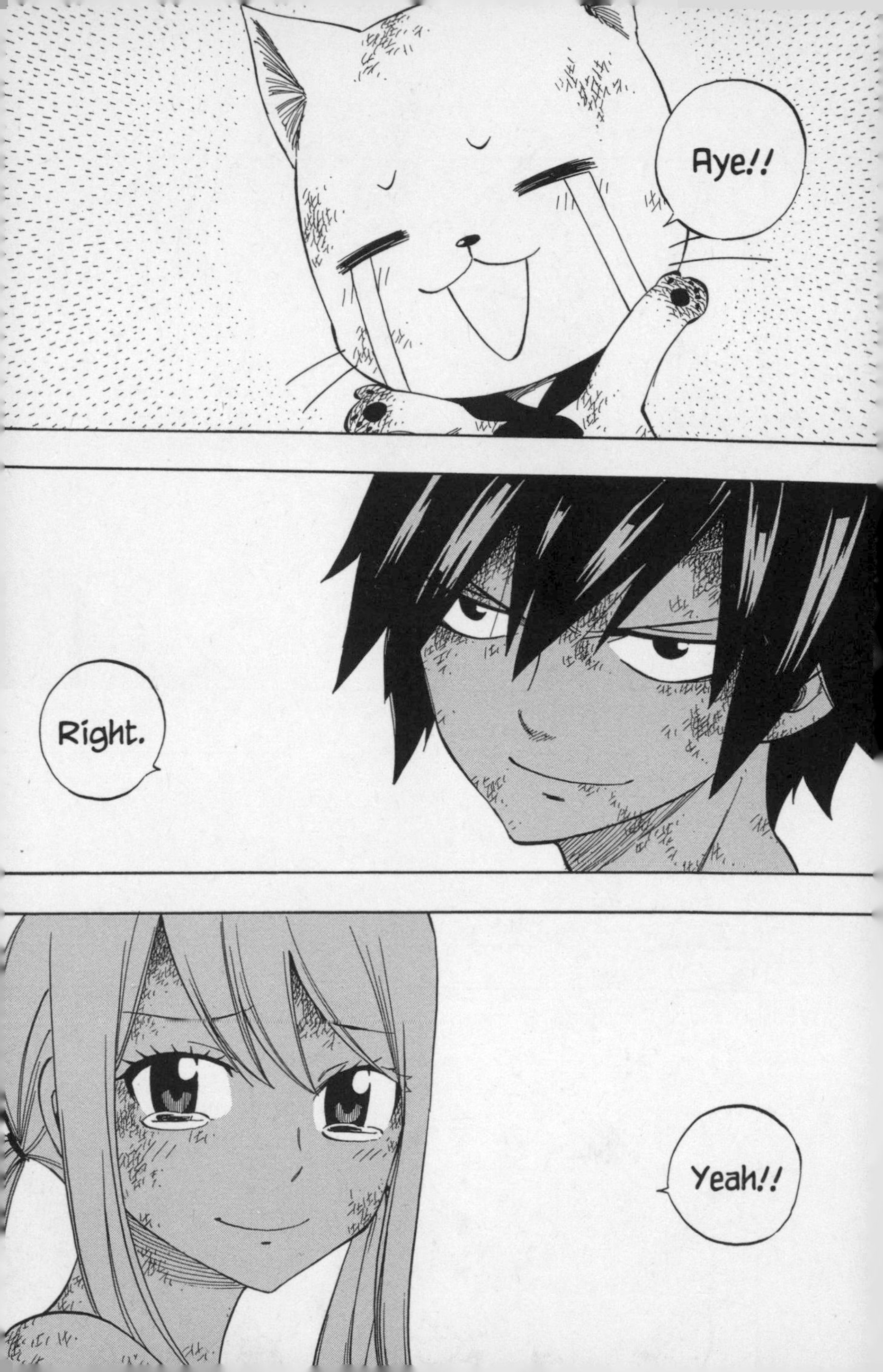
Aye!!
Right.
Yeah!!

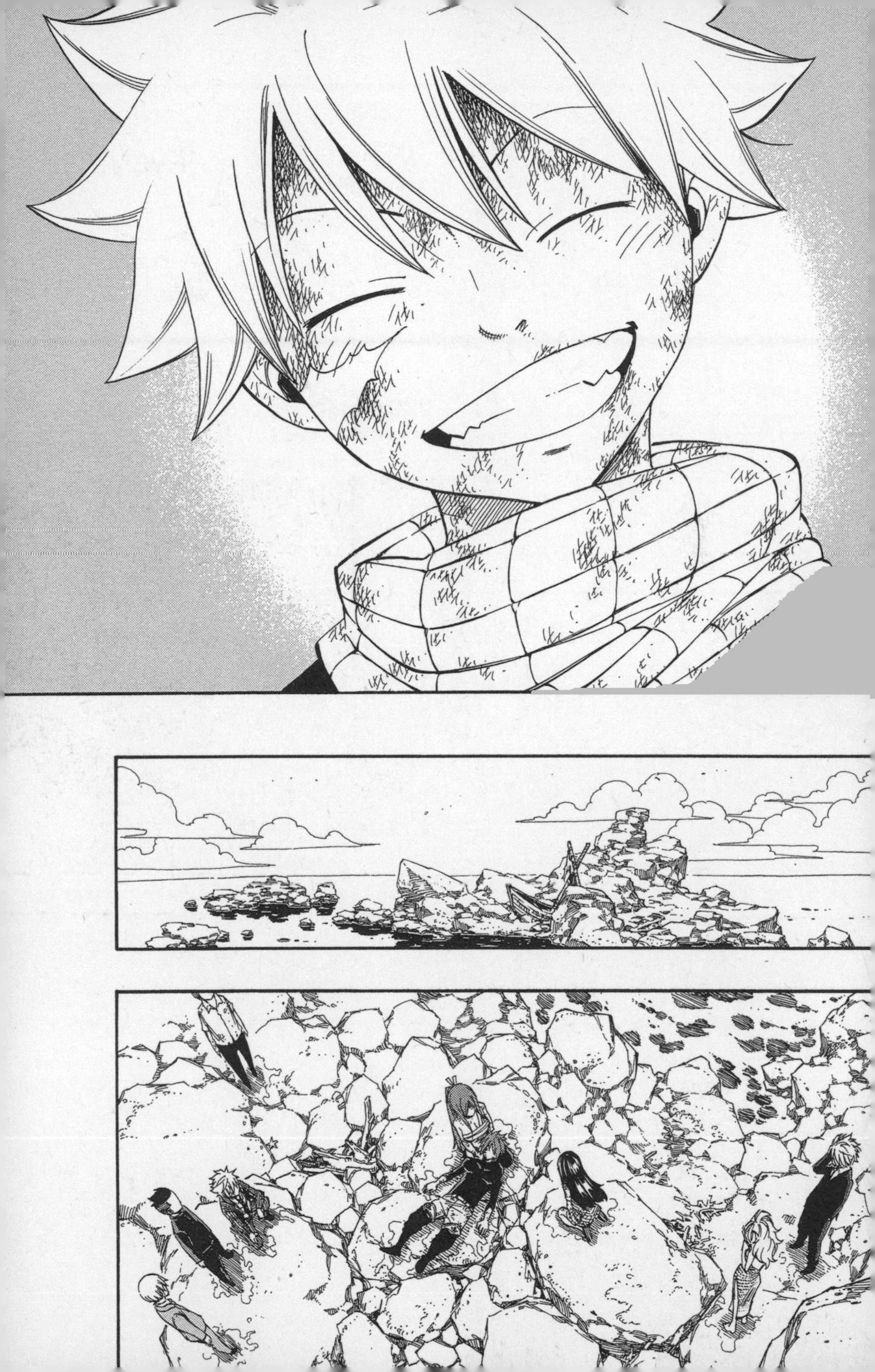

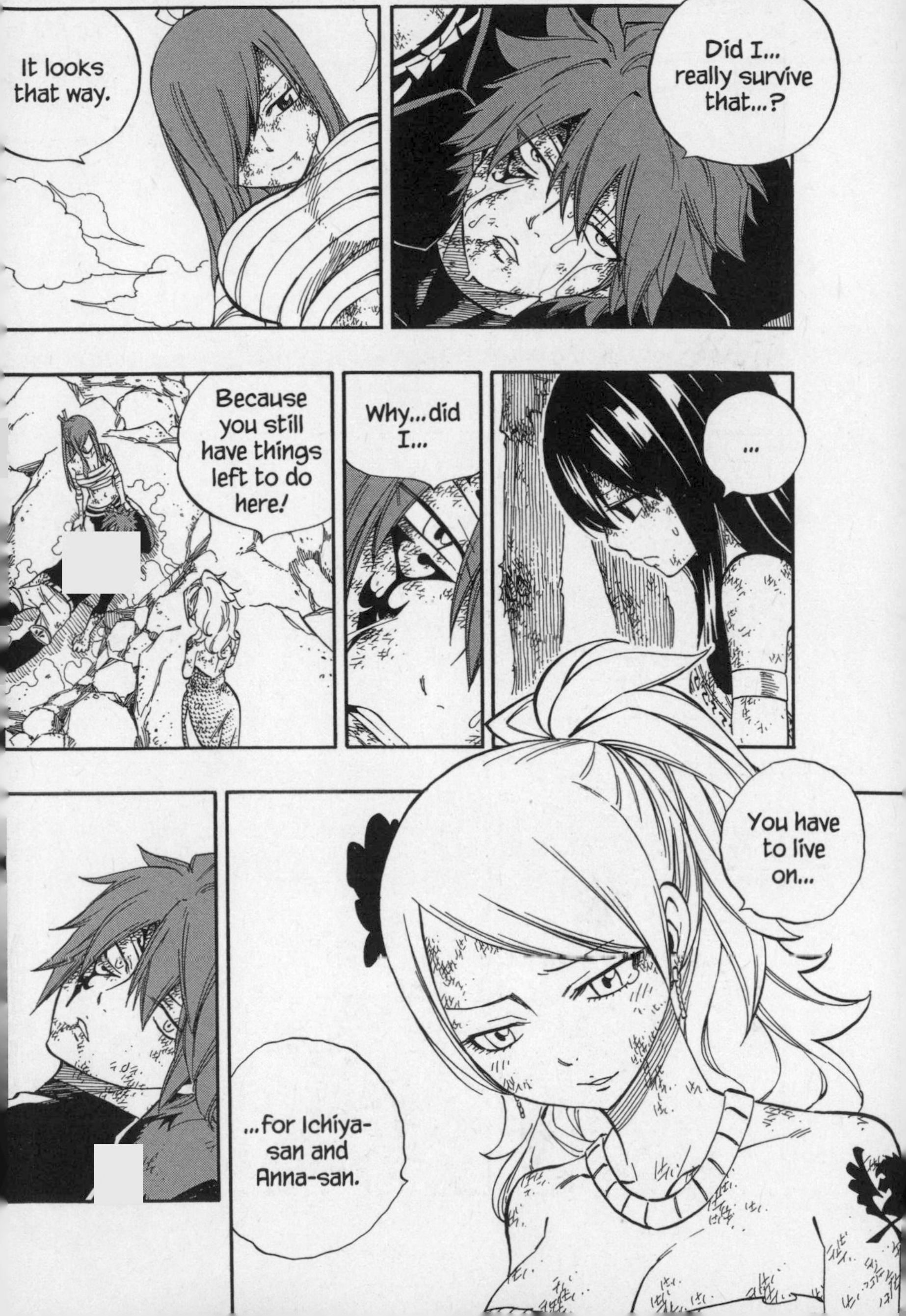
Did I... really survive that...?
It looks that way.
...
Why...did I...
Because you still have things left to do here!
You have to live on...
...for Ichiya-san and Anna-san.

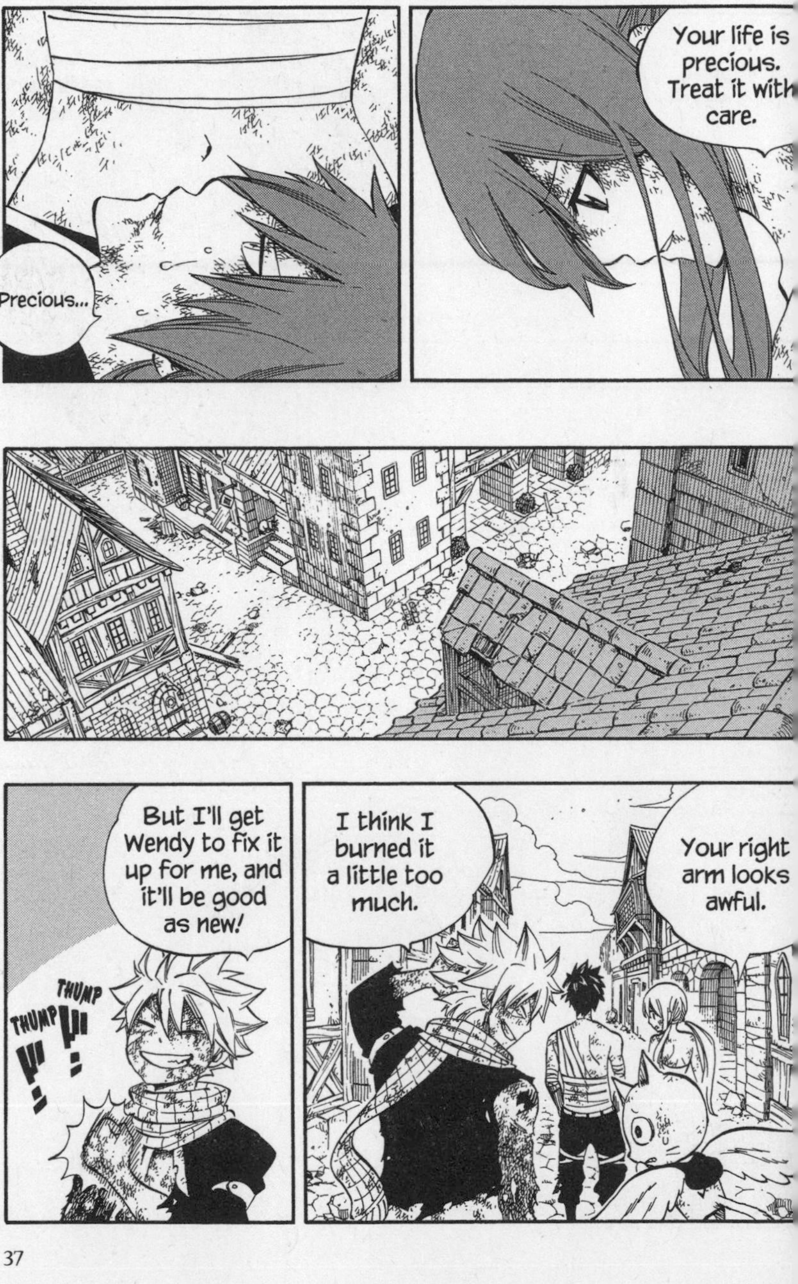
Your life is precious. Treat it with care.
Precious...
Your right arm looks awful.
I think I burned it a little too much.
But I'll get Wendy to fix it up for me, and it'll be good as new!
THUMP
THUMP

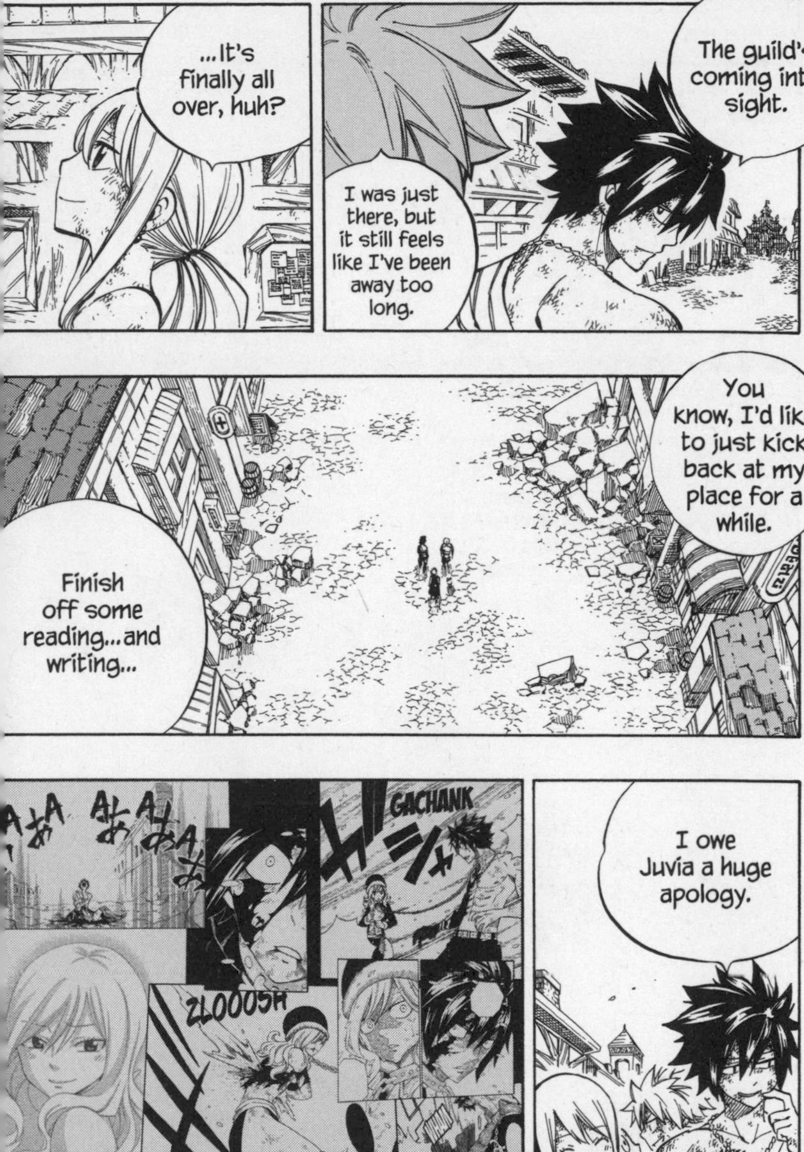

The guild's coming into sight.
I was just there, but it still feels like I've been away too long.
...It's finally all over, huh?
You know, I'd like to just kick back at my place for a while.
Finish off some reading...and writing...
I owe Juvia a huge apology.
GACHANK
ZLOOOSH

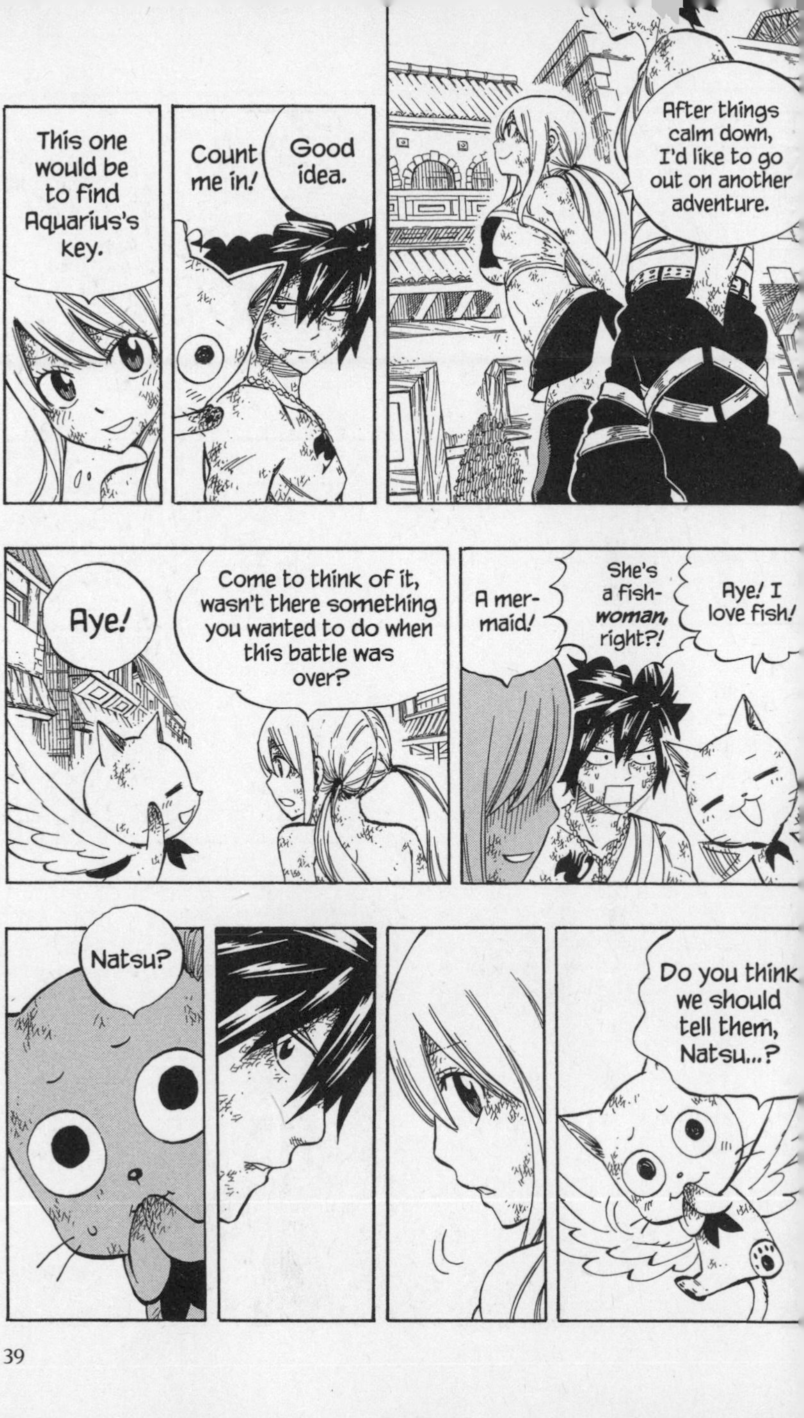
After things calm down, I'd like to go out on another adventure.
Good idea.
Count me in!
This one would be to find Aquarius's key.
Aye! I love fish!
She's a fish-*woman*, right?!
A mer-maid!
Come to think of it, wasn't there something you wanted to do when this battle was over?
Aye!
Do you think we should tell them, Natsu...?
Natsu?

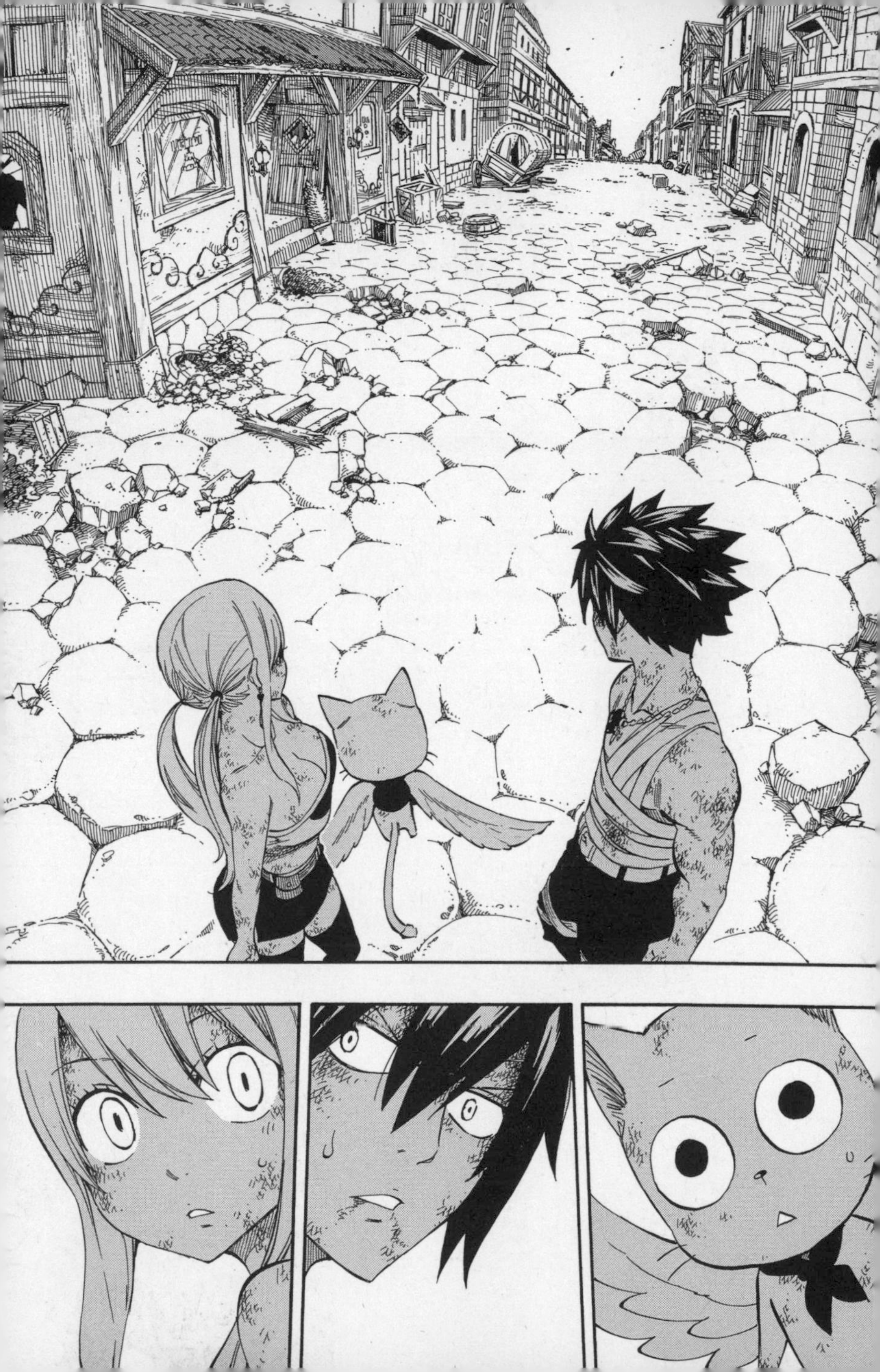

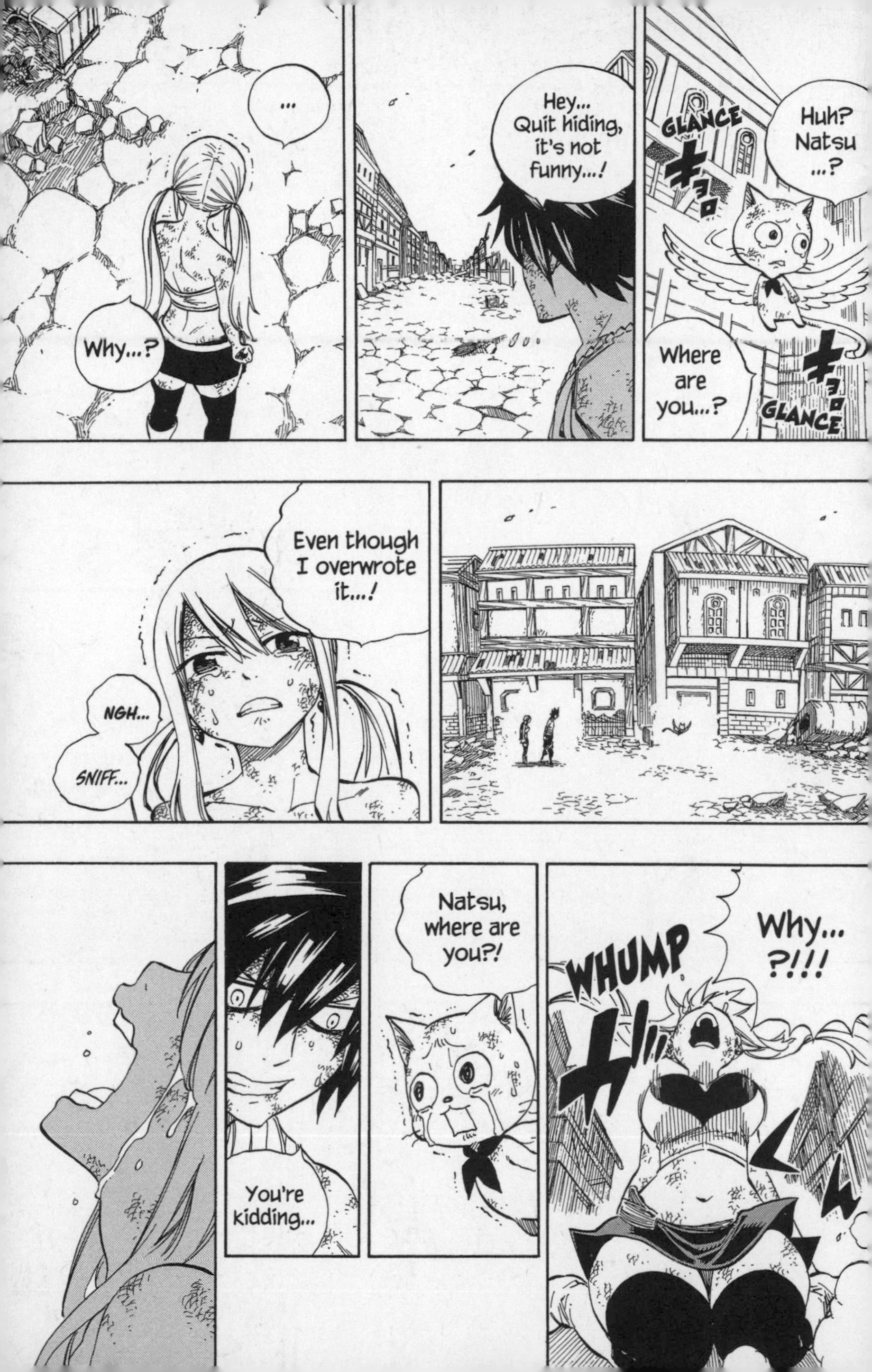
GLANCE
キョロ
Huh? Natsu ...?
Where are you...?
キョロ
GLANCE
Hey... Quit hiding, it's not funny...!
...
Why...?
Even though I overwrote it...!
NGH...
SNIFF...
WHUMP
Why... ?!!!
Natsu, where are you?!
You're kidding...

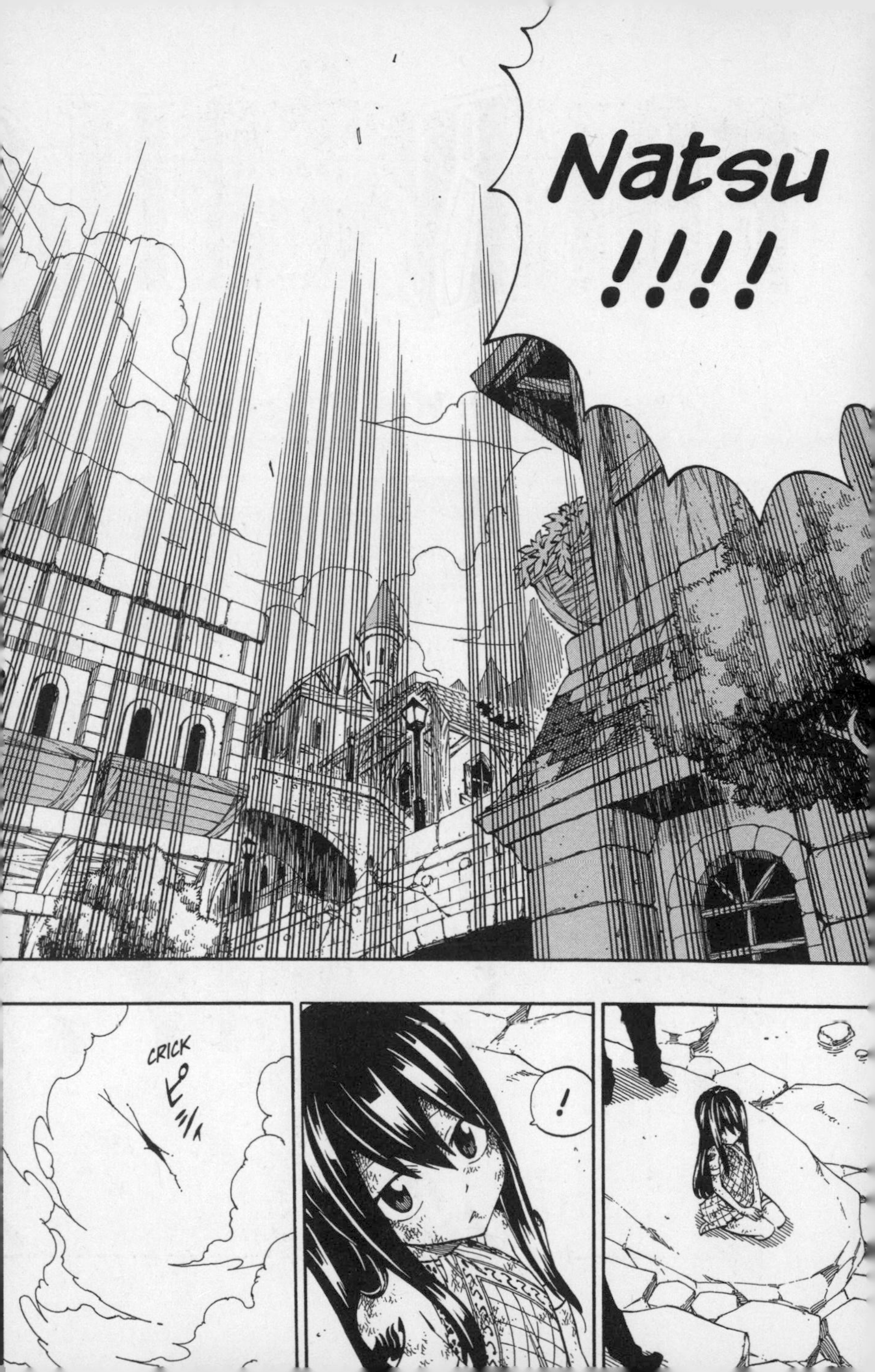
Natsu !!!!
!
CRICK

FAIRY TAIL

フェアリーテイル

Chapter 539: World Destruction

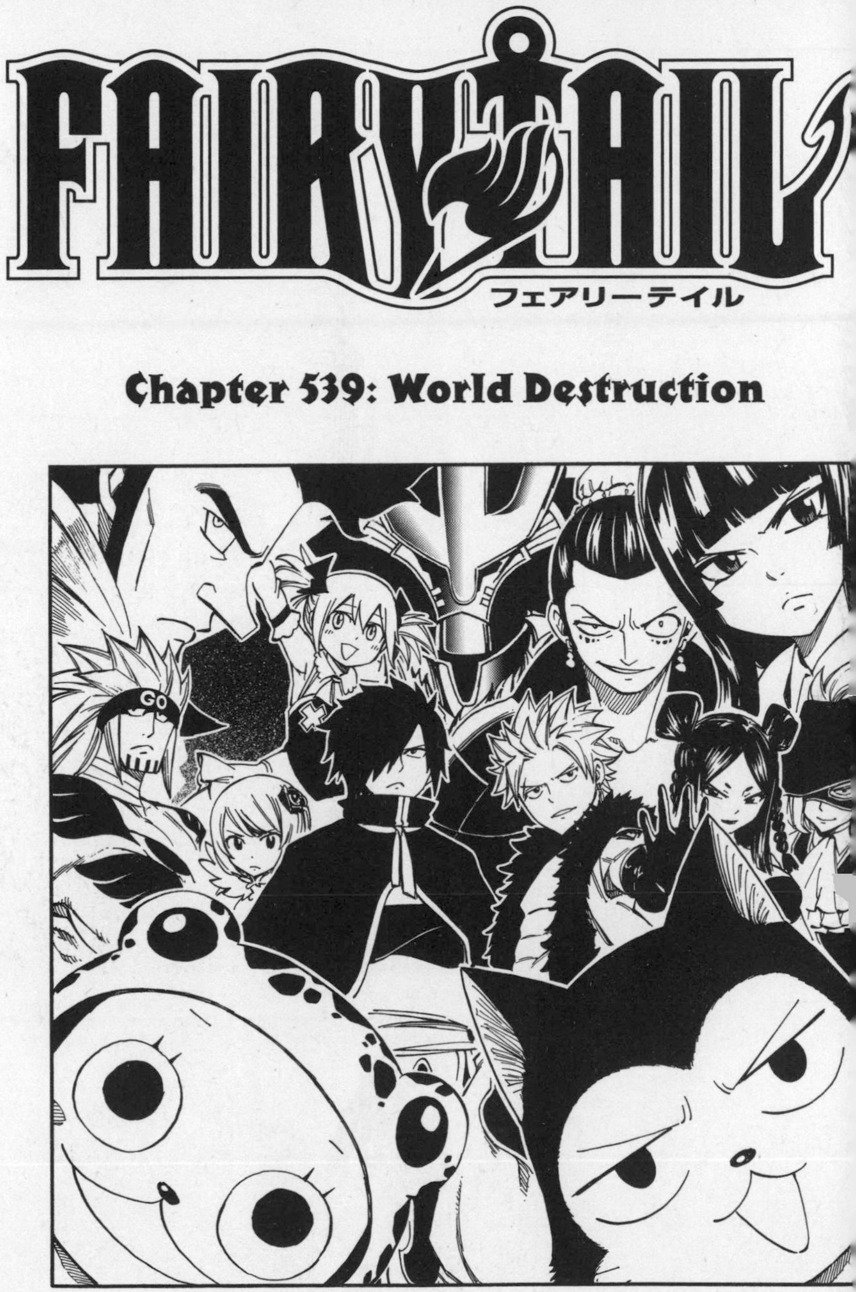
GO

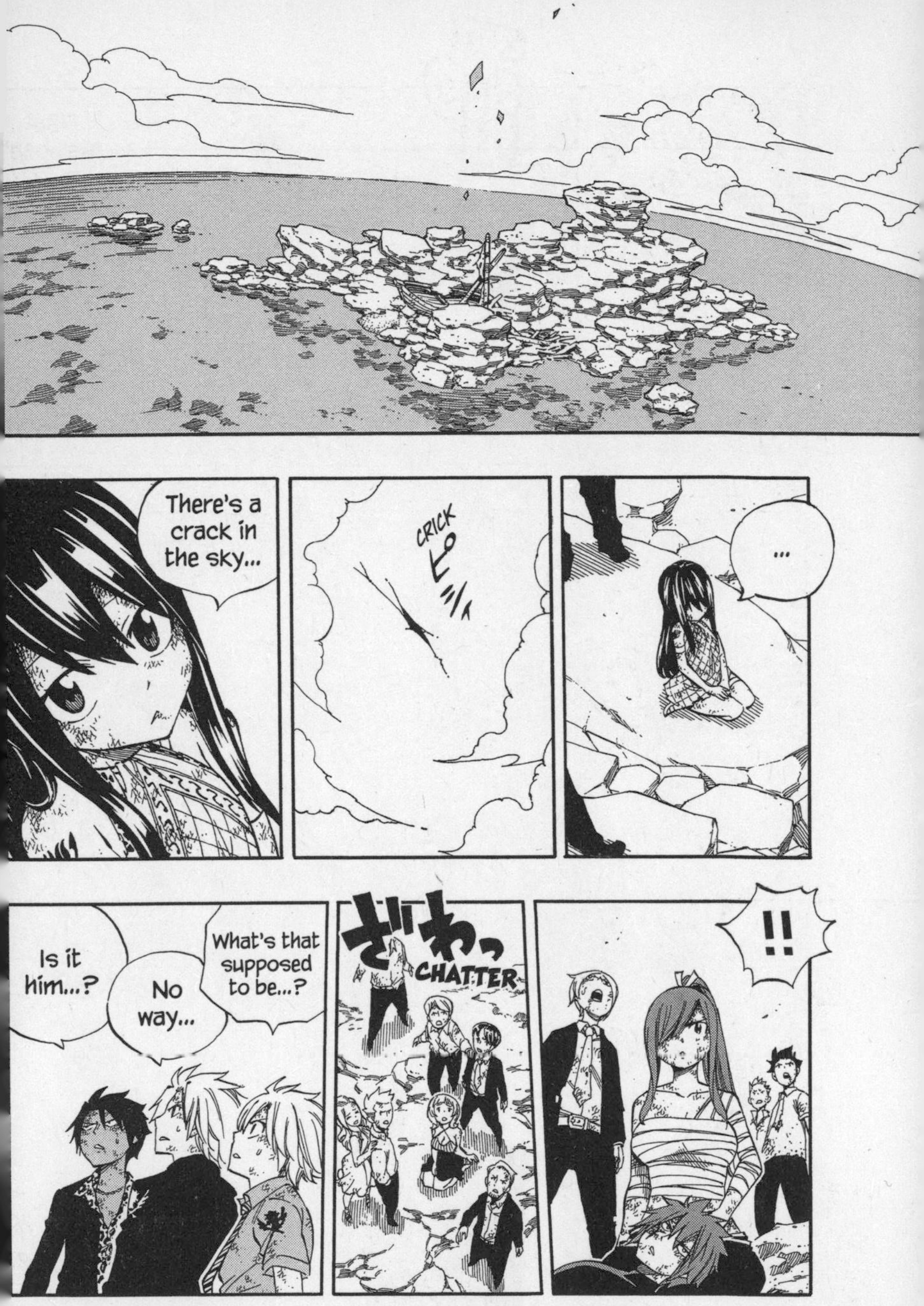
...
CRICK
There's a crack in the sky...
!!
ざわっ
CHATTER
What's that supposed to be...?
No way...
Is it him...?

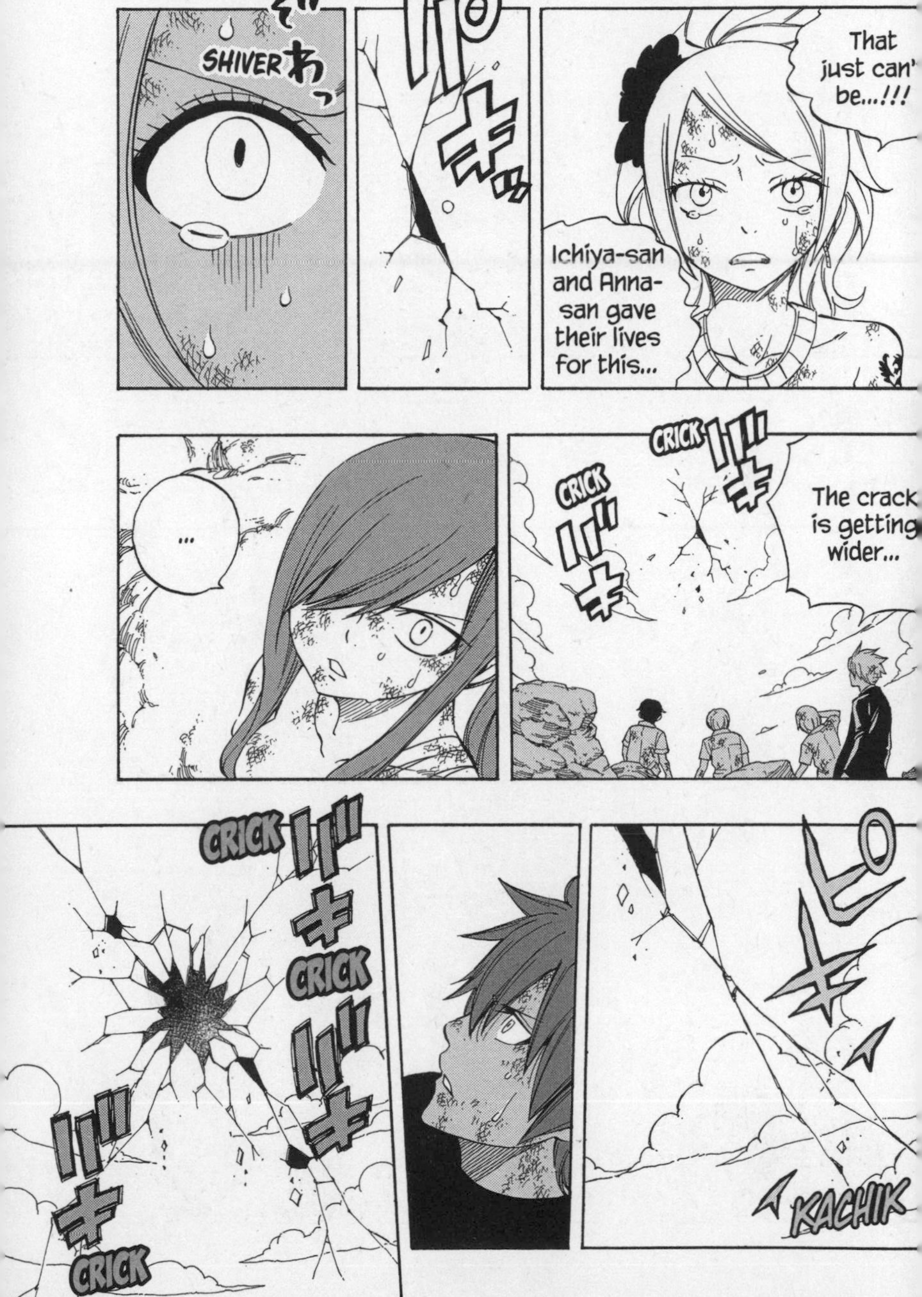
That just can' be...!!!
Ichiya-san and Anna-san gave their lives for this...
CRACK
SHIVER
CRICK
CRICK
The crack is getting wider...
...
KACHIK
CRICK
CRICK
CRICK

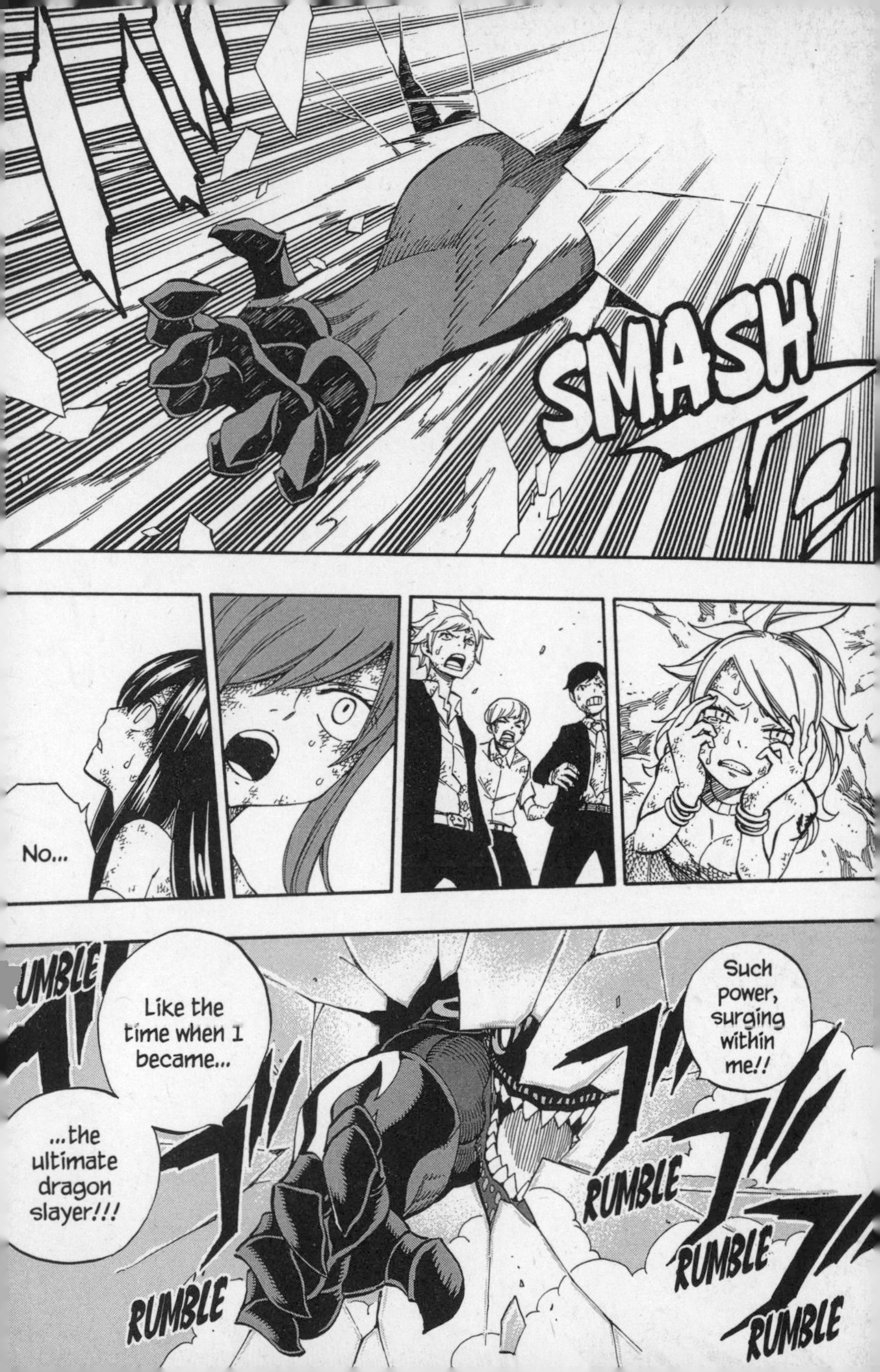
SMASH
No...
Such power, surging within me!!
Like the time when I became...
...the ultimate dragon slayer!!!
RUMBLE
RUMBLE
RUMBLE
RUMBLE
UMBLE

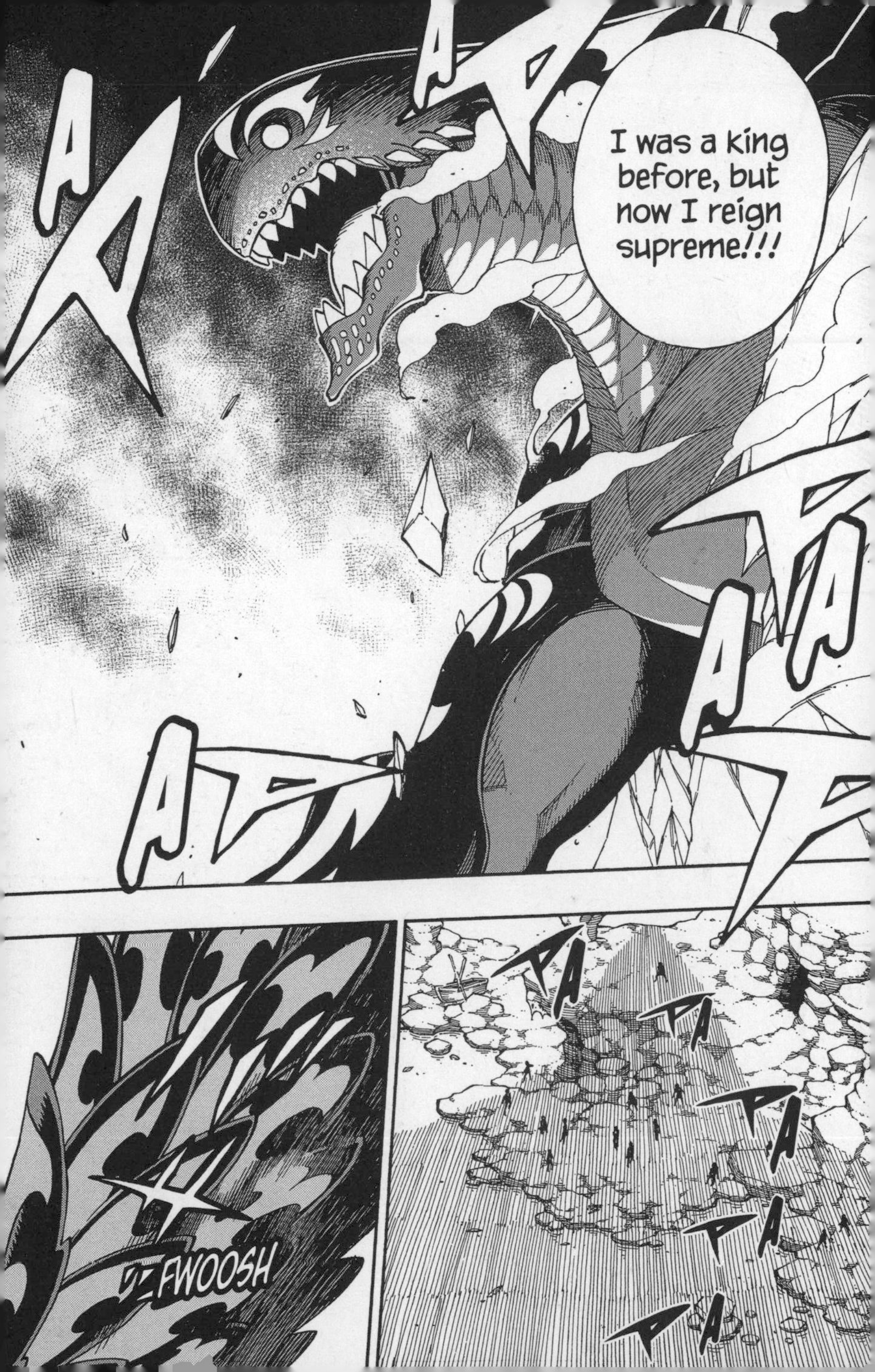
I was a king before, but now I reign supreme!!!
PA PA PA PA PA PA PA
FWOOSH

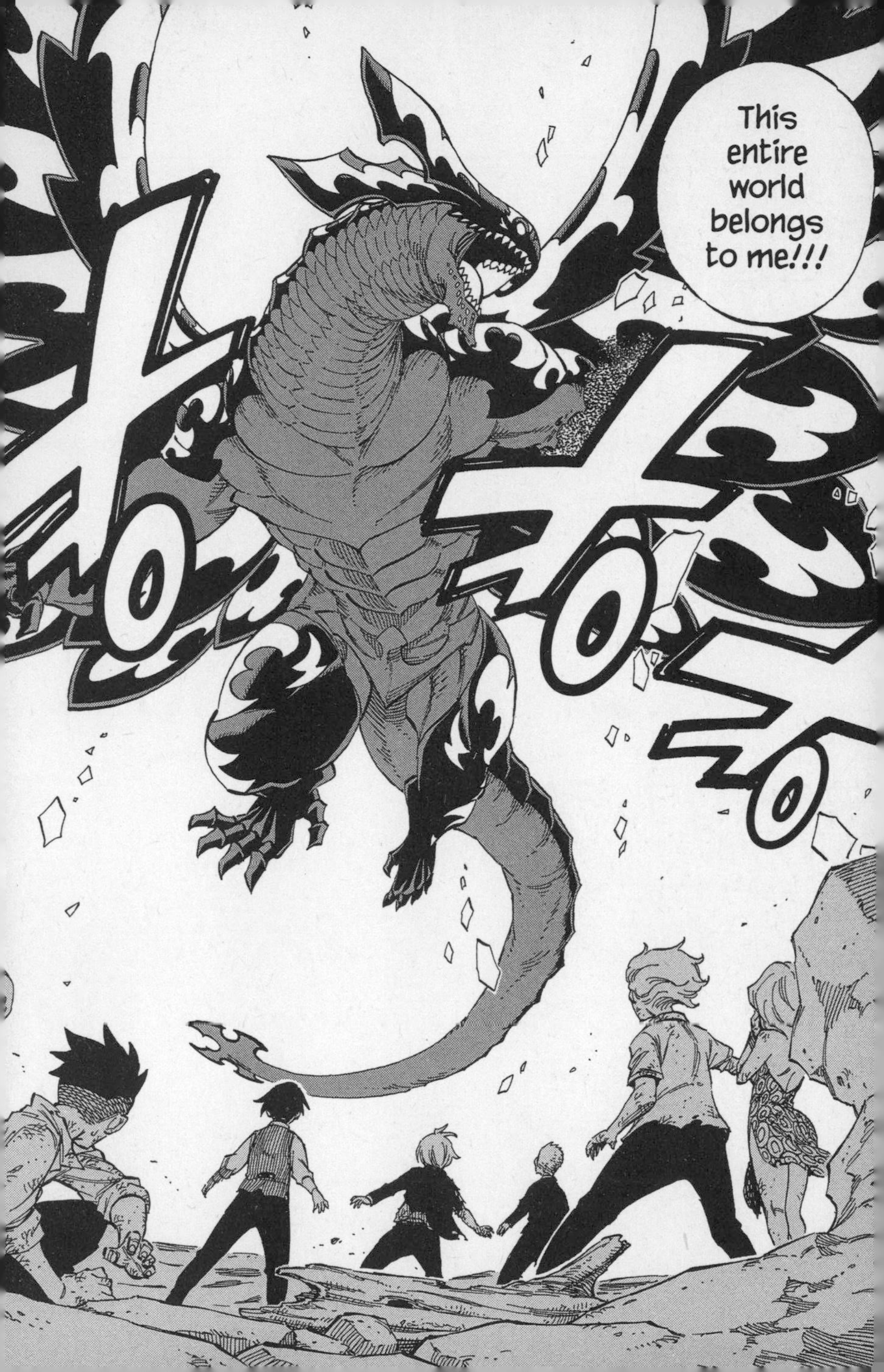
This entire world belongs to me!!!

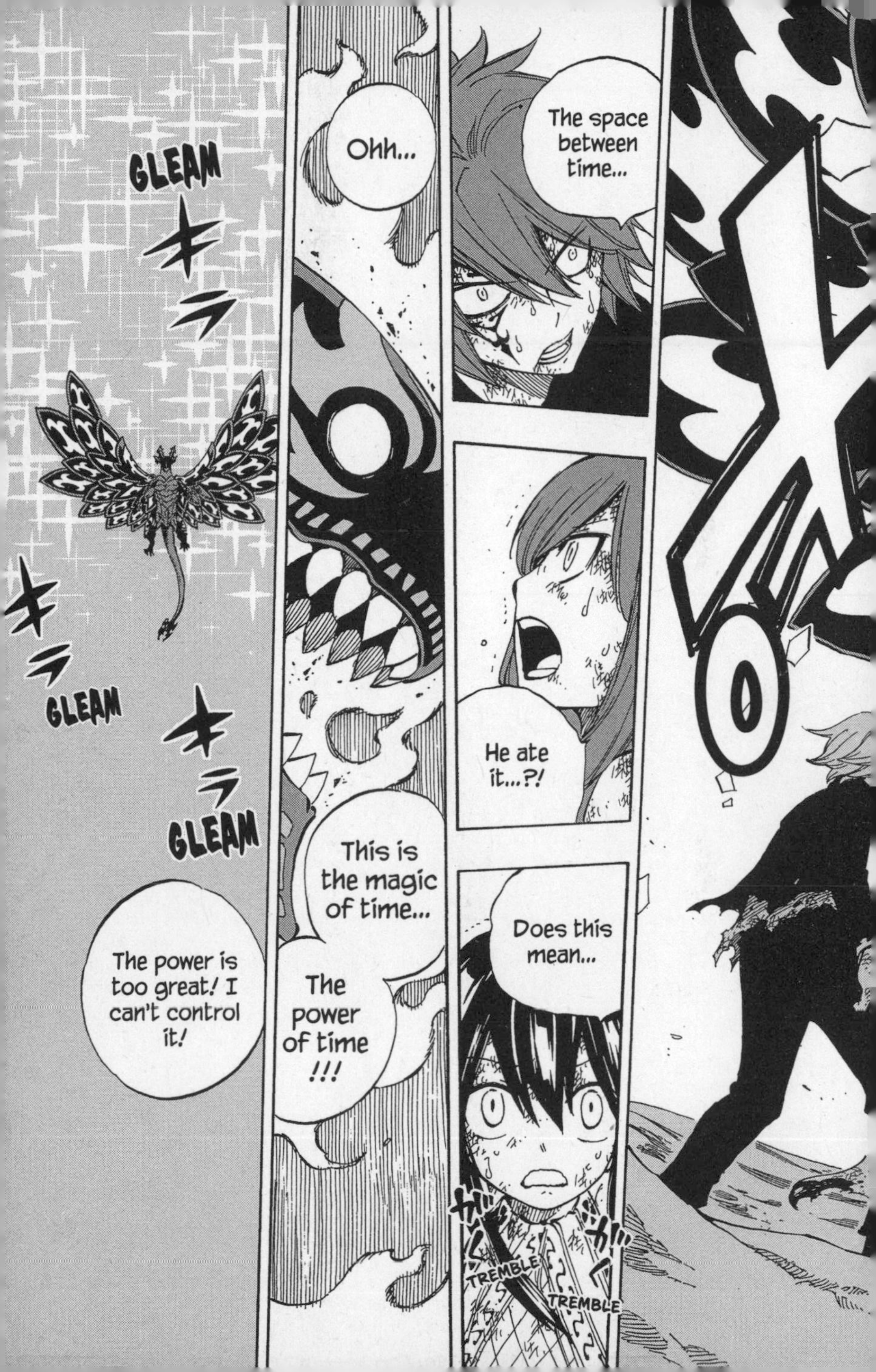
The space between time...
He ate it...?!
Does this mean...
TREMBLE
TREMBLE
Ohh...
This is the magic of time...
The power of time!!!
GLEAM
GLEAM
GLEAM
The power is too great! I can't control it!

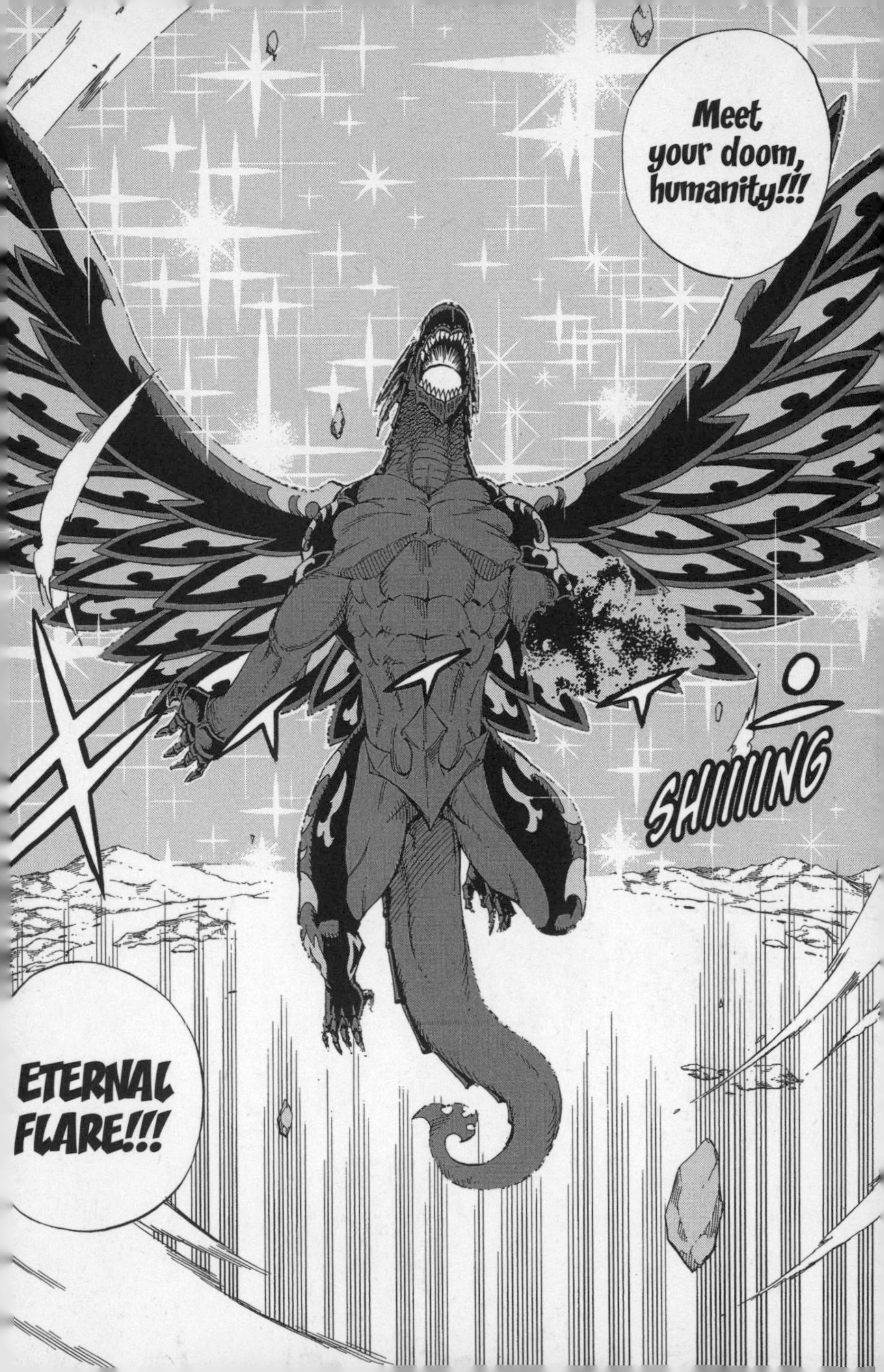
Meet your doom, humanity!!!
SHIIIING
ETERNAL FLARE!!!

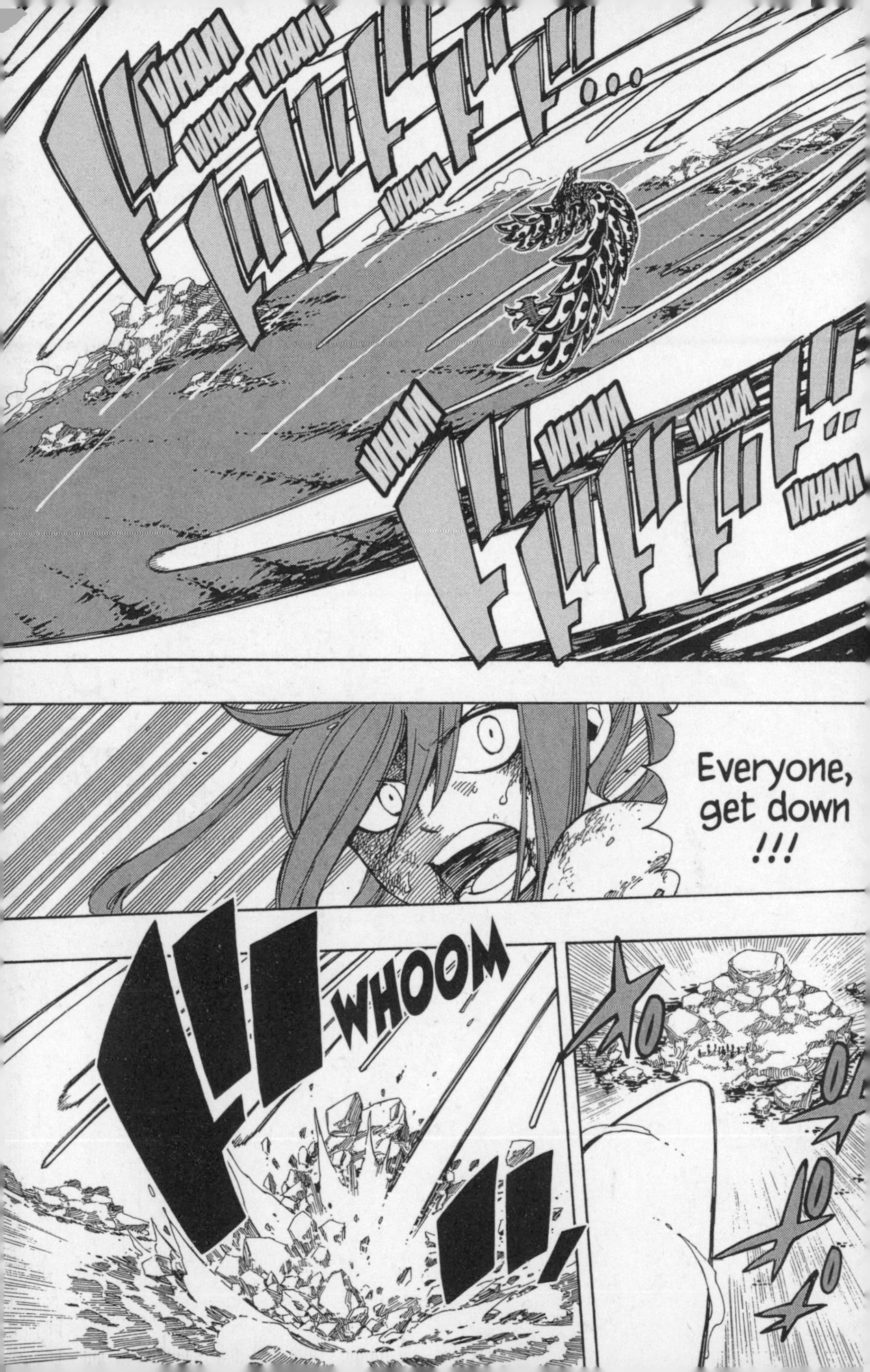
WHAM
WHAM
WHAM
WHAM
WHAM
WHAM
WHAM
WHAM
Everyone, get down !!!
WHOOM

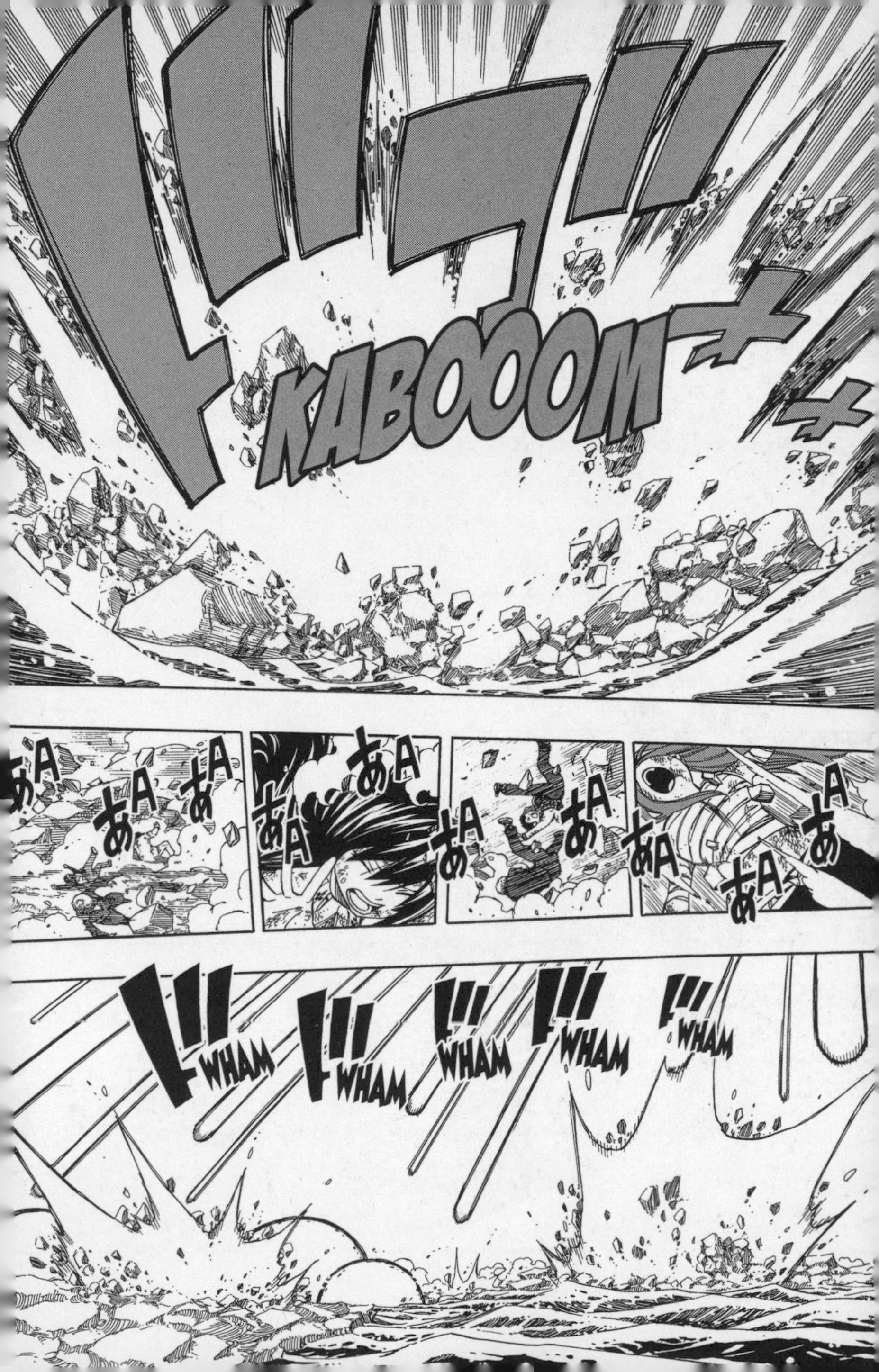
KABOOOM
あA あA
あA あA あA
あA あA
あA あA
WHAM
WHAM
WHAM
WHAM
WHAM

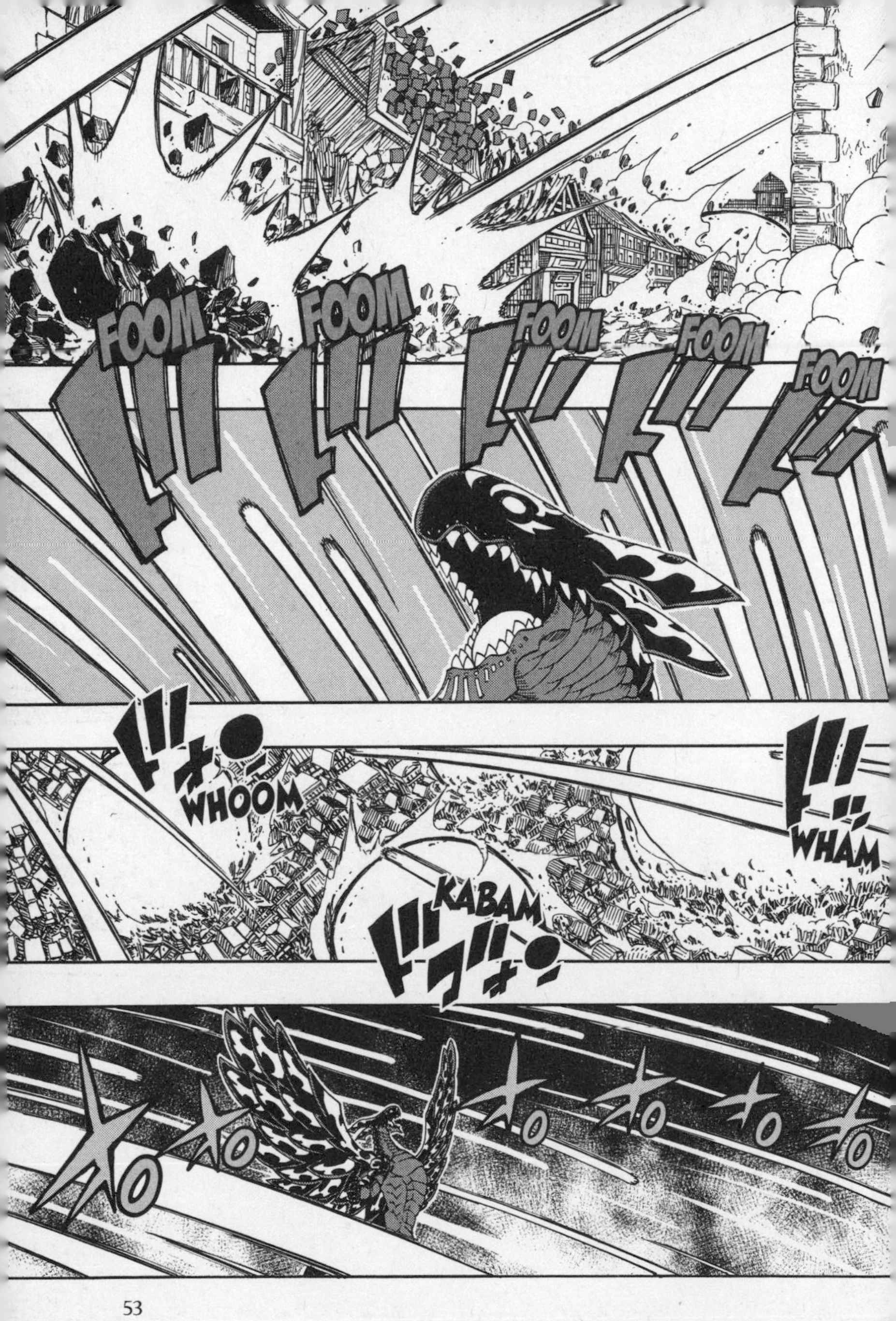
FOOM
FOOM
FOOM
FOOM
FOOM
WHAM
KABAM
WHOOM

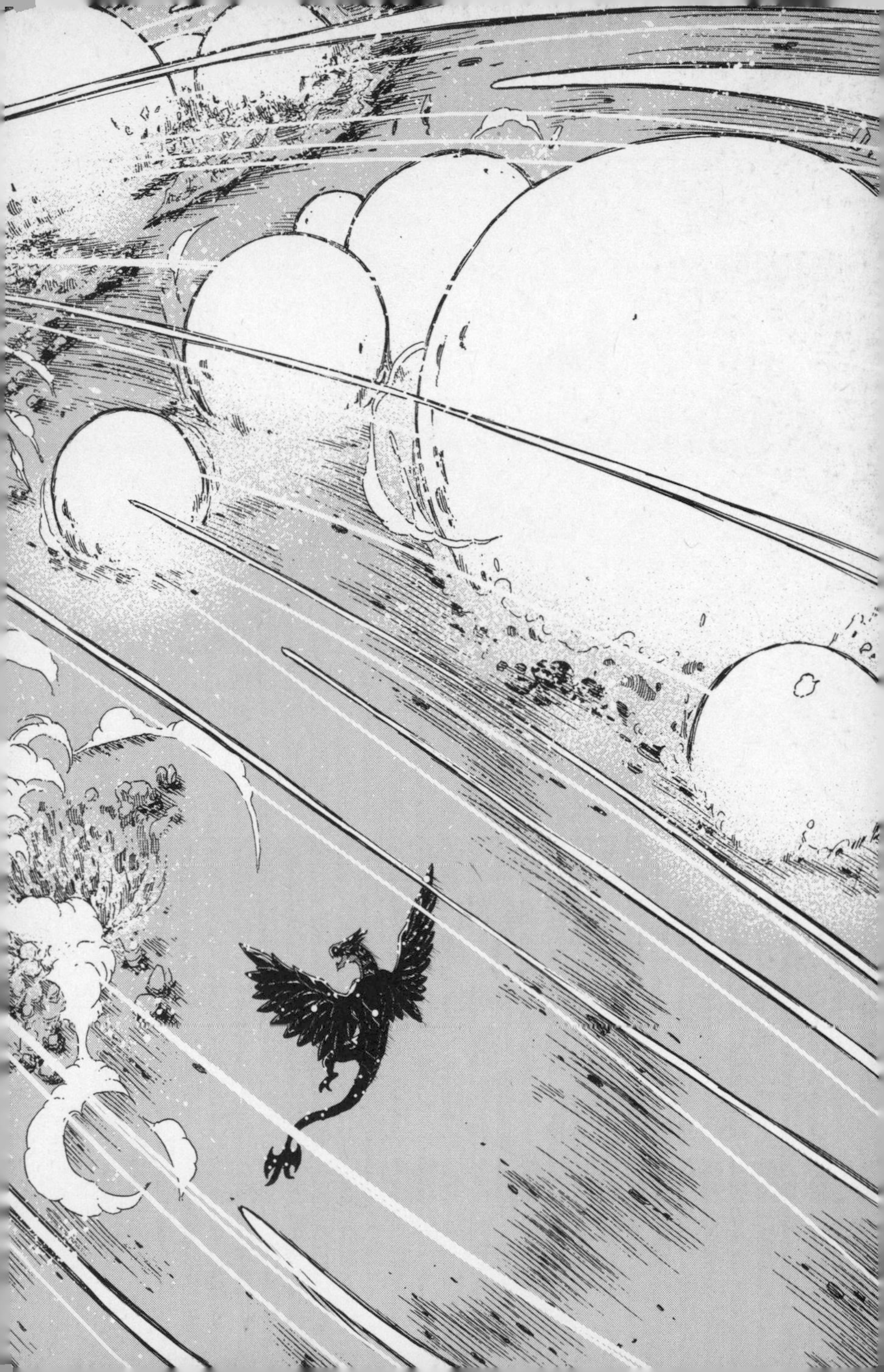

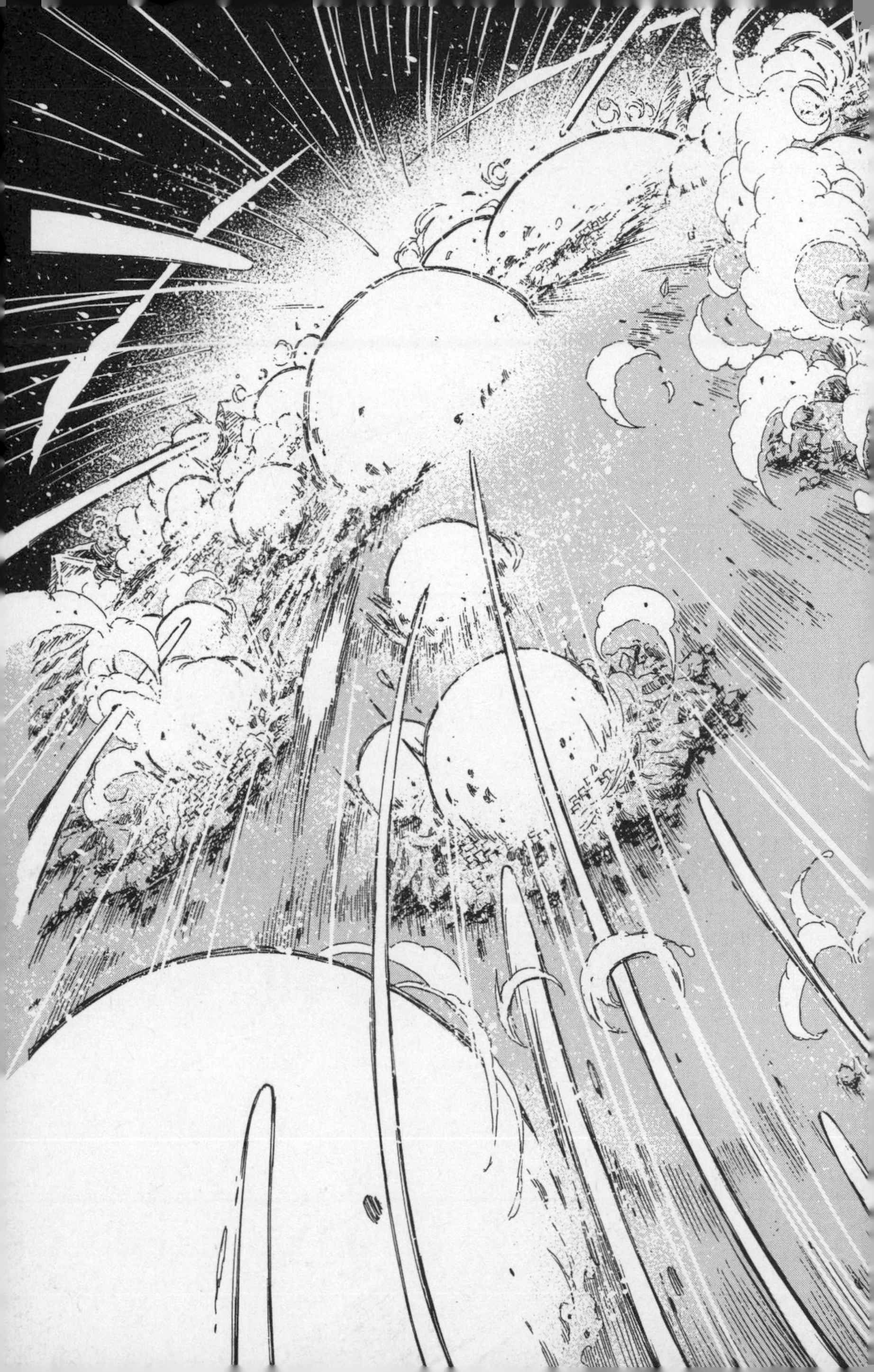

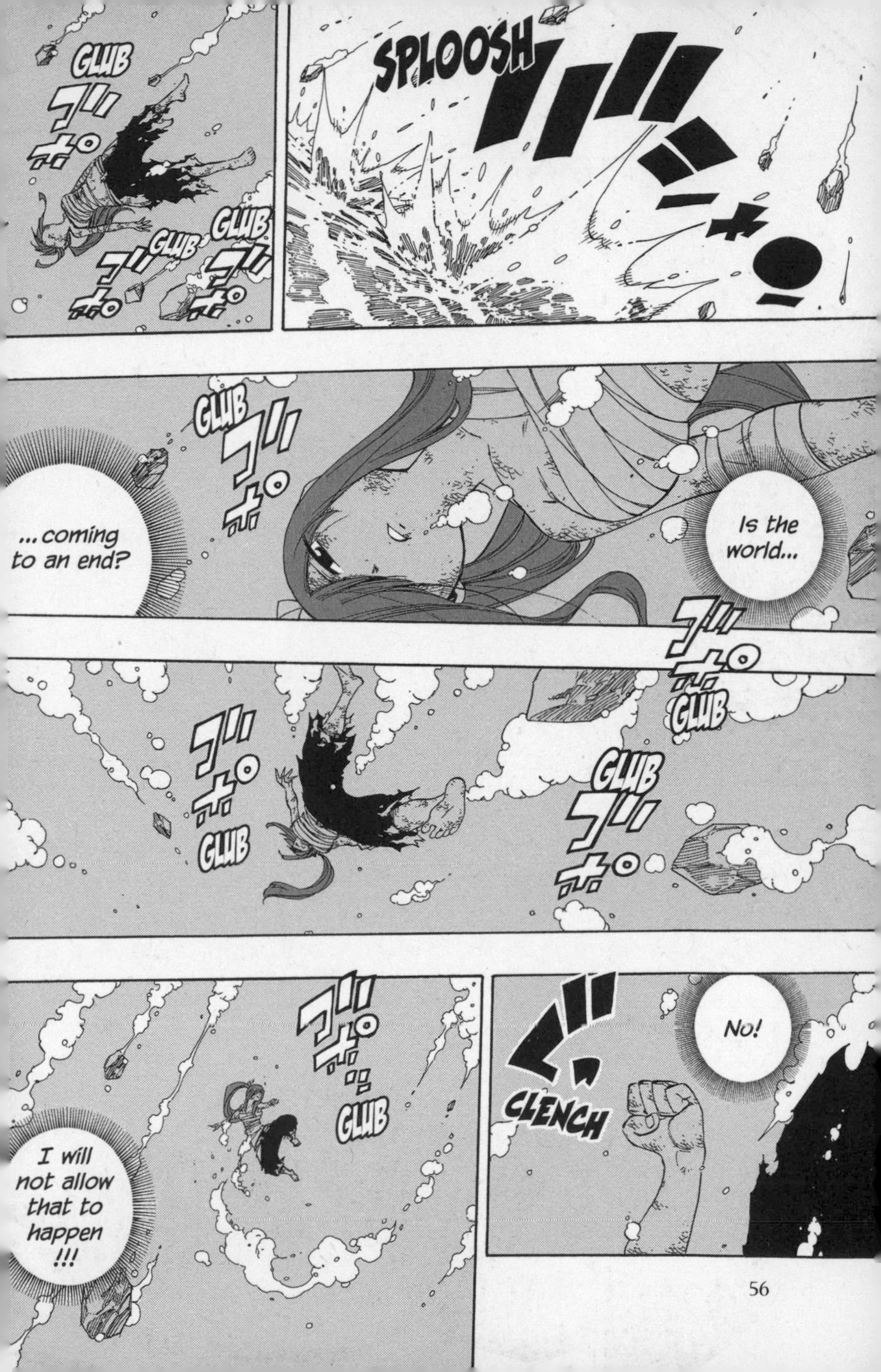
SPLOOSH
GLUB
GLUB
GLUB
Is the world...
GLUB
...coming to an end?
GLUB
GLUB
GLUB
No!
CLENCH
GLUB
I will not allow that to happen !!!

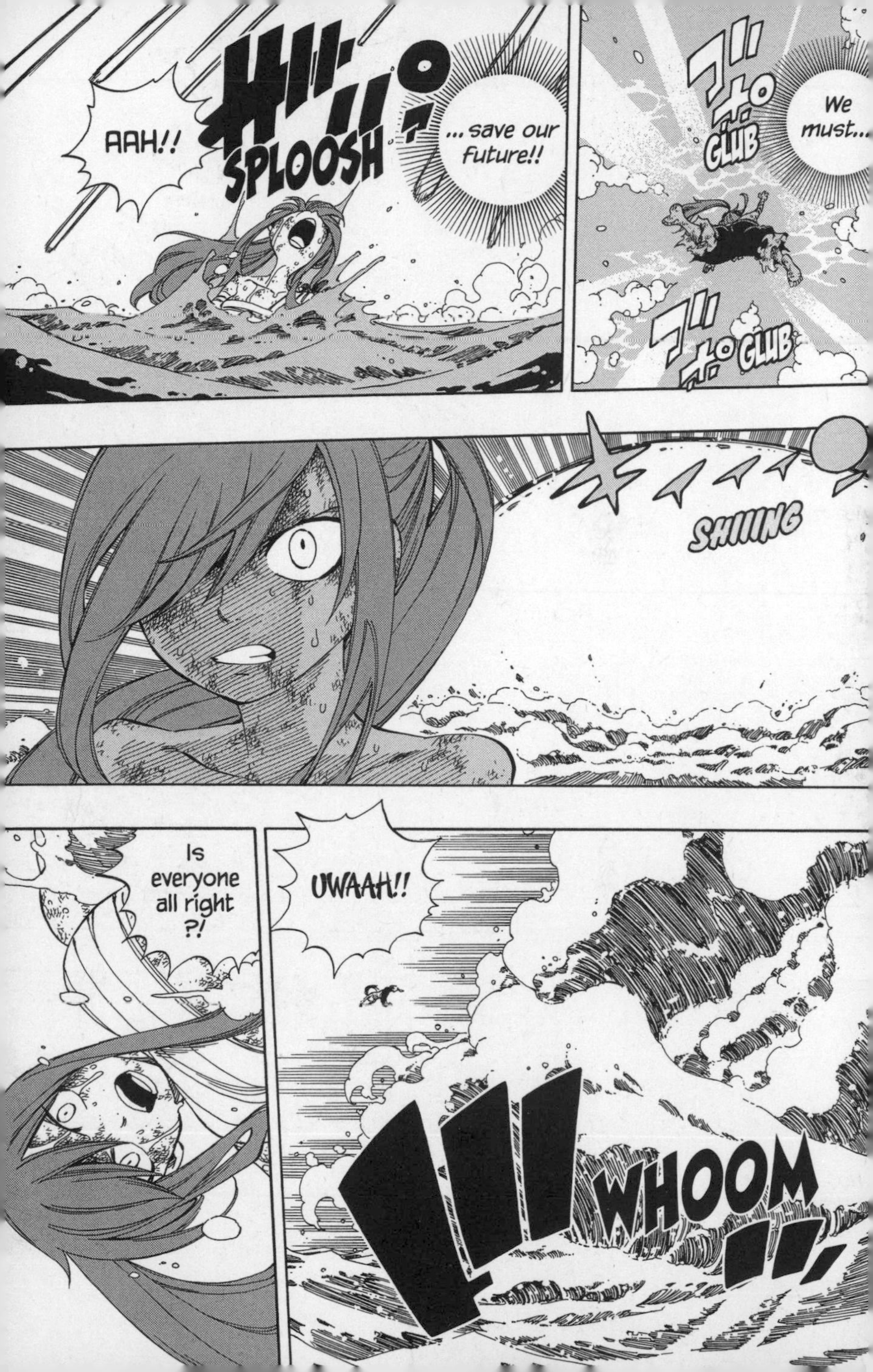
We must...
GLUB
GLUB
...save our future!!
SPLOOSH
AAH!!
SHIIING
UWAAH!!
WHOOM
Is everyone all right?!

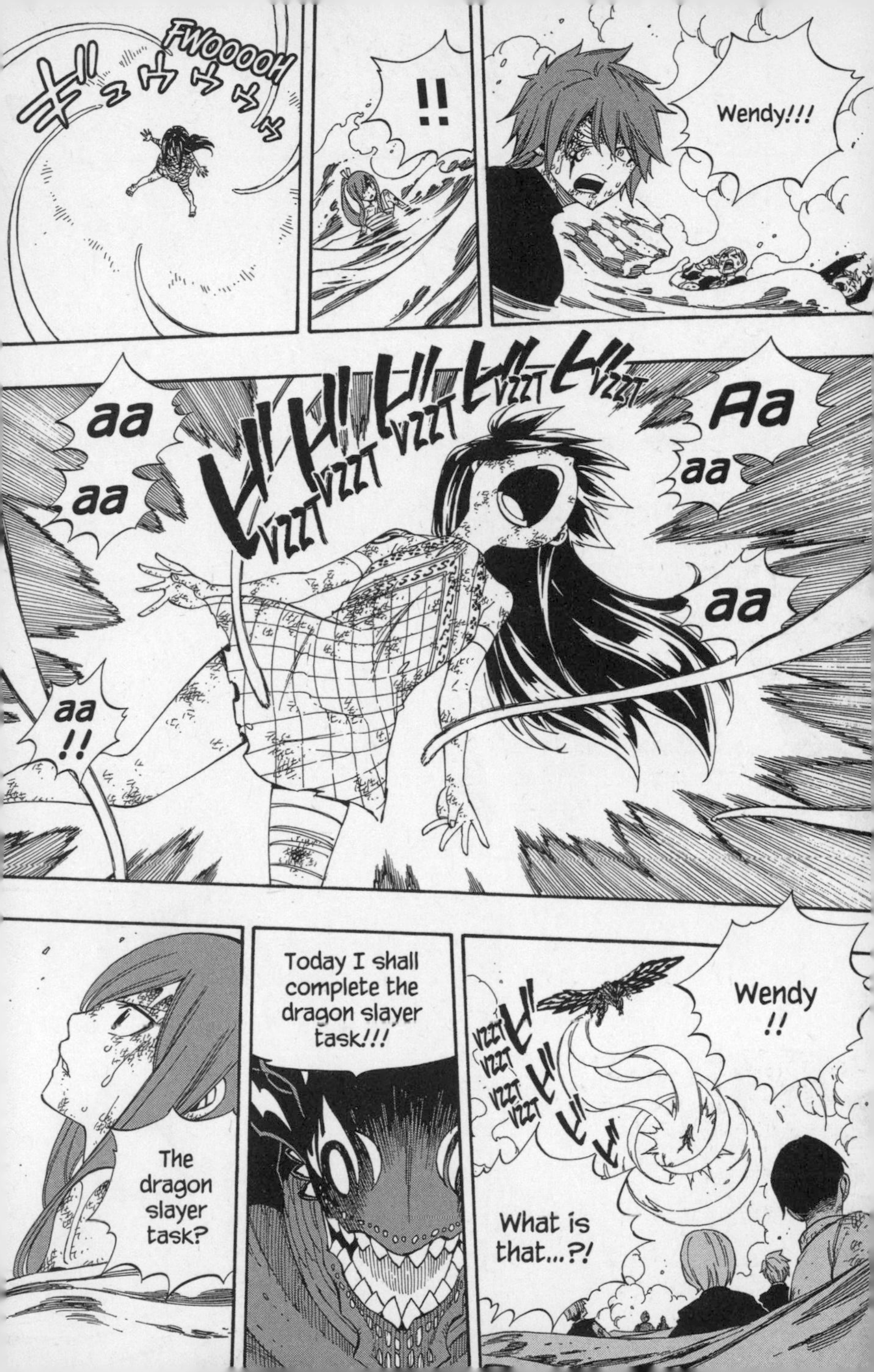
Wendy!!!
!!
FWOOOOH
Aa
aa
VZZT VZZT VZZT VZZT VZZT VZZT
aa
aa
aa
aa
!!
Wendy
!!
VZZT
VZZT
VZZT
VZZT
What is that...?!
Today I shall complete the dragon slayer task!!!
The dragon slayer task?

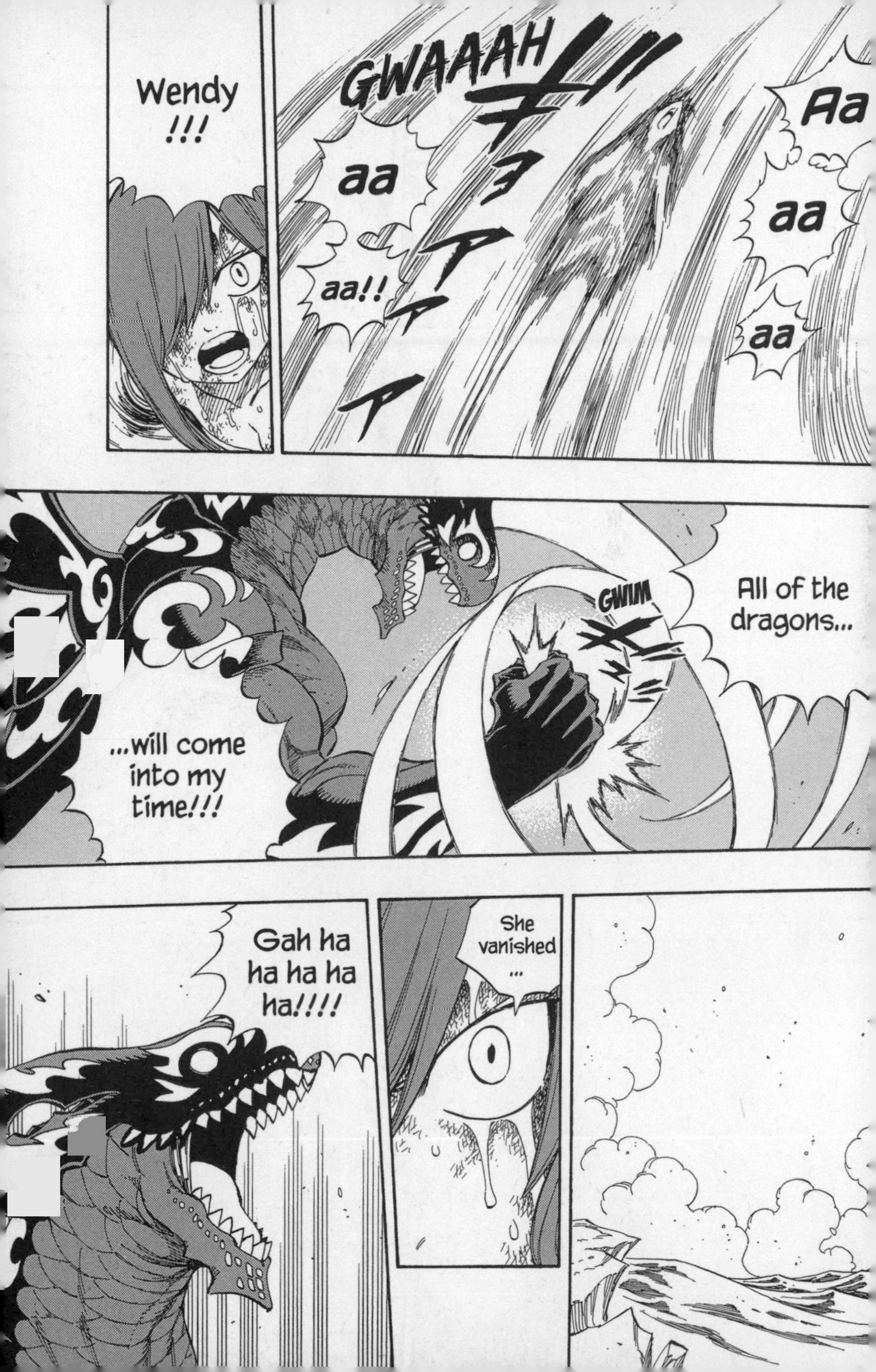
Aa
aa
aa
GWAAAH
aa
aa!!
Wendy !!!
All of the dragons...
GWIM
...will come into my time!!!
She vanished ...
Gah ha ha ha ha ha!!!!

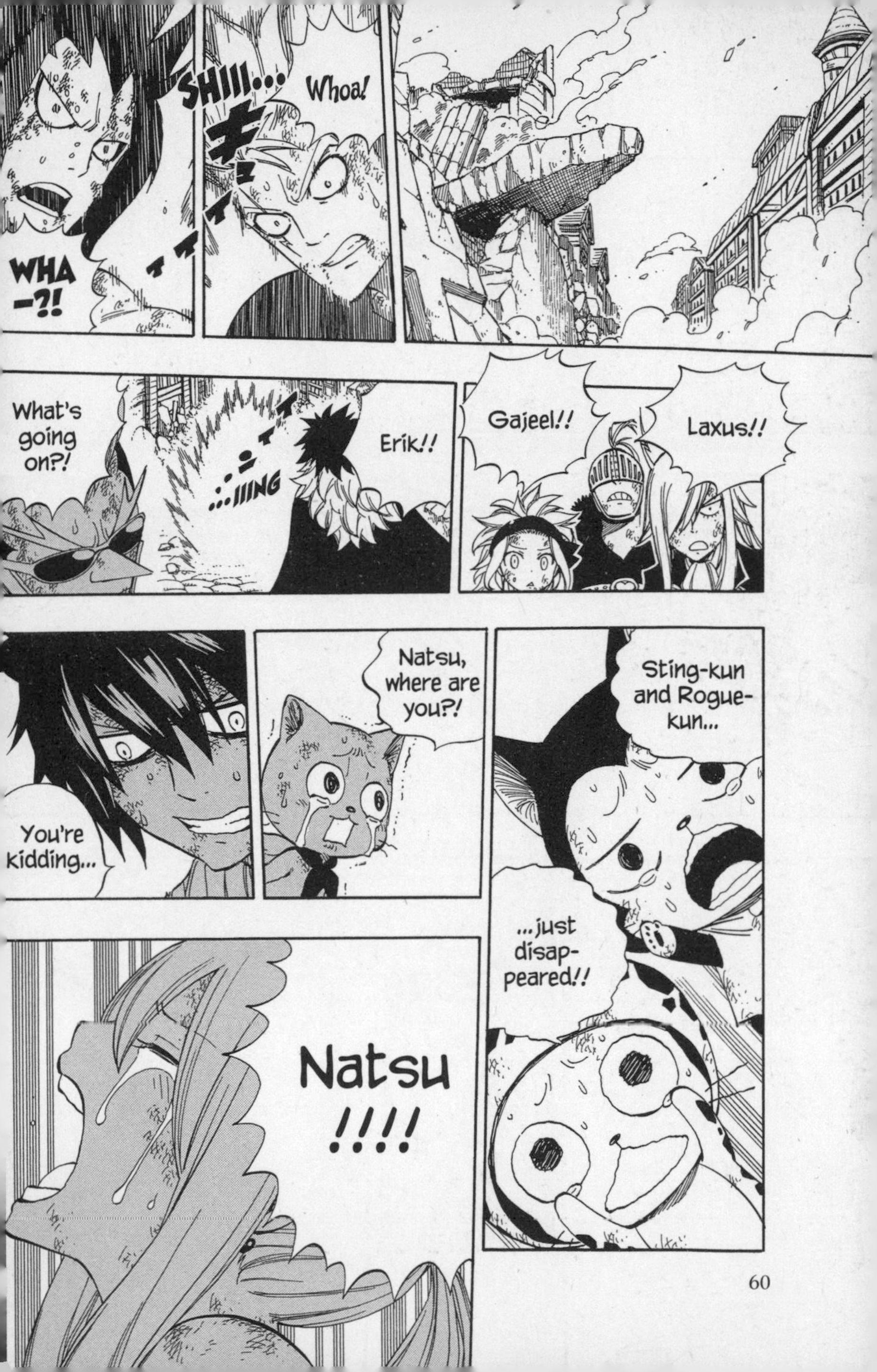

Whoa!
SHIII...
WHA-?!
Laxus!!
Gajeel!!
Erik!!
...IIING
What's going on?!
Sting-kun and Rogue-kun...
...just disappeared!!
Natsu, where are you?!
You're kidding...
Natsu !!!!

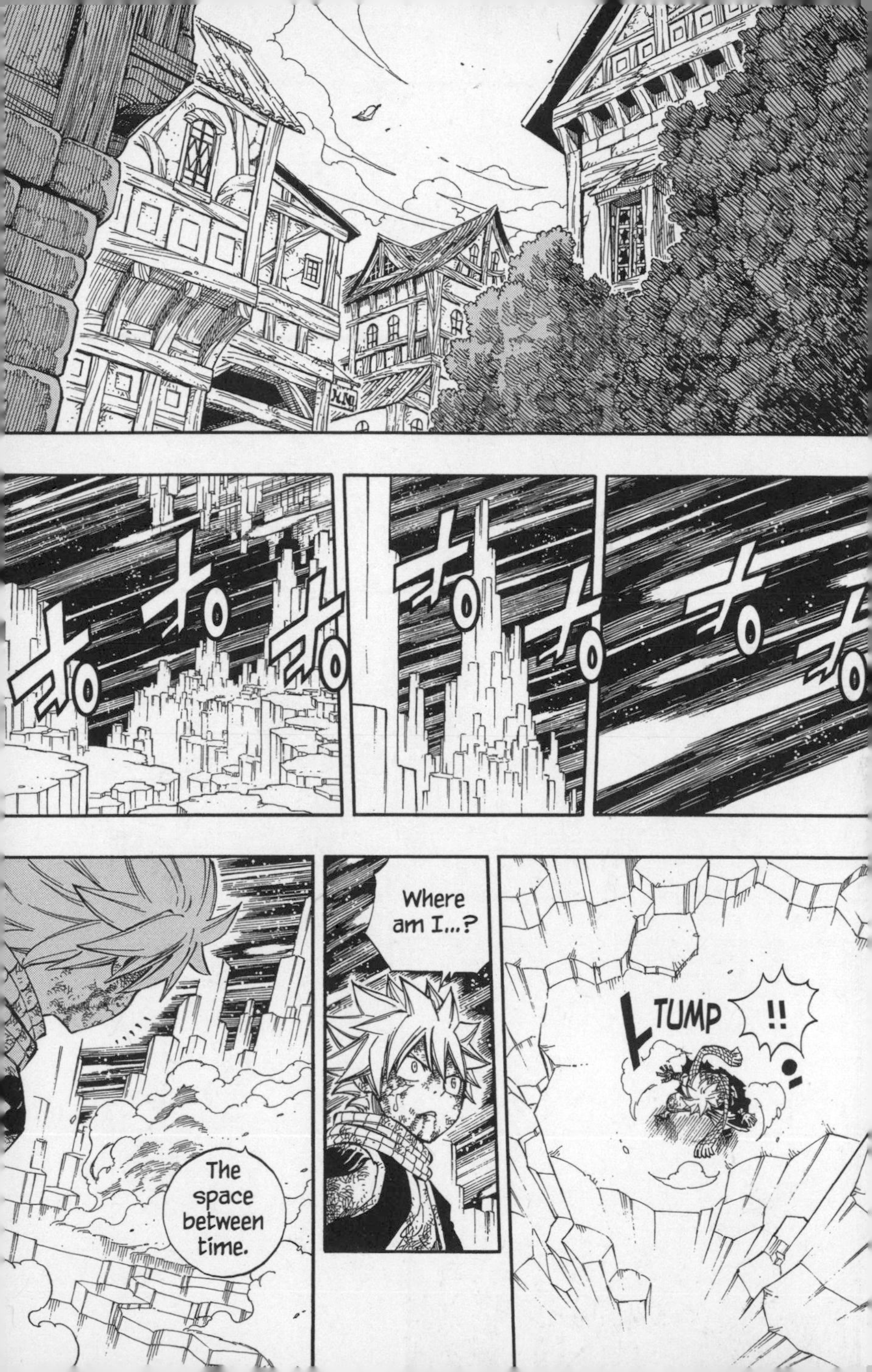
TUMP
!!
Where am I...?
...
The space between time.

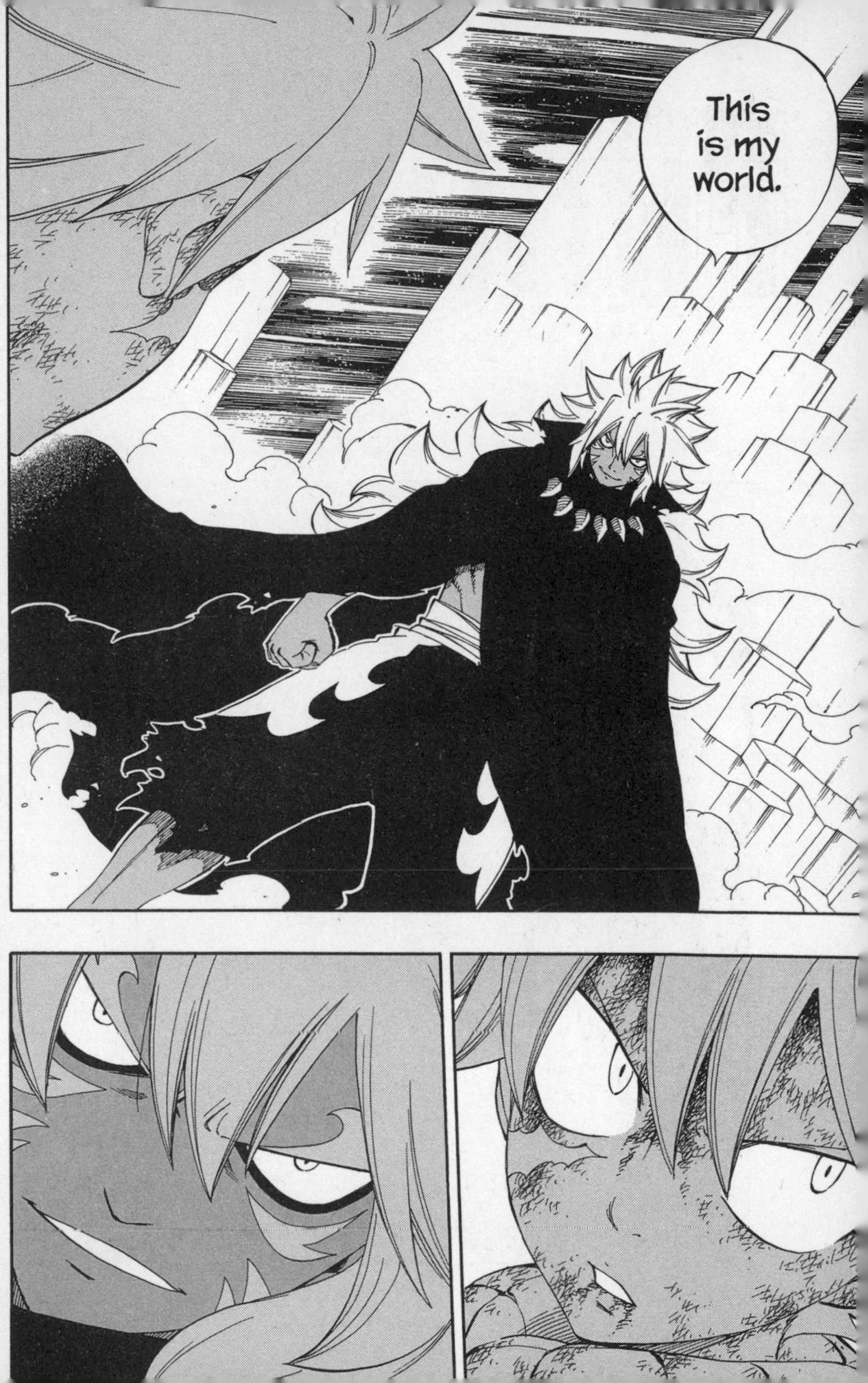
This is my world.

FAIRY TAIL

フェアリーテイル

Chapter 540: Balance

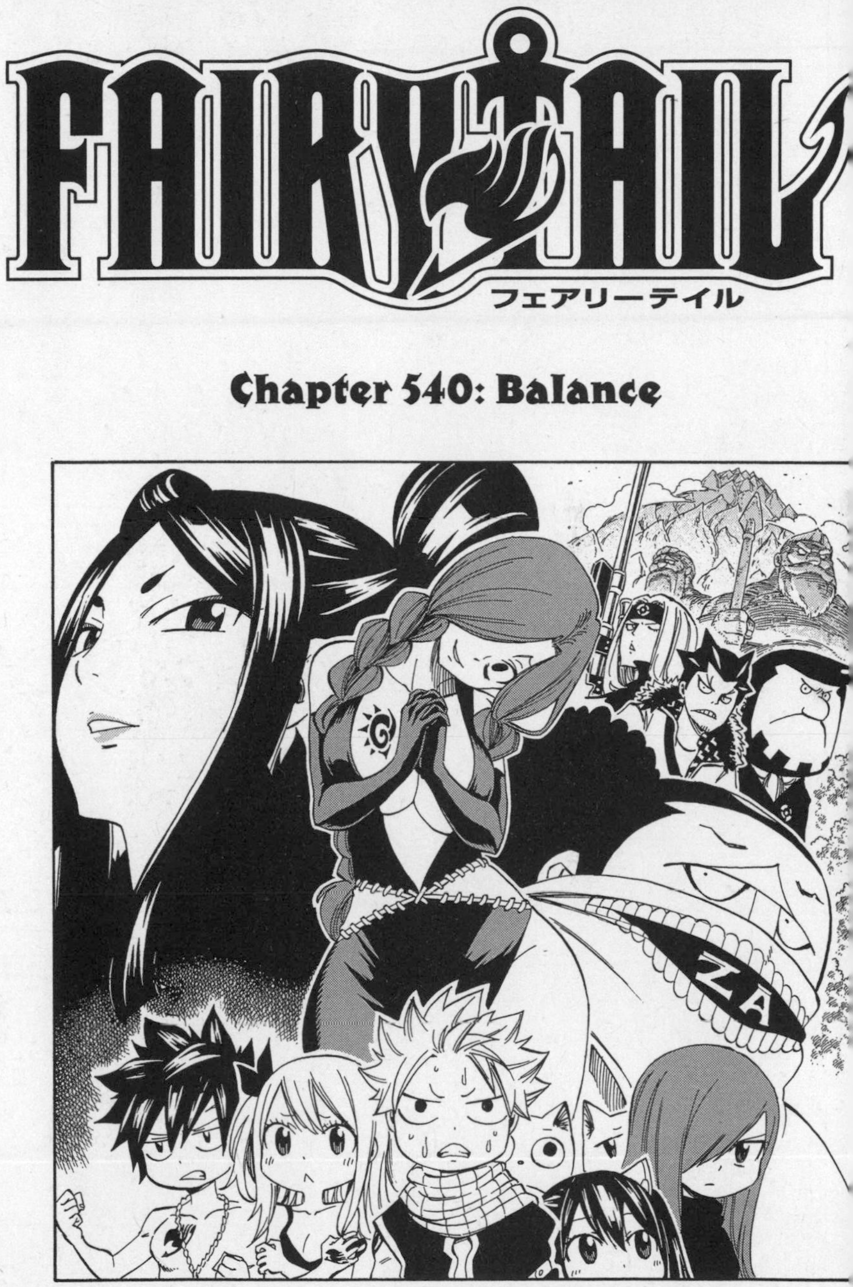

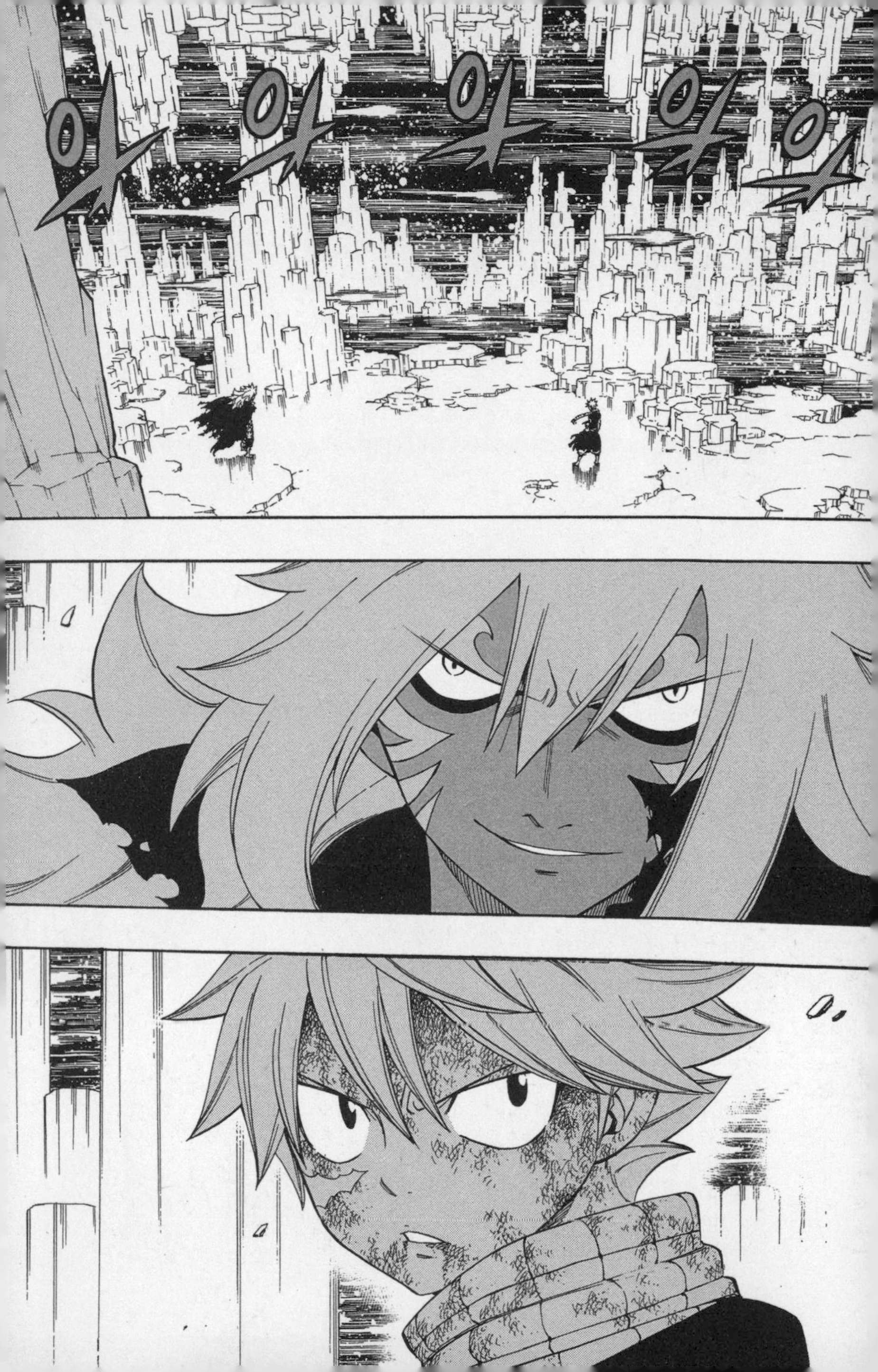

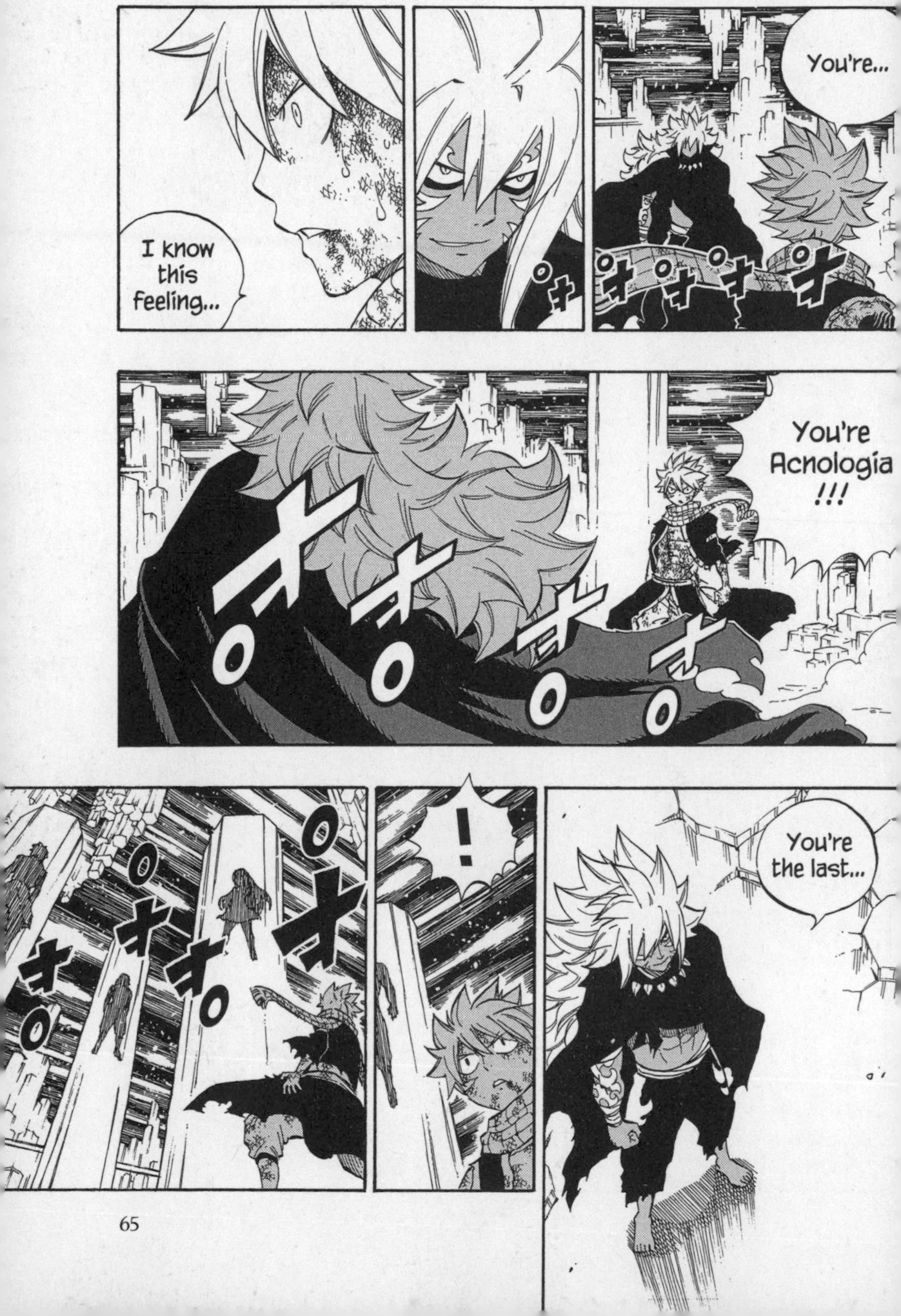
You're...
I know this feeling...
You're Acnologia !!!
You're the last...
!

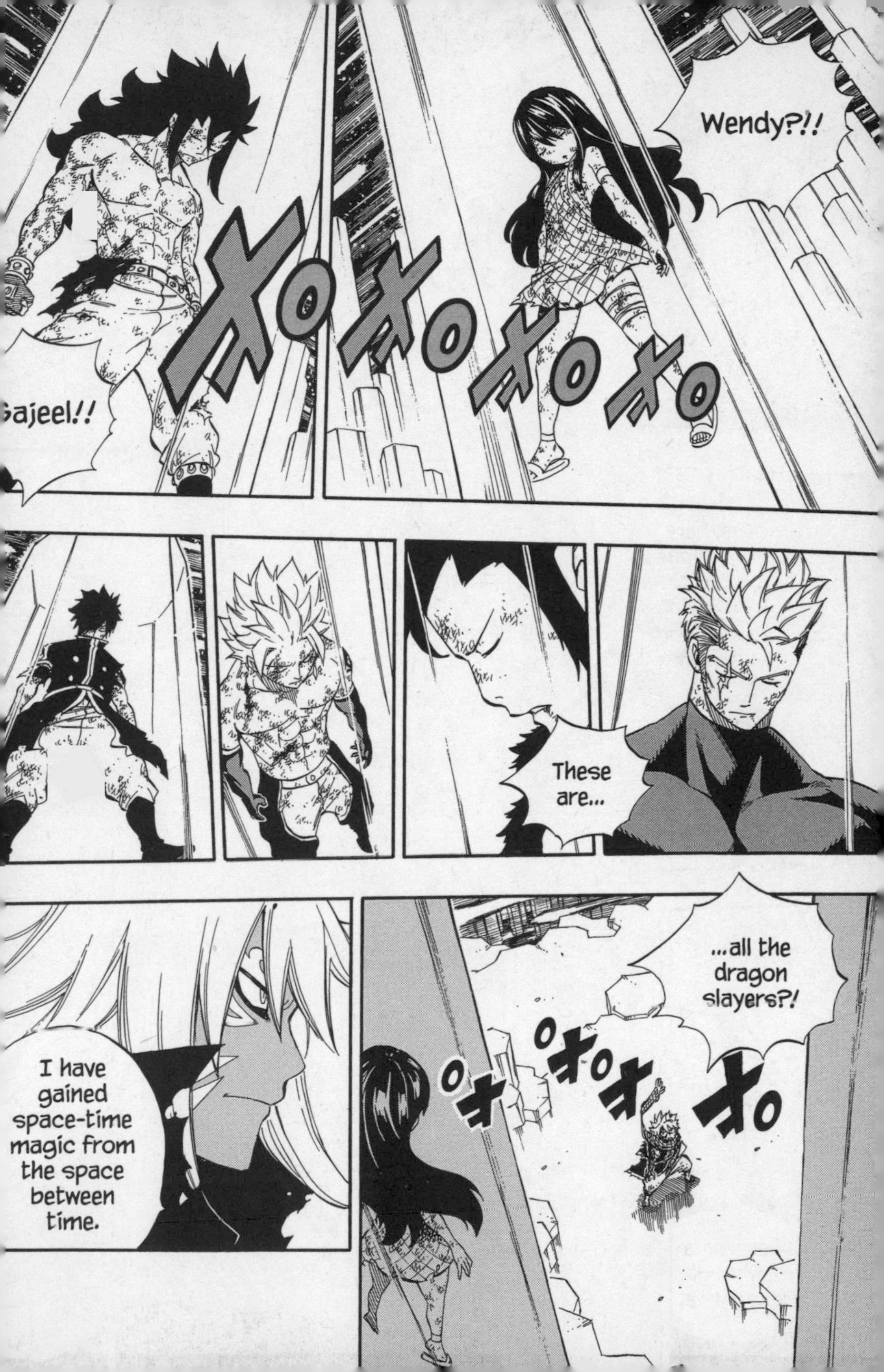
Wendy?!!
Gajeel!!
These are...
...all the dragon slayers?!
I have gained space-time magic from the space between time.

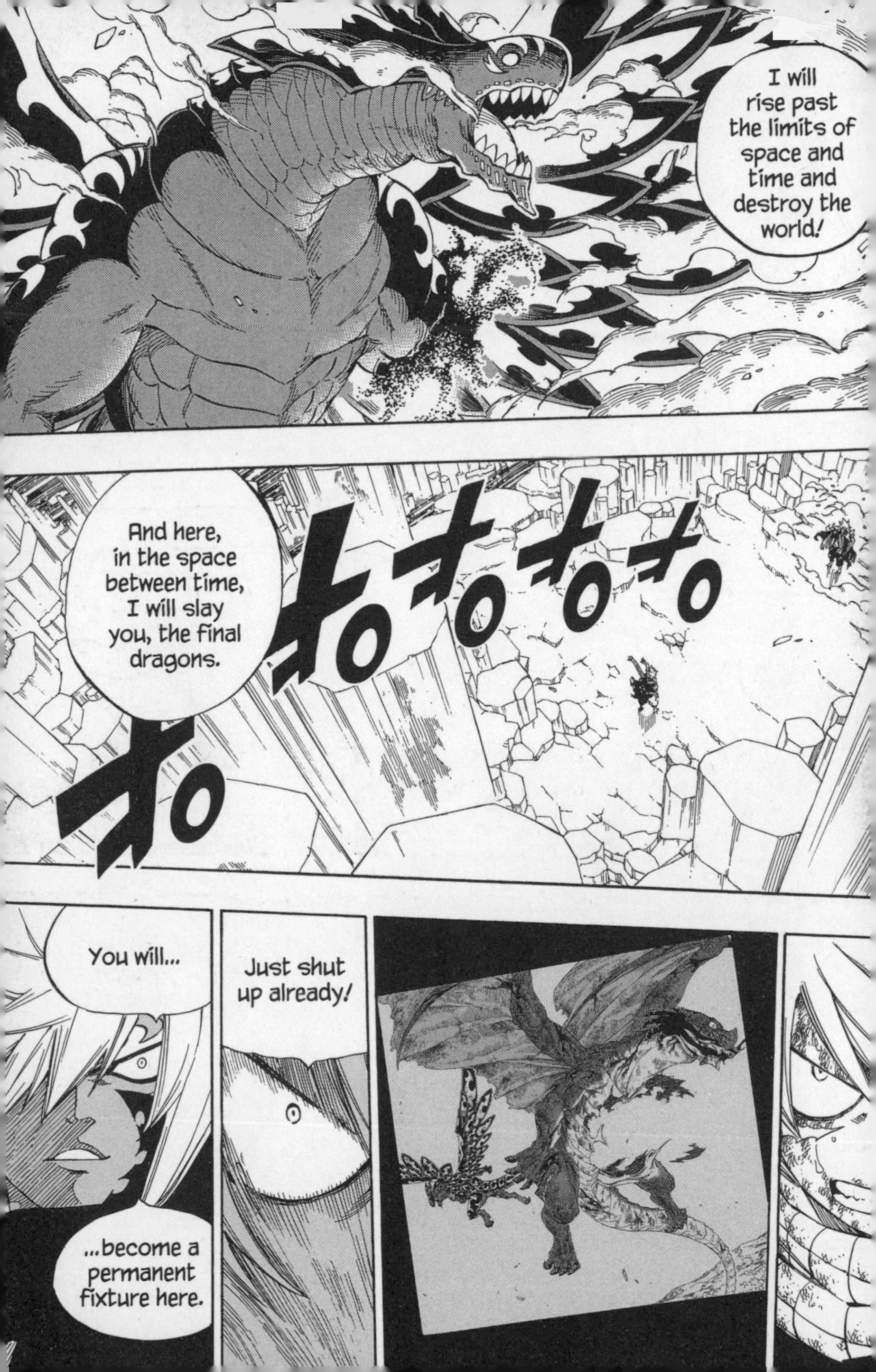
I will rise past the limits of space and time and destroy the world!
And here, in the space between time, I will slay you, the final dragons.
Just shut up already!
You will...
...become a permanent fixture here.

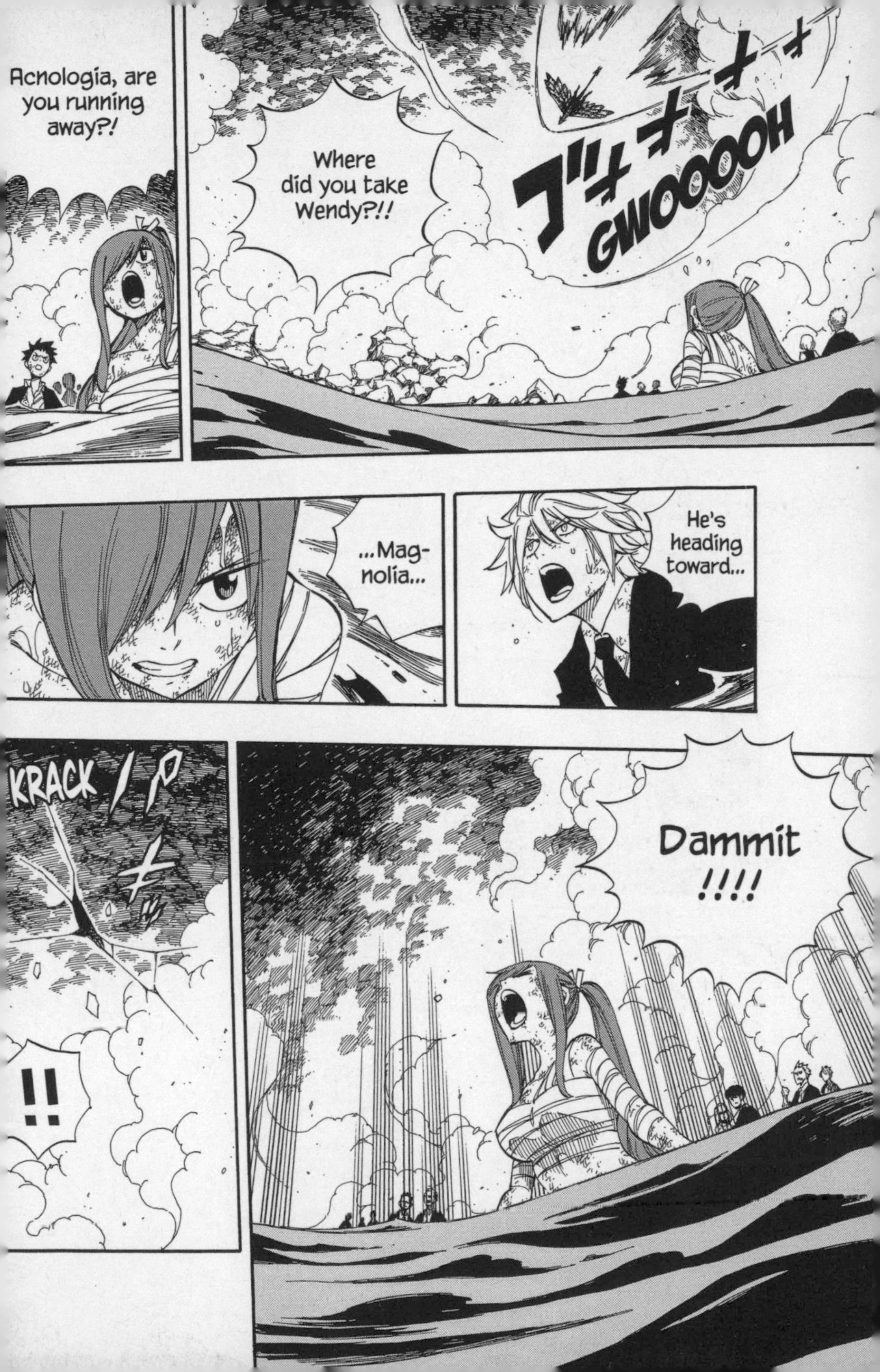
GWOOOOH
Where did you take Wendy?!!
Acnologia, are you running away?!
He's heading toward...
...Mag-nolia...
Dammit!!!!
KRACK
!!

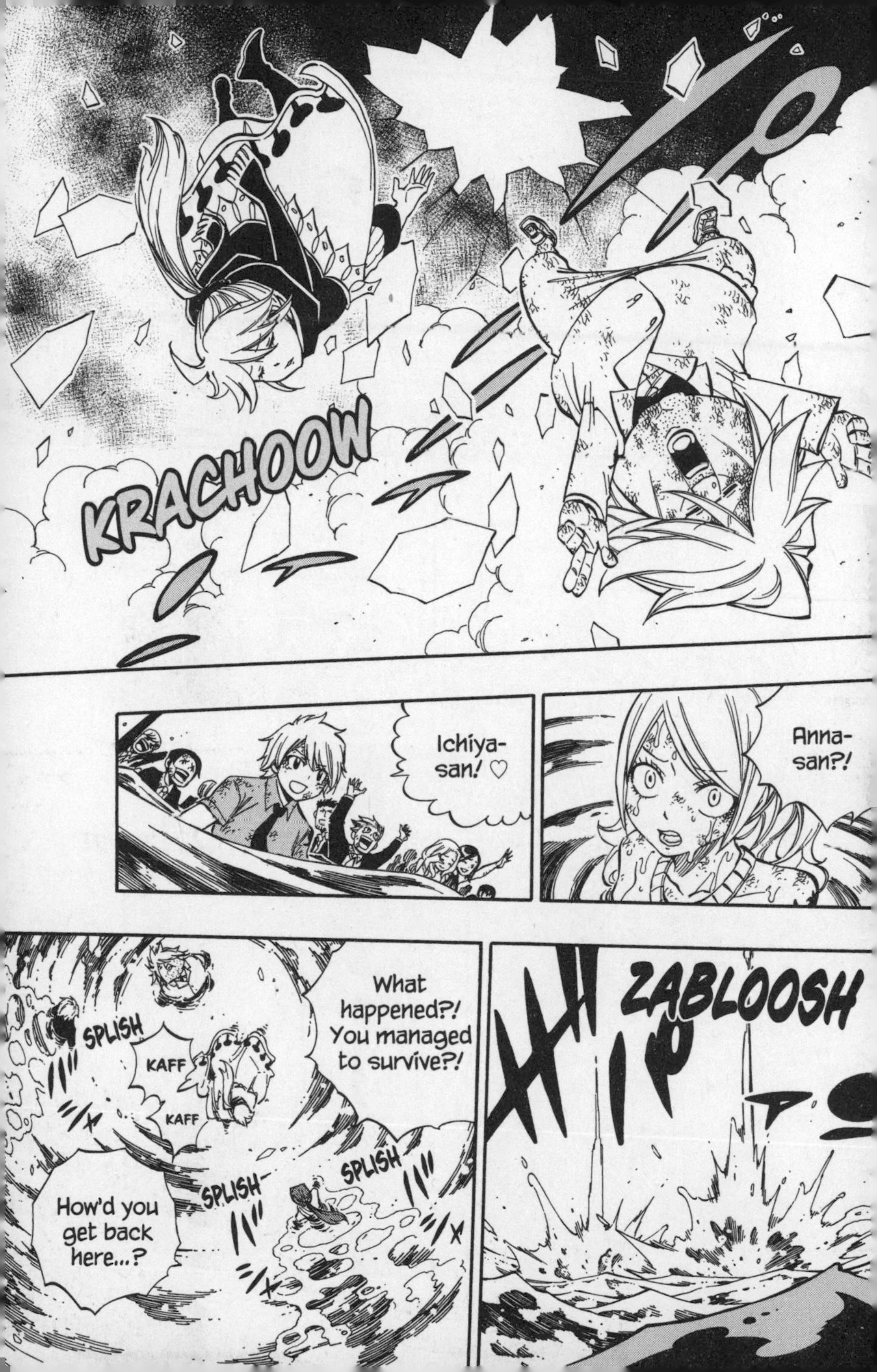
KRACHOOW
Anna-san?!
Ichiya-san! ♡
ZABLOOSH
What happened?! You managed to survive?!
SPLISH
KAFF
KAFF
SPLISH
SPLISH
How'd you get back here...?

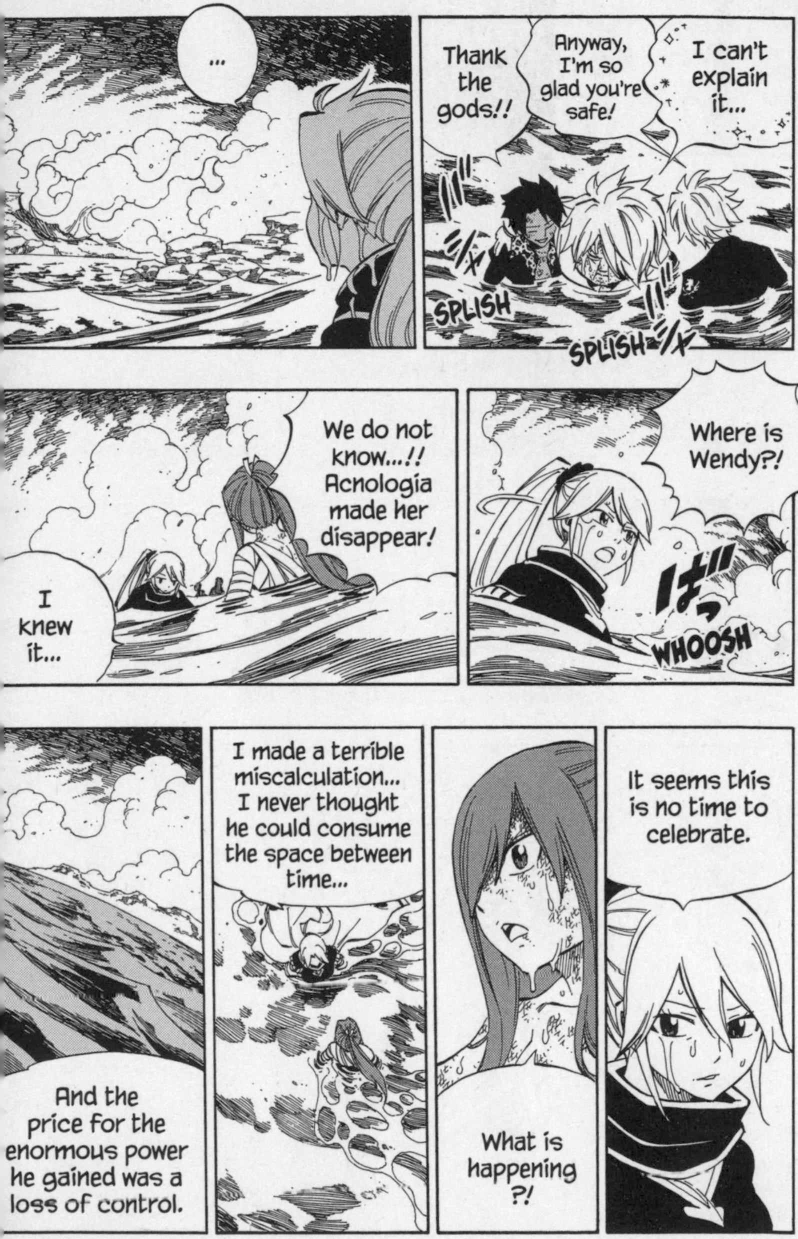
I can't explain it...
Anyway, I'm so glad you're safe!
Thank the gods!!
SPLISH
SPLISH
...
Where is Wendy?!
ばっ
WHOOSH
We do not know...!! Acnologia made her disappear!
I knew it...
It seems this is no time to celebrate.
What is happening ?!
I made a terrible miscalculation... I never thought he could consume the space between time...
And the price for the enormous power he gained was a loss of control.

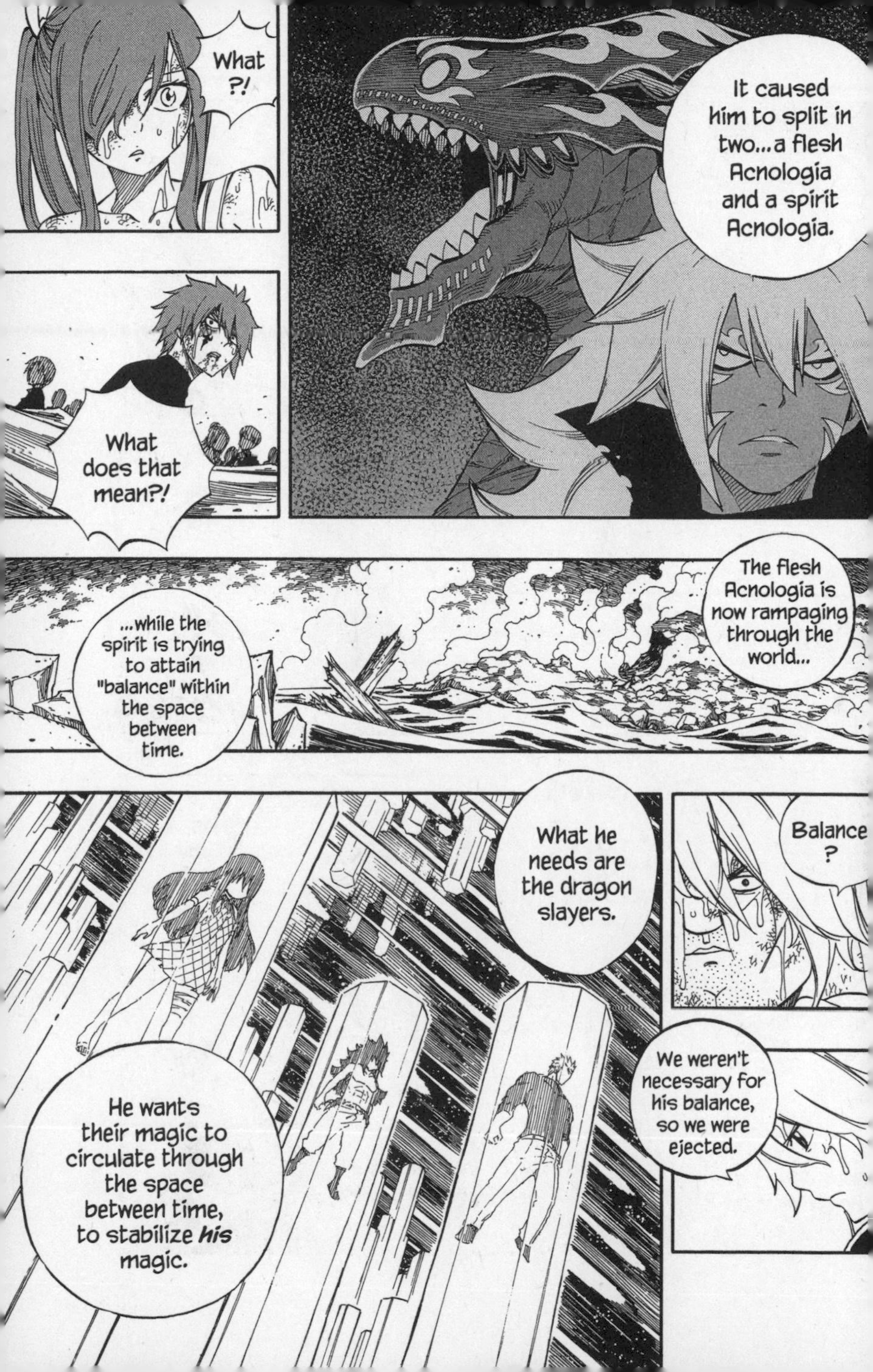
It caused him to split in two...a flesh Acnologia and a spirit Acnologia.
What ?!
What does that mean?!
The flesh Acnologia is now rampaging through the world...
...while the spirit is trying to attain "balance" within the space between time.
Balance ?
We weren't necessary for his balance, so we were ejected.
What he needs are the dragon slayers.
He wants their magic to circulate through the space between time, to stabilize *his* magic.

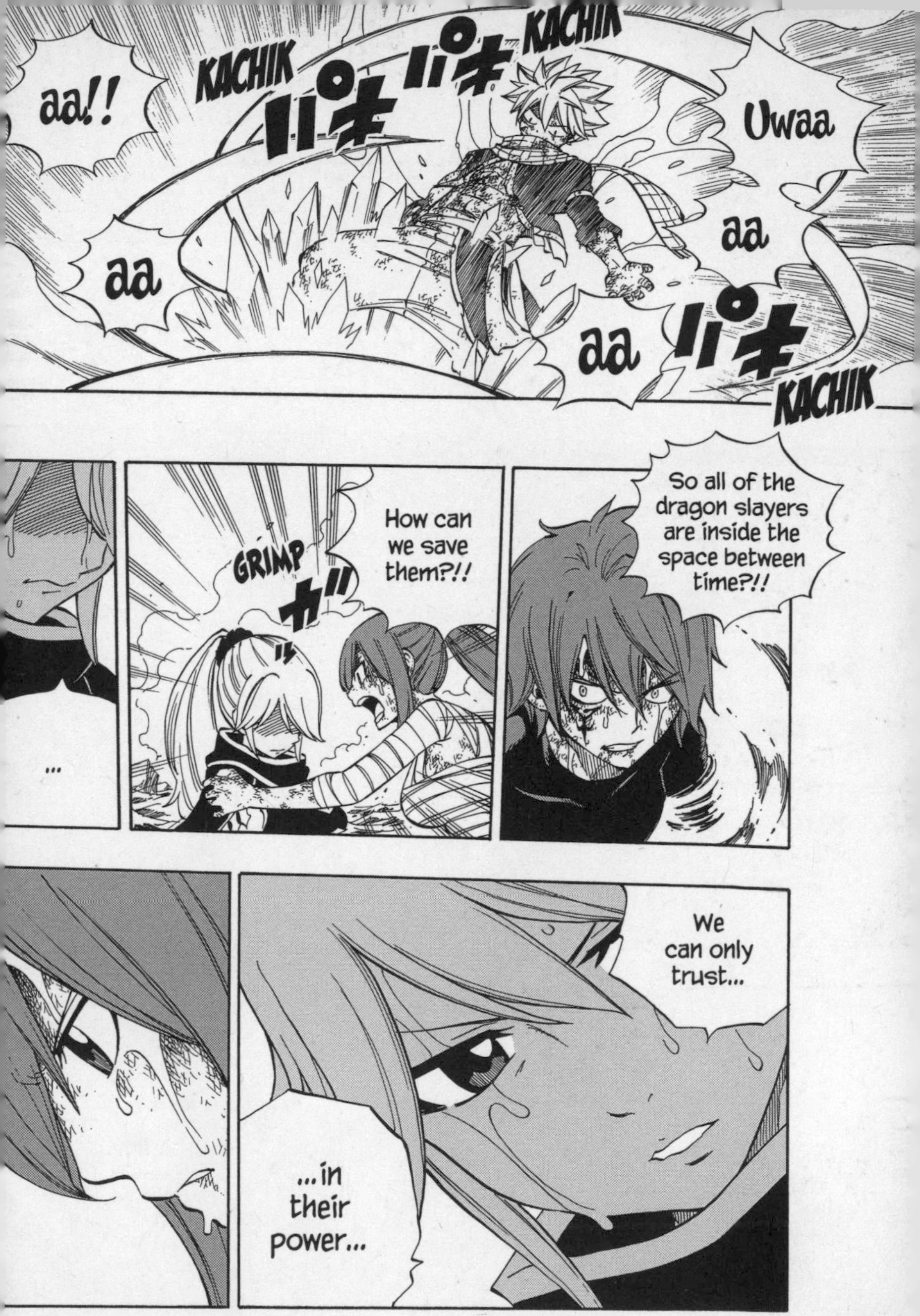
Uwaa
aa
KACHIK
パキ
aa
パキパキ
KACHIK
KACHIK
aa!!
aa
So all of the dragon slayers are inside the space between time?!!
How can we save them?!!
GRIMP
ガッ
...
We can only trust...
...in their power...

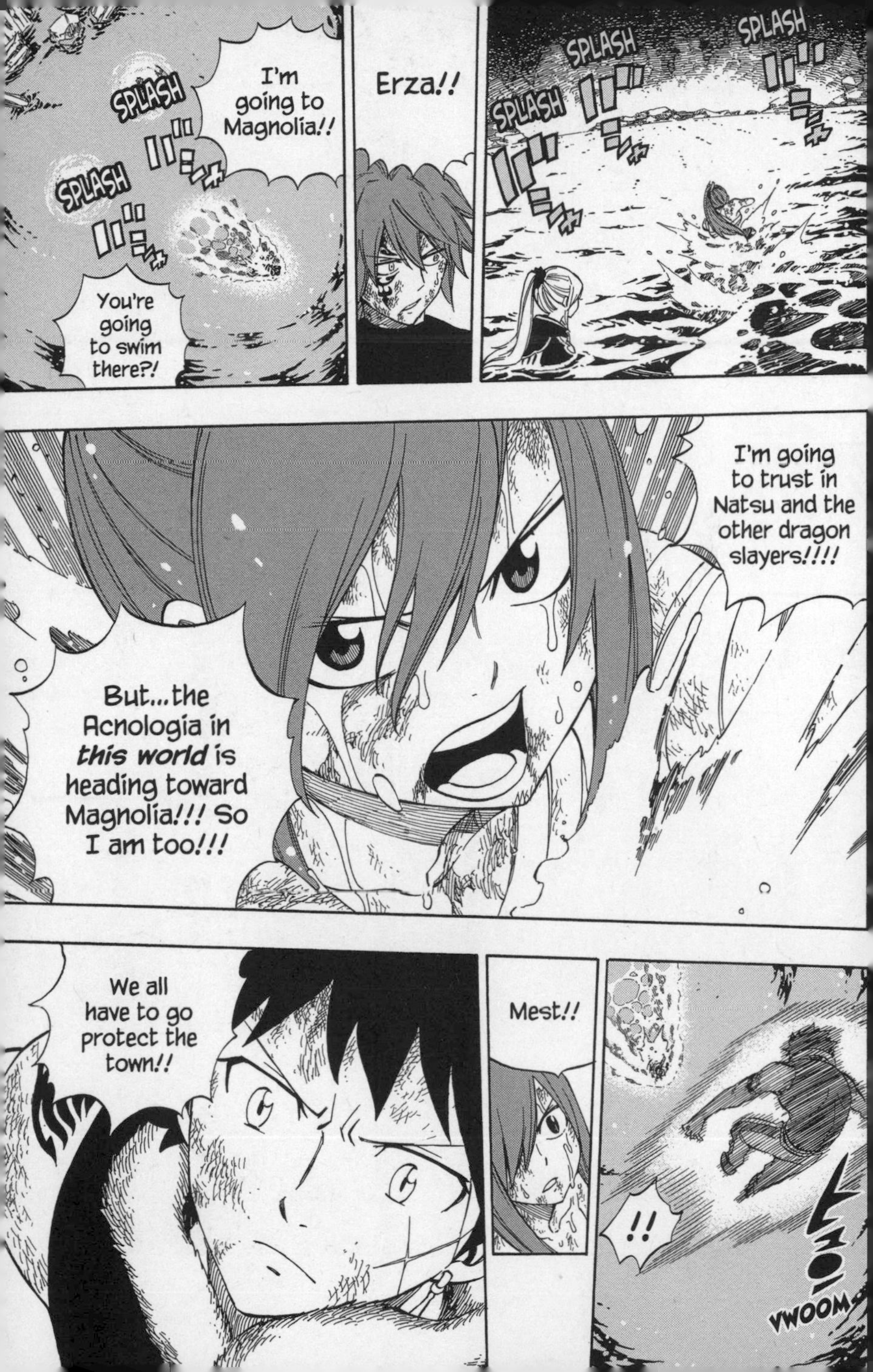
SPLASH
SPLASH
SPLASH
Erza!!
I'm going to Magnolia!!
SPLASH
SPLASH
You're going to swim there?!
I'm going to trust in Natsu and the other dragon slayers!!!!
But...the Acnologia in ***this world*** is heading toward Magnolia!!! So I am too!!!
!!
VWOOM
Mest!!
We all have to go protect the town!!

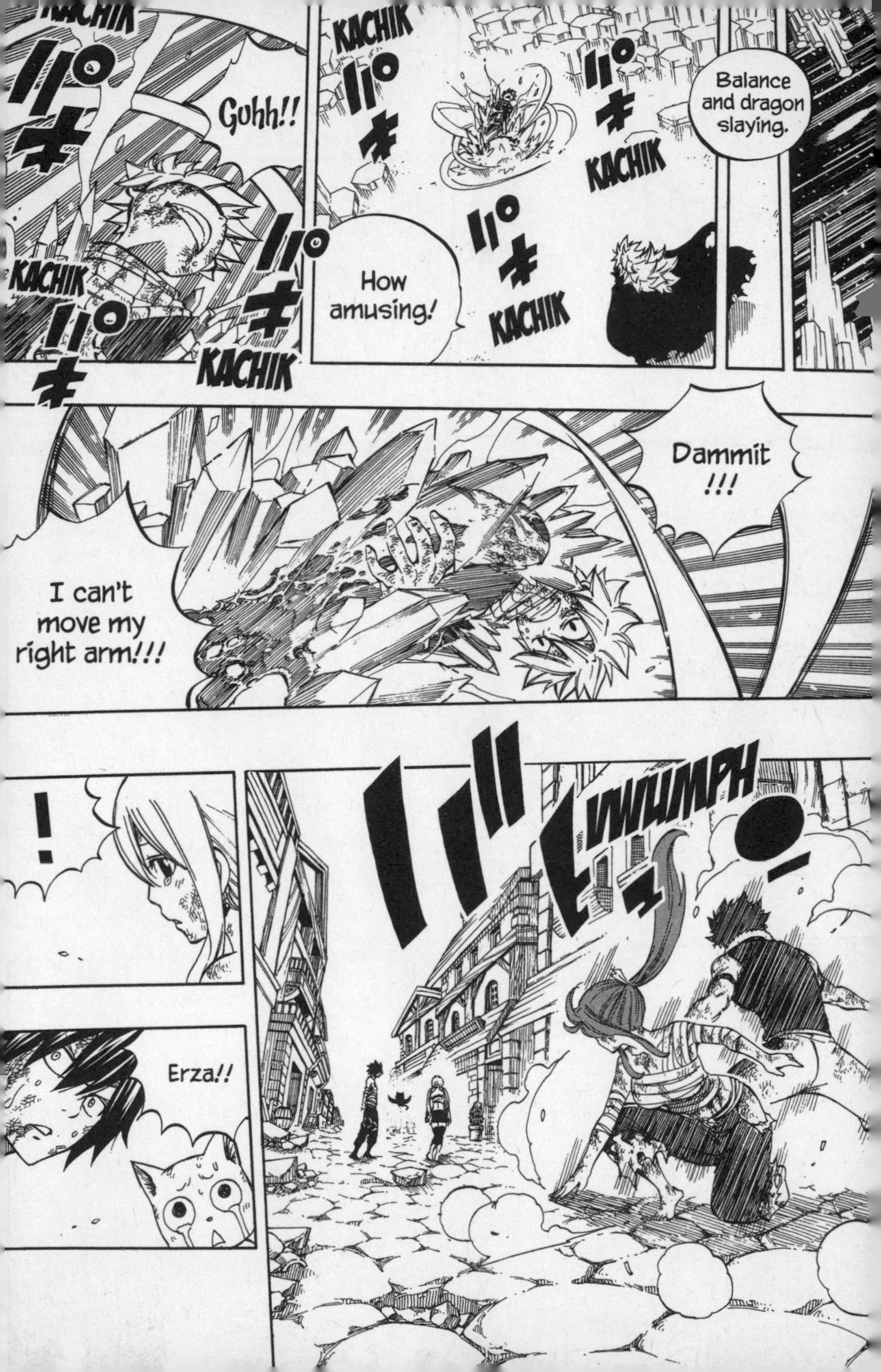
Balance and dragon slaying.
KACHIK
How amusing!
KACHIK
KACHIK
KACHIK
Guhh!!
KACHIK
KACHIK
Dammit!!!
I can't move my right arm!!!
VWUMPH
!
Erza!!

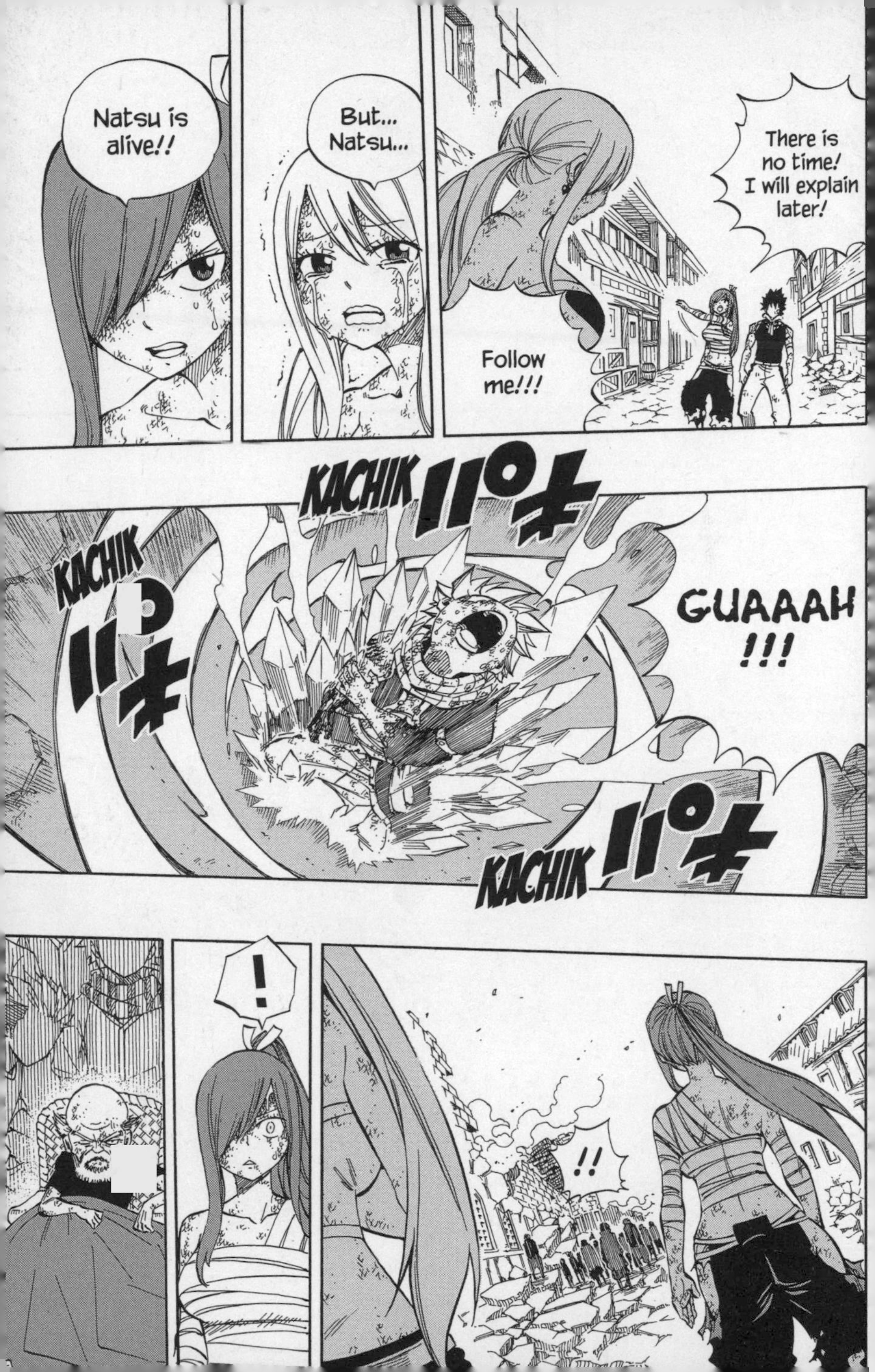
There is no time! I will explain later!
Follow me!!!
But... Natsu...
Natsu is alive!!
KACHIK
パキ
GUAAAH !!!
KACHIK
パキ
KACHIK
パキ
!!
!

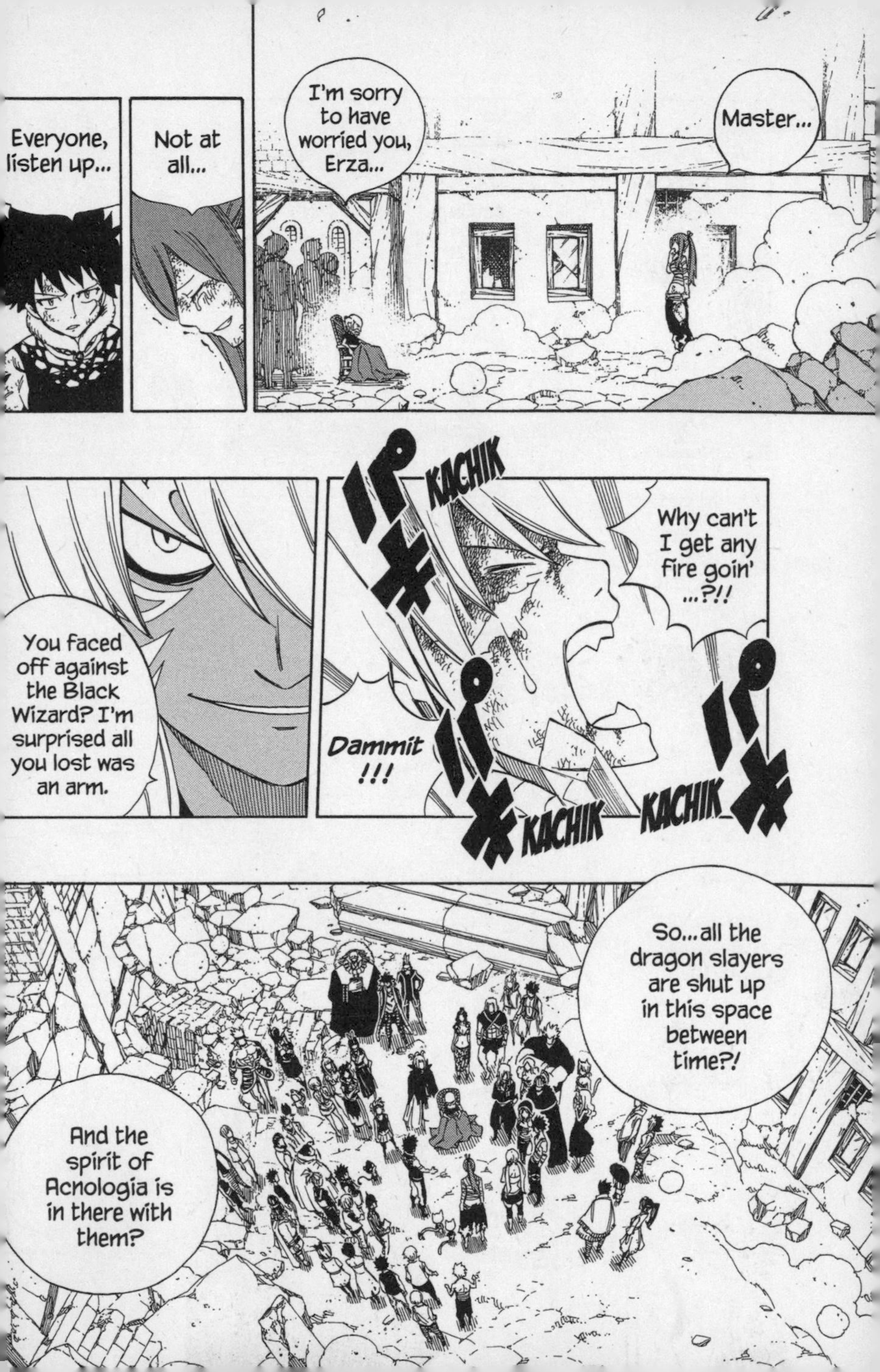
Master...
I'm sorry to have worried you, Erza...
Not at all...
Everyone, listen up...
KACHIK
Why can't I get any fire goin' ...?!!
KACHIK
KACHIK
Dammit !!!
You faced off against the Black Wizard? I'm surprised all you lost was an arm.
So...all the dragon slayers are shut up in this space between time?!
And the spirit of Acnologia is in there with them?

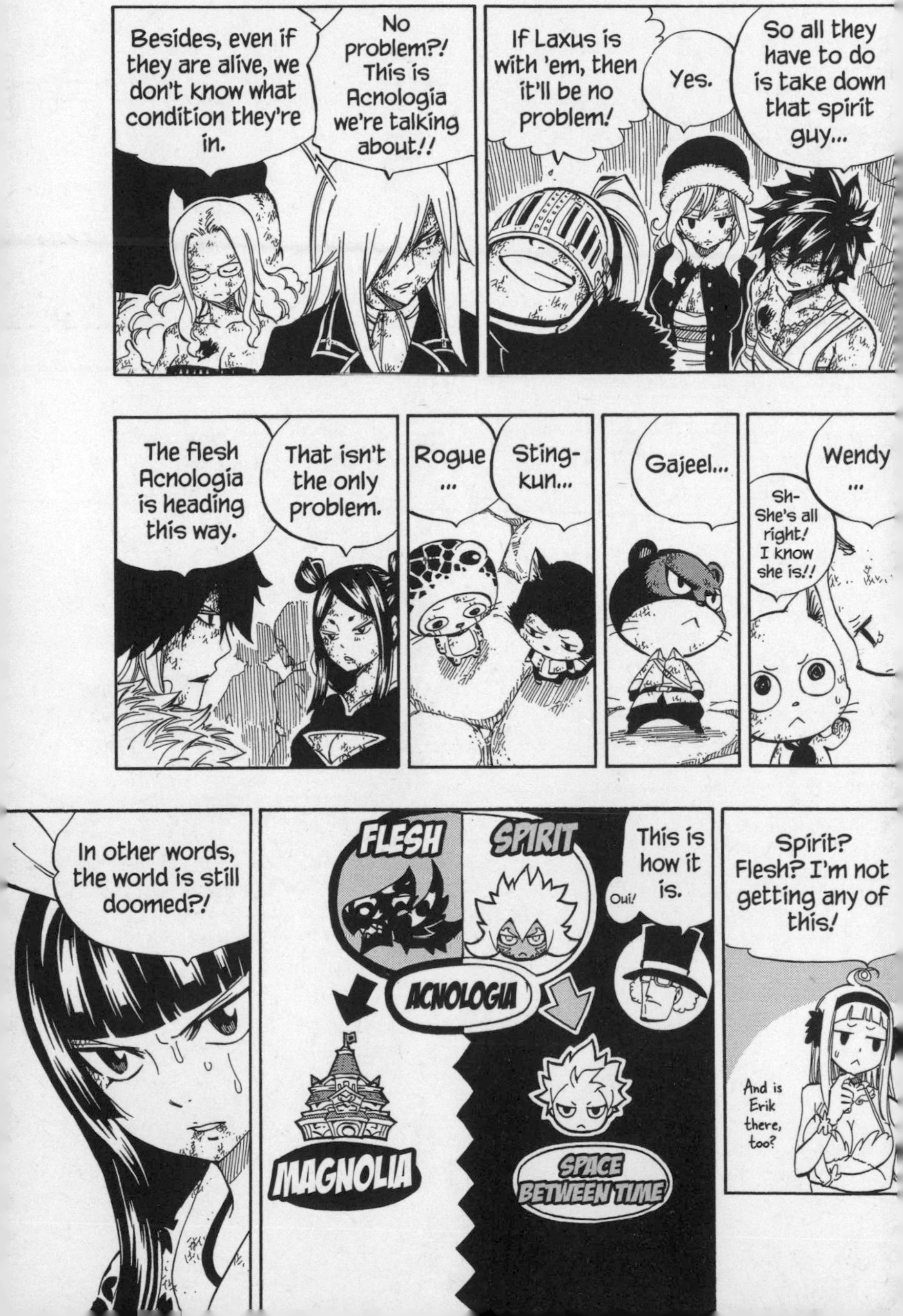
So all they have to do is take down that spirit guy...
Yes.
If Laxus is with 'em, then it'll be no problem!
No problem?! This is Acnologia we're talking about!!
Besides, even if they are alive, we don't know what condition they're in.
Wendy ...
Sh- She's all right! I know she is!!
Gajeel...
Sting-kun...
Rogue ...
That isn't the only problem.
The flesh Acnologia is heading this way.
Spirit? Flesh? I'm not getting any of this!
And is Erik there, too?
This is how it is.
Oui!
FLESH
SPIRIT
ACNOLOGIA
MAGNOLIA
SPACE BETWEEN TIME
In other words, the world is still doomed?!

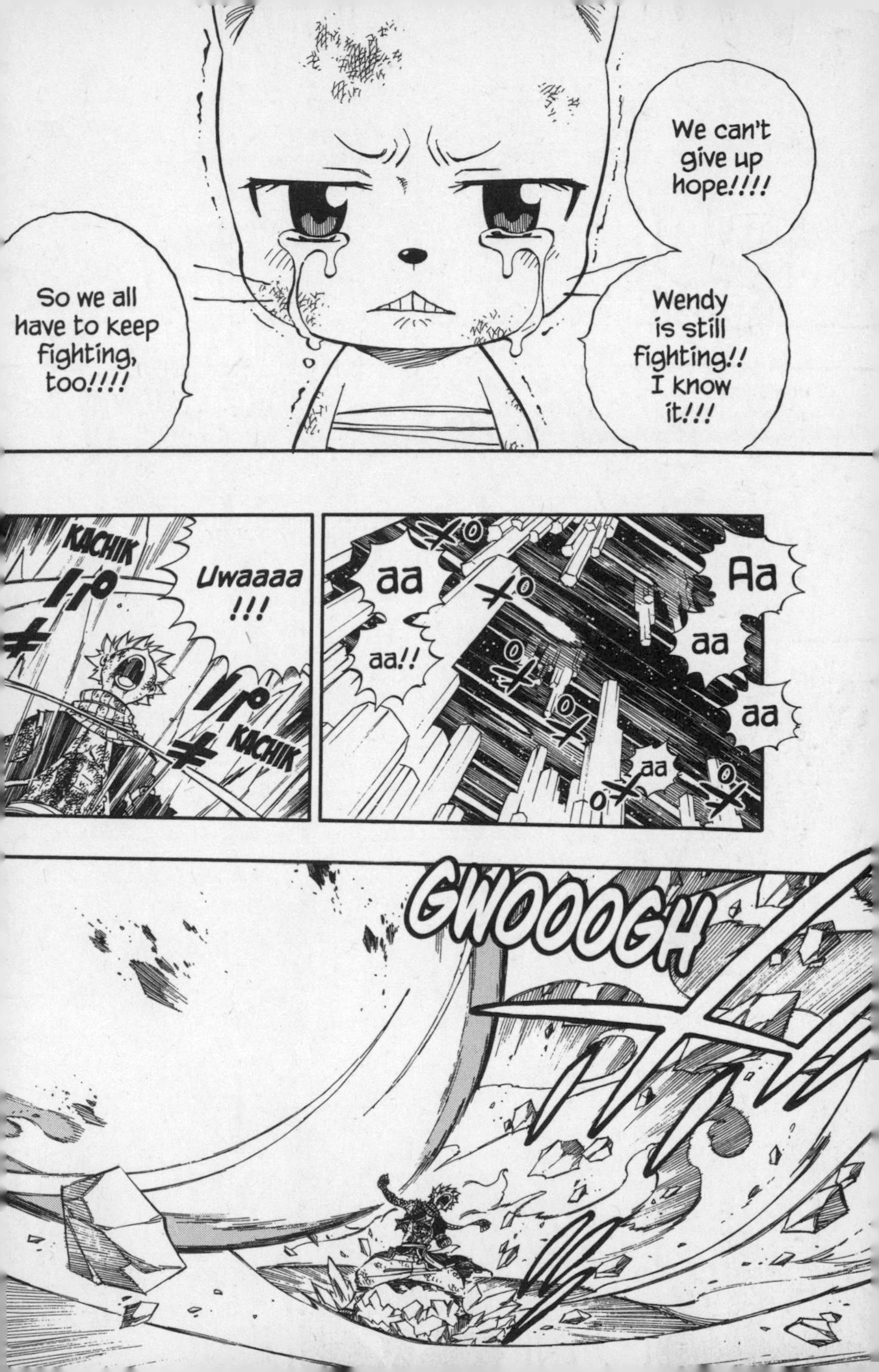
We can't give up hope!!!!
Wendy is still fighting!! I know it!!!
So we all have to keep fighting, too!!!!
Aa aa aa aa
aa aa!!
KACHIK
Uwaaaa!!!
KACHIK
GWOOOGH

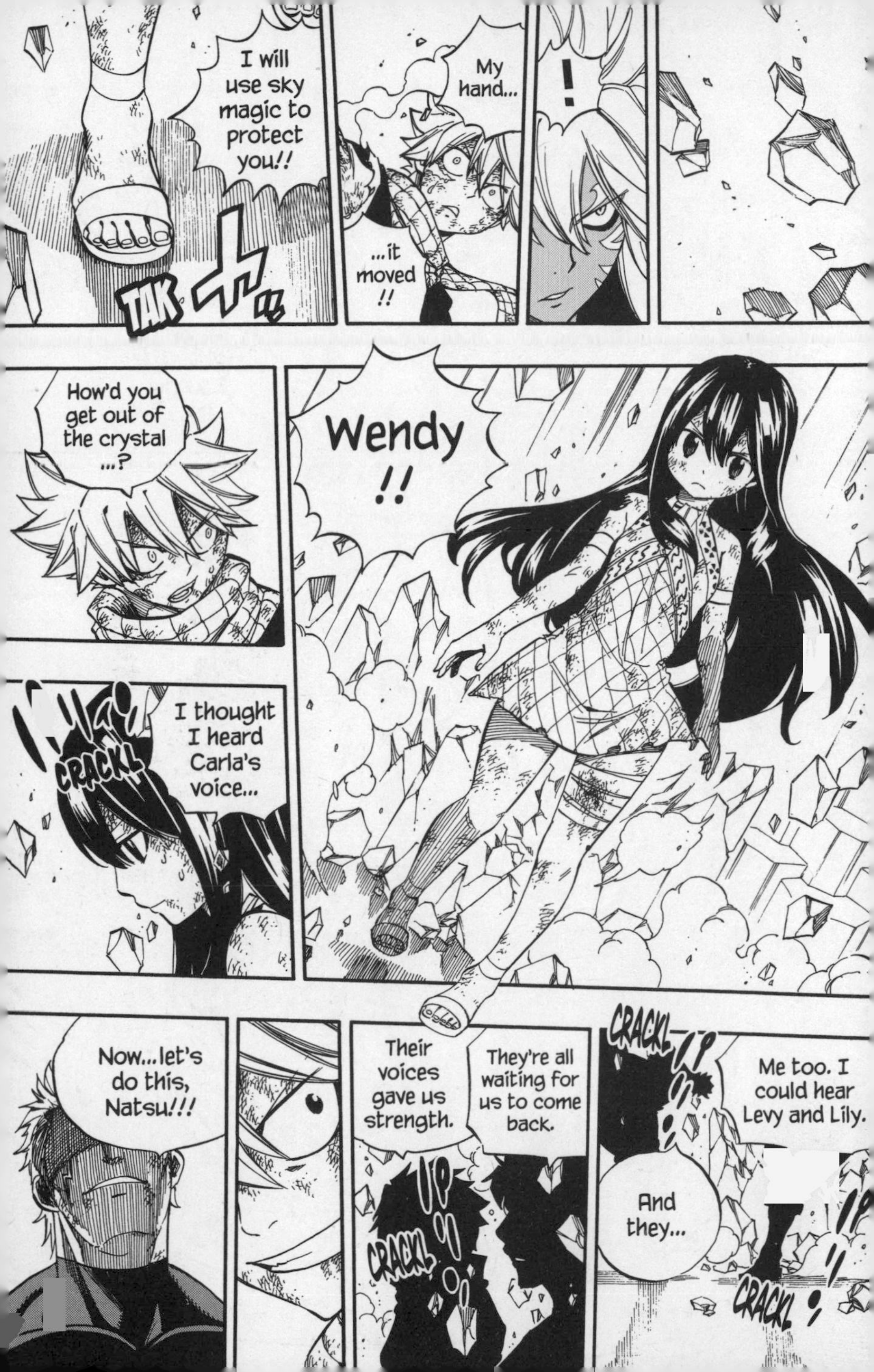
!
My hand...
...it moved !!
I will use sky magic to protect you!!
TAK
Wendy !!
How'd you get out of the crystal ...?
CRACKL
I thought I heard Carla's voice...
CRACKL
Me too. I could hear Levy and Lily.
And they...
CRACKL
They're all waiting for us to come back.
Their voices gave us strength.
CRACKL
Now...let's do this, Natsu!!!

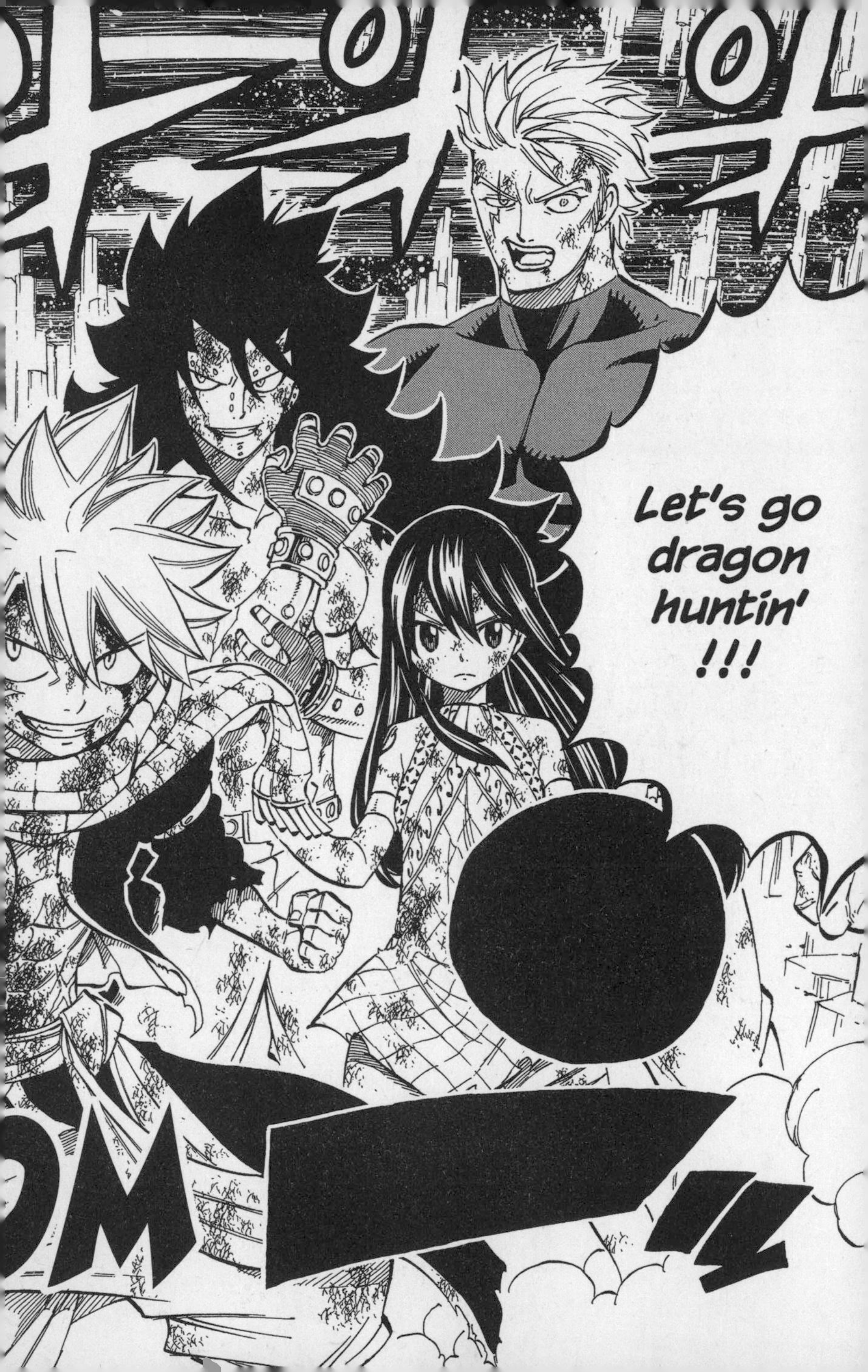
Let's go dragon huntin' !!!

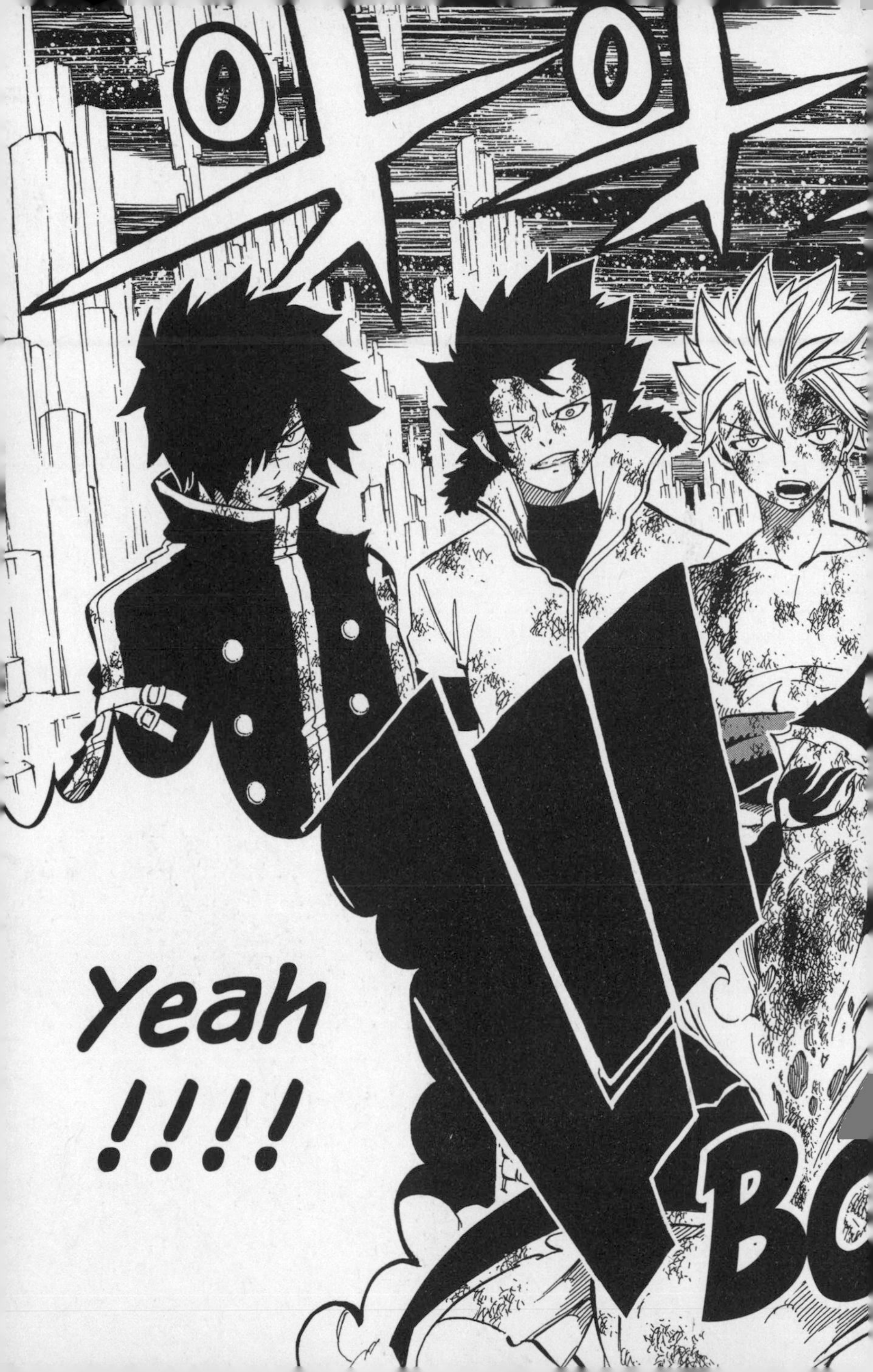
Yeah !!!!

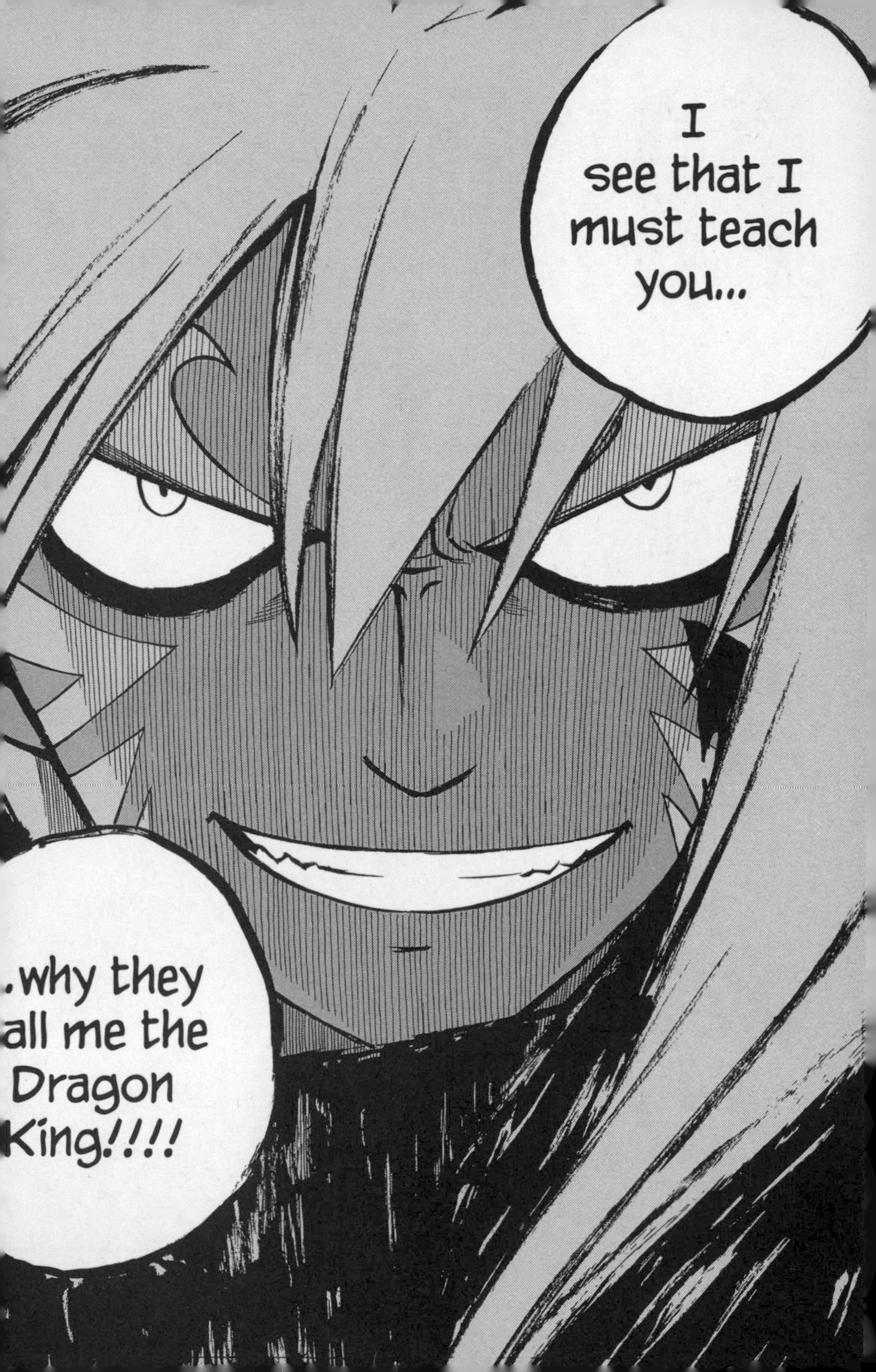
I see that I must teach you...
.why they all me the Dragon King!!!!

FAIRY TAIL
フェアリーテイル

Chapter 541: The Magic of Hope

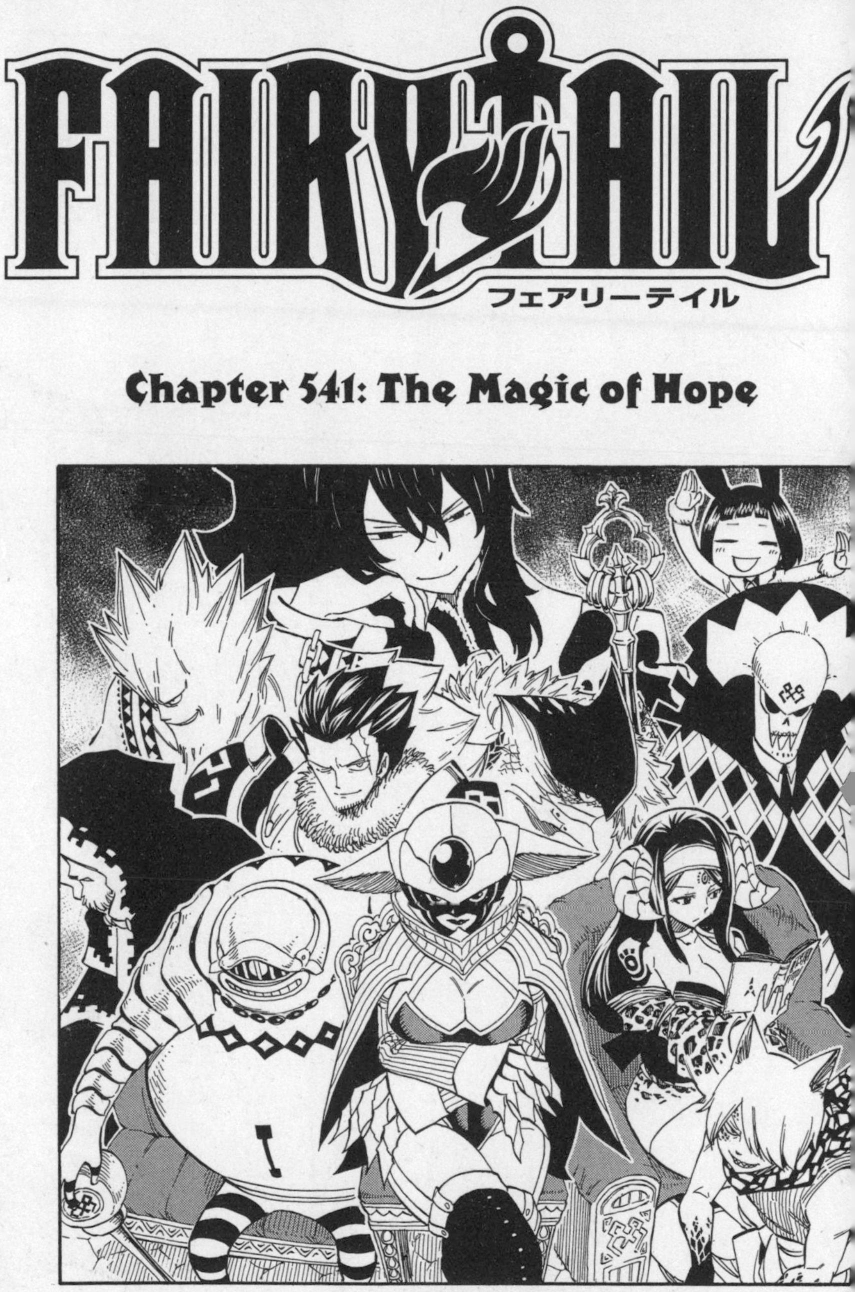

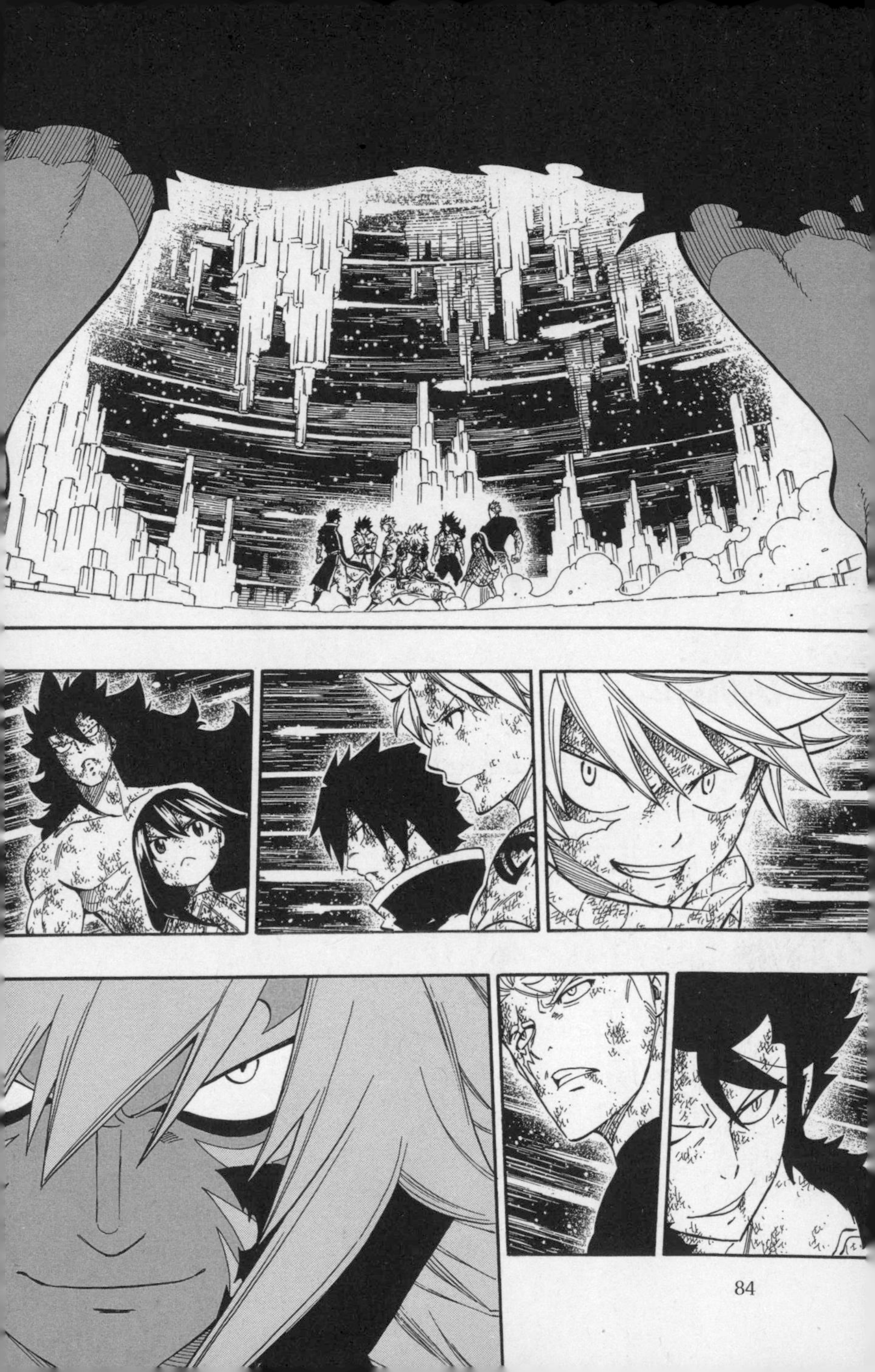

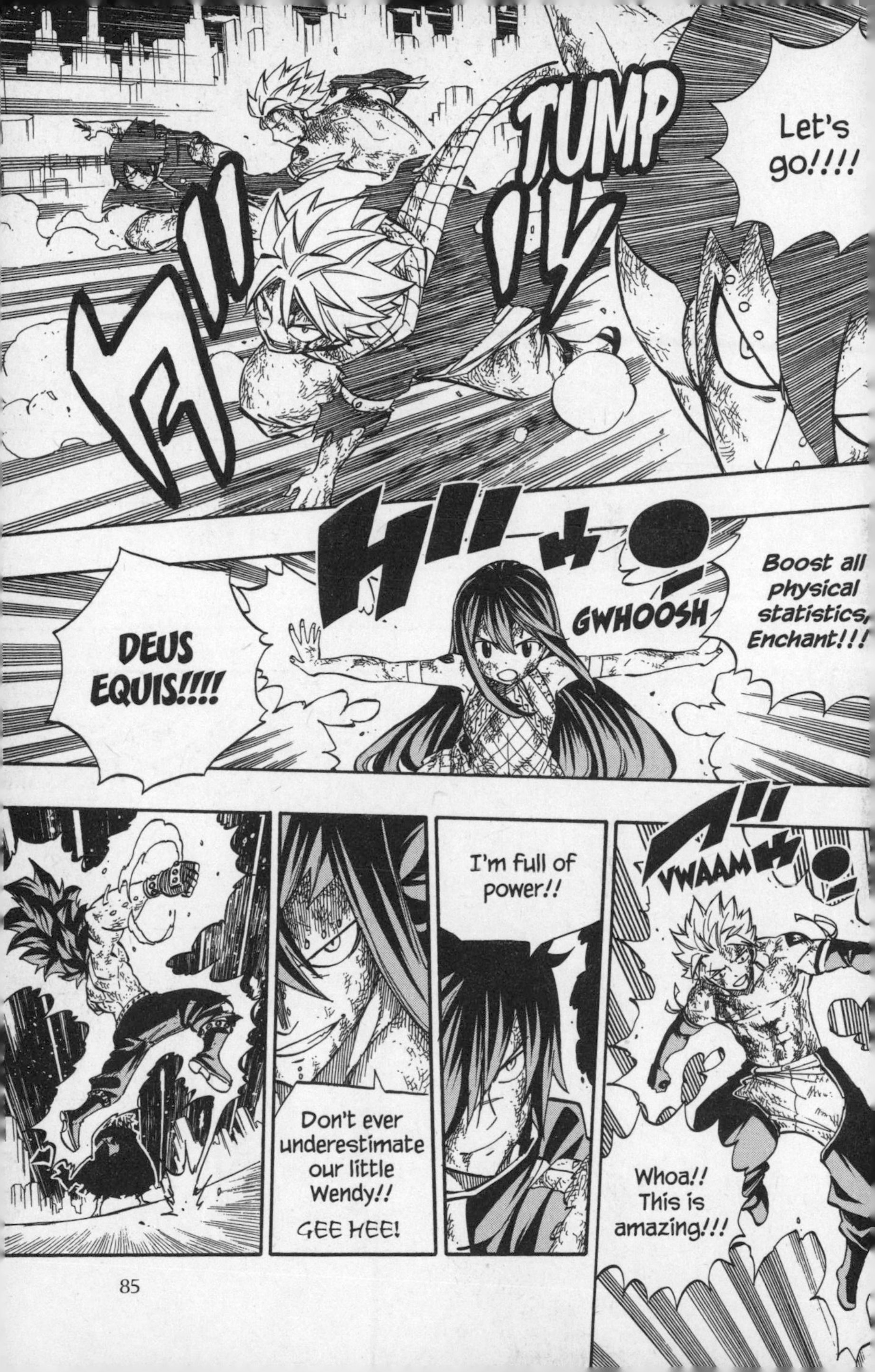

Let's go!!!!
TUMP
Boost all physical statistics, Enchant!!!
GWHOOSH
DEUS EQUIS!!!!
VWAAM
Whoa!! This is amazing!!!
I'm full of power!!
Don't ever underestimate our little Wendy!!
GEE HEE!

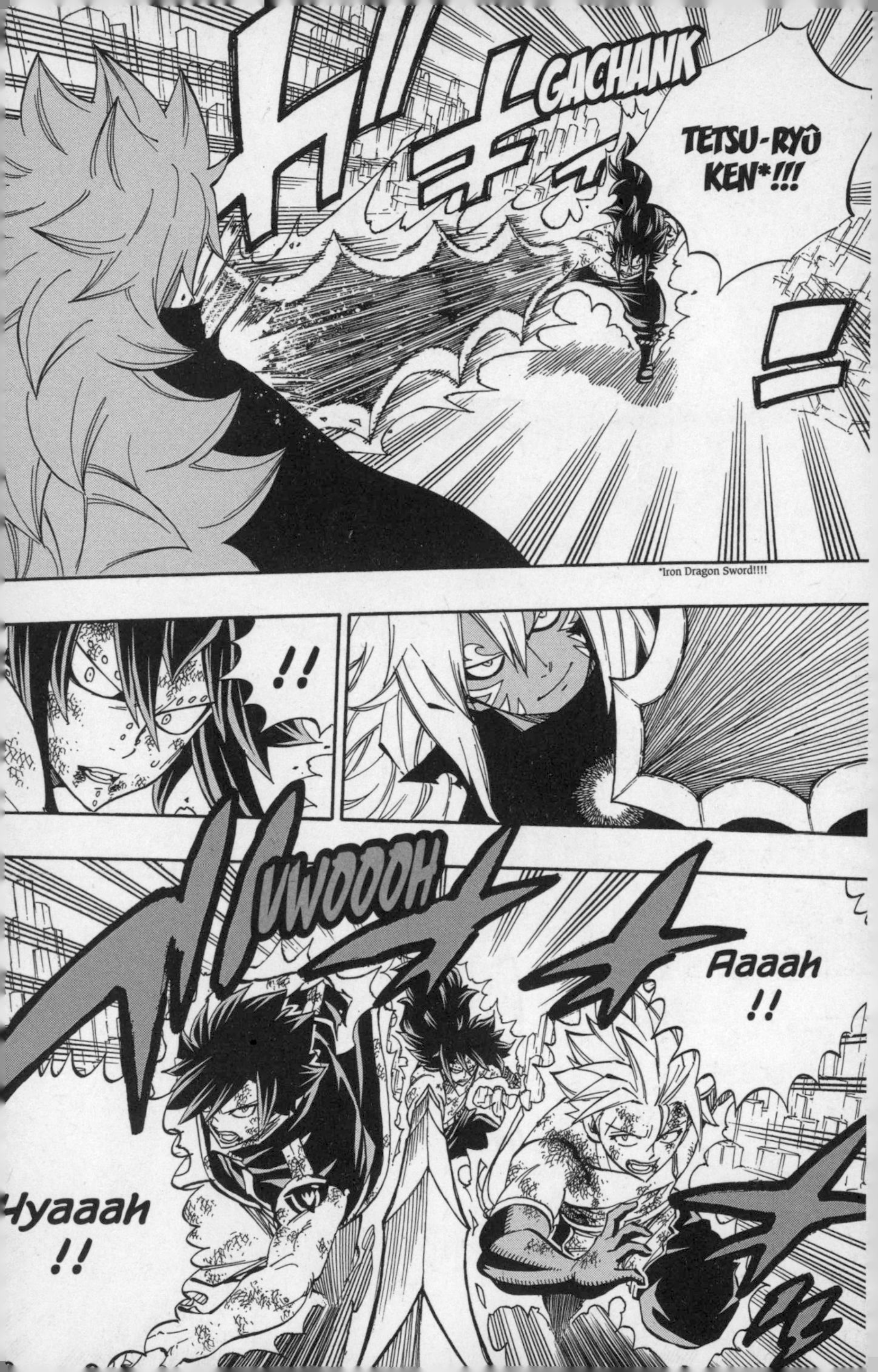
GACHANK
TETSU-RYÔ KEN*!!!
!
*Iron Dragon Sword!!!!
!!
VWOOOH
Aaaah !!
Hyaaah !!

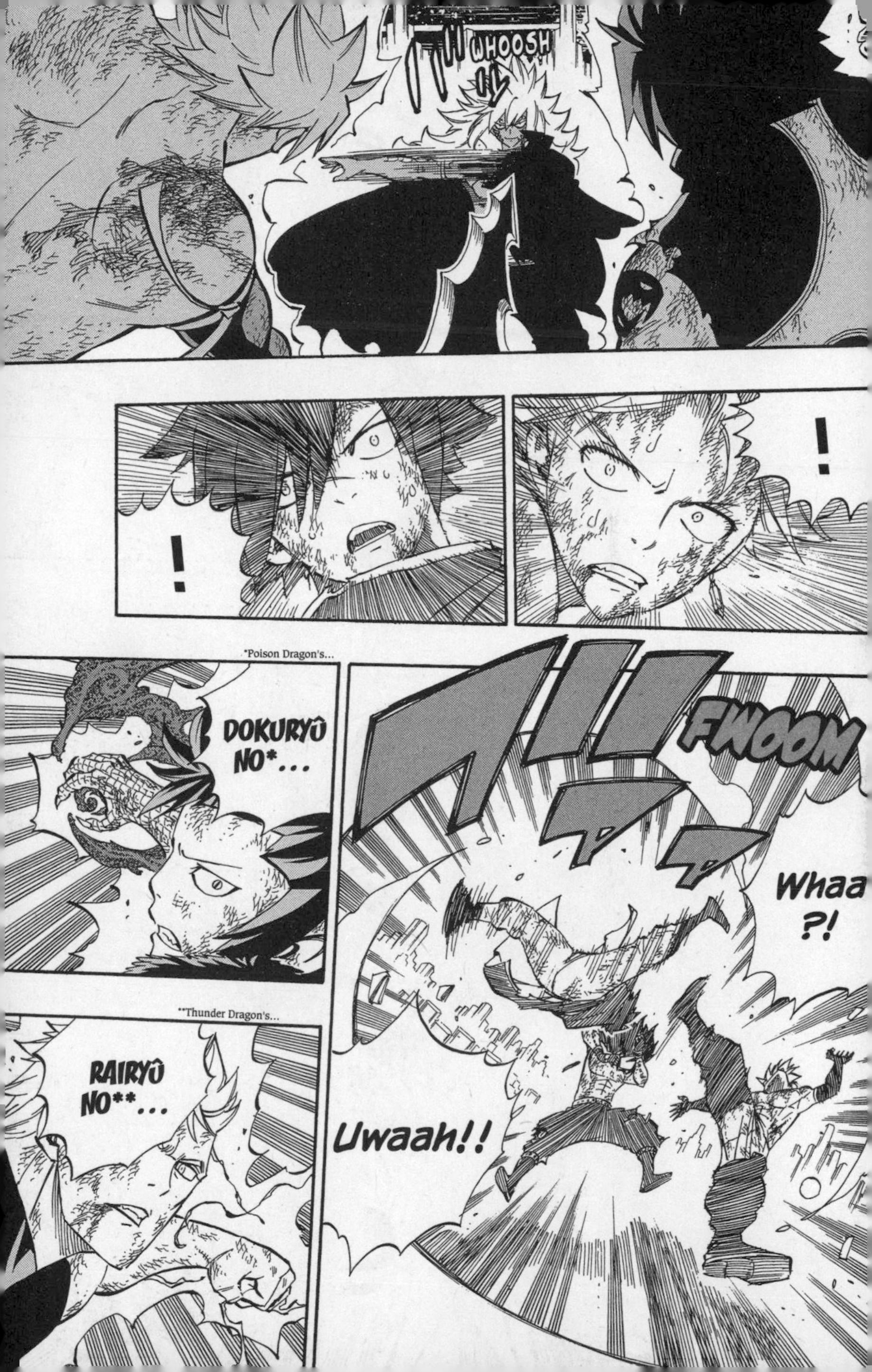
WHOOSH
!
!
FWOOM
Whaa?!
Uwaah!!
DOKURYÛ NO*...
RAIRYÛ NO**...
*Poison Dragon's...
**Thunder Dragon's...

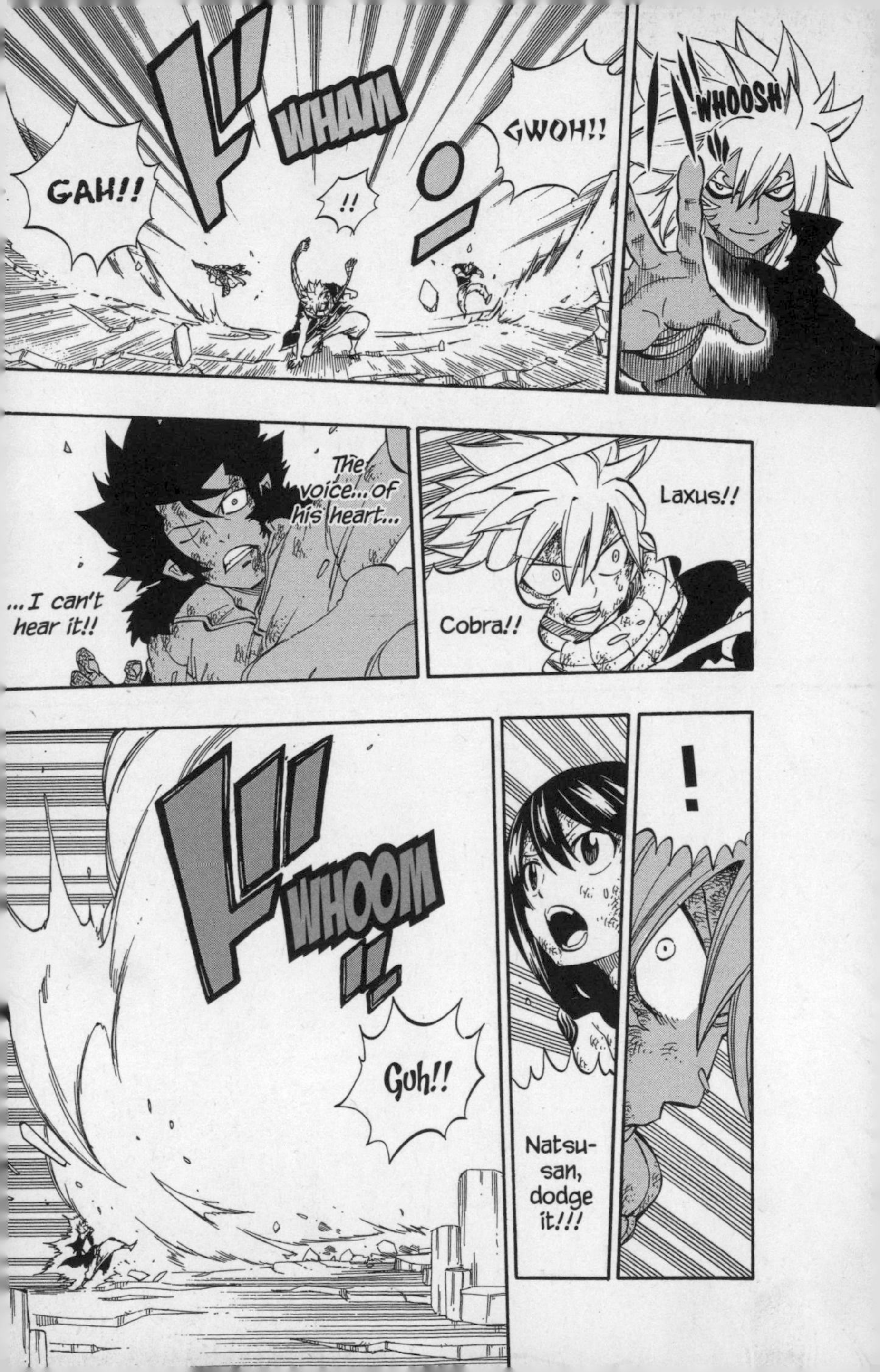
WHOOSH
GWOH!!
WHAM
!!
GAH!!
Laxus!!
Cobra!!
The voice... of his heart...
...I can't hear it!!
!
Natsu-san, dodge it!!!
WHOOM!!
Guh!!

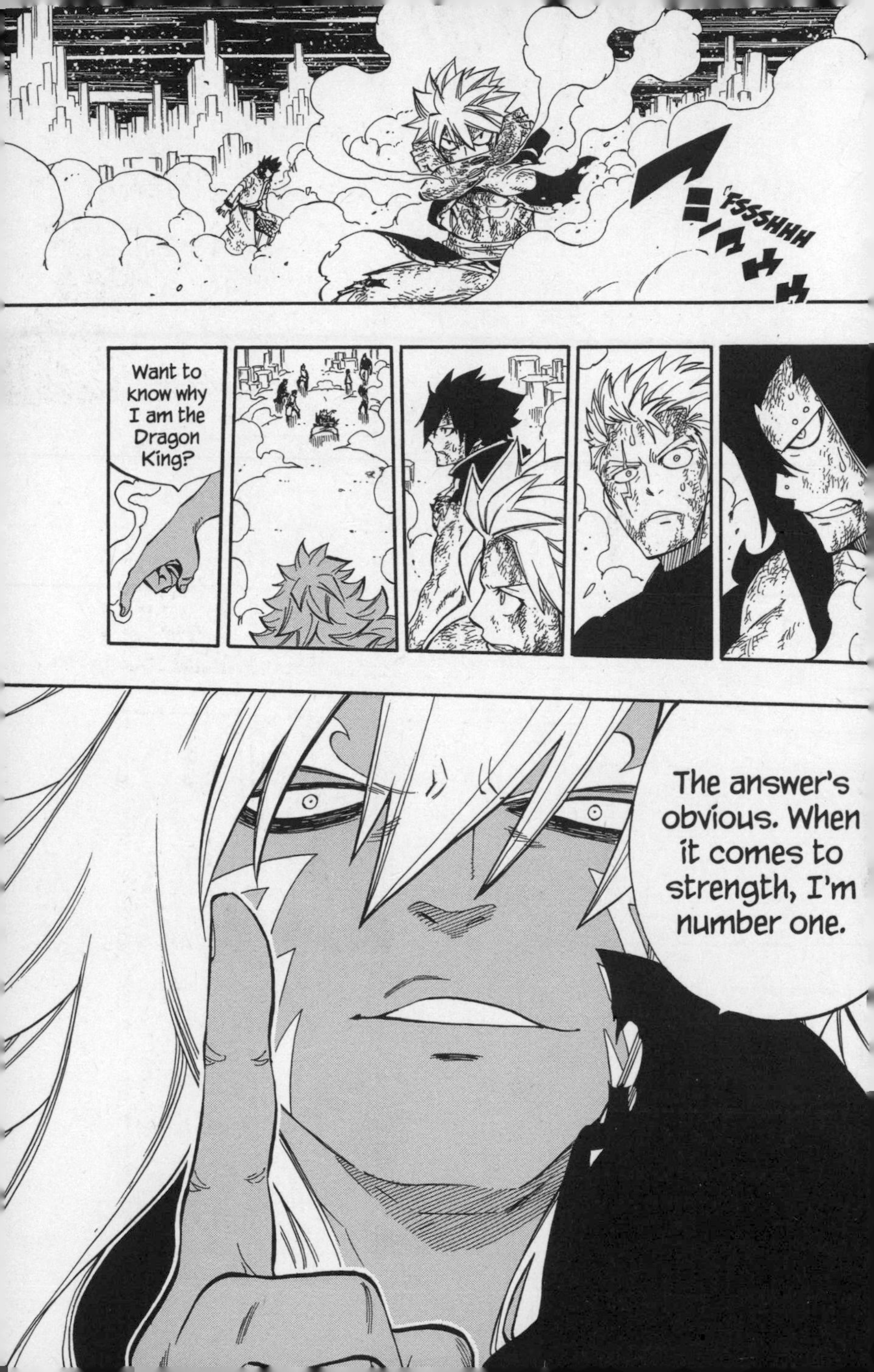
FSSSHHH
Want to know why I am the Dragon King?
The answer's obvious. When it comes to strength, I'm number one.

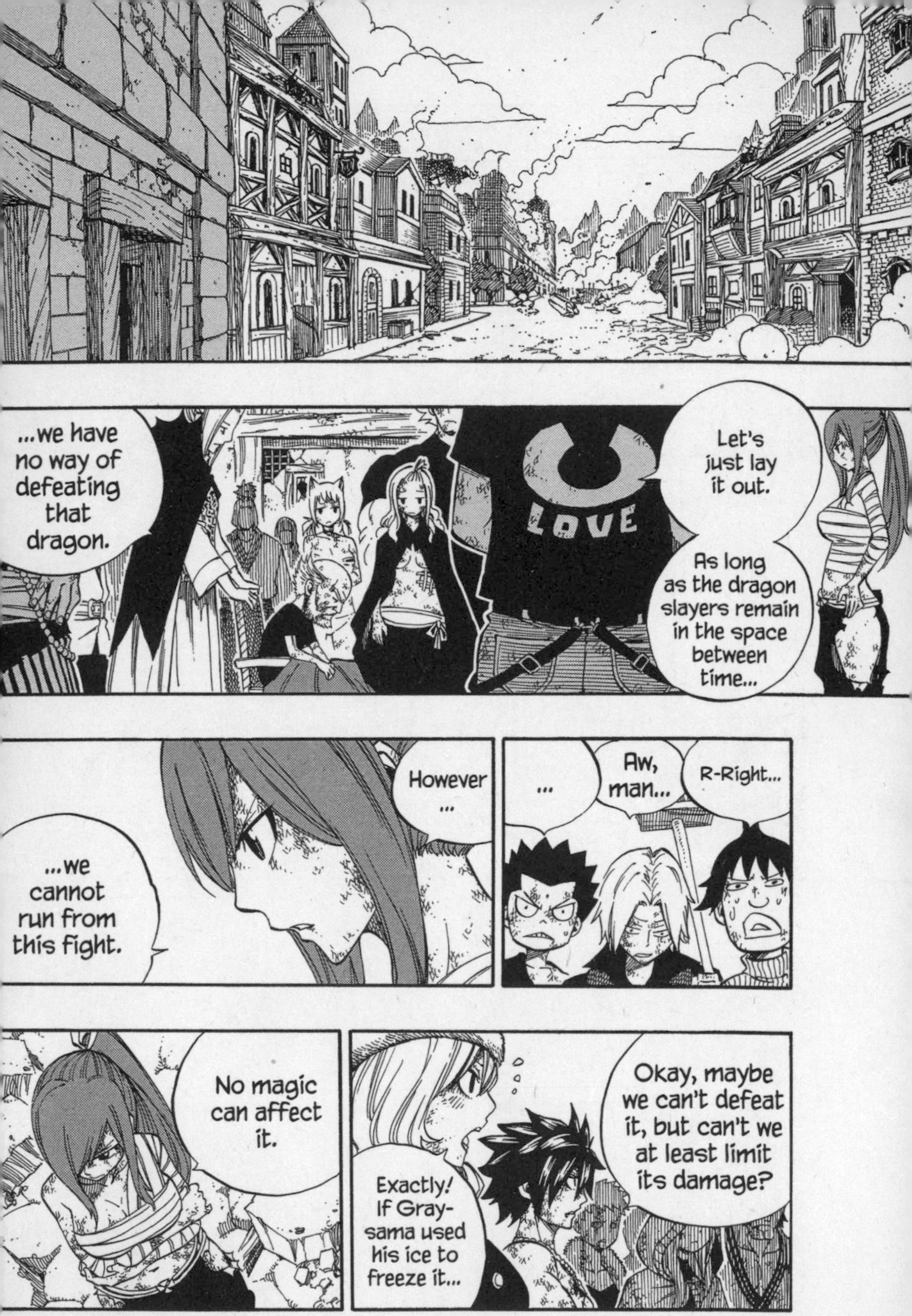
Let's just lay it out.
As long as the dragon slayers remain in the space between time...
...we have no way of defeating that dragon.
R-Right...
Aw, man...
...
However ...
...we cannot run from this fight.
Okay, maybe we can't defeat it, but can't we at least limit its damage?
Exactly! If Gray-sama used his ice to freeze it...
No magic can affect it.

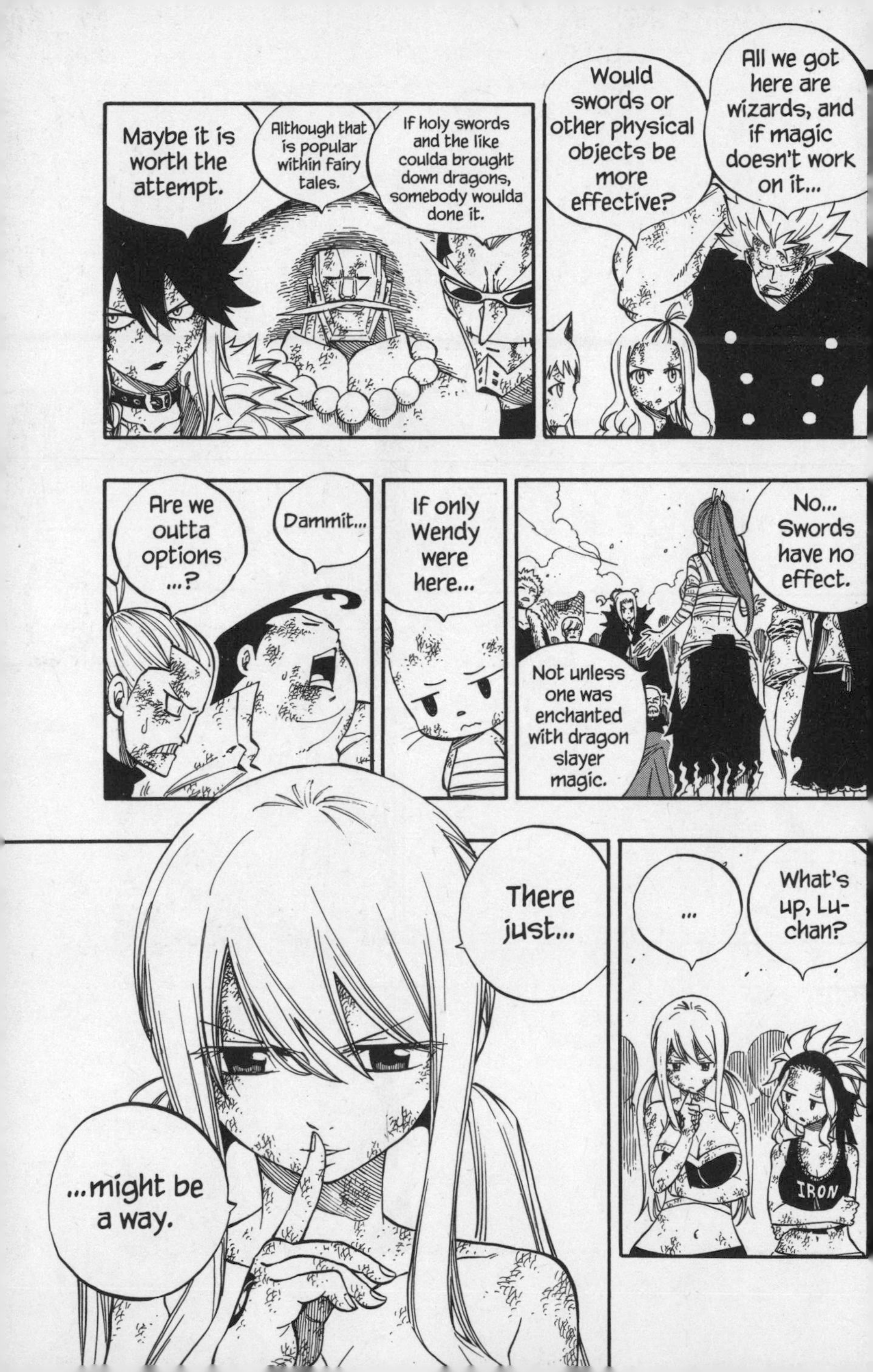
All we got here are wizards, and if magic doesn't work on it...
Would swords or other physical objects be more effective?
If holy swords and the like coulda brought down dragons, somebody woulda done it.
Although that is popular within fairy tales.
Maybe it is worth the attempt.
No... Swords have no effect.
Not unless one was enchanted with dragon slayer magic.
If only Wendy were here...
Dammit...
Are we outta options ...?
What's up, Lu-chan?
...
There just...
...might be a way.

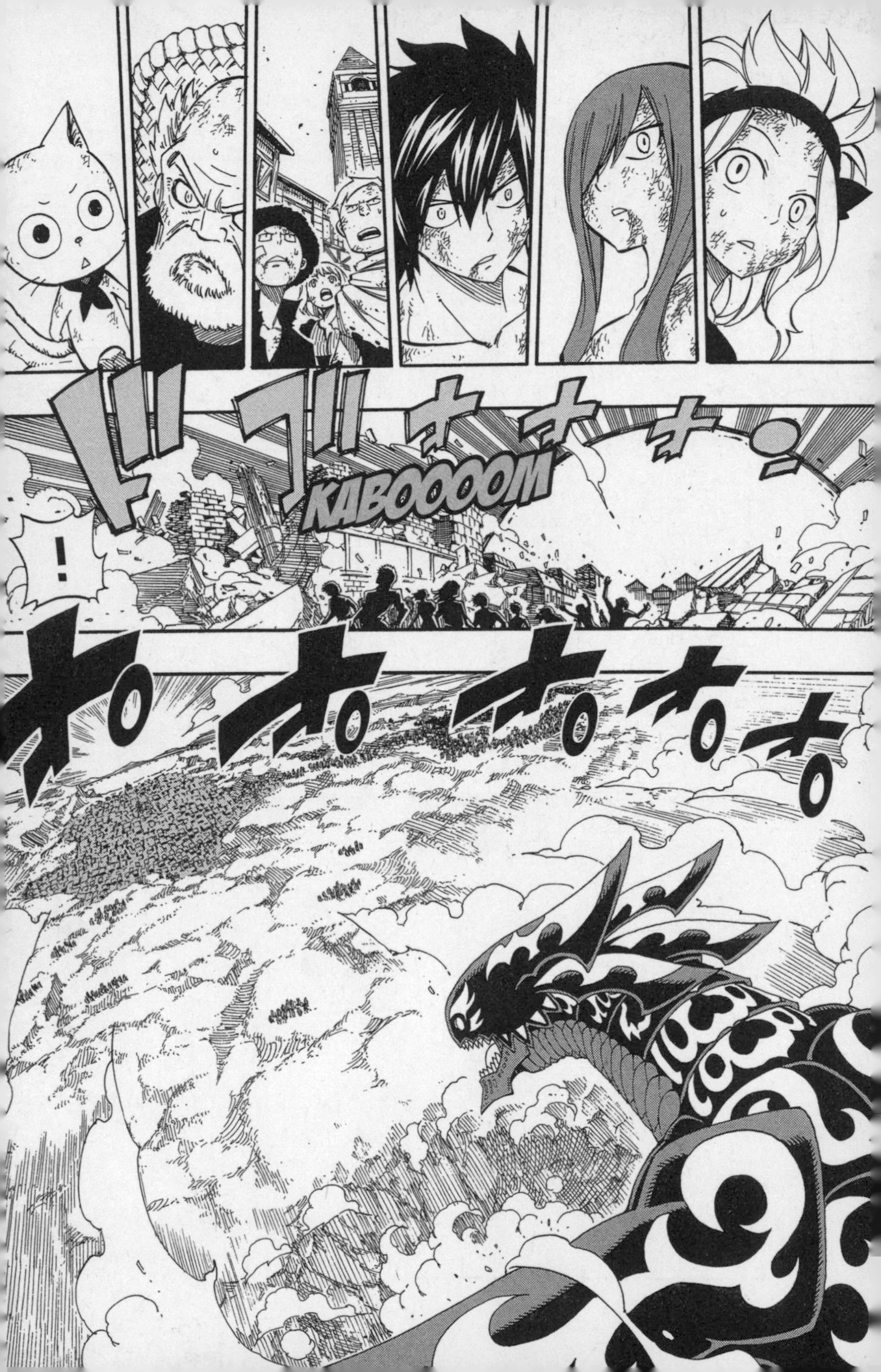
KABOOOOM
!

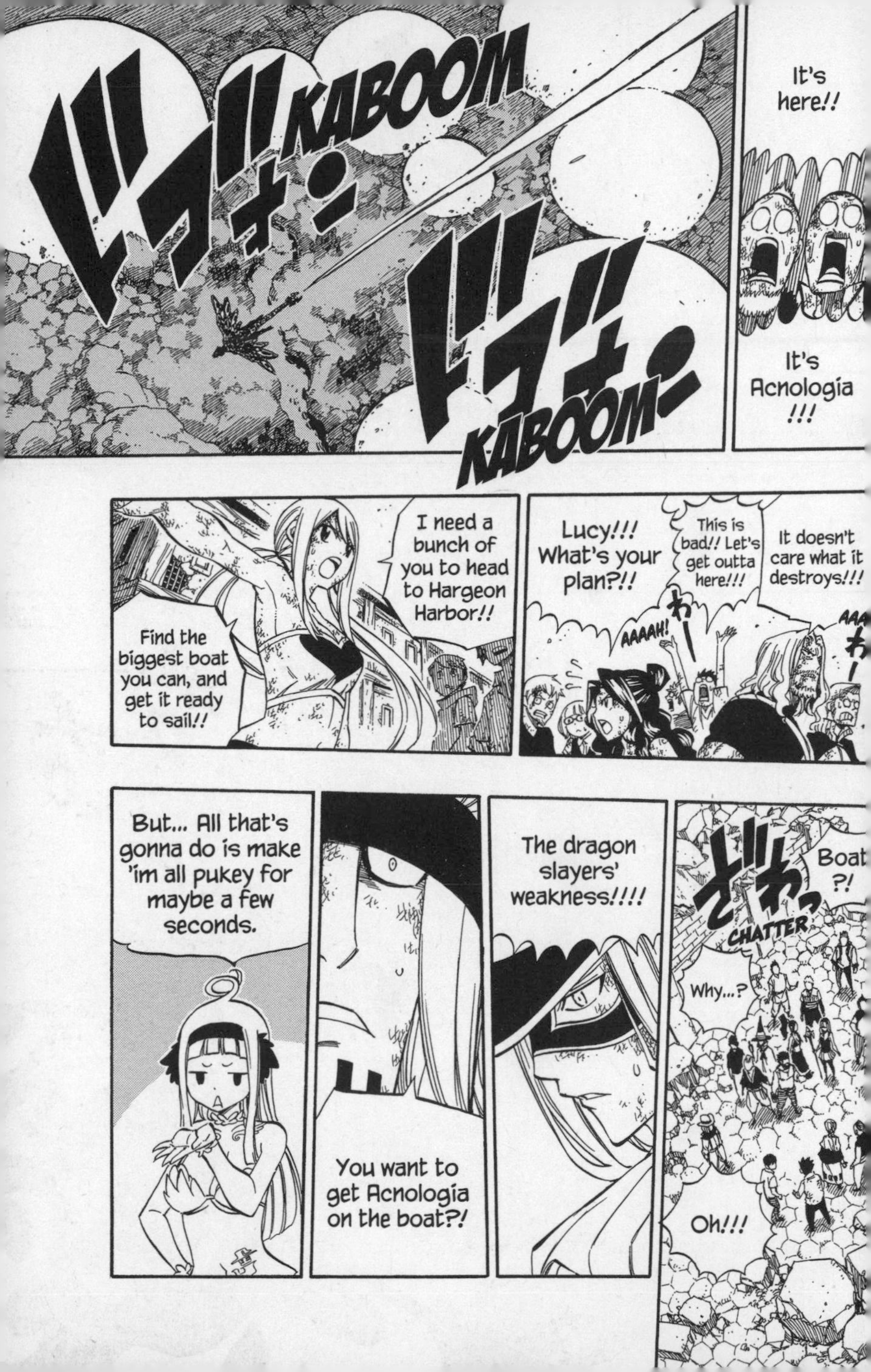
It's here!!
It's Acnologia!!!
KABOOM
KABOOM
It doesn't care what it destroys!!!
This is bad!! Let's get outta here!!!
Lucy!!! What's your plan?!!
AAAAH!
I need a bunch of you to head to Hargeon Harbor!!
Find the biggest boat you can, and get it ready to sail!!
Boat?!
CHATTER
Why...?
Oh!!!
The dragon slayers' weakness!!!!
You want to get Acnologia on the boat?!
But... All that's gonna do is make 'im all pukey for maybe a few seconds.

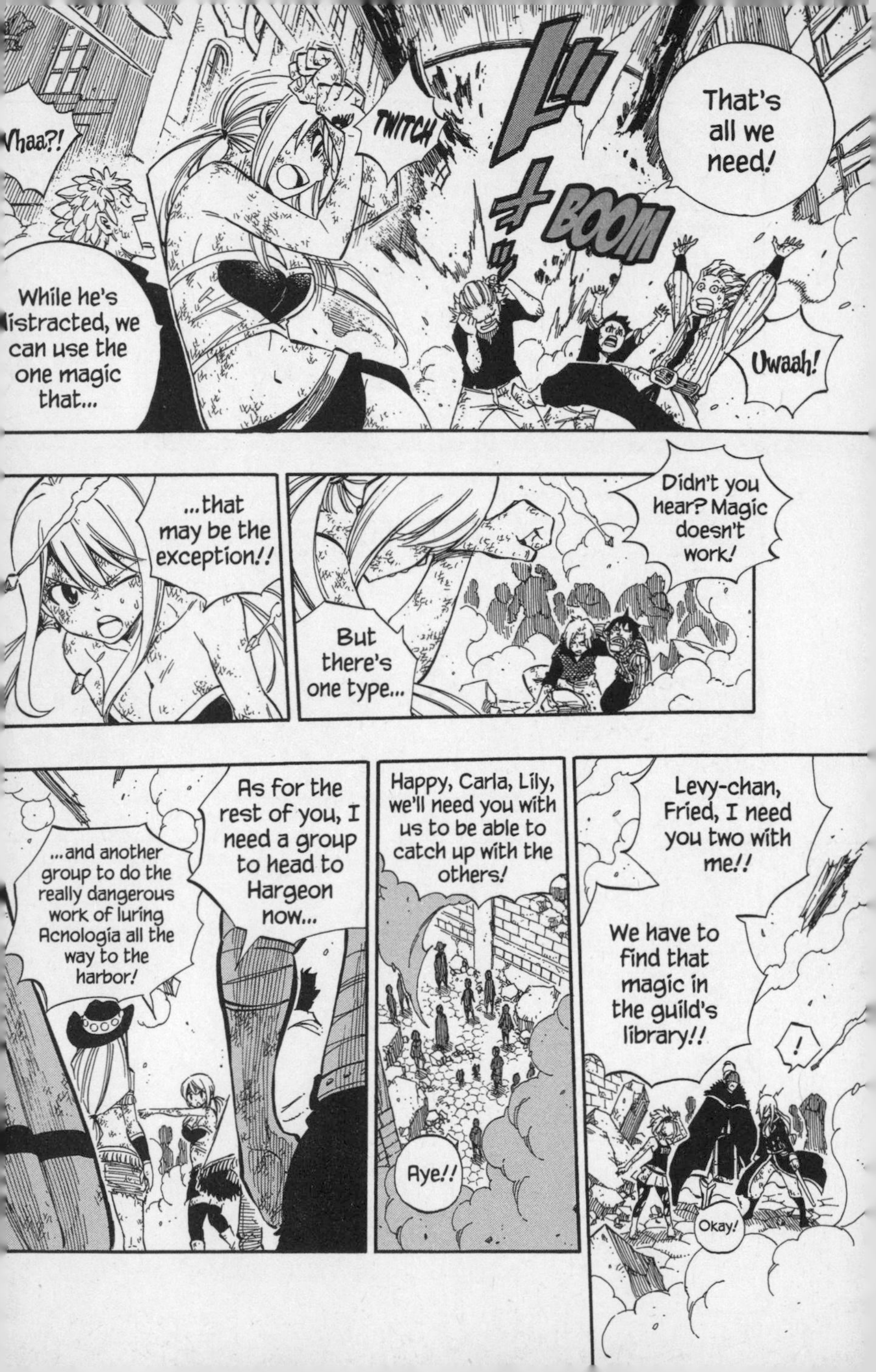

That's all we need!
TWITCH
BOOM
Uwaah!
Vhaa?!
While he's
istracted, we can use the one magic that...
Didn't you hear? Magic doesn't work!
But there's one type...
...that may be the exception!!
Levy-chan, Fried, I need you two with me!!
We have to find that magic in the guild's library!!
!
Okay!
Happy, Carla, Lily, we'll need you with us to be able to catch up with the others!
Aye!!
As for the rest of you, I need a group to head to Hargeon now...
...and another group to do the really dangerous work of luring Acnologia all the way to the harbor!

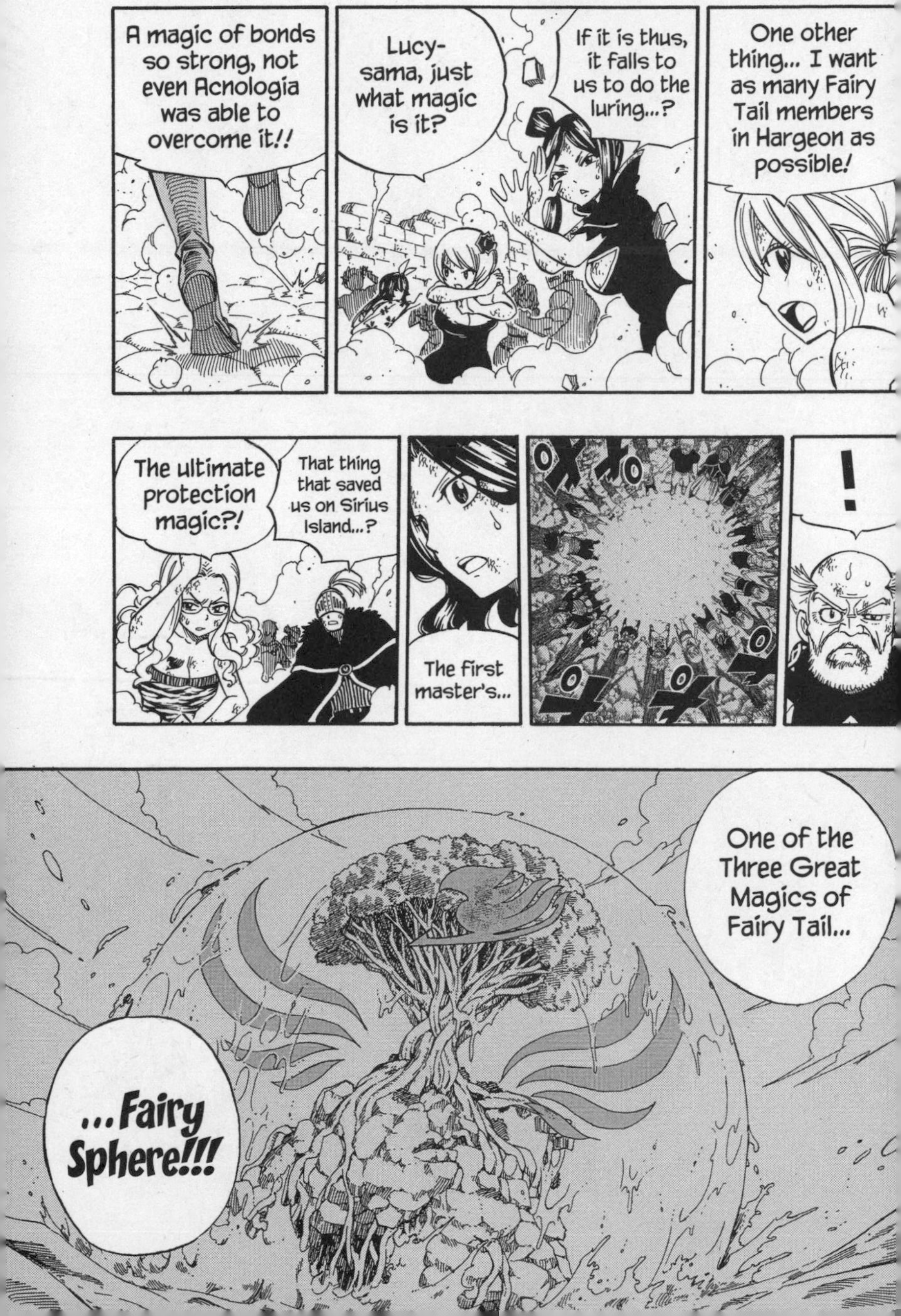
One other thing... I want as many Fairy Tail members in Hargeon as possible!
If it is thus, it falls to us to do the luring...?
Lucy-sama, just what magic is it?
A magic of bonds so strong, not even Acnologia was able to overcome it!!
!
The first master's...
That thing that saved us on Sirius Island...?
The ultimate protection magic?!
One of the Three Great Magics of Fairy Tail...
...Fairy Sphere!!!

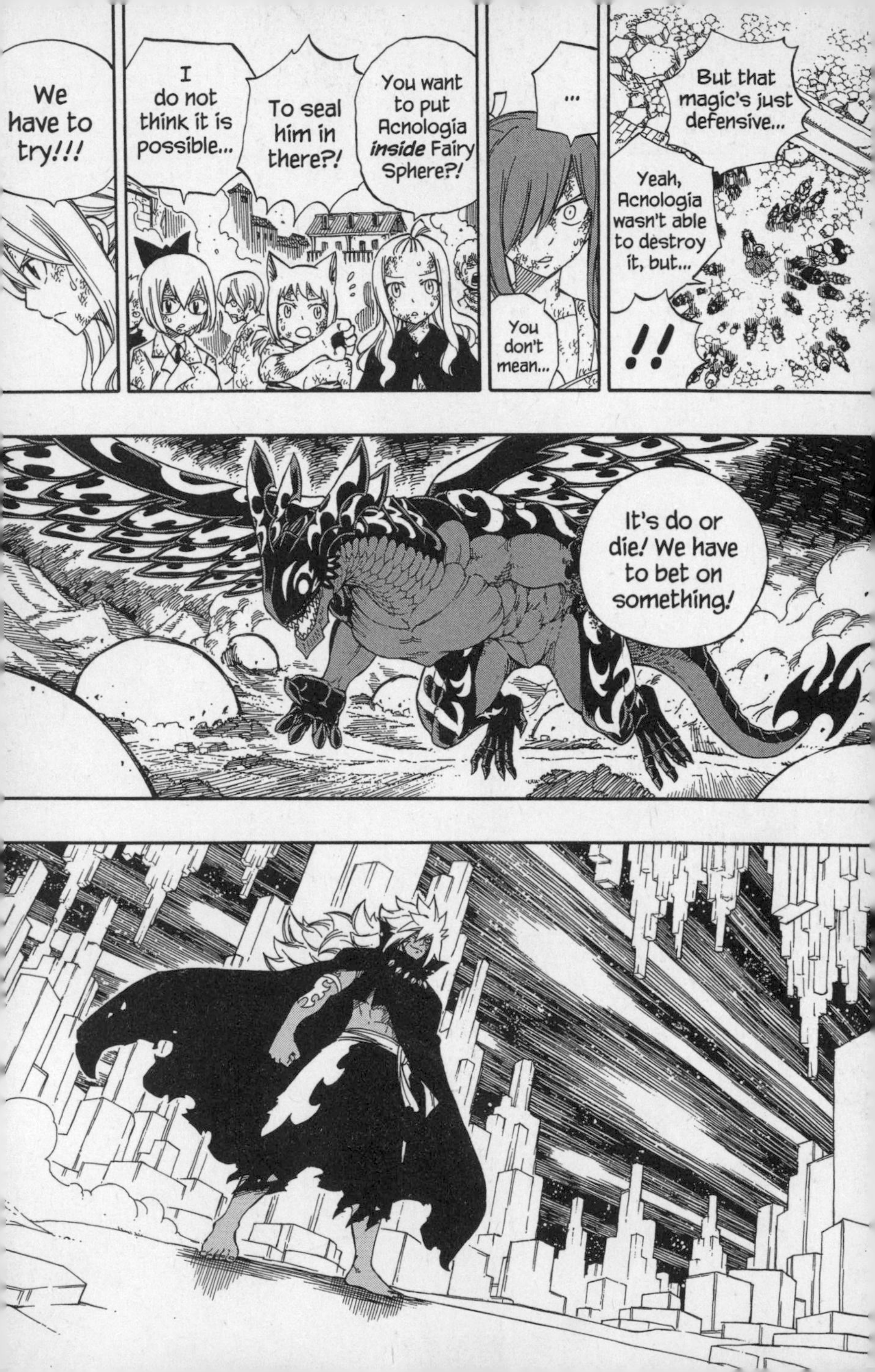
But that magic's just defensive...
Yeah, Acnologia wasn't able to destroy it, but...
!!
...
You don't mean...
You want to put Acnologia *inside* Fairy Sphere?!
To seal him in there?!
I do not think it is possible...
We have to try!!!
It's do or die! We have to bet on something!

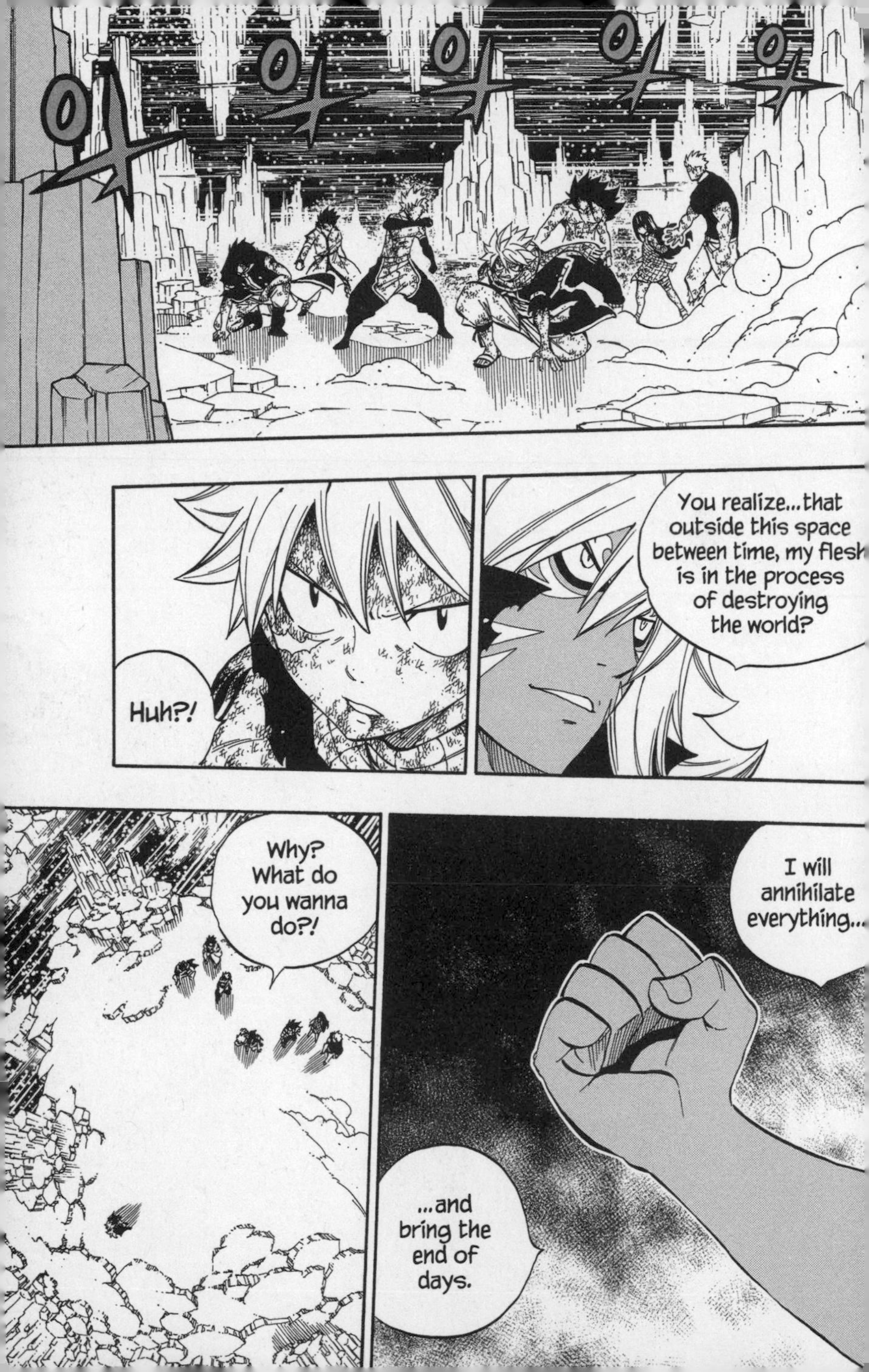
You realize...that outside this space between time, my flesh is in the process of destroying the world?
Huh?!
I will annihilate everything...
...and bring the end of days.
Why? What do you wanna do?!

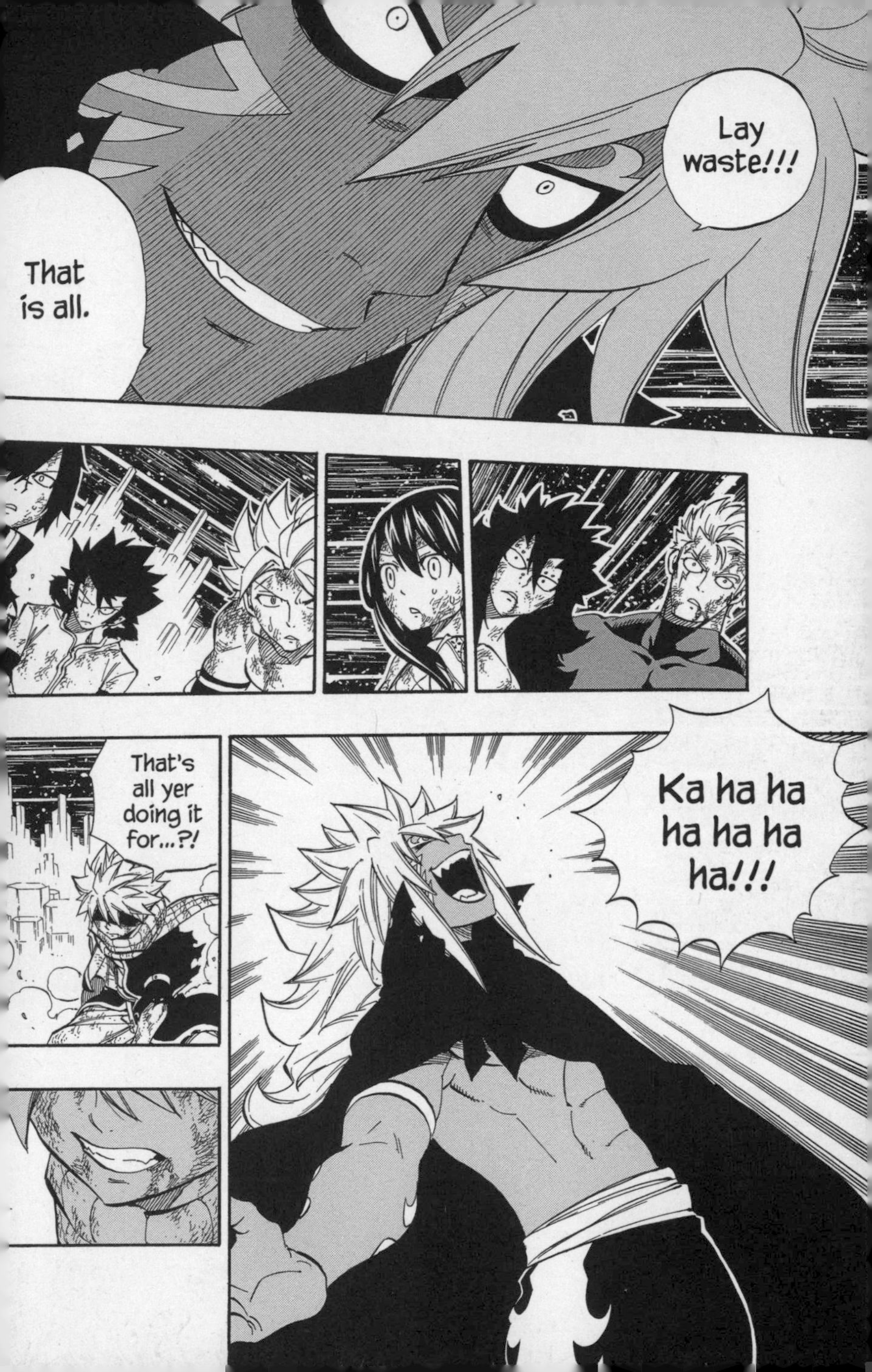
Lay waste!!!
That is all.
Ka ha ha ha ha ha ha!!!
That's all yer doing it for...?!

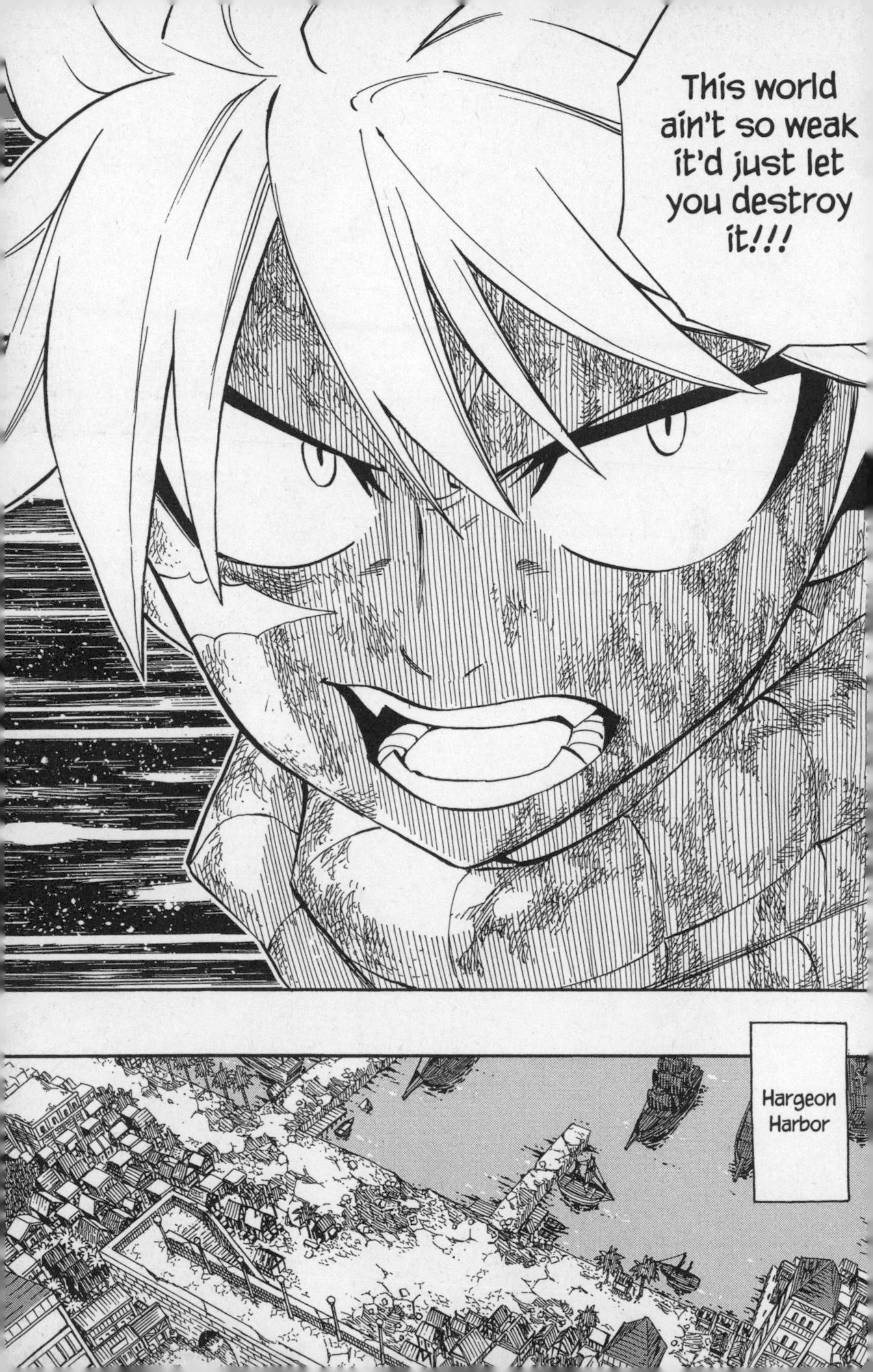
This world ain't so weak it'd just let you destroy it!!!
Hargeon Harbor

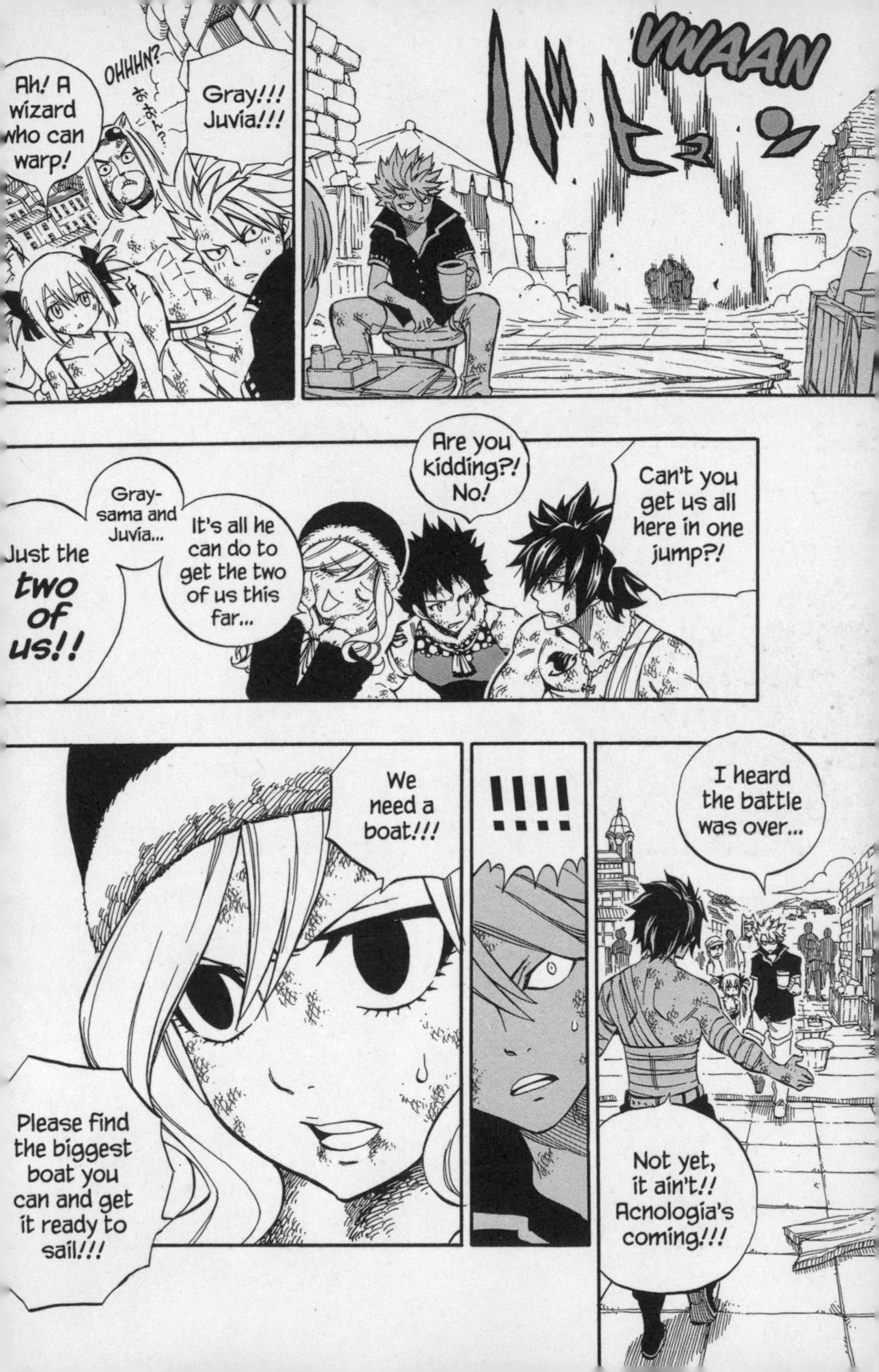
VWAAN
Gray!!! Juvia!!!
OHHHN?
おおん?
Ah! A wizard who can warp!
Can't you get us all here in one jump?!
Are you kidding?! No!
It's all he can do to get the two of us this far...
Gray-sama and Juvia...
Just the two of us!!
I heard the battle was over...
Not yet, it ain't!! Acnologia's coming!!!
!!!!
We need a boat!!!
Please find the biggest boat you can and get it ready to sail!!!

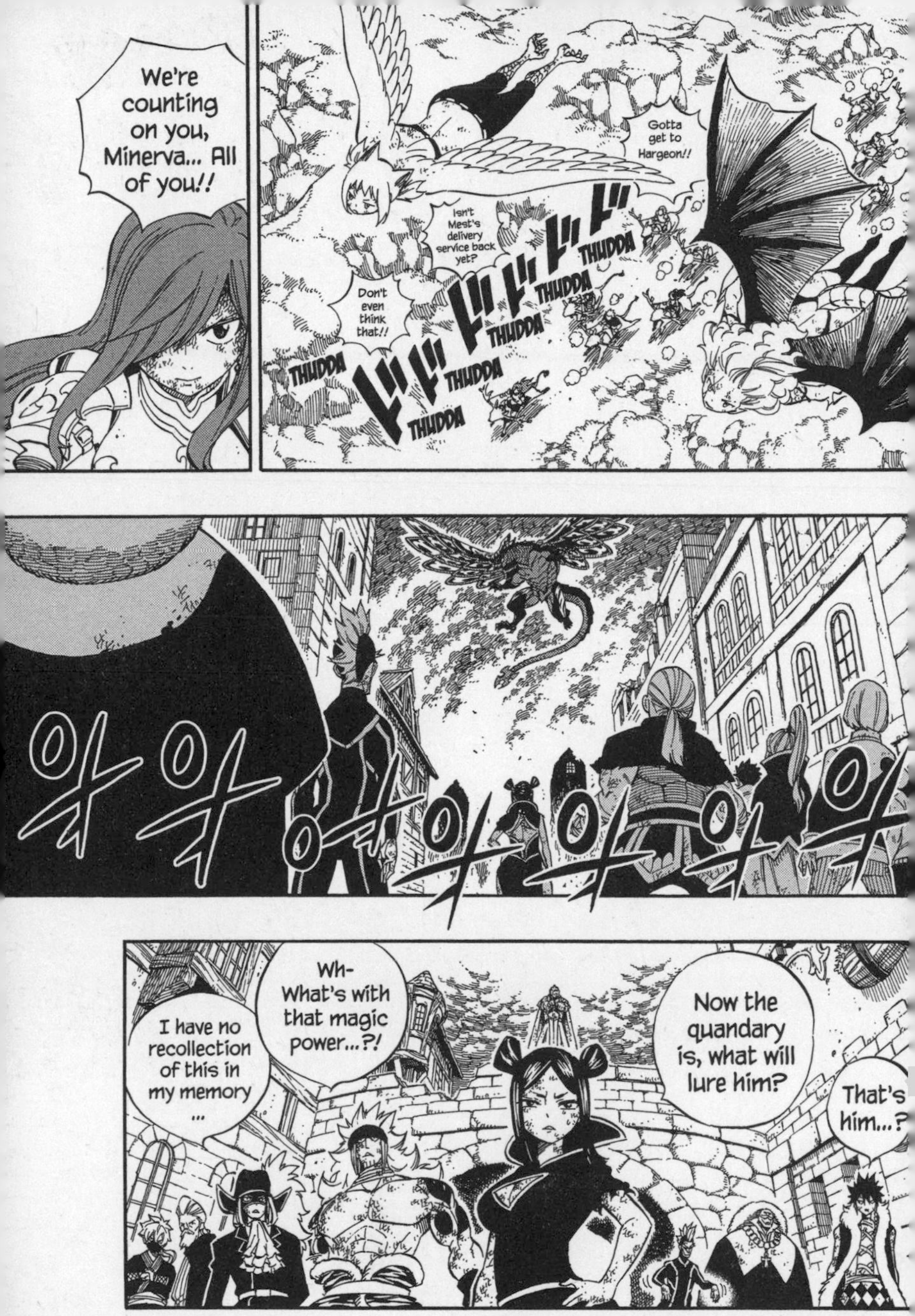
Gotta get to Hargeon!!
Isn't Mest's delivery service back yet?
THUDDA THUDDA THUDDA THUDDA THUDDA THUDDA
Don't even think that!!
We're counting on you, Minerva... All of you!!
That's him...?
Now the quandary is, what will lure him?
Wh- What's with that magic power...?!
I have no recollection of this in my memory ...

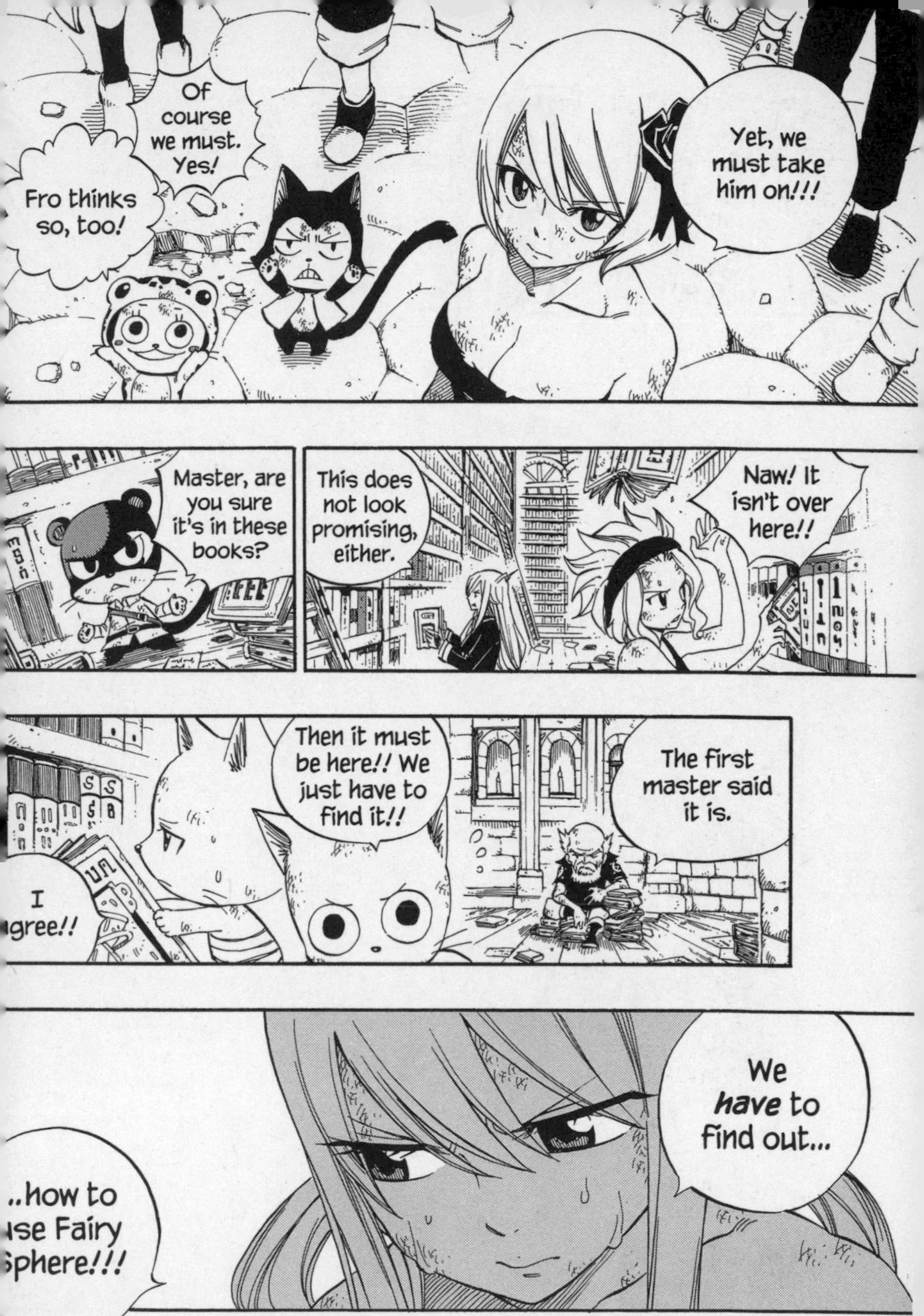
Yet, we must take him on!!!
Of course we must. Yes!
Fro thinks so, too!
Naw! It isn't over here!!
This does not look promising, either.
Master, are you sure it's in these books?
The first master said it is.
Then it must be here!! We just have to find it!!
I agree!!
We *have* to find out...
..how to use Fairy Sphere!!!

FAIRY TAIL

フェアリーテイル

Chapter 542: Instinct

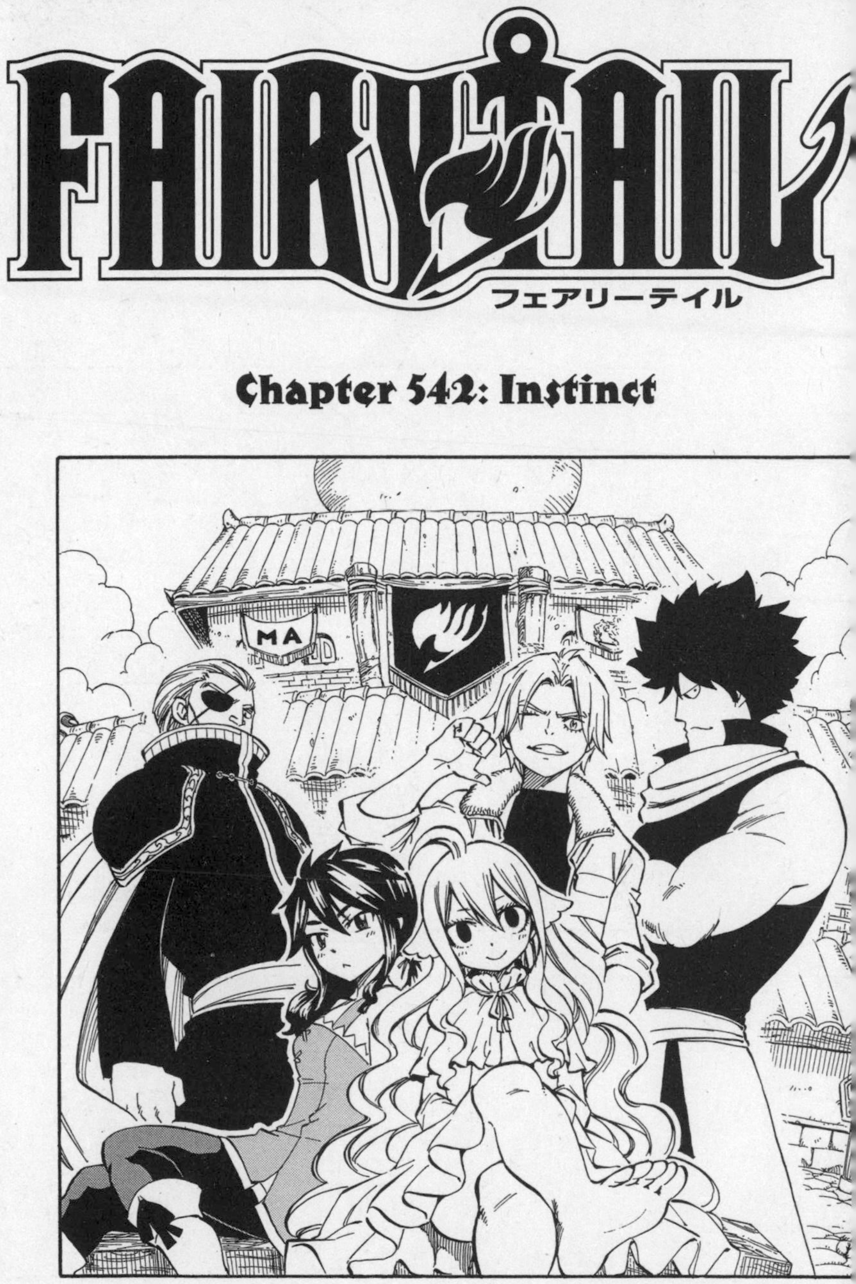
MA

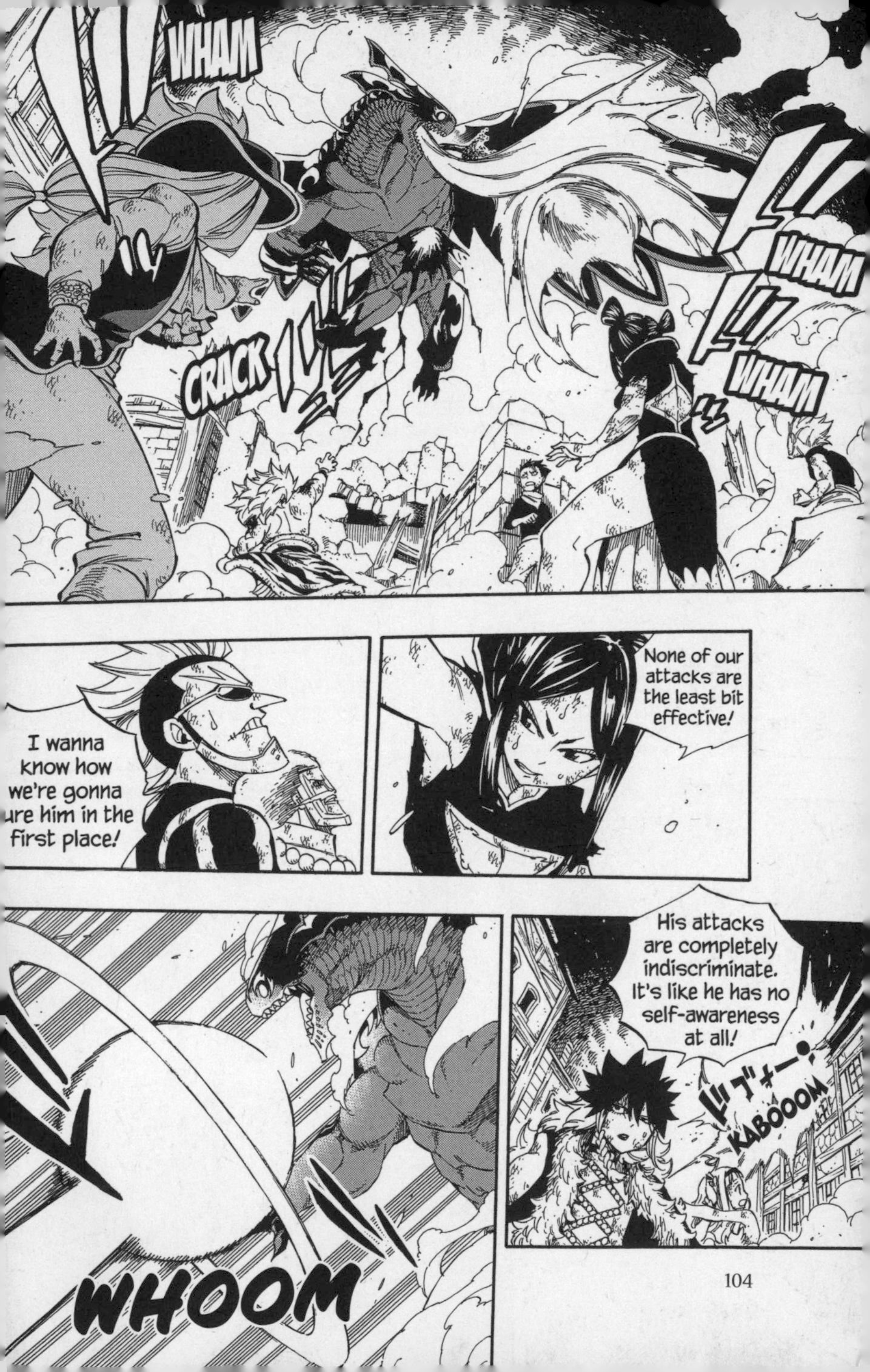
WHAM
WHAM
WHAM
CRACK
None of our attacks are the least bit effective!
I wanna know how we're gonna ure him in the first place!
His attacks are completely indiscriminate. It's like he has no self-awareness at all!
KABOOOM
WHOOM

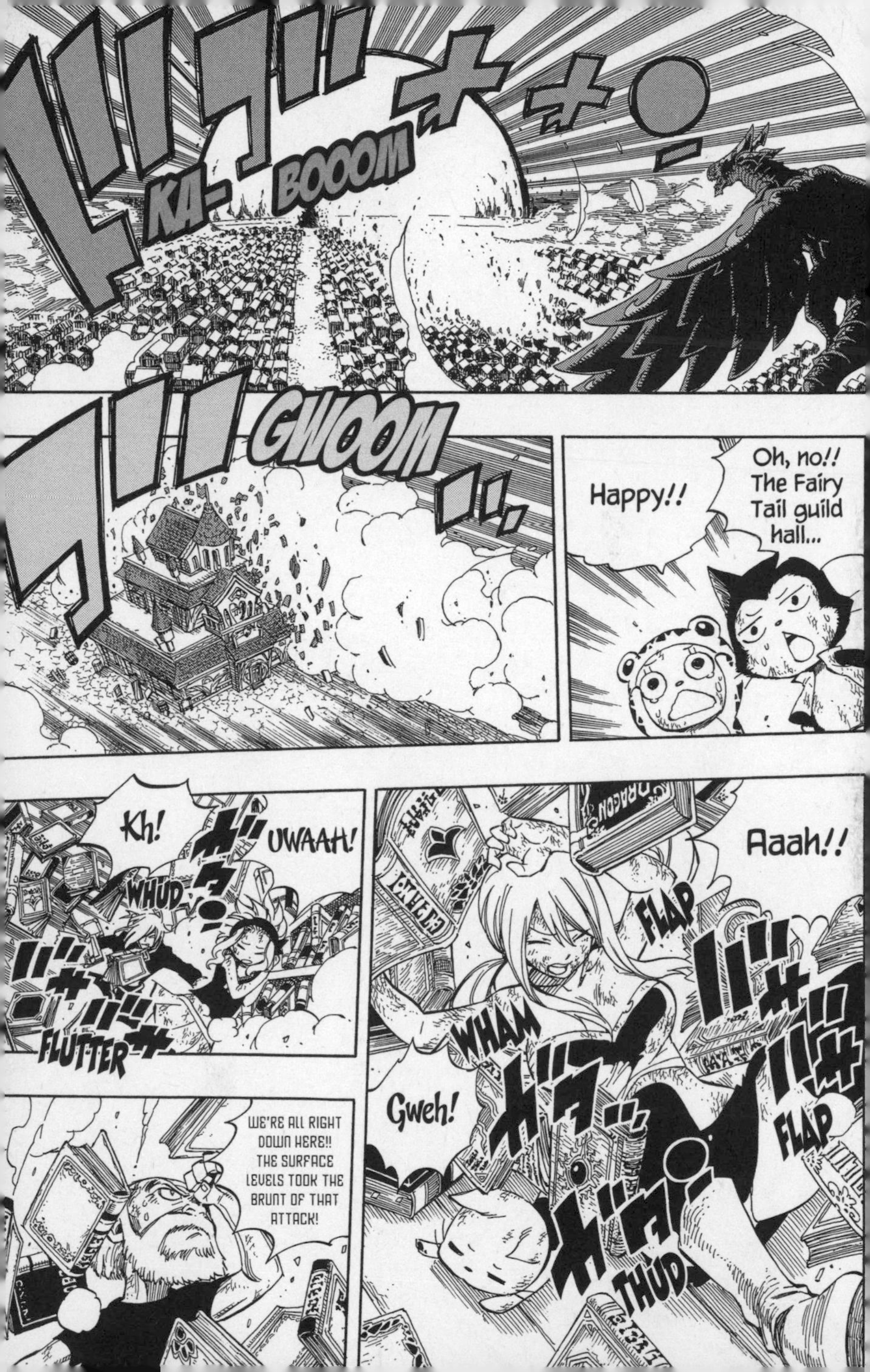
KA-BOOOM
Oh, no!! The Fairy Tail guild hall...
Happy!!
GWOOM
Aaah!!
FLAP
FLAP
WHAM
Gweh!
THUD
Kh!
UWAAH!
WHUD
FLUTTER
WE'RE ALL RIGHT DOWN HERE!! THE SURFACE LEVELS TOOK THE BRUNT OF THAT ATTACK!

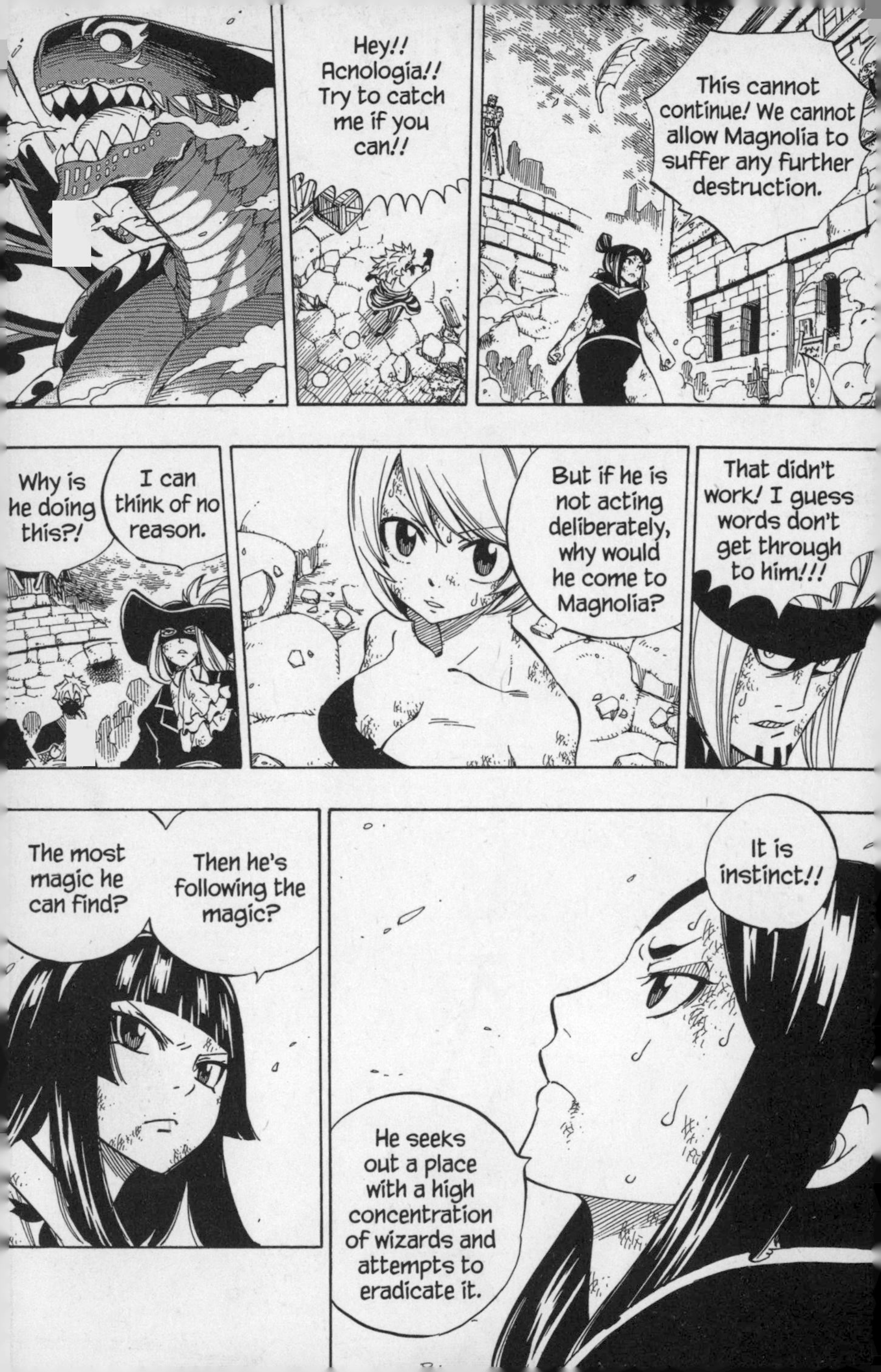
This cannot continue! We cannot allow Magnolia to suffer any further destruction.
Hey!! Acnologia!! Try to catch me if you can!!
That didn't work! I guess words don't get through to him!!!
But if he is not acting deliberately, why would he come to Magnolia?
I can think of no reason.
Why is he doing this?!
It is instinct!!
He seeks out a place with a high concentration of wizards and attempts to eradicate it.
Then he's following the magic?
The most magic he can find?

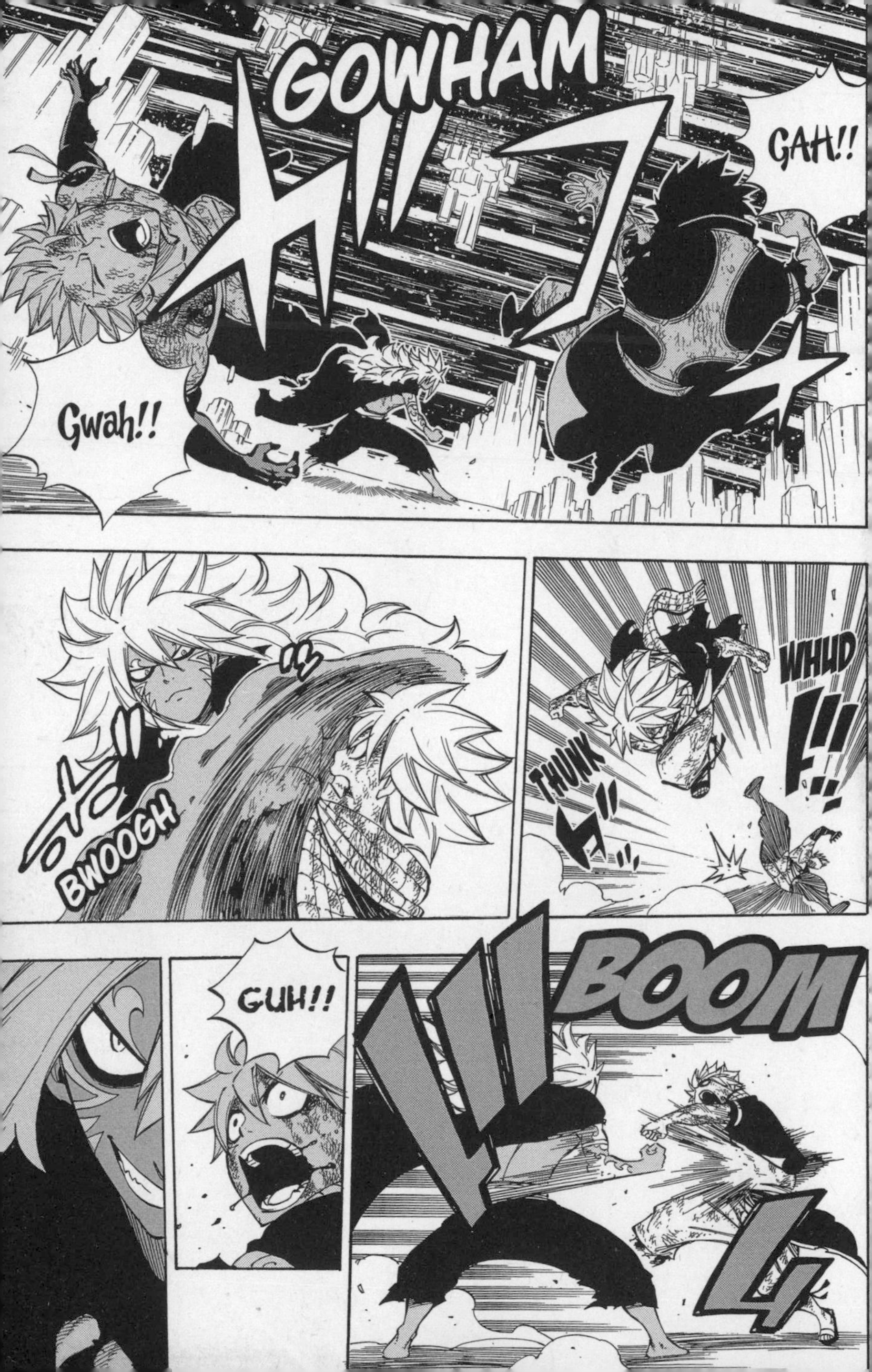
GOWHAM
GAH!!
Gwah!!
WHUD
THUNK
BWOOGH
BOOM
GUH!!

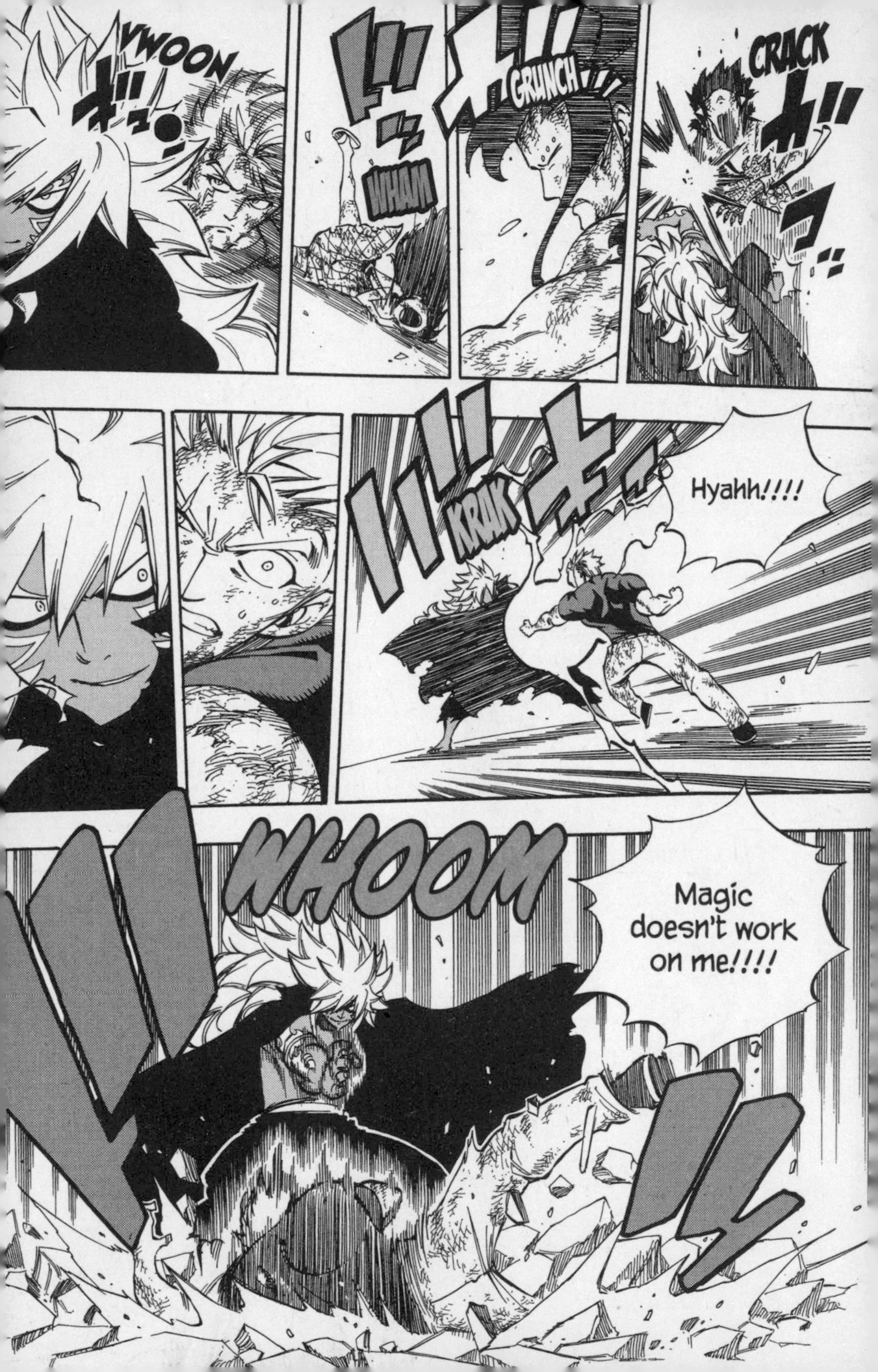
CRACK
GRUNCH
WHAM
VWOON
Hyahh!!!!
KRAK
Magic doesn't work on me!!!!
WHOOM

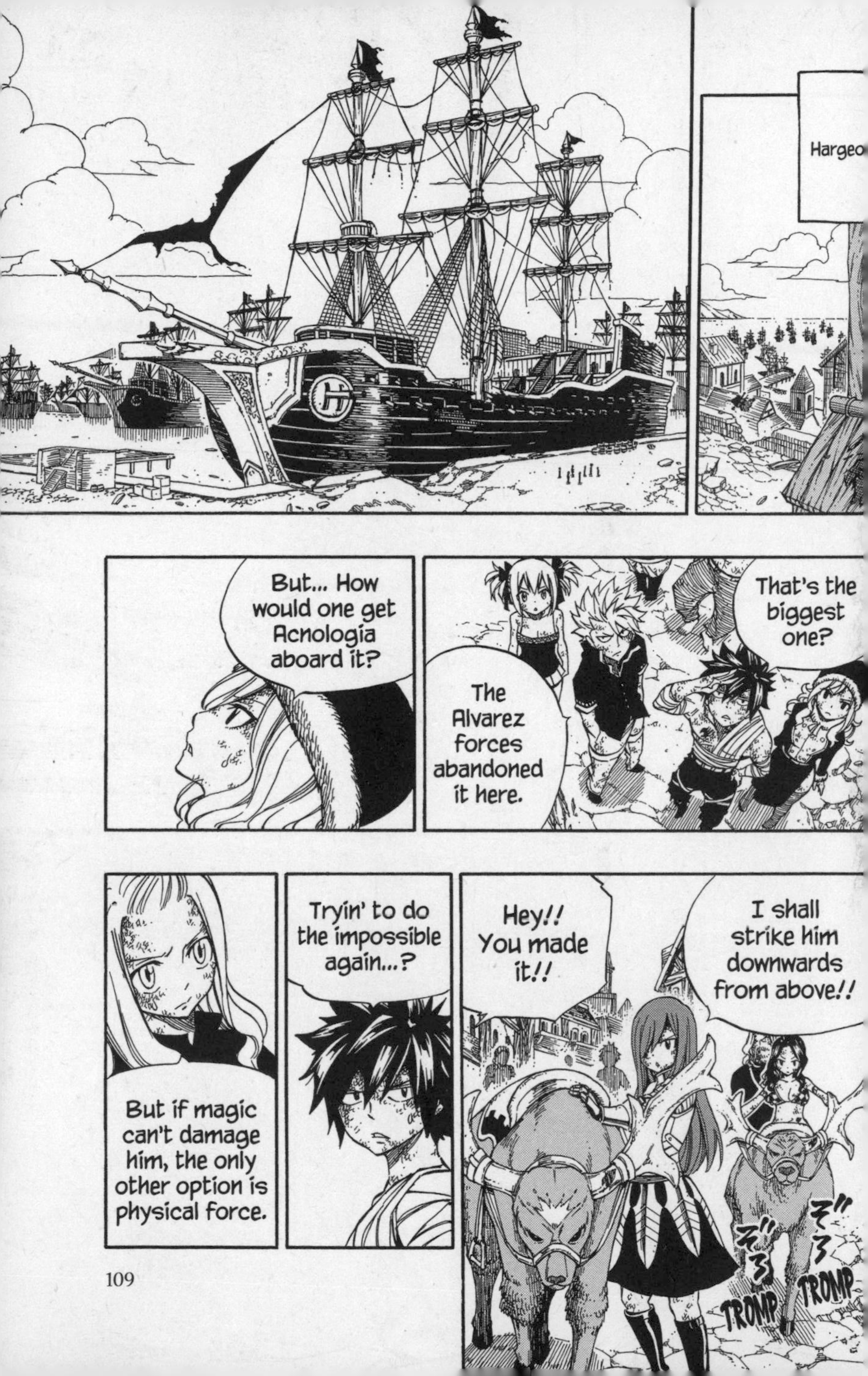
Hargeo
That's the biggest one?
The Alvarez forces abandoned it here.
But... How would one get Acnologia aboard it?
I shall strike him downwards from above!!
Hey!! You made it!!
ぞろ
ぞろ
TROMP
TROMP
Tryin' to do the impossible again...?
But if magic can't damage him, the only other option is physical force.

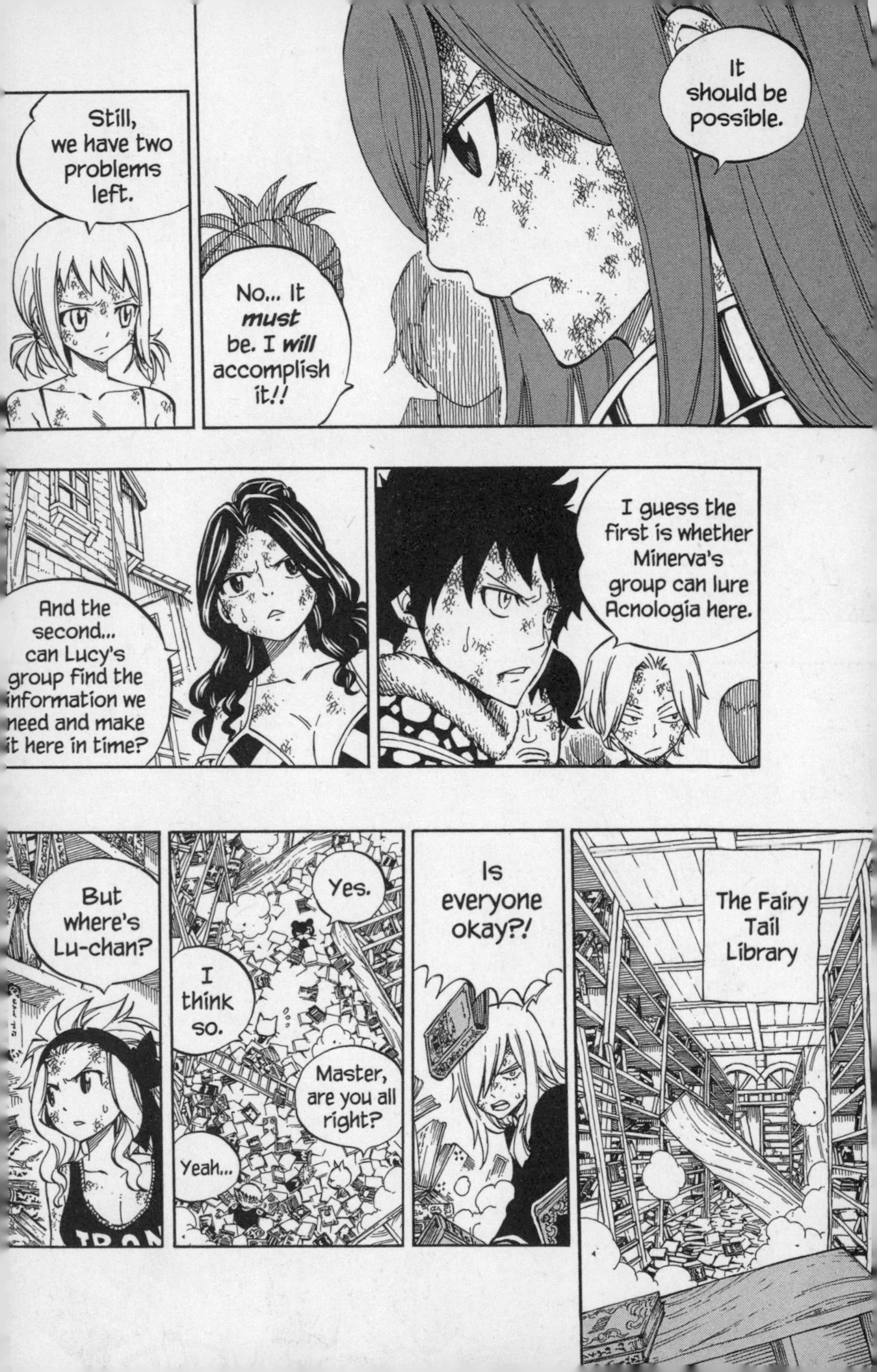
It should be possible.
No... It *must* be. I *will* accomplish it!!
Still, we have two problems left.
I guess the first is whether Minerva's group can lure Acnologia here.
And the second... can Lucy's group find the information we need and make it here in time?
The Fairy Tail Library
Is everyone okay?!
Yes.
I think so.
Master, are you all right?
Yeah...
But where's Lu-chan?

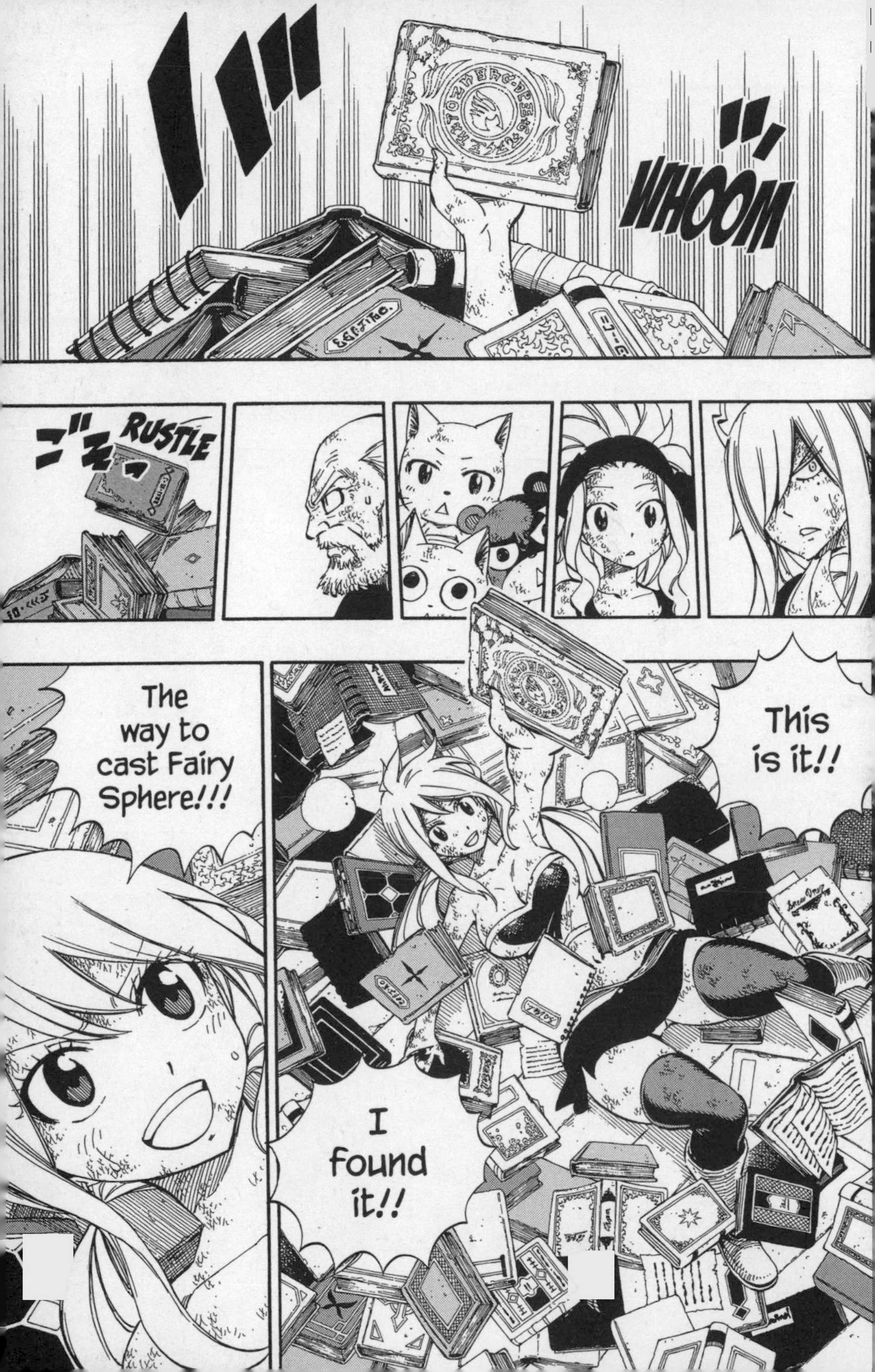
WHOOM
RUSTLE
This is it!!
I found it!!
The way to cast Fairy Sphere!!!

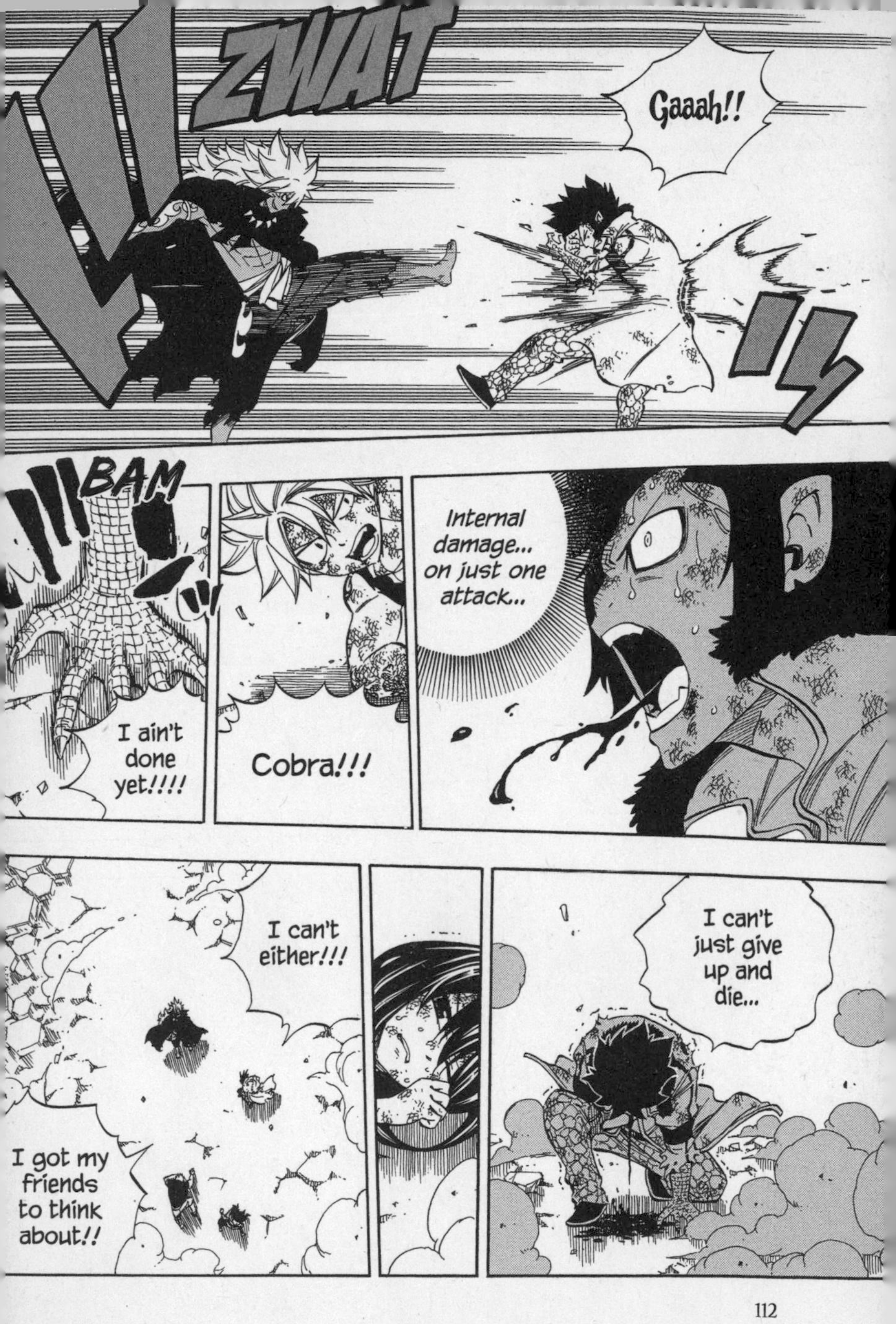
Gaaah!!
ZWAT
Internal damage... on just one attack...
Cobra!!!
BAM
I ain't done yet!!!!
I can't just give up and die...
I can't either!!!
I got my friends to think about!!

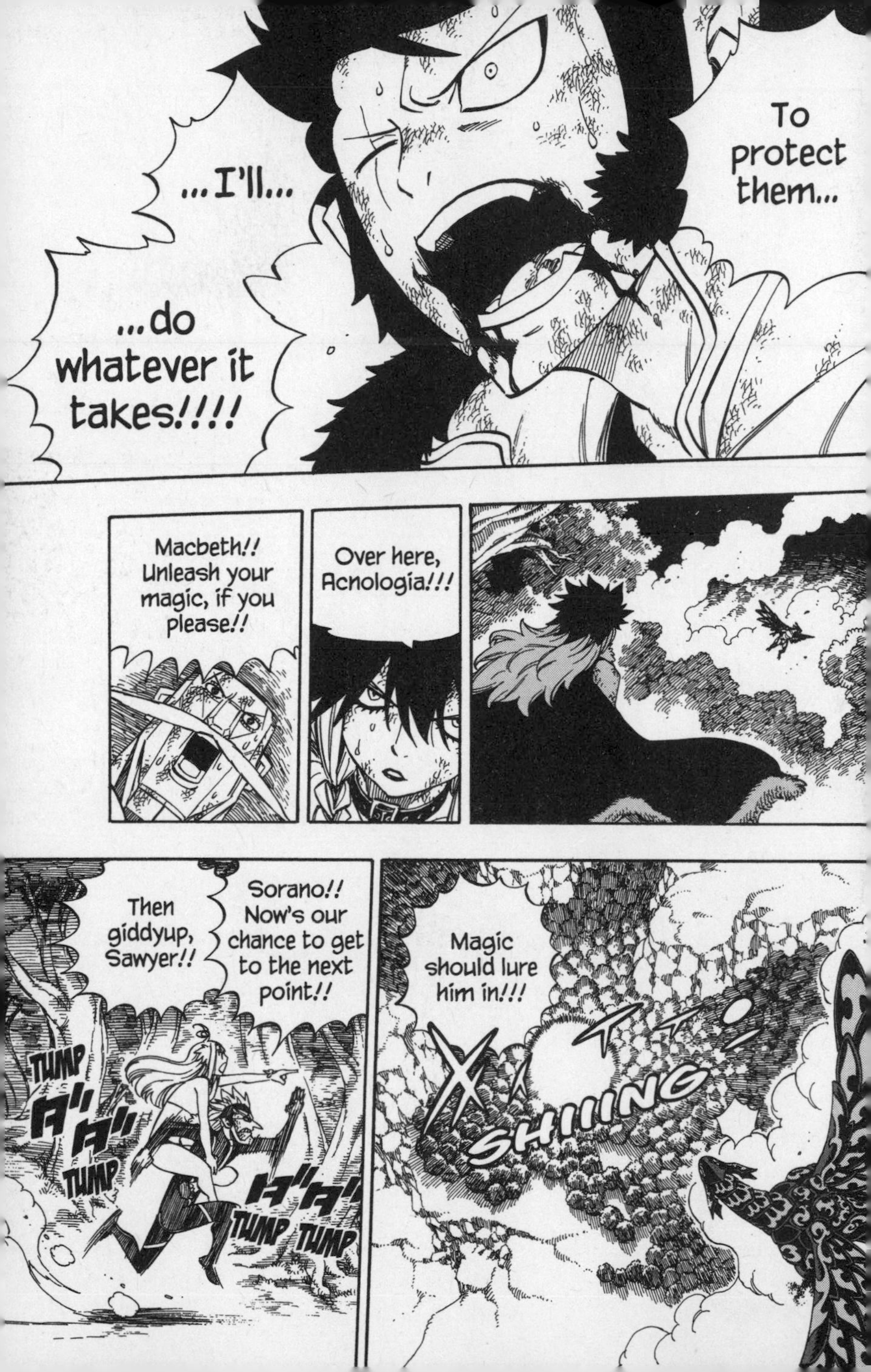
To protect them...
...I'll...
...do whatever it takes!!!!
Over here, Acnologia!!!
Macbeth!! Unleash your magic, if you please!!
Magic should lure him in!!!
SHIIIING
Sorano!! Now's our chance to get to the next point!!
Then giddyup, Sawyer!!
TUMP TUMP
TUMP
TUMP
TUMP

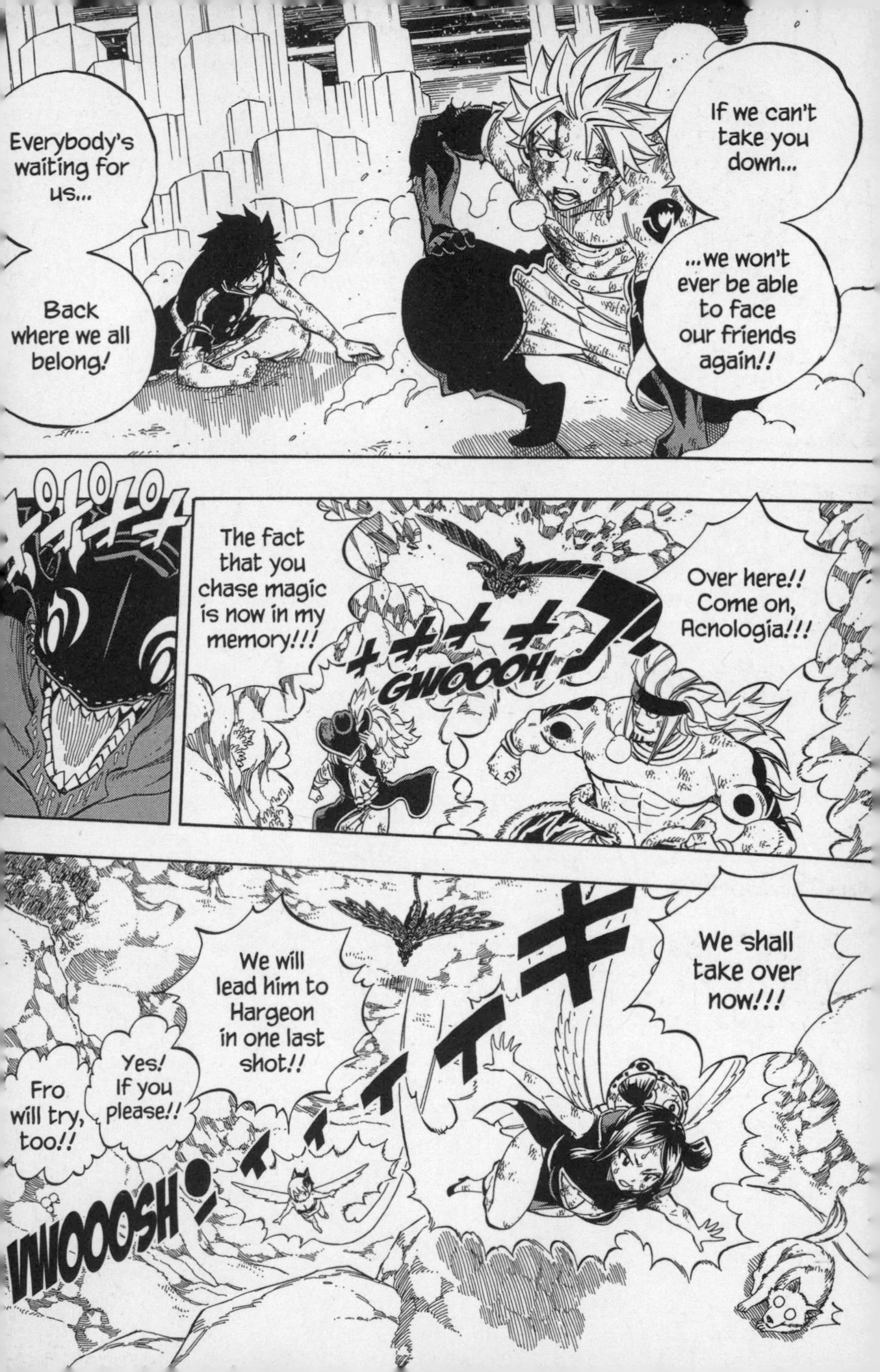

If we can't take you down...
...we won't ever be able to face our friends again!!
Everybody's waiting for us...
Back where we all belong!
Over here!! Come on, Acnologia!!!
GWOOOH
The fact that you chase magic is now in my memory!!!
We shall take over now!!!
We will lead him to Hargeon in one last shot!!
Yes! If you please!!
Fro will try, too!!
VWOOOSH

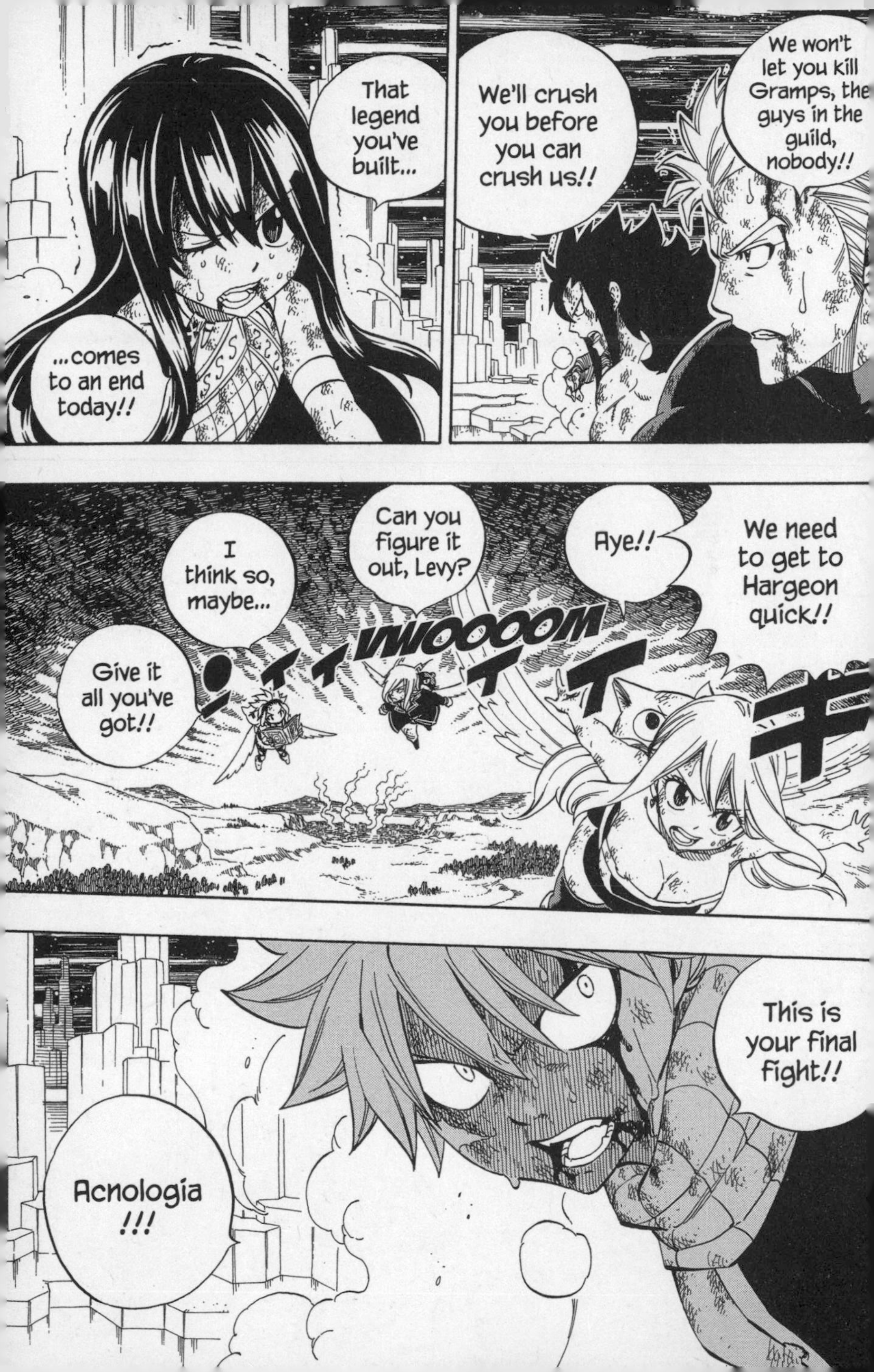

We won't let you kill Gramps, the guys in the guild, nobody!!
We'll crush you before you can crush us!!
That legend you've built...
...comes to an end today!!
We need to get to Hargeon quick!!
Aye!!
VWOOOOM
Can you figure it out, Levy?
I think so, maybe...
Give it all you've got!!
This is your final fight!!
Acnologia!!!

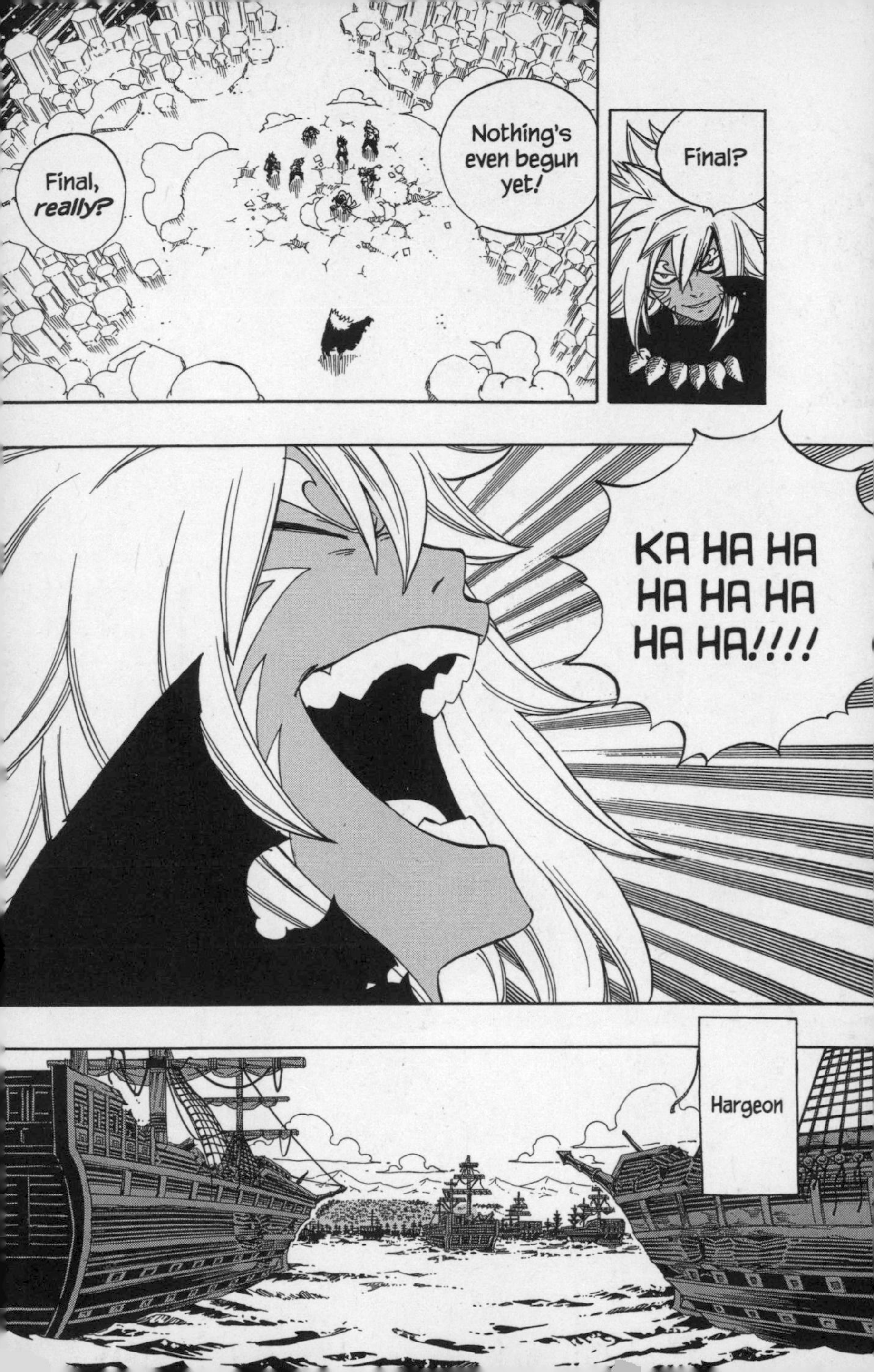
Final?
Nothing's even begun yet!
Final, *really?*
KA HA HA HA HA HA HA HA!!!!
Hargeon

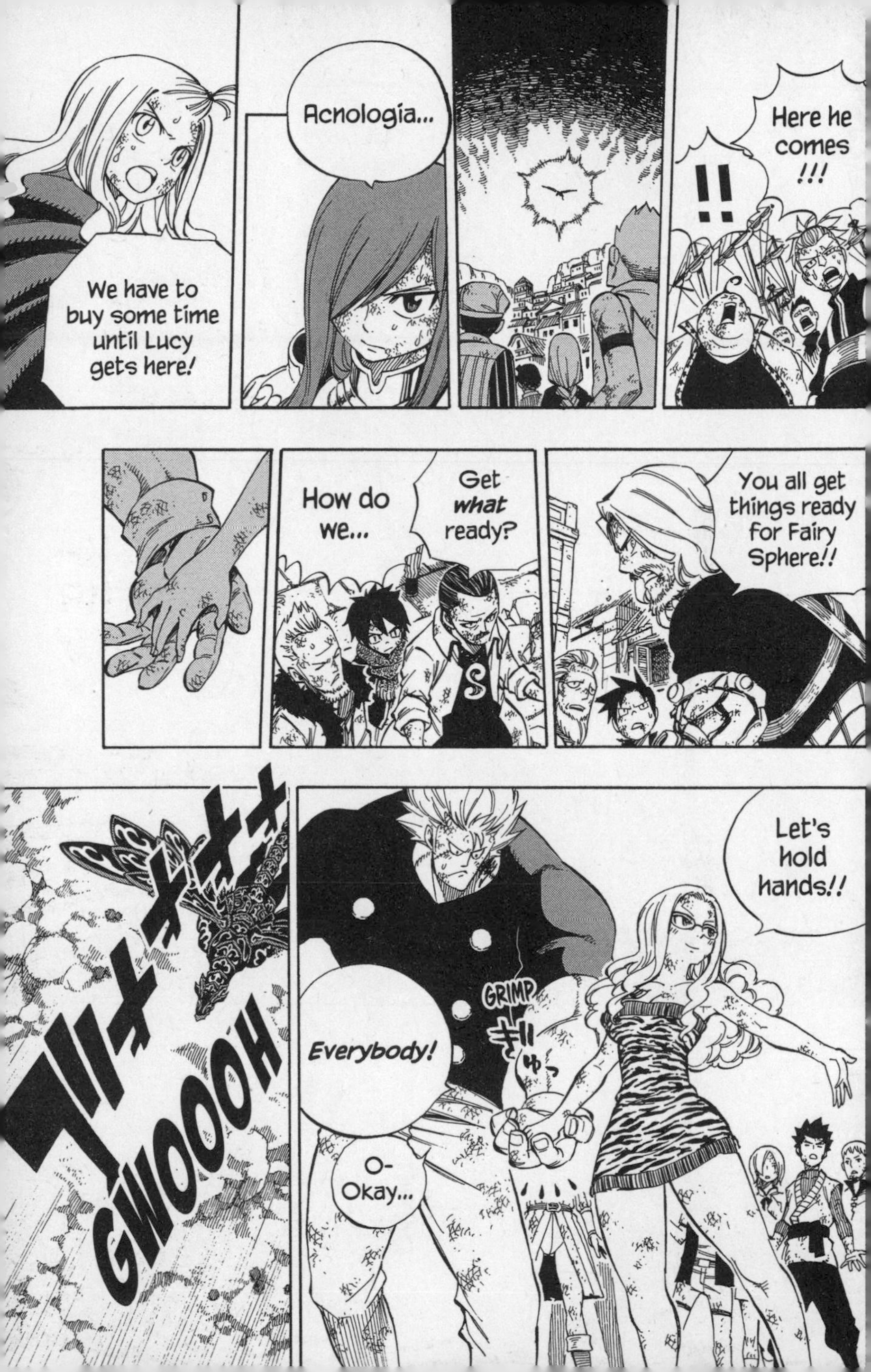
!!
Here he comes !!!
Acnologia...
We have to buy some time until Lucy gets here!
You all get things ready for Fairy Sphere!!
Get *what* ready?
How do we...
Let's hold hands!!
GRIMP
Everybody!
O- Okay...
GWOOOH

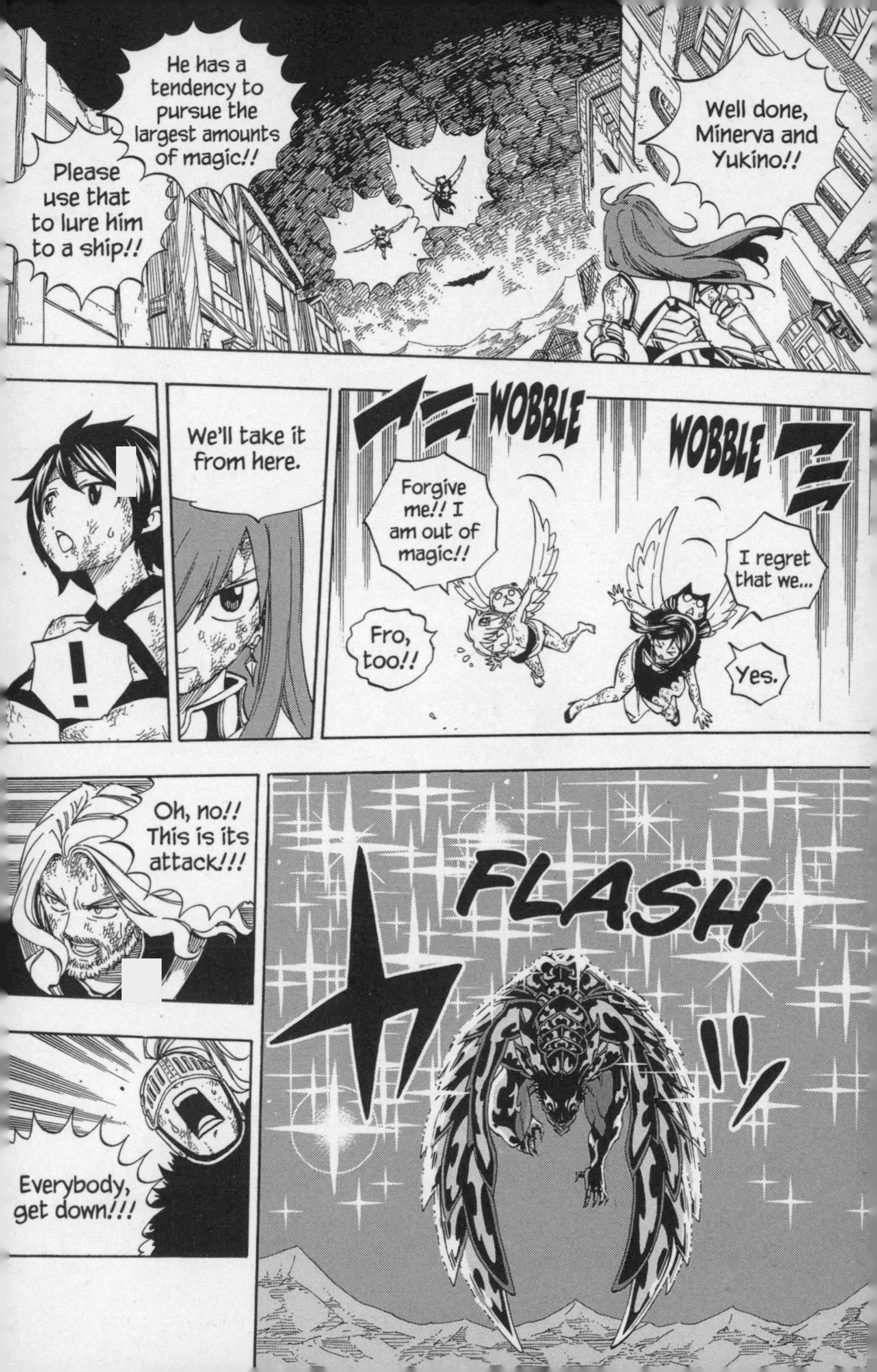

Well done, Minerva and Yukino!!
He has a tendency to pursue the largest amounts of magic!!
Please use that to lure him to a ship!!
WOBBLE
WOBBLE
I regret that we...
Yes.
Forgive me!! I am out of magic!!
Fro, too!!
We'll take it from here.
!
FLASH
!!
Oh, no!! This is its attack!!!
Everybody, get down!!!

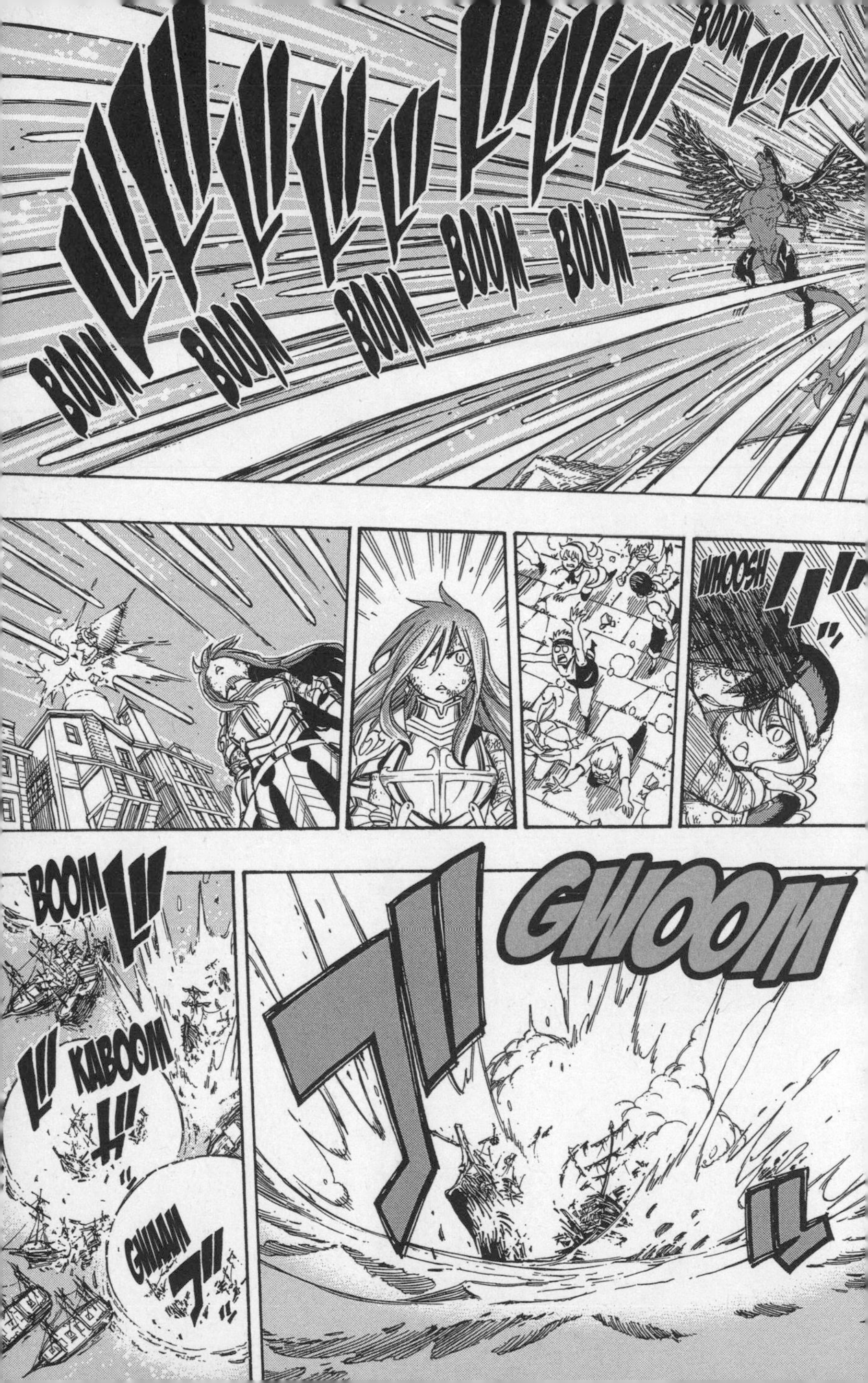
BOOM
BOOM
BOOM
BOOM
BOOM
BOOM
WHOOSH
GWOOM
BOOM
KABOOM
GWAAM

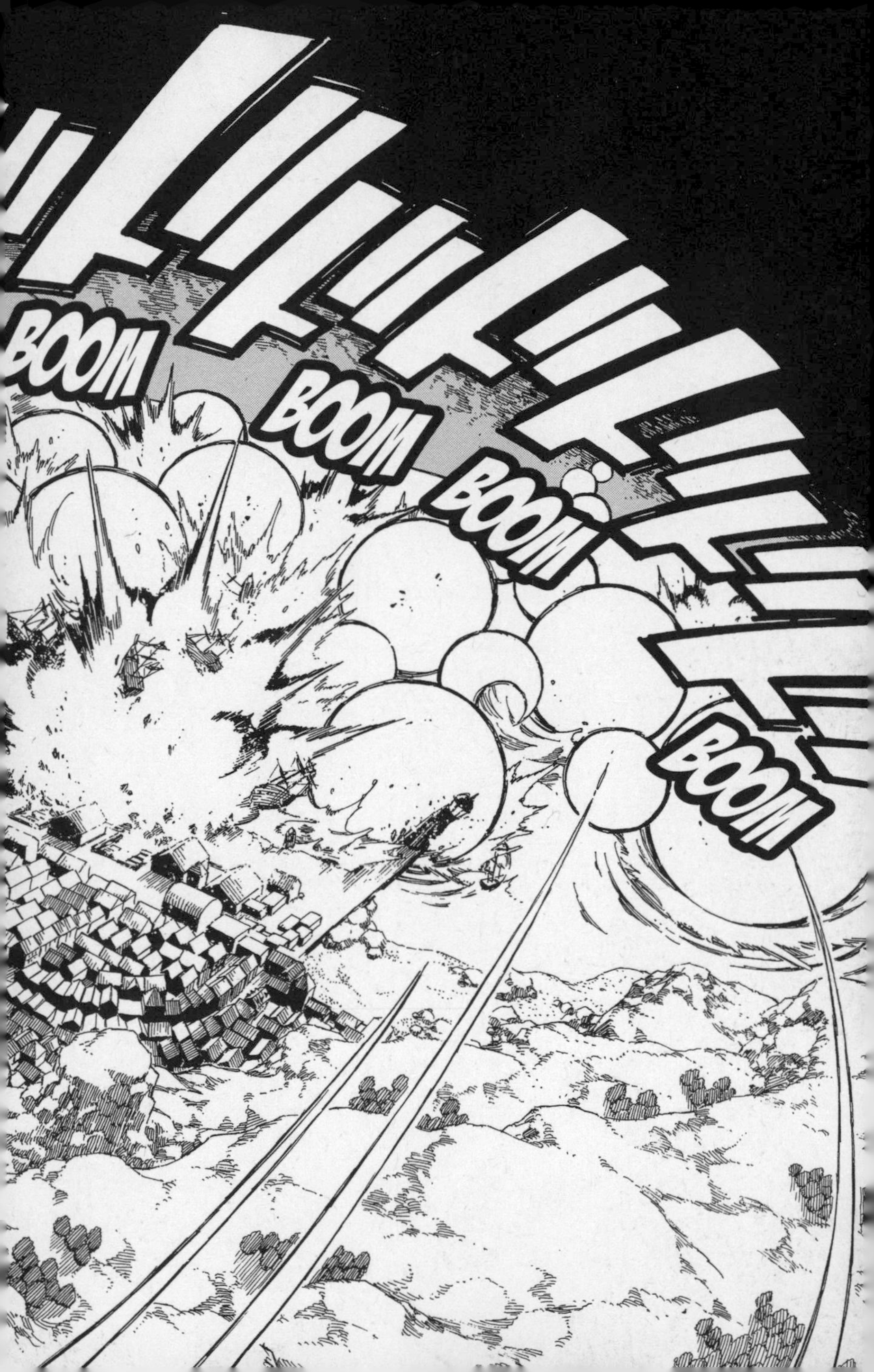
BOOM
BOOM
BOOM
BOOM

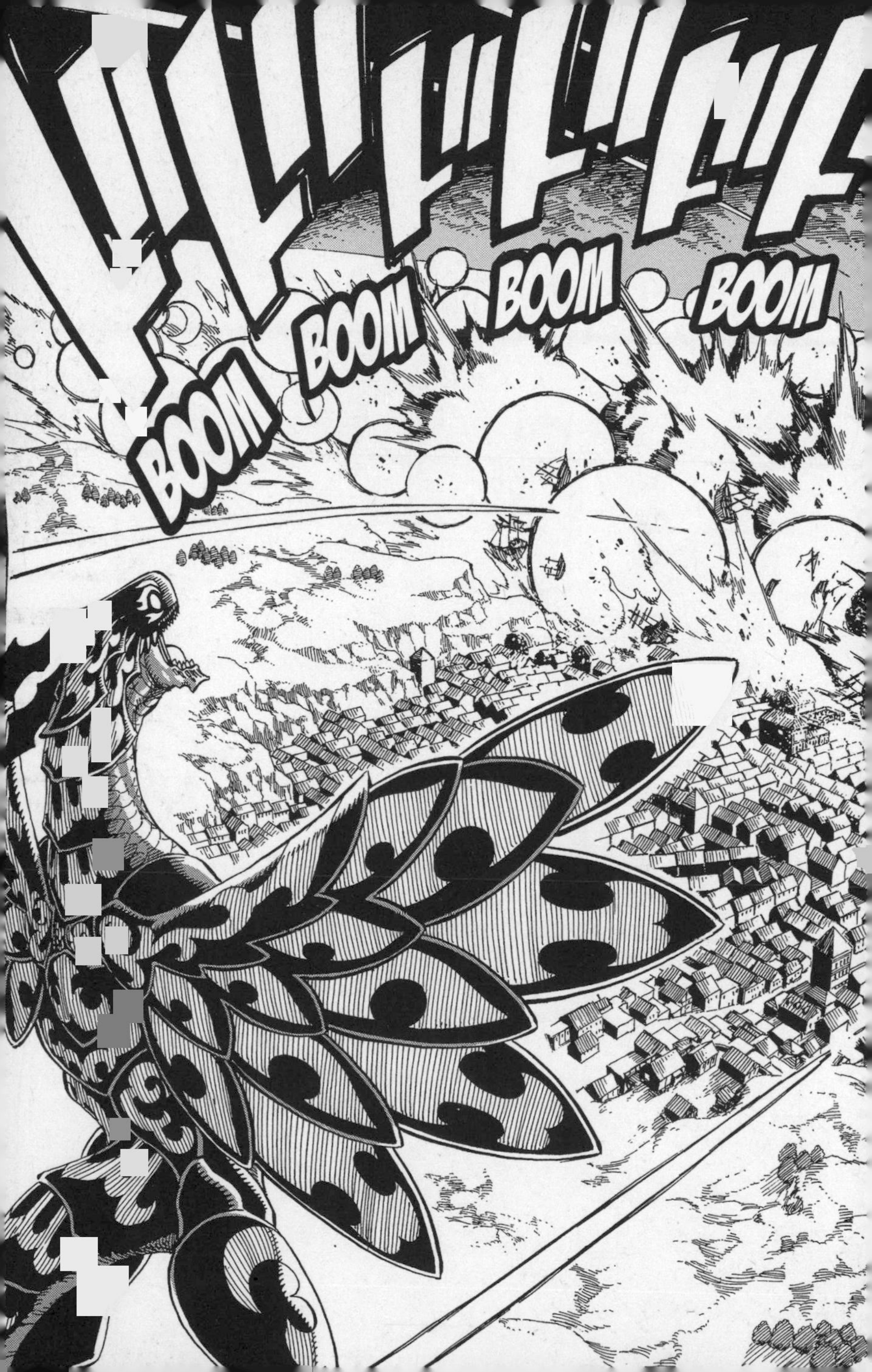
BOOM
BOOM
BOOM
BOOM

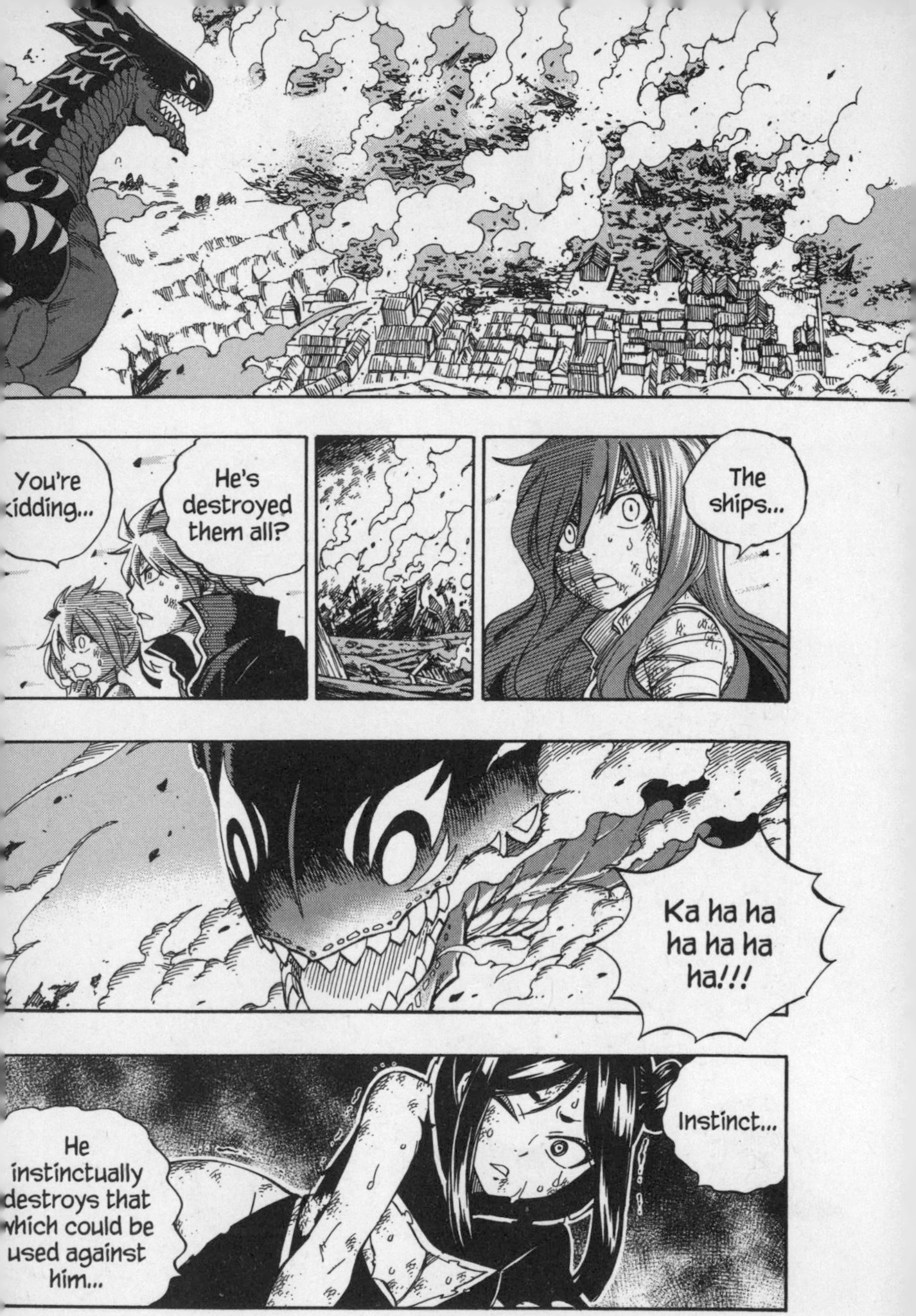
The ships...
He's destroyed them all?
You're kidding...
Ka ha ha ha ha ha ha!!!
Instinct...
He instinctually destroys that which could be used against him...

FAIRY TAIL
フェアリーテイル

Chapter 543: Hearts Connected

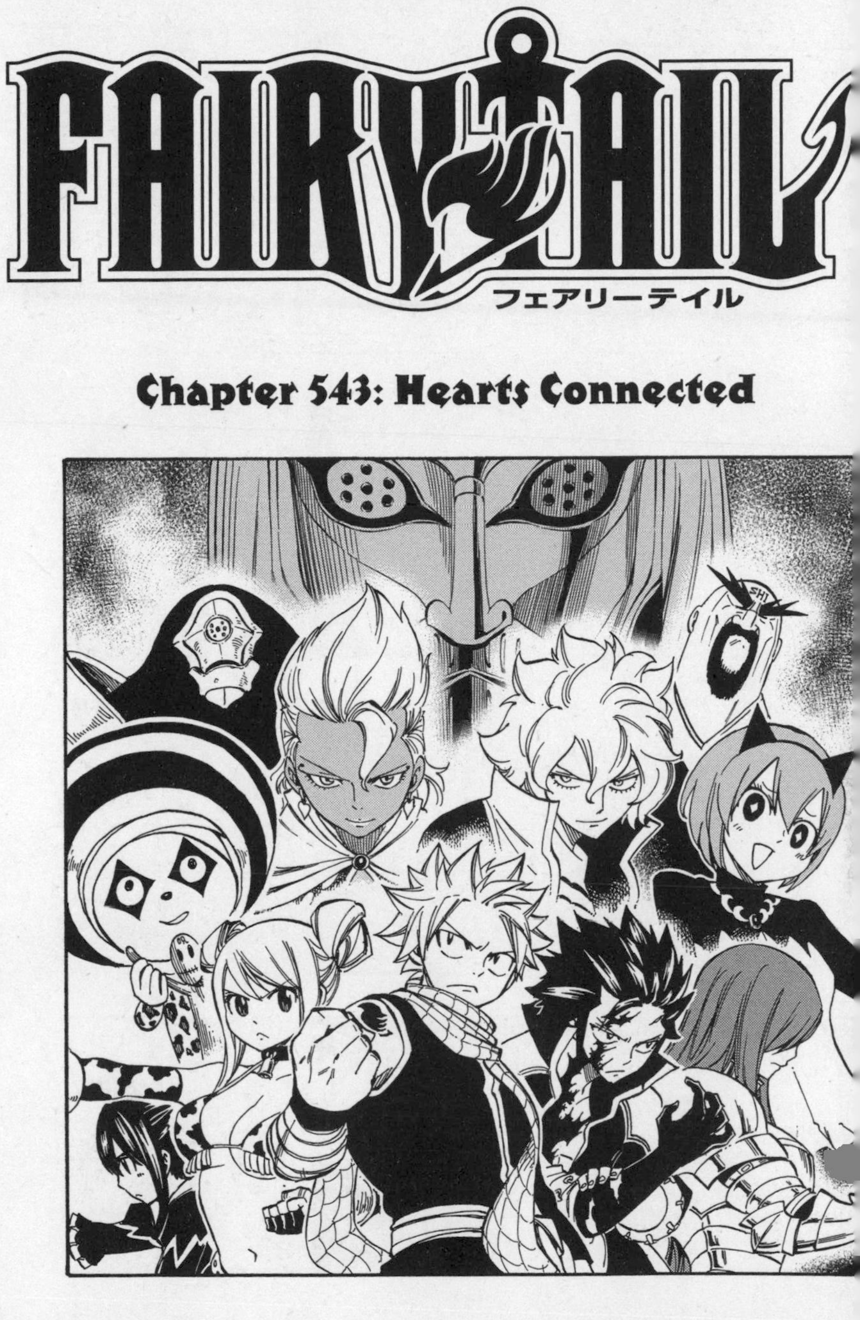

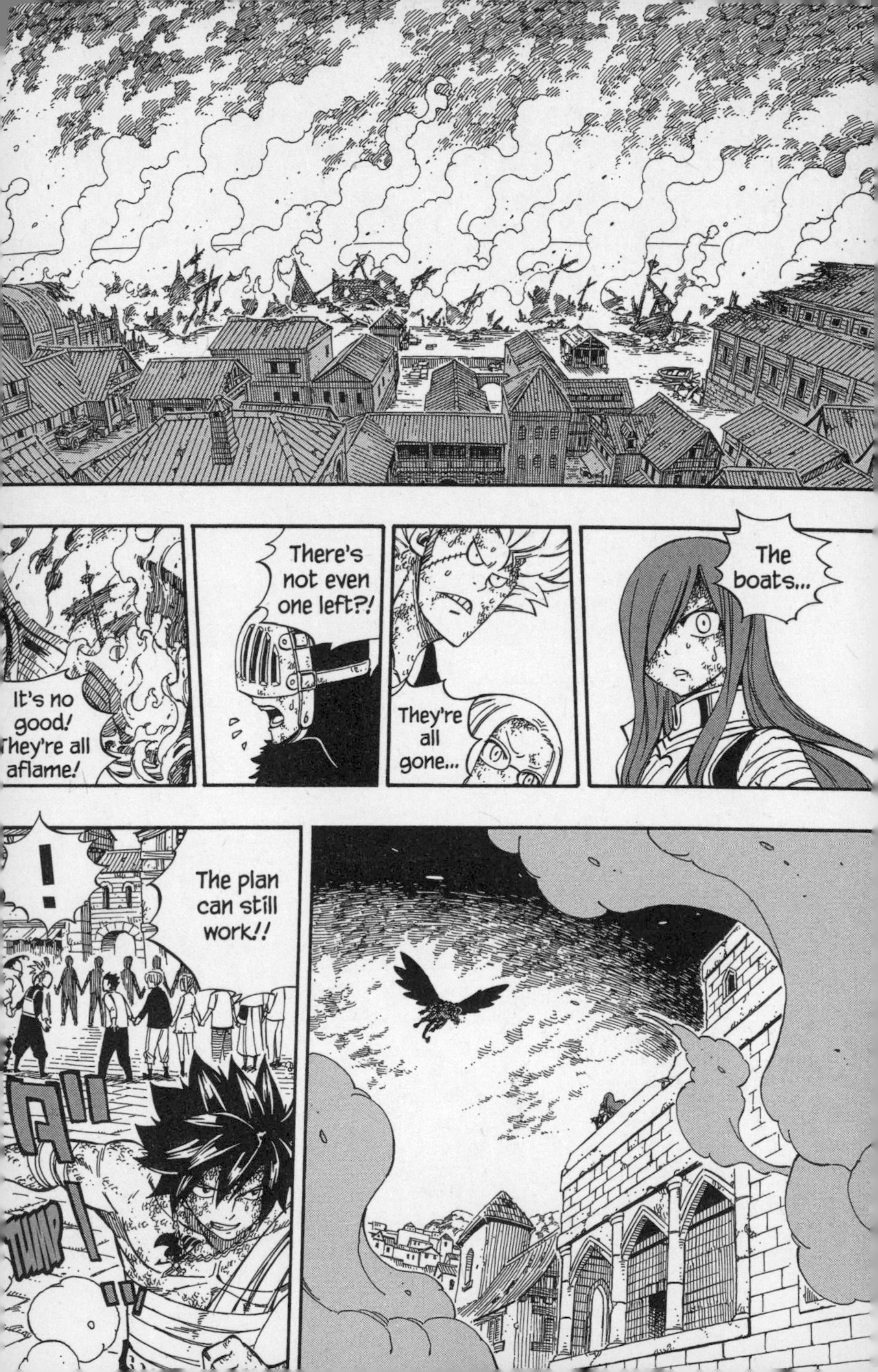
The boats...
They're all gone...
There's not even one left?!
It's no good! They're all aflame!
!
The plan can still work!!
THUMP

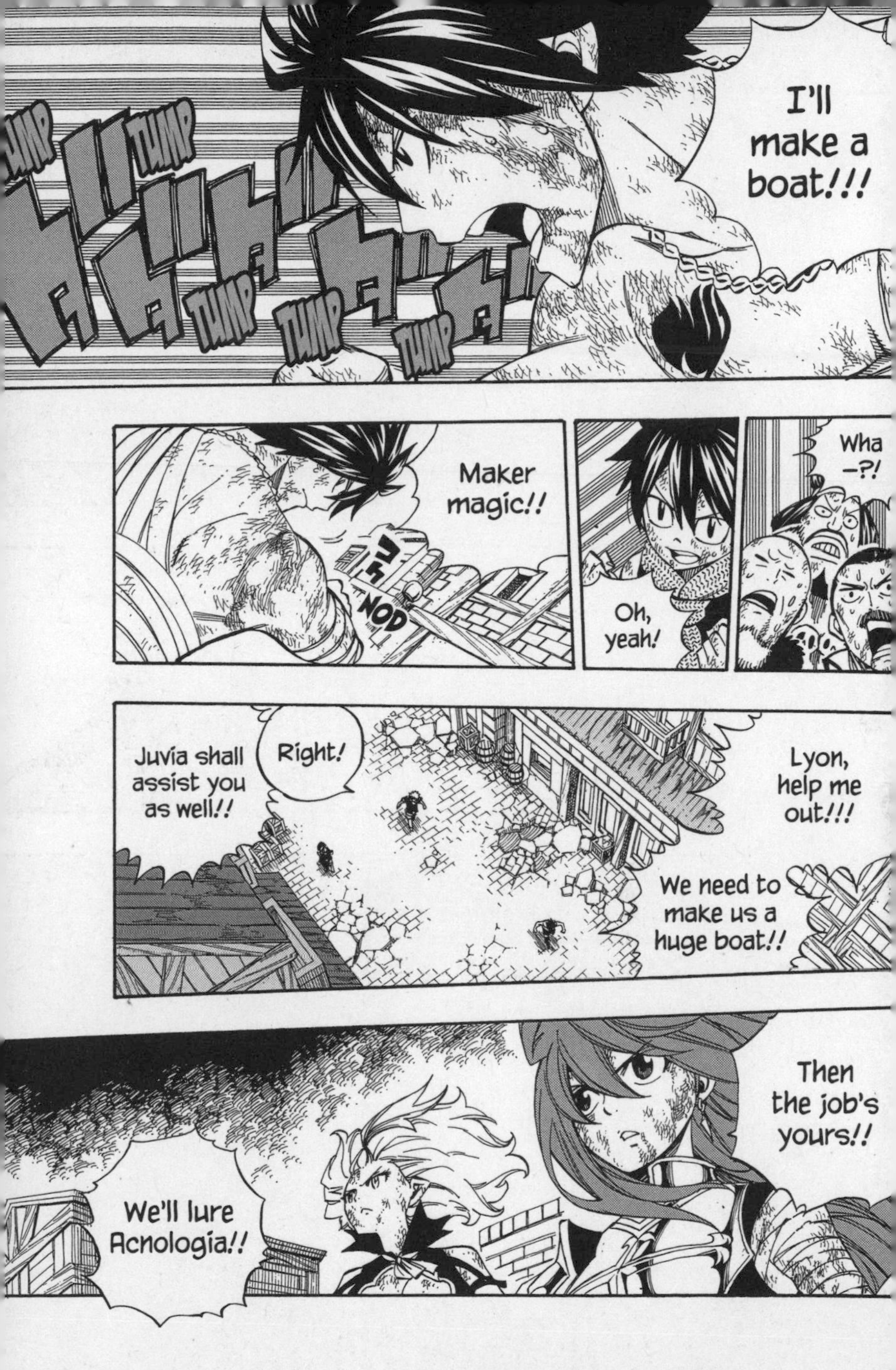
I'll make a boat!!!
TUMP
TUMP
TUMP
TUMP
Wha —?!
Oh, yeah!
Maker magic!!
NOD
Lyon, help me out!!!
We need to make us a huge boat!!
Right!
Juvia shall assist you as well!!
Then the job's yours!!
We'll lure Acnologia!!

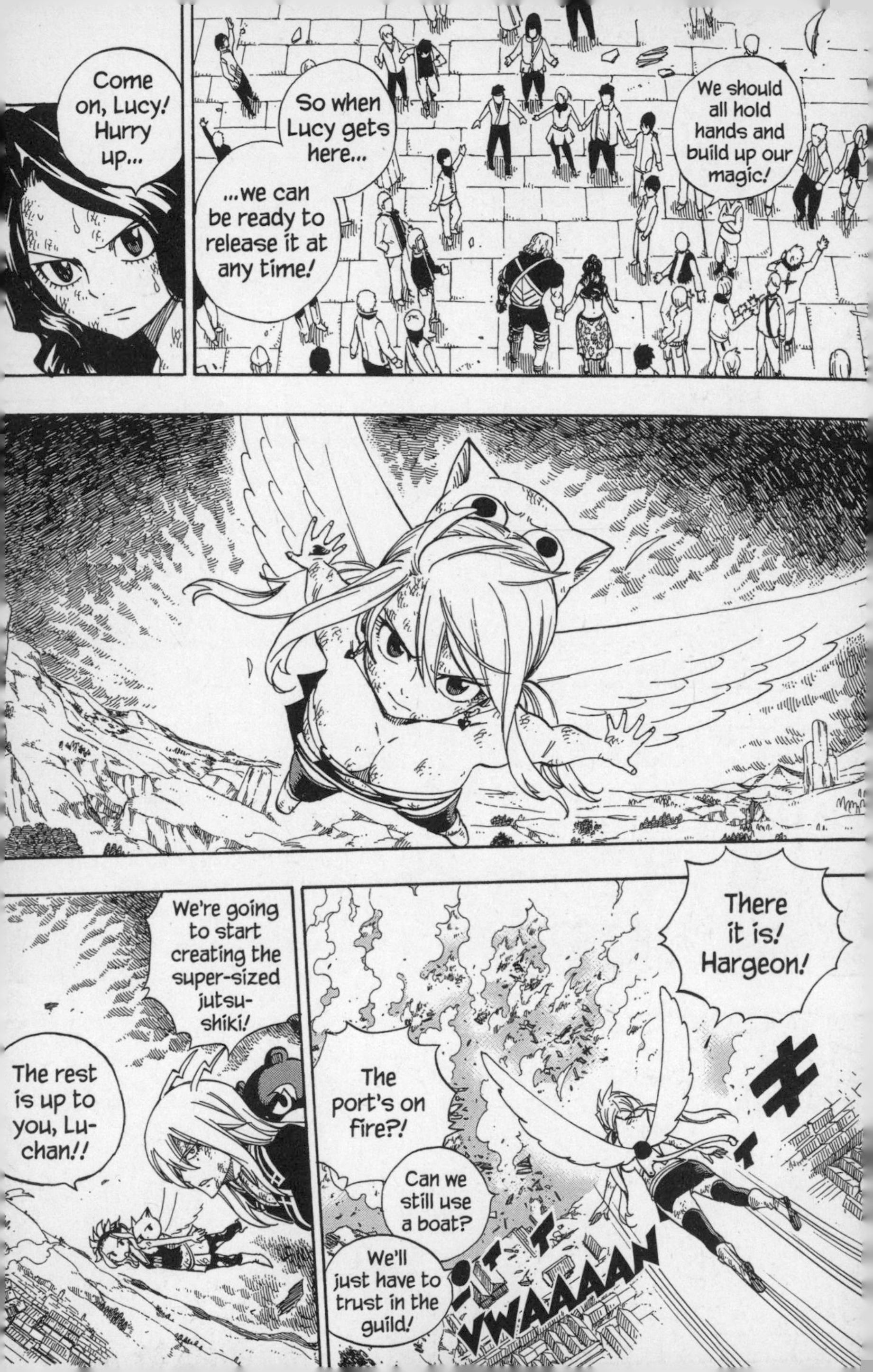
We should all hold hands and build up our magic!
So when Lucy gets here...
...we can be ready to release it at any time!
Come on, Lucy! Hurry up...
There it is! Hargeon!
The port's on fire?!
Can we still use a boat?
We'll just have to trust in the guild!
VWAAAAN
We're going to start creating the super-sized jutsu-shiki!
The rest is up to you, Lu-chan!!

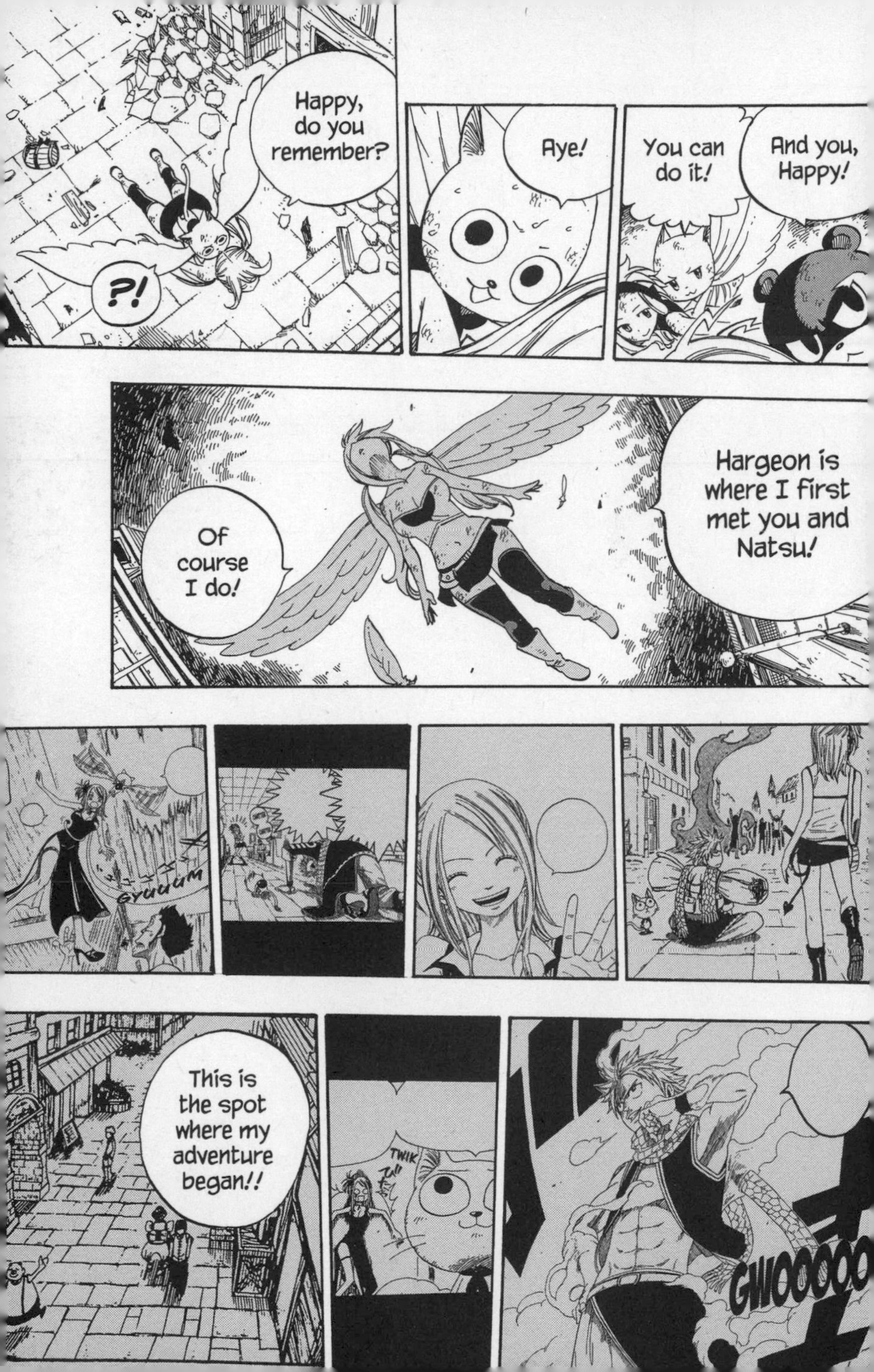
And you, Happy!
You can do it!
Aye!
Happy, do you remember?
?!
Hargeon is where I first met you and Natsu!
Of course I do!
Gruuum
GWOOOOO
TWIK
This is the spot where my adventure began!!

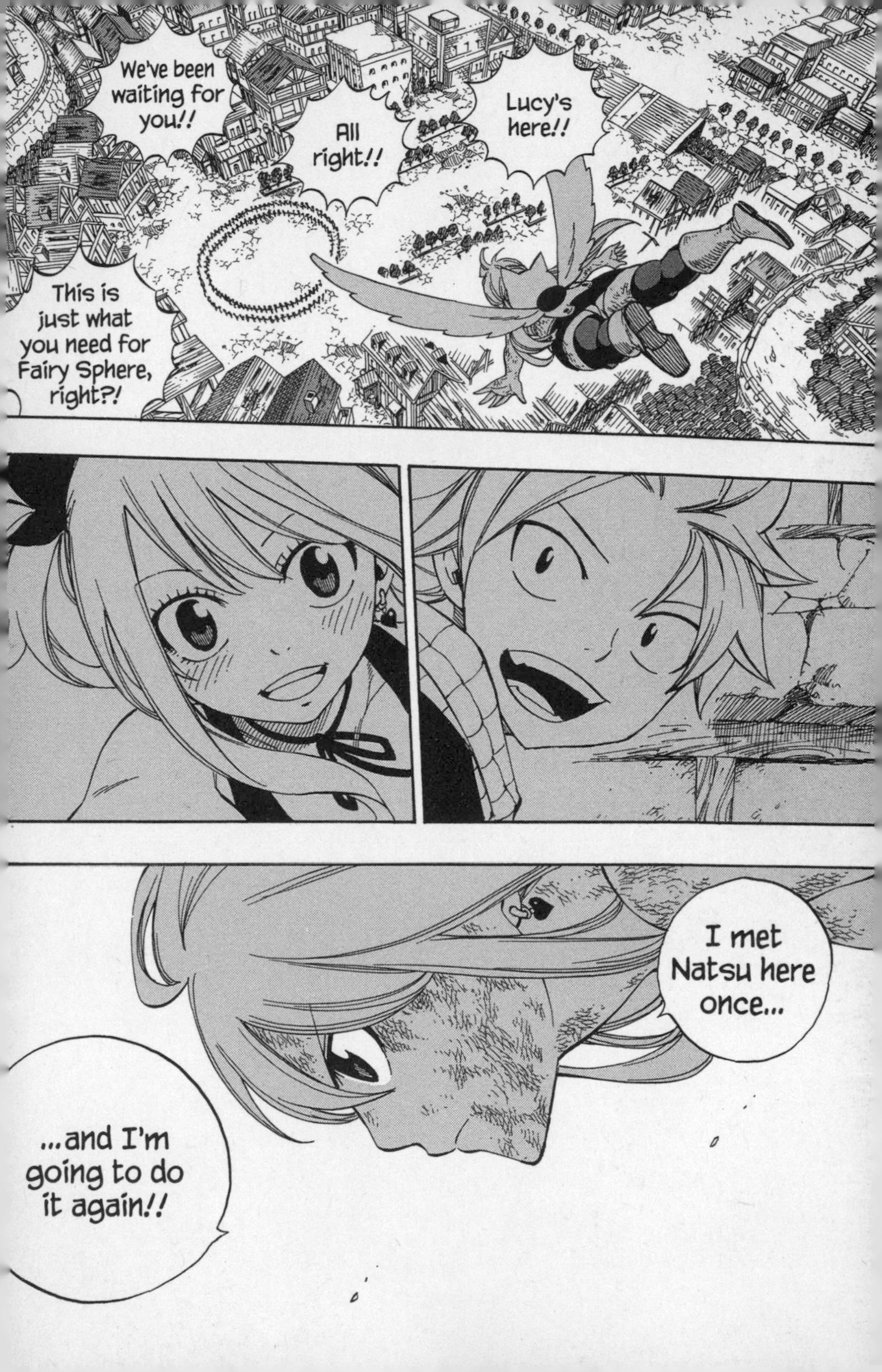
Lucy's here!!
All right!!
We've been waiting for you!!
This is just what you need for Fairy Sphere, right?!
I met Natsu here once...
...and I'm going to do it again!!

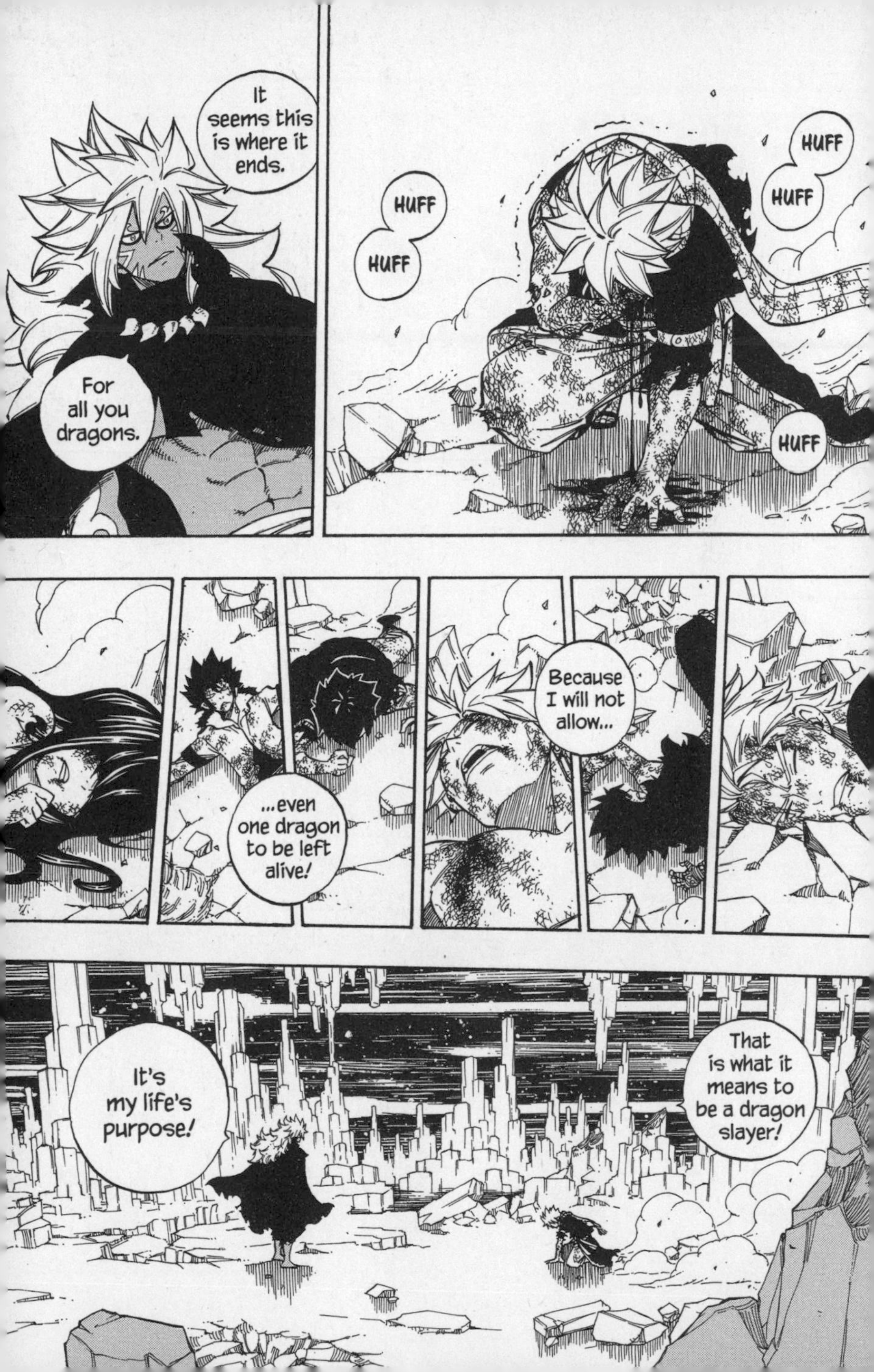
HUFF
HUFF
HUFF
HUFF
HUFF
It seems this is where it ends.
For all you dragons.
Because I will not allow...
...even one dragon to be left alive!
That is what it means to be a dragon slayer!
It's my life's purpose!

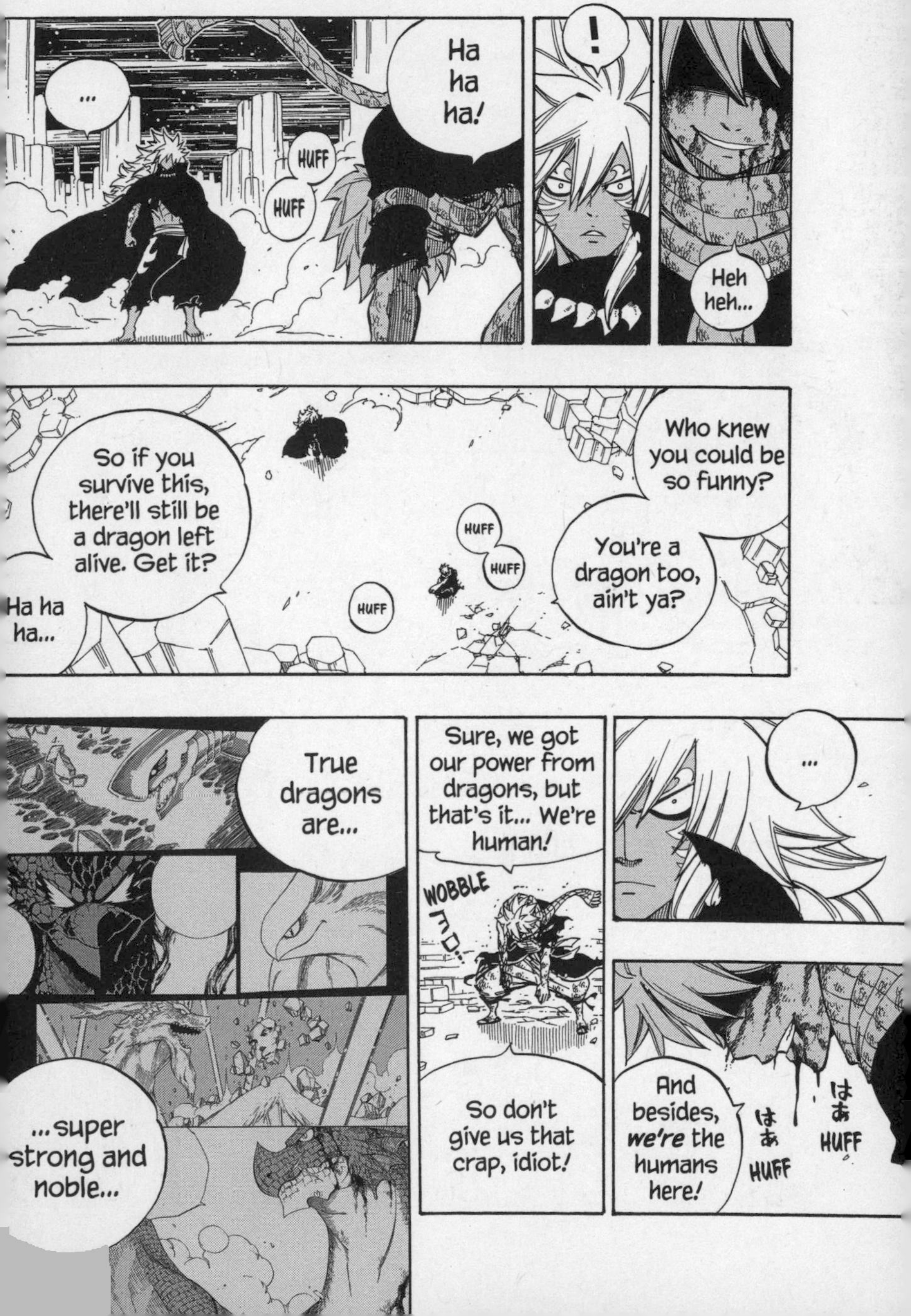
Heh heh...
!
Ha ha ha!
...
HUFF
HUFF
Who knew you could be so funny?
You're a dragon too, ain't ya?
HUFF
HUFF
So if you survive this, there'll still be a dragon left alive. Get it?
HUFF
Ha ha ha...
...
はあ HUFF
And besides, *we're* the humans here!
はあ HUFF
Sure, we got our power from dragons, but that's it... We're human!
WOBBLE ヨロ...
So don't give us that crap, idiot!
True dragons are...
...super strong and noble...

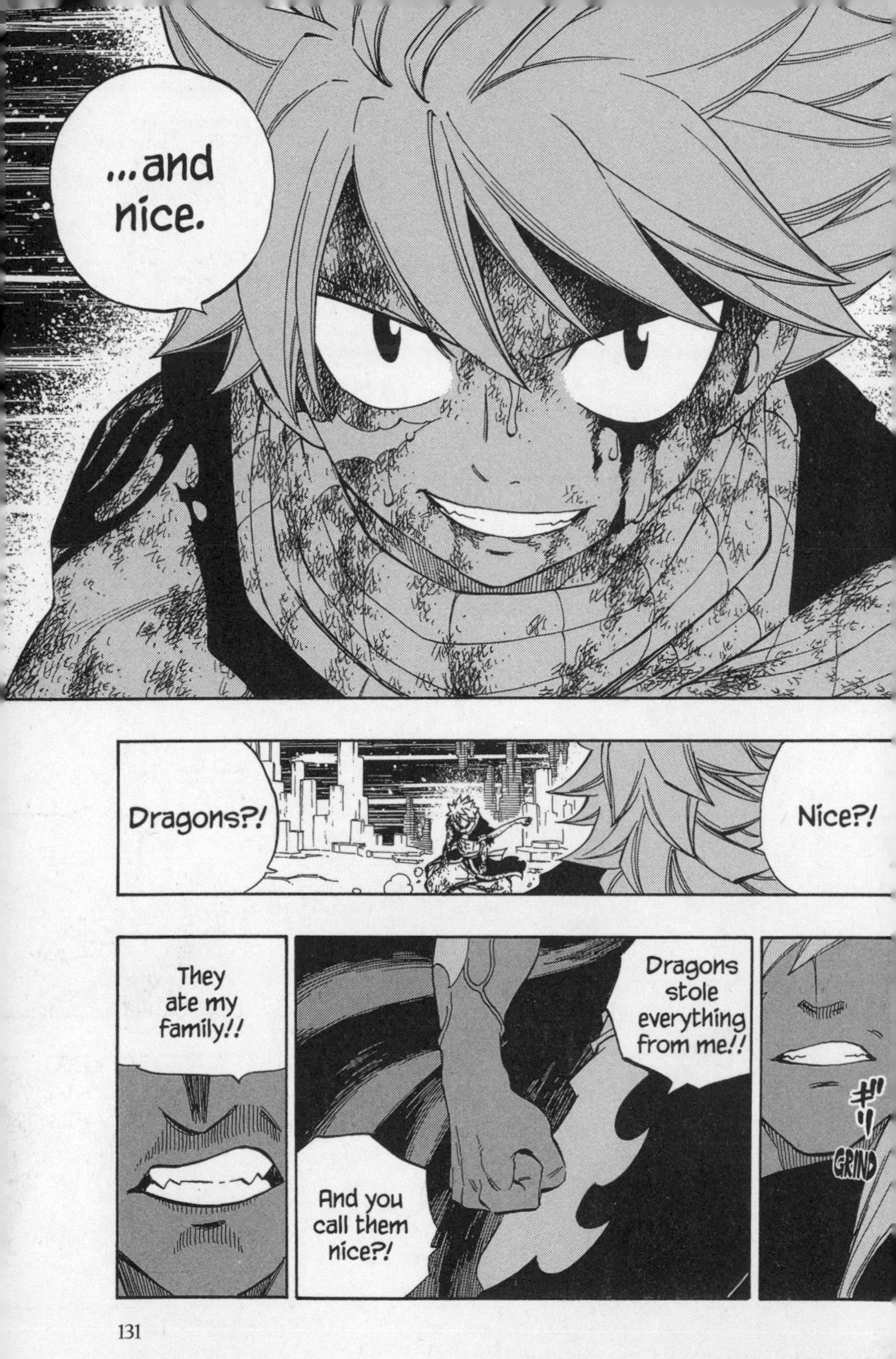
...and nice.
Nice?!
Dragons?!
ギリ
GRIND
Dragons stole everything from me!!
And you call them nice?!
They ate my family!!

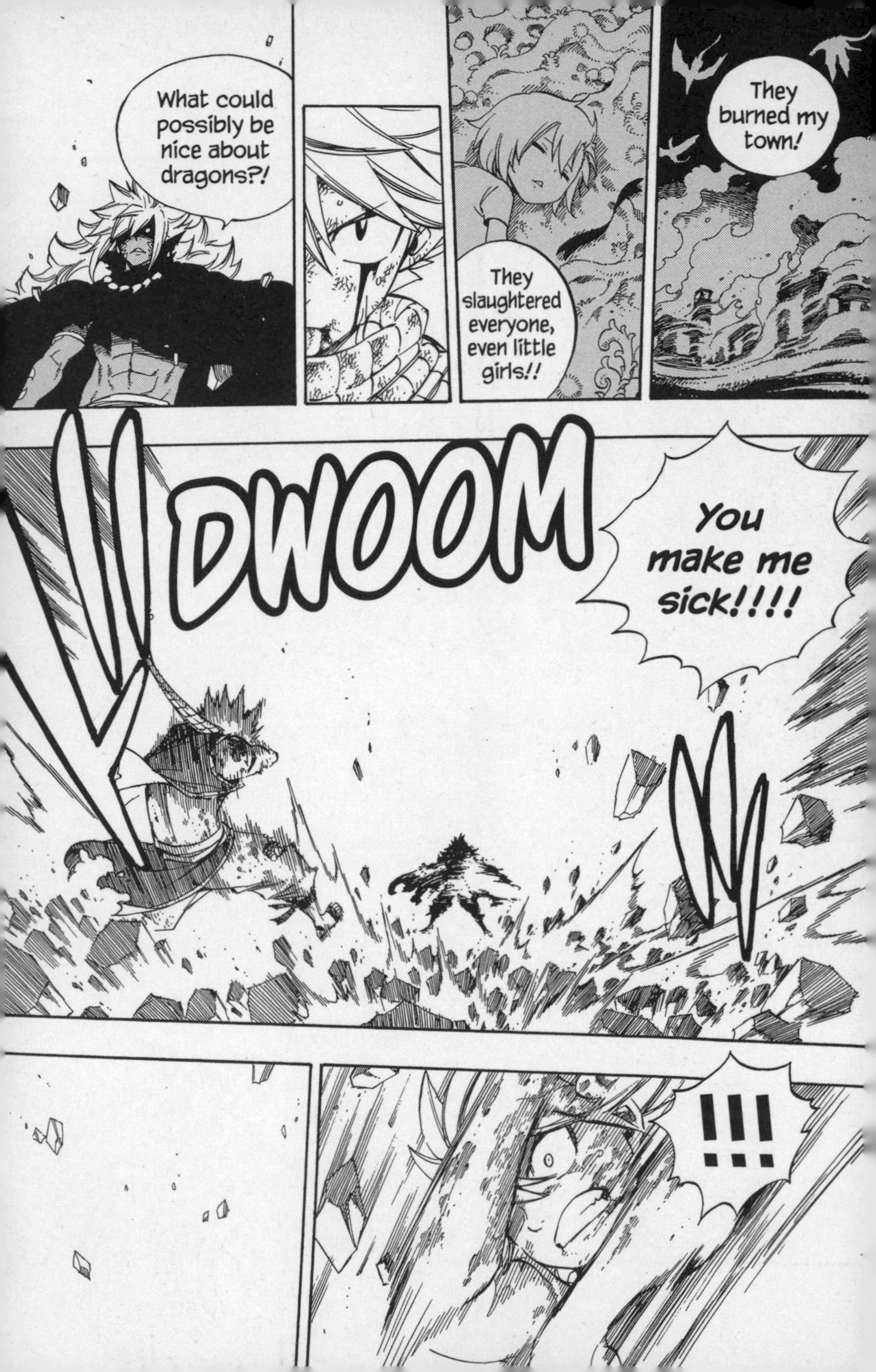
They burned my town!
They slaughtered everyone, even little girls!!
What could possibly be nice about dragons?!
You make me sick!!!!
DWOOM
!!!

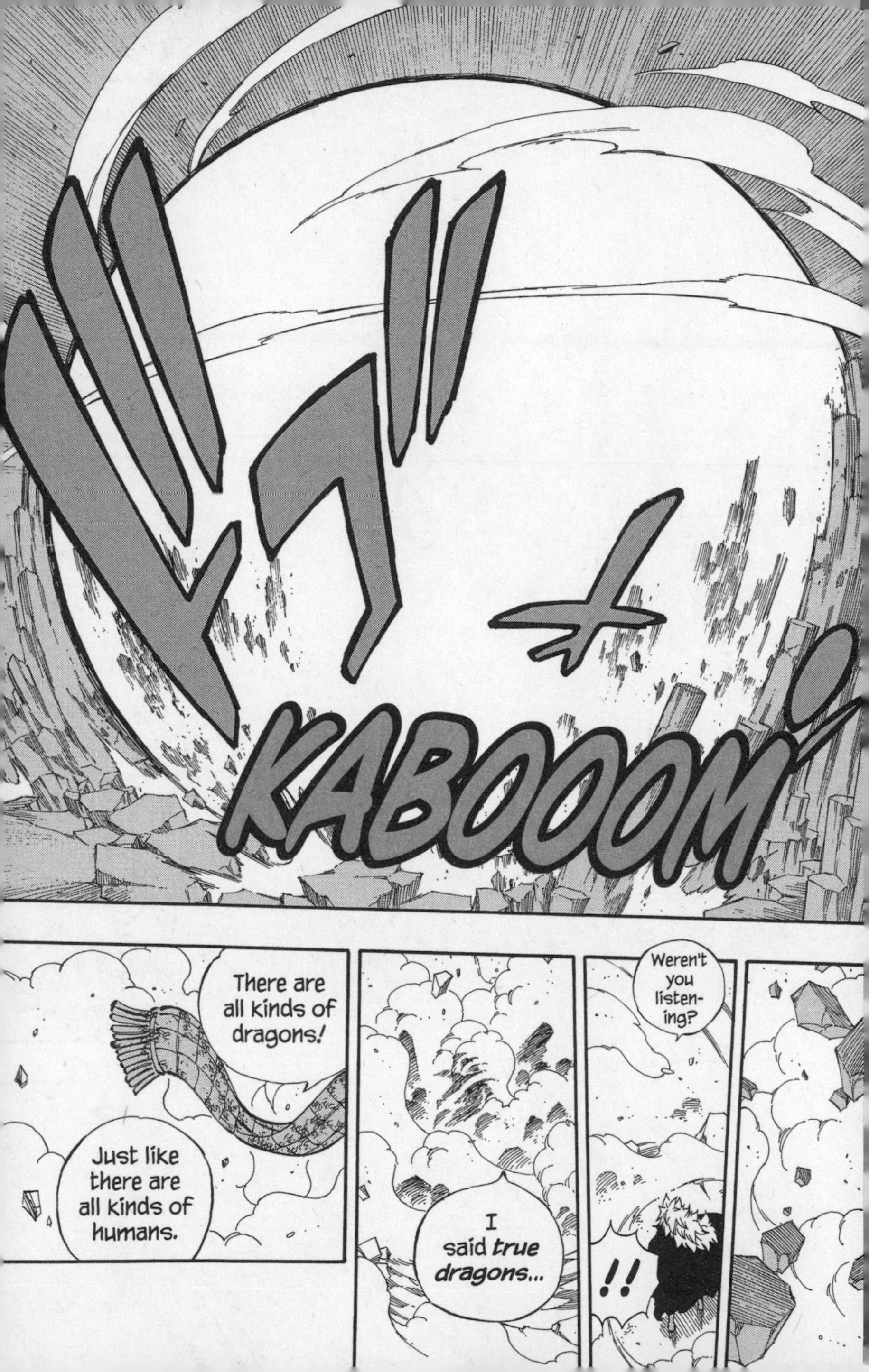
KABOOOM
Weren't you listening?
!!
I said *true dragons*...
There are all kinds of dragons!
Just like there are all kinds of humans.

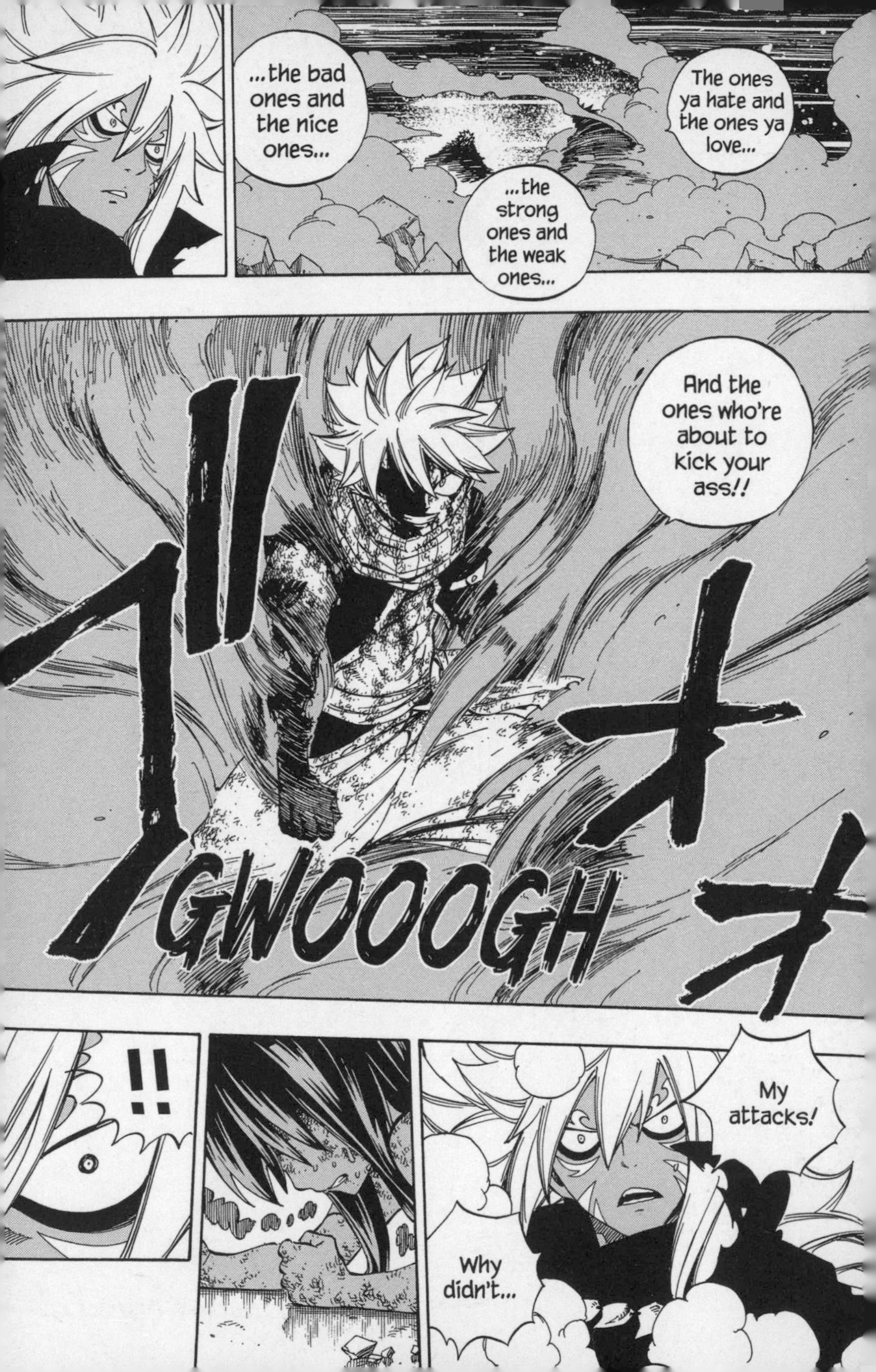

The ones ya hate and the ones ya love...
...the bad ones and the nice ones...
...the strong ones and the weak ones...
And the ones who're about to kick your ass!!
GWOOOGH
My attacks!
Why didn't...
!!

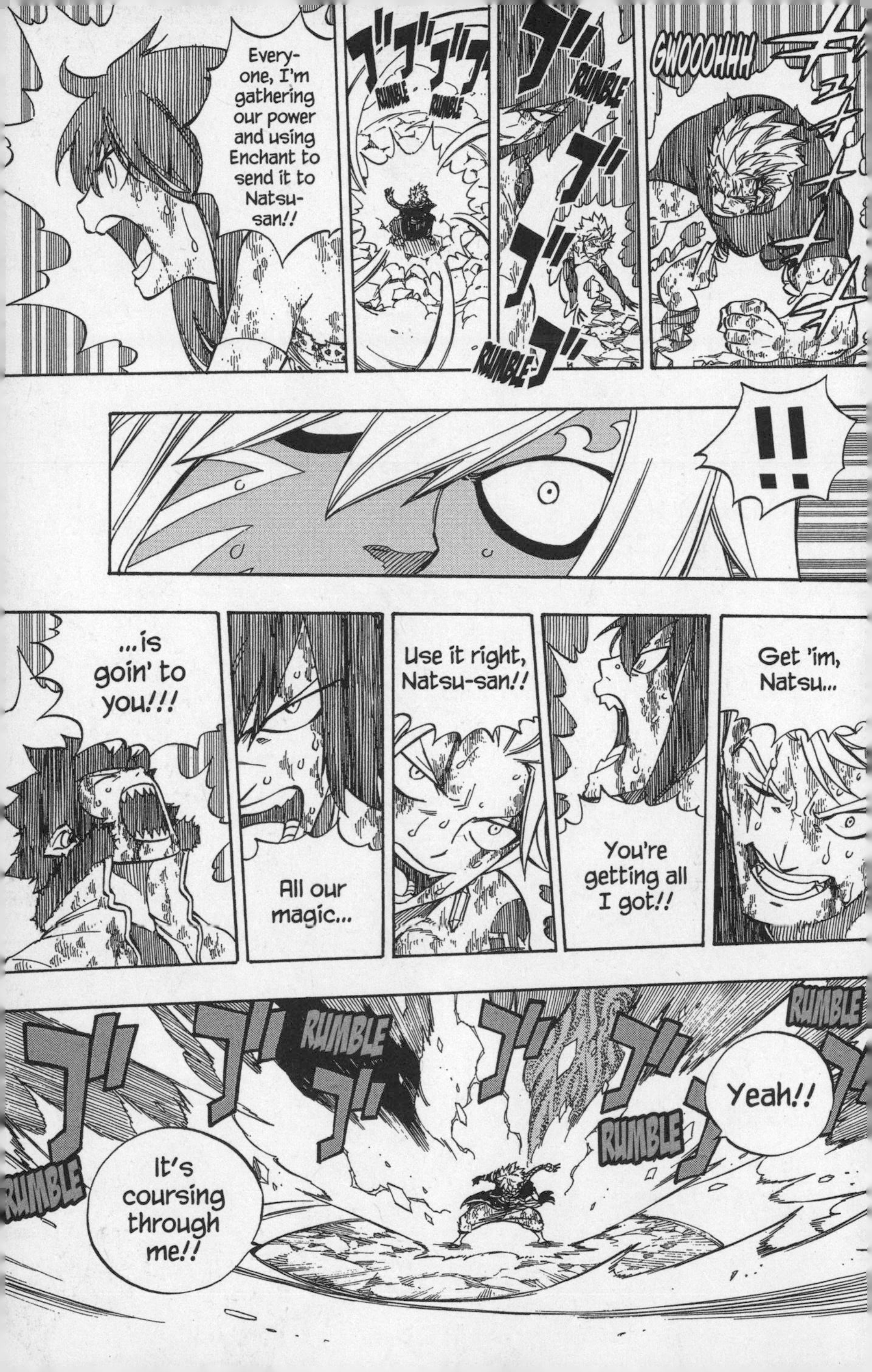
GWOOOHHH
RUMBLE
RUMBLE
RUMBLE
RUMBLE
Every-one, I'm gathering our power and using Enchant to send it to Natsu-san!!
!!
Get 'im, Natsu...
You're getting all I got!!
Use it right, Natsu-san!!
All our magic...
...is goin' to you!!!
RUMBLE
Yeah!!
RUMBLE
RUMBLE
It's coursing through me!!
RUMBLE

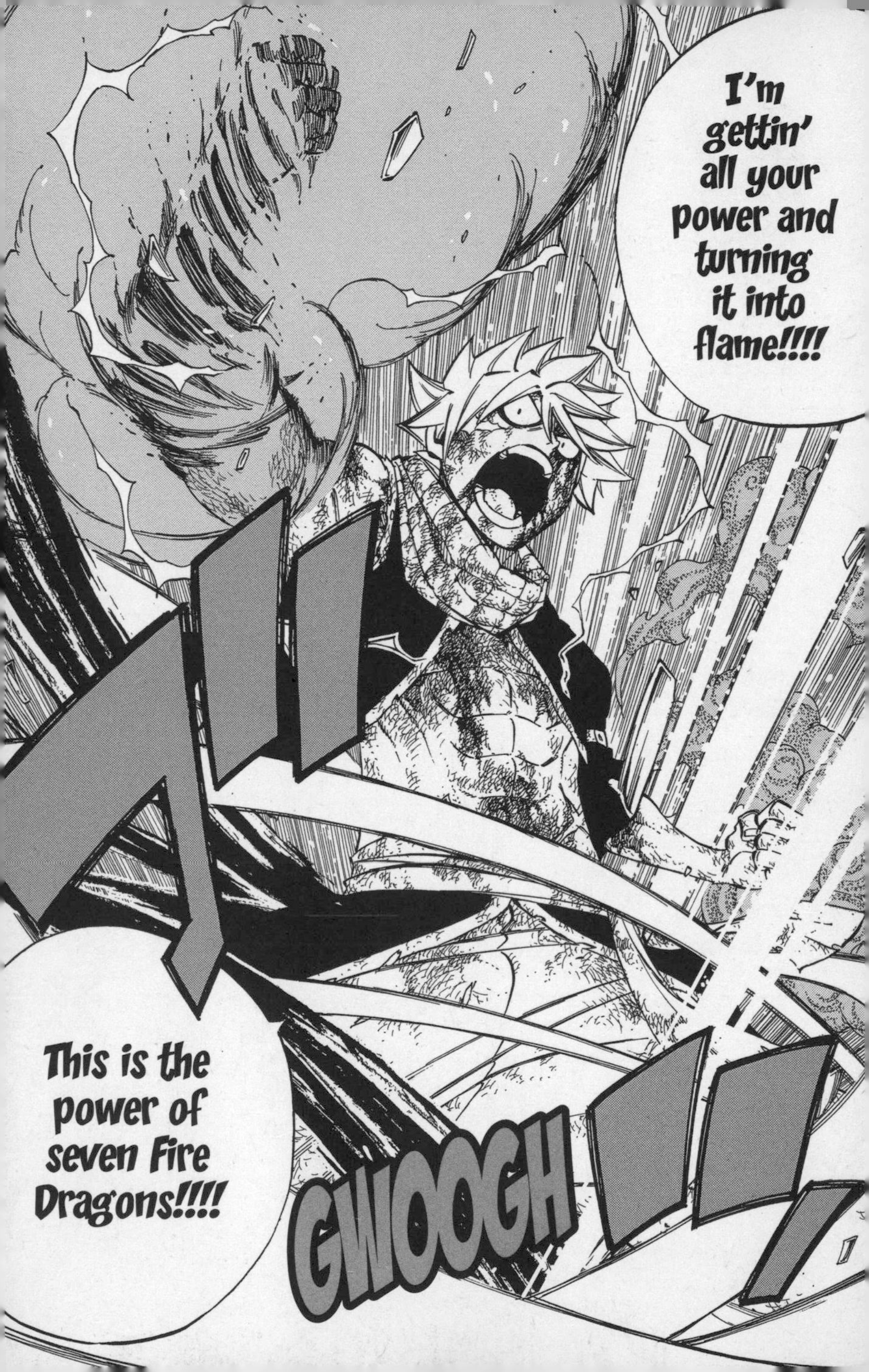
I'm gettin' all your power and turning it into flame!!!!
This is the power of seven Fire Dragons!!!!
GWOOGH

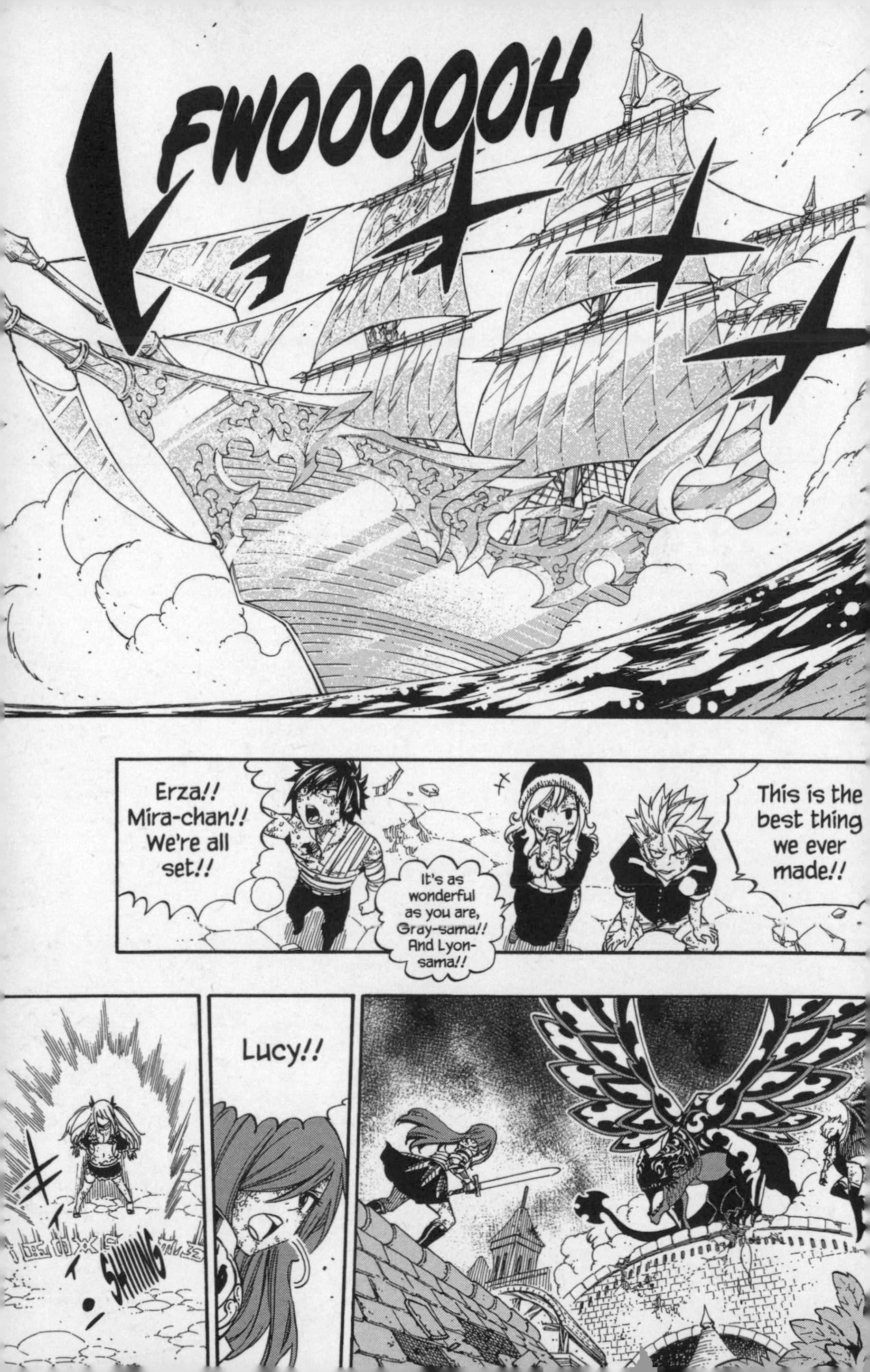
FWOOOOOH
This is the best thing we ever made!!
It's as wonderful as you are, Gray-sama!! And Lyon-sama!!
Erza!! Mira-chan!! We're all set!!
Lucy!!
SHIING

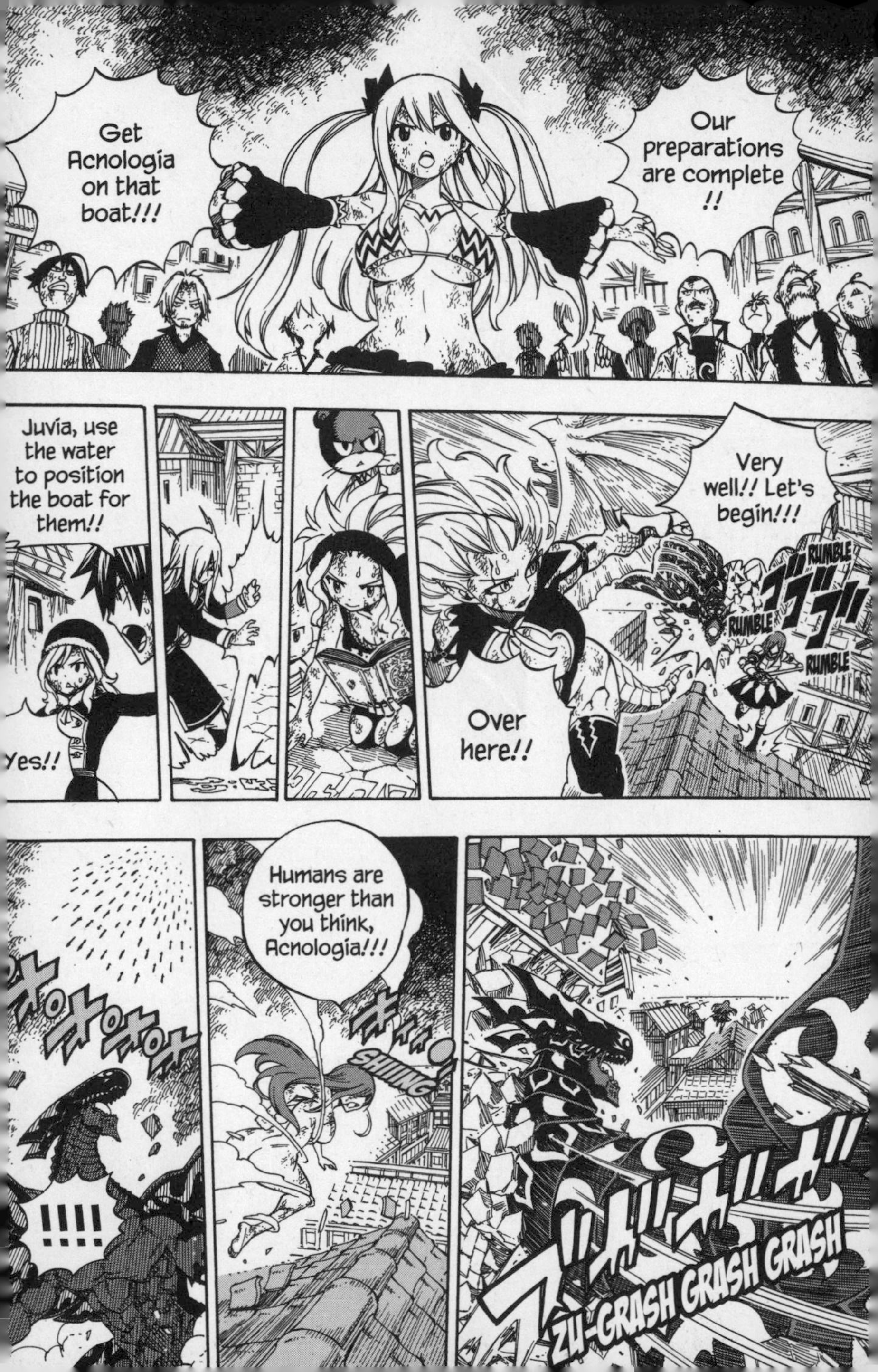
Our preparations are complete!!
Get Acnologia on that boat!!!
Very well!! Let's begin!!!
RUMBLE
RUMBLE
RUMBLE
Over here!!
Juvia, use the water to position the boat for them!!
Yes!!
ZU-GRASH GRASH GRASH
Humans are stronger than you think, Acnologia!!!
SHIIING
!!!!

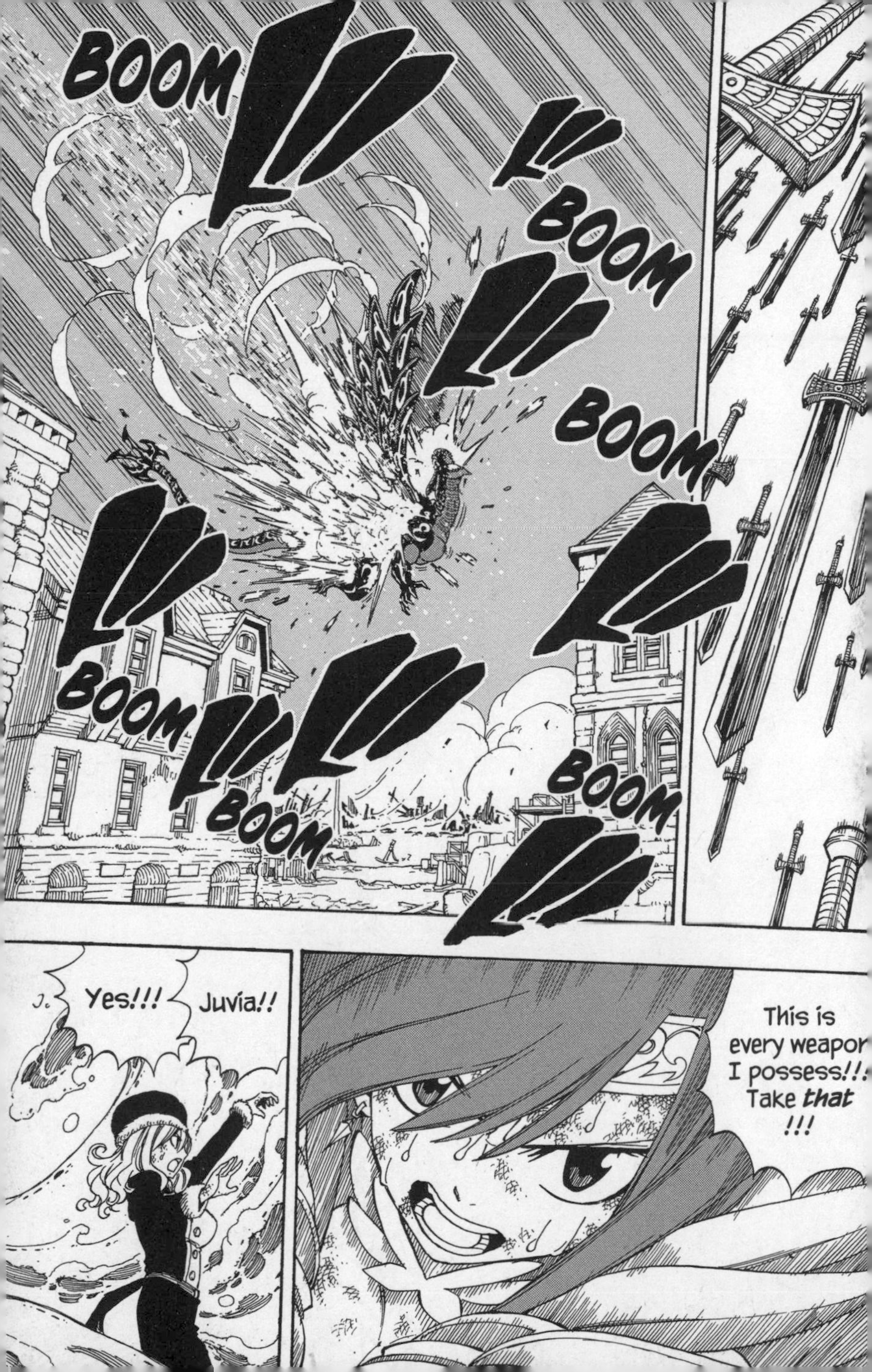
BOOM
BOOM
BOOM
BOOM
BOOM
BOOM
This is every weapo I possess!!! Take *that* !!!
Juvia!!
Yes!!!
J.

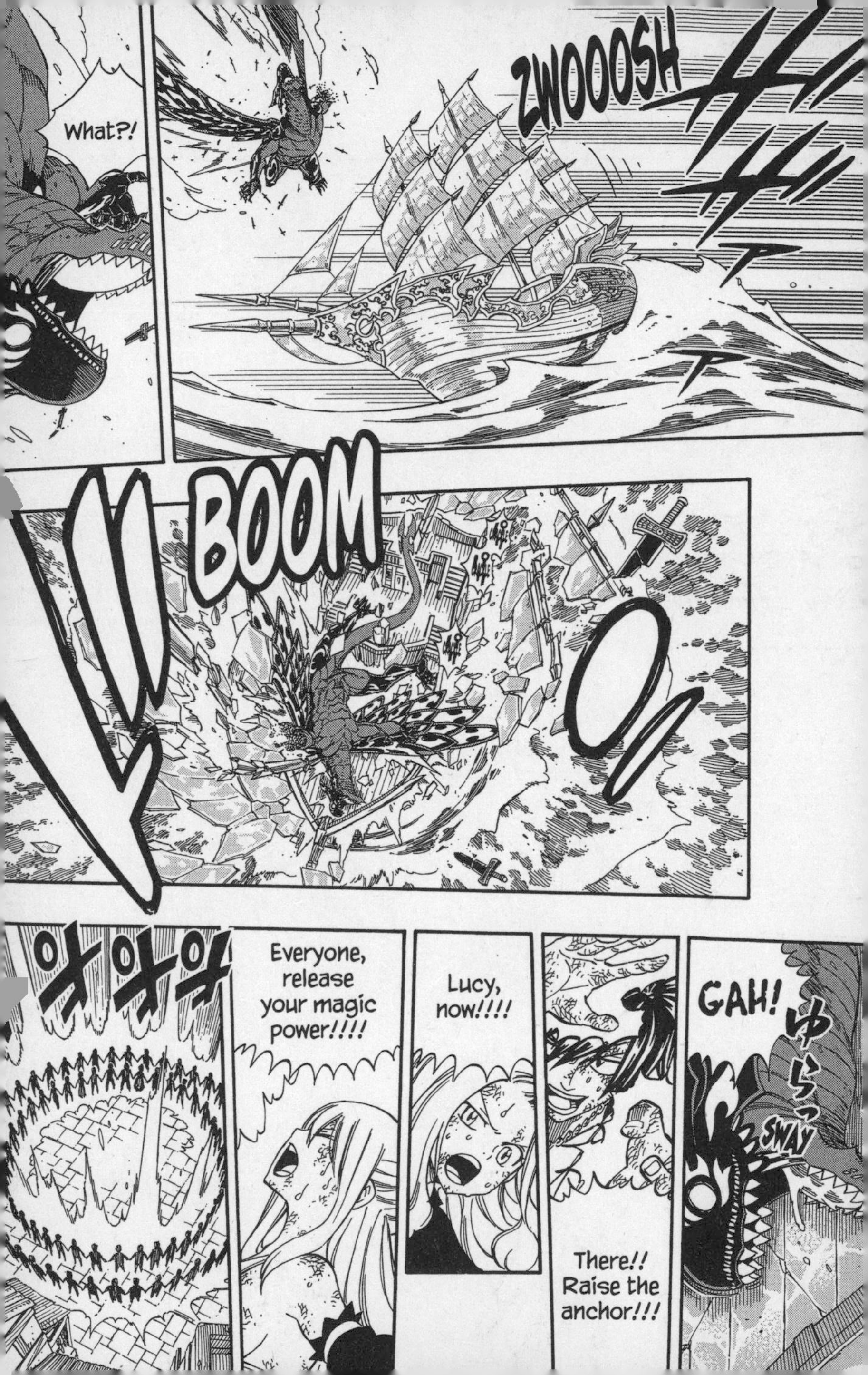
ZWOOOSH
What?!
BOOM
GAH!
ゆらっ
SWAY
There!! Raise the anchor!!!
Lucy, now!!!!
Everyone, release your magic power!!!!

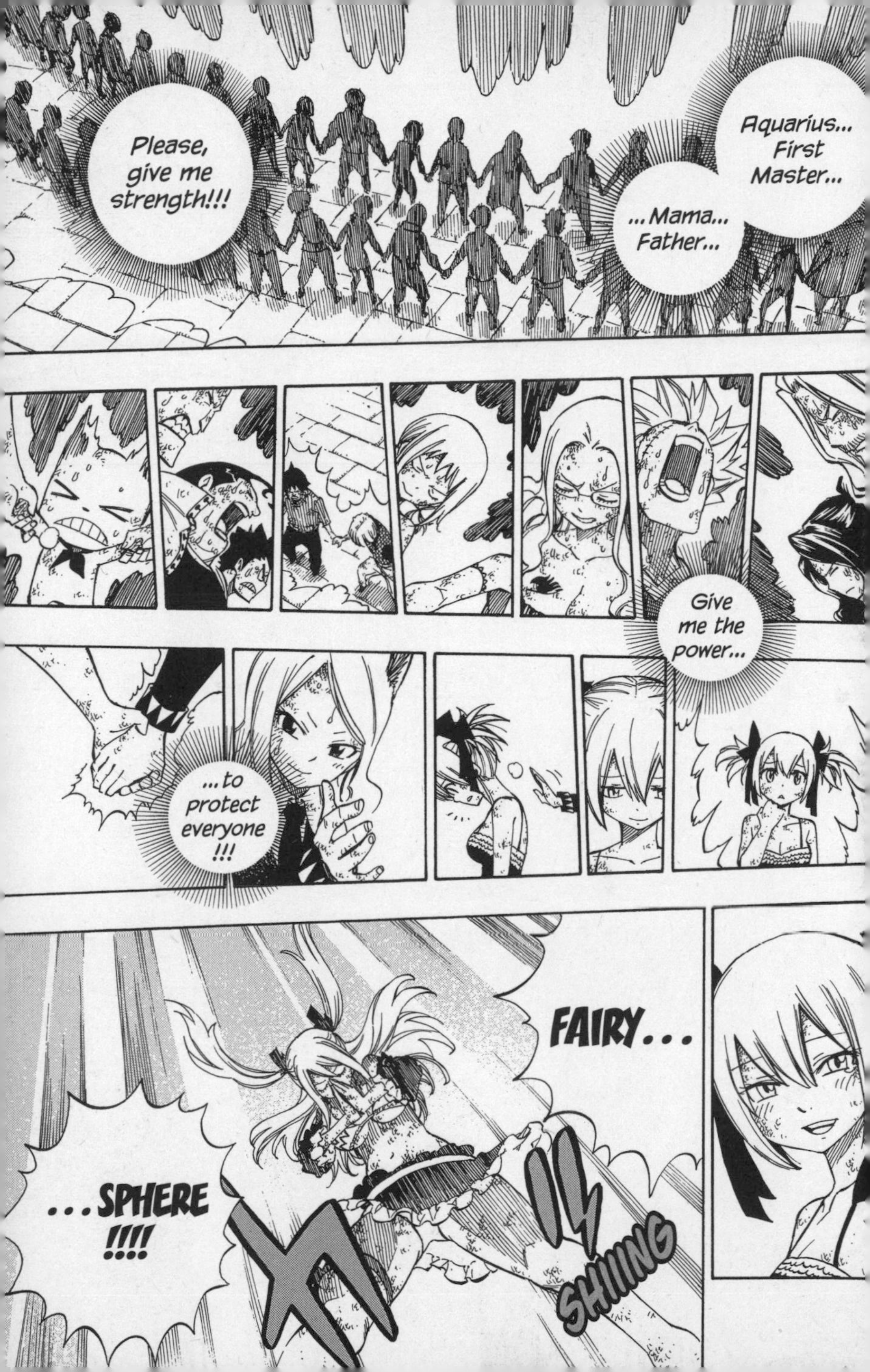
Aquarius... First Master...
...Mama... Father...
Please, give me strength!!!
Give me the power...
...to protect everyone!!!
FAIRY...
SHIIING
...SPHERE!!!!

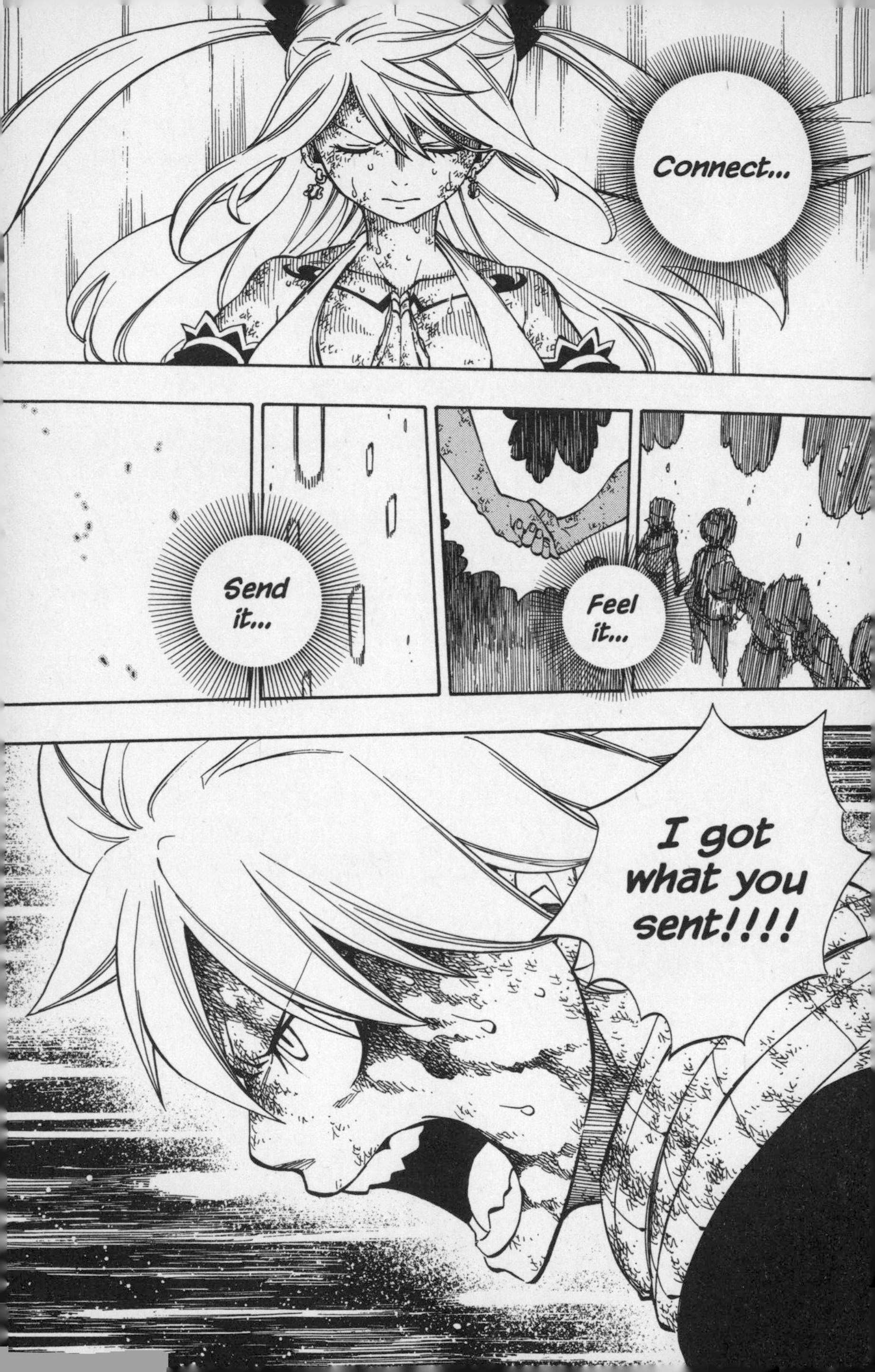
Connect...
Feel it...
Send it...
I got what you sent!!!!

FAIRY TAIL

#544 You're the king

HIRO MASHIMA

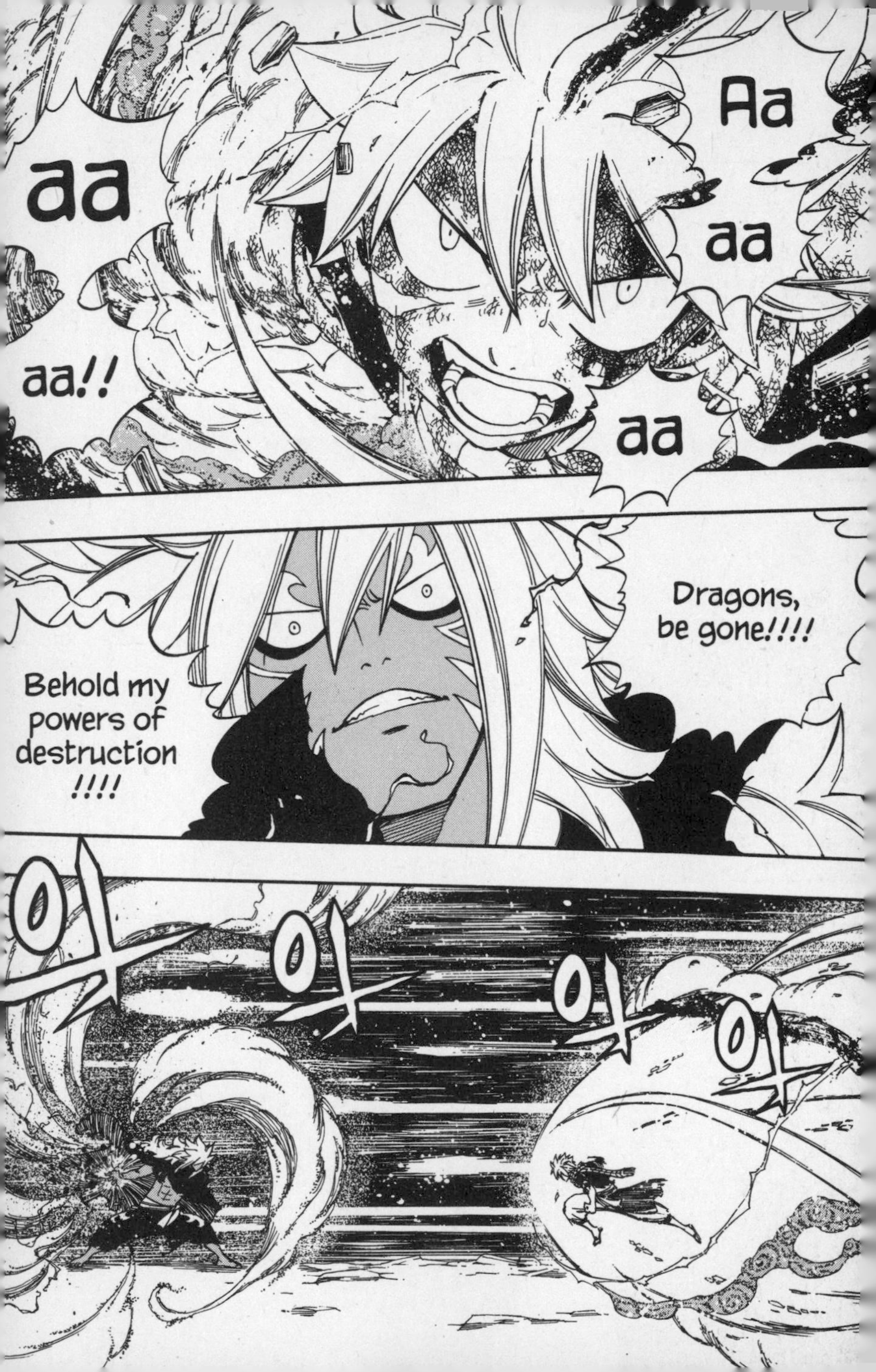
Aa
aa
aa
aa
aa!!
Dragons, be gone!!!!
Behold my powers of destruction !!!!

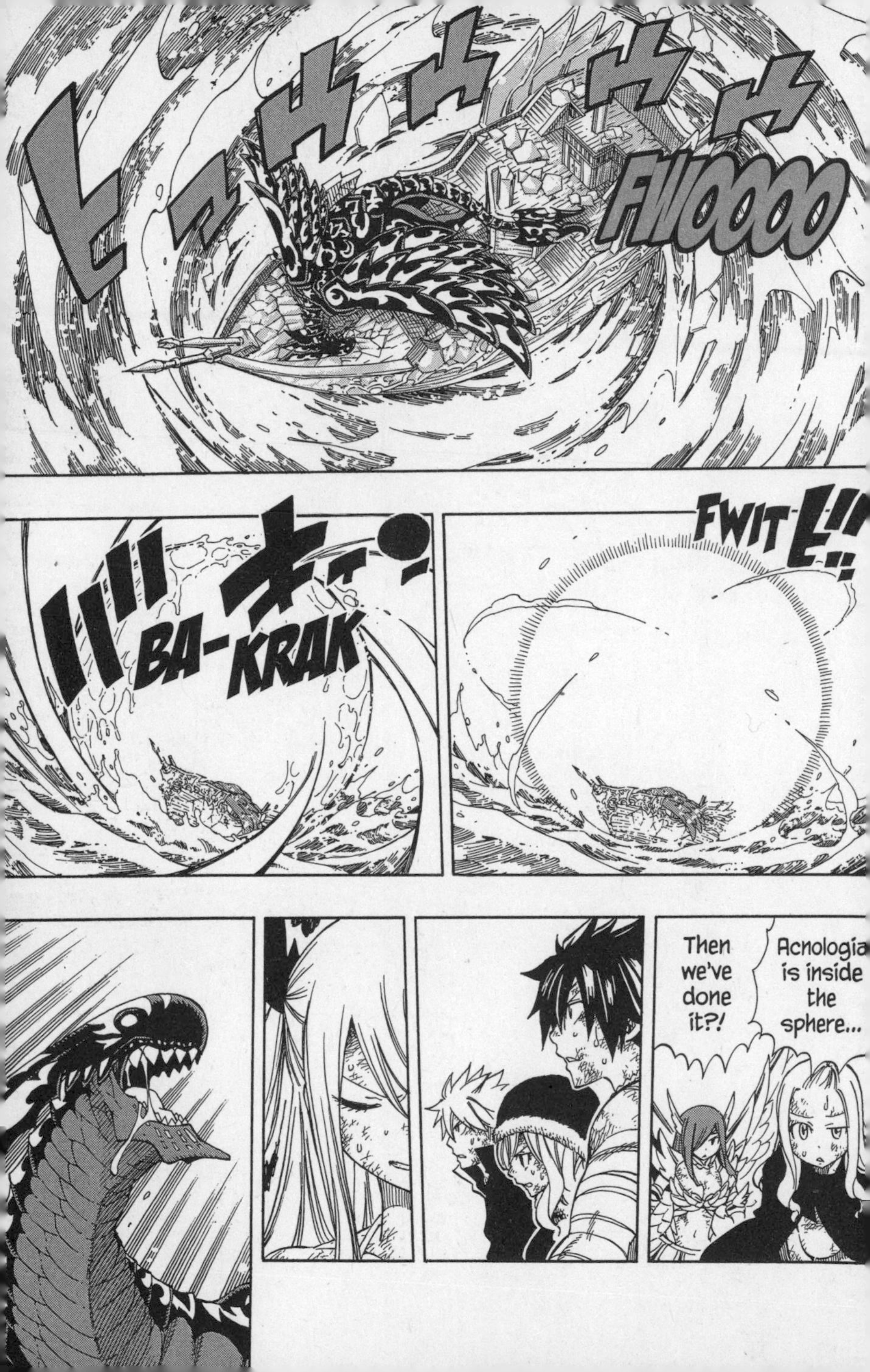
FWOOOO
FWIT
BA-KRAK
Acnologia is inside the sphere...
Then we've done it?!

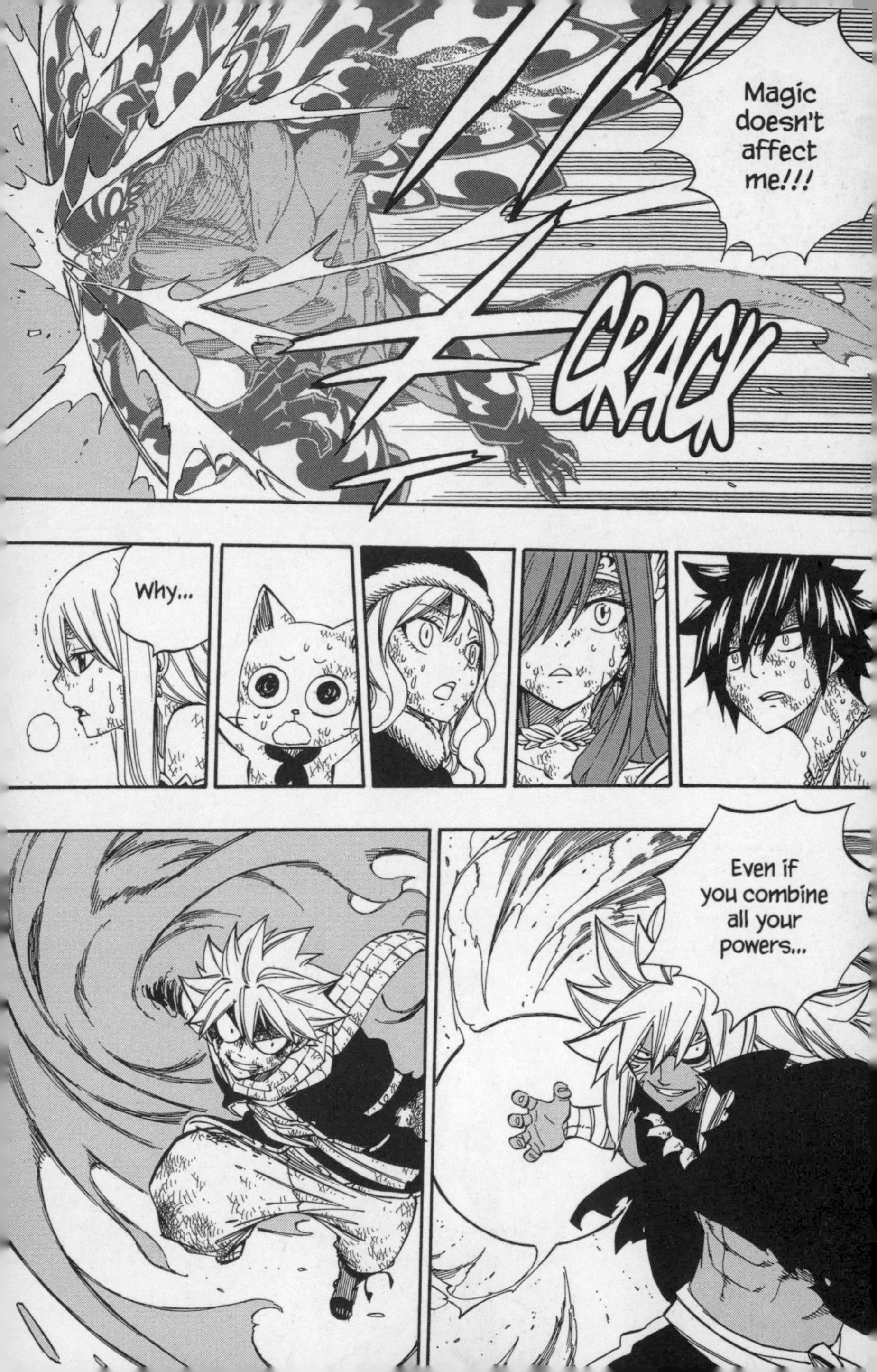
Magic doesn't affect me!!!
CRACK
Why...
Even if you combine all your powers...

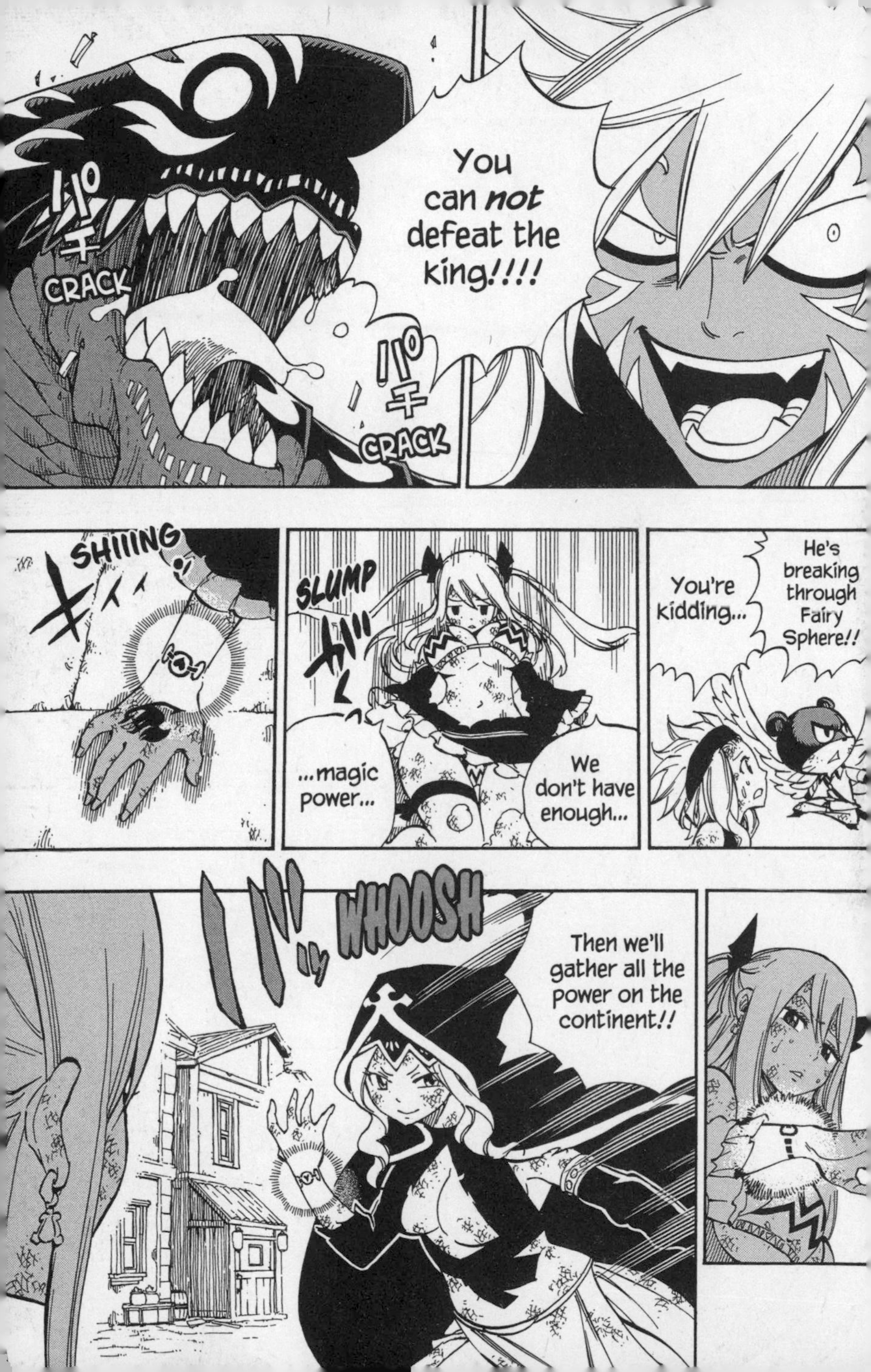
You can not defeat the king!!!!
CRACK
CRACK
He's breaking through Fairy Sphere!!
You're kidding...
SLUMP
We don't have enough...
...magic power...
SHIIING
WHOOSH
Then we'll gather all the power on the continent!!

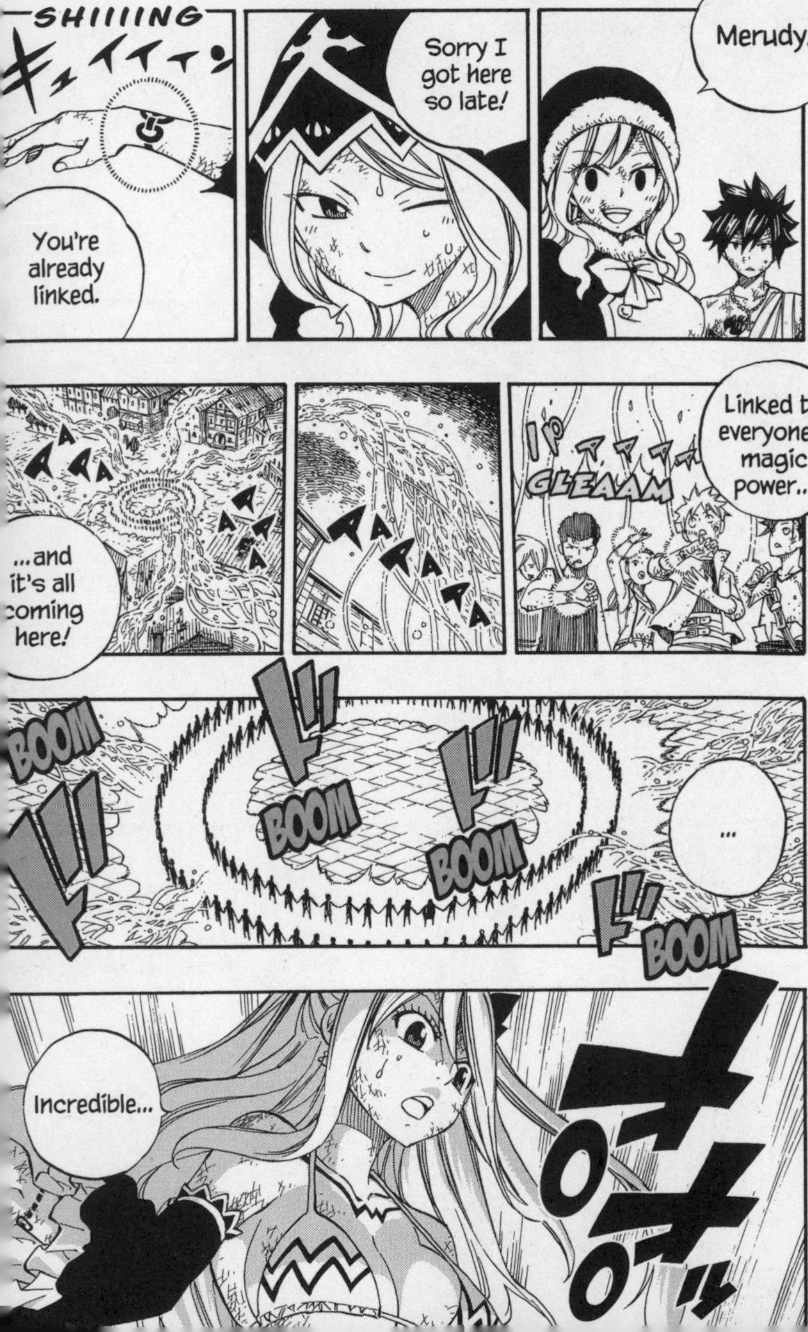
Merudy!!
Sorry I got here so late!
SHIIIING
You're already linked.
Linked to everyone's magic power...
GLEAAM
...and it's all coming here!
BOOM
...
BOOM
BOOM
BOOM
Incredible...

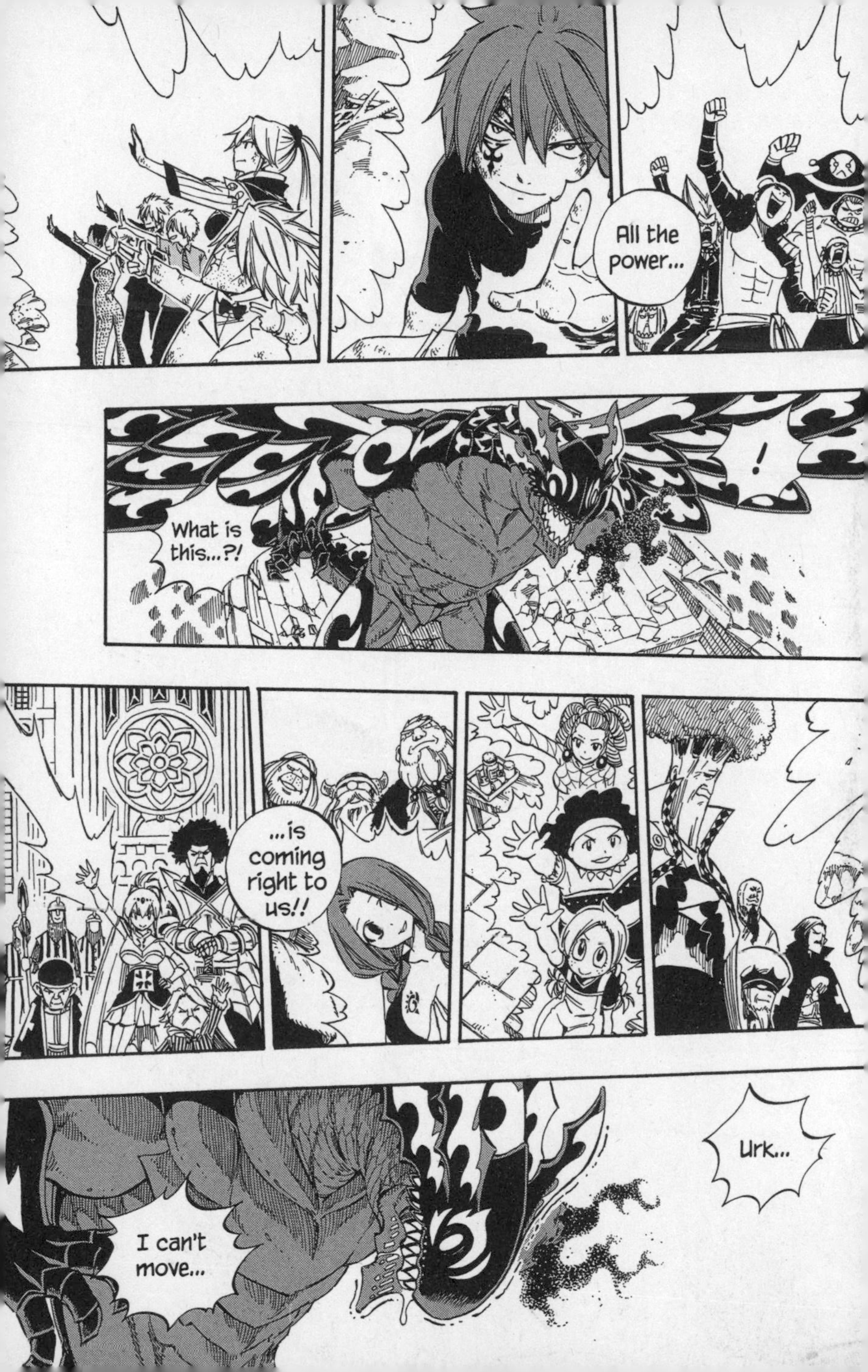
All the power...
!
What is this...?!
...is coming right to us!!
Urk...
I can't move...

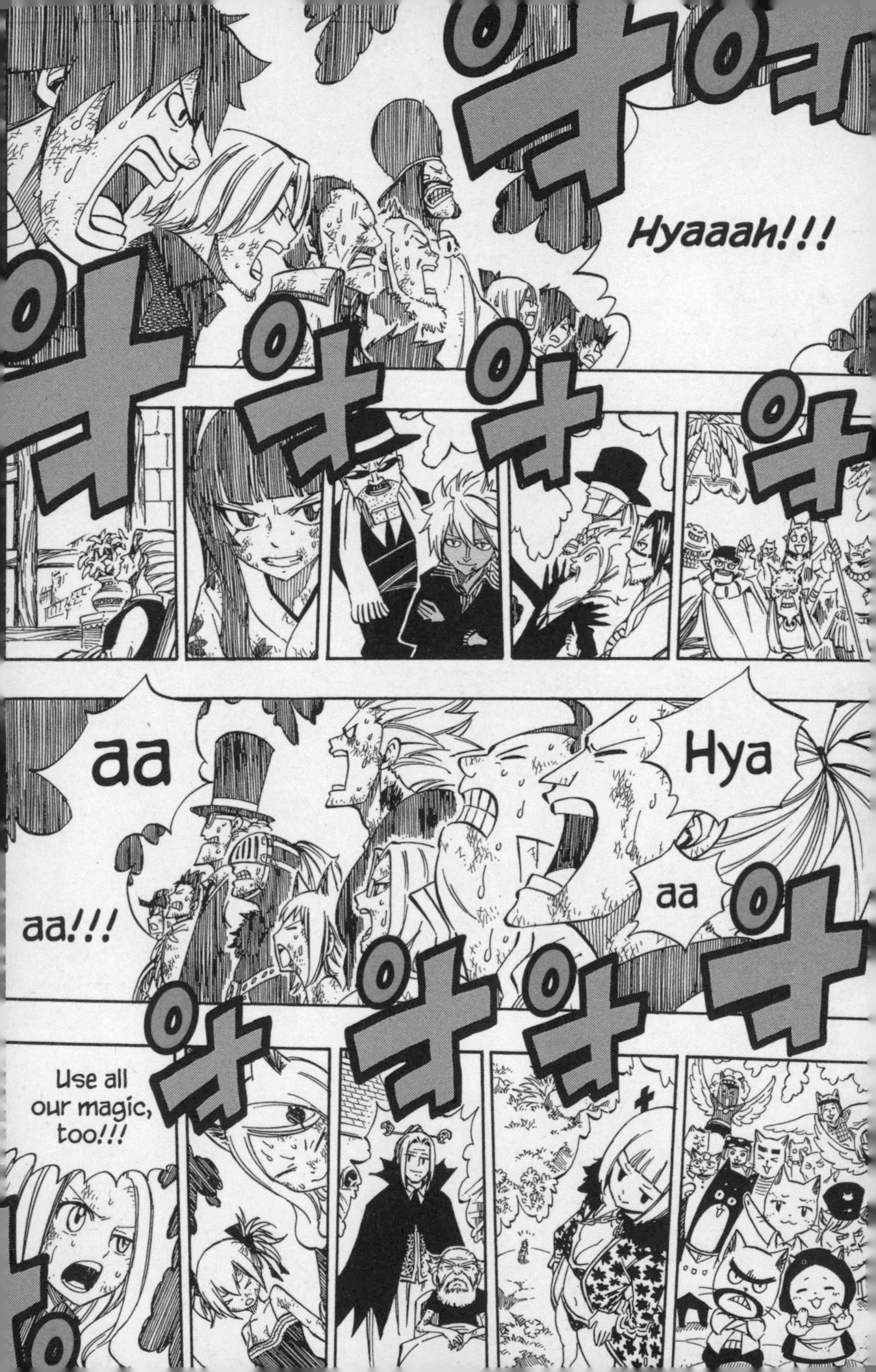
Hyaaah!!!
Hya
aa
aa
aa!!!
Use all our magic, too!!!

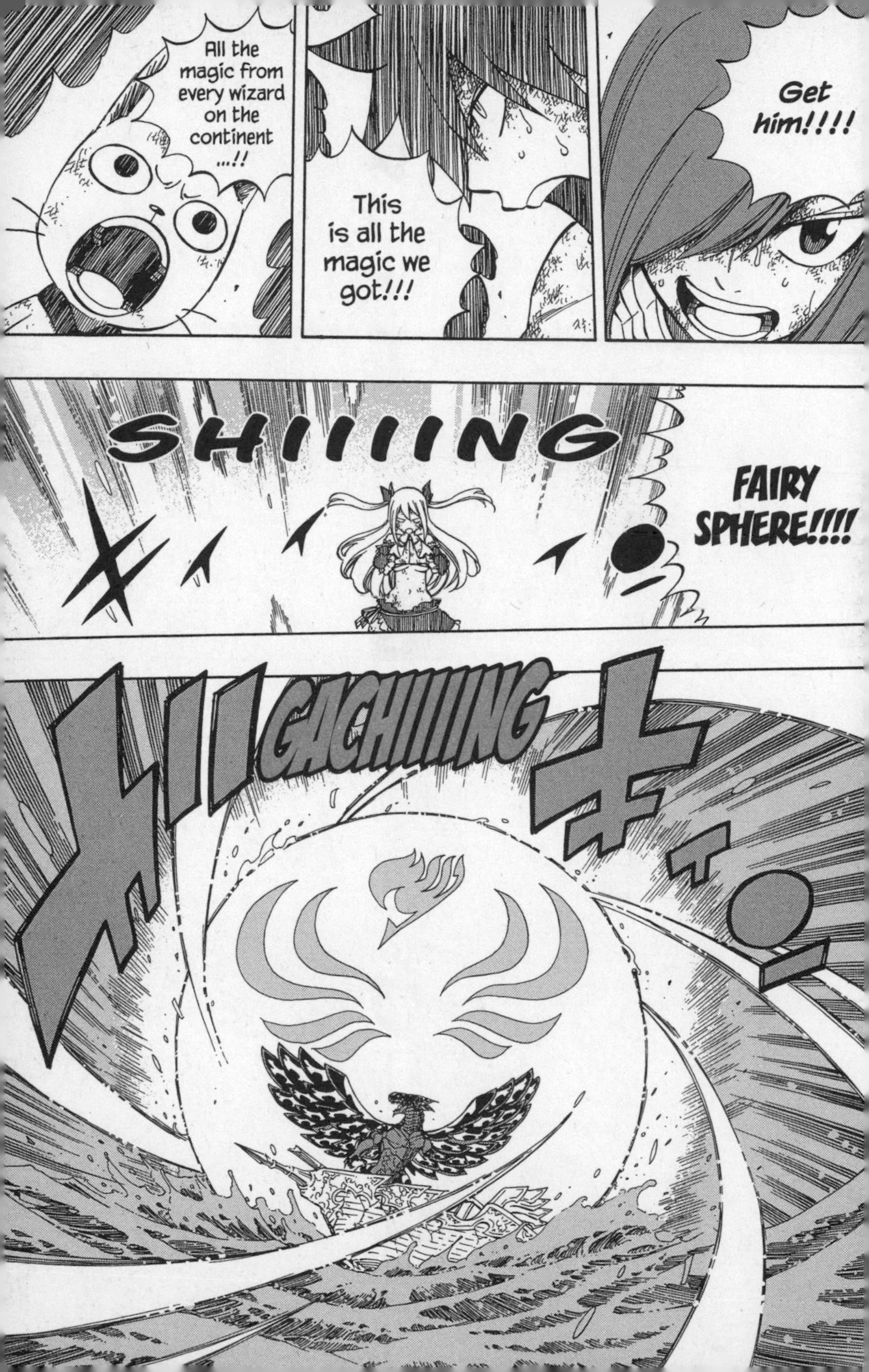
Get him!!!!
This is all the magic we got!!!
All the magic from every wizard on the continent ...!!
FAIRY SPHERE!!!!
SHIIIING
GACHIIIING

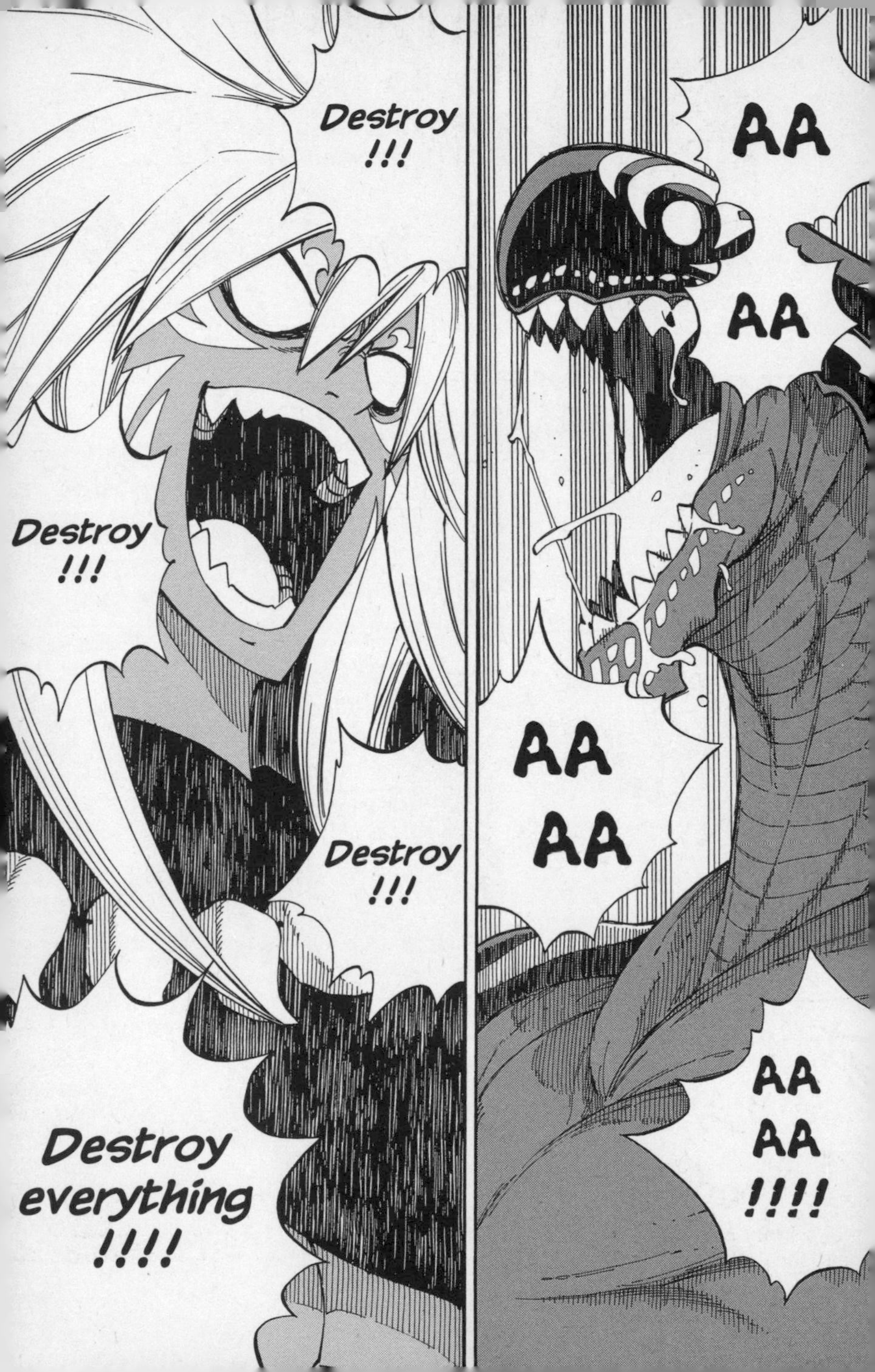
AA AA
AA AA
AA AA !!!!
Destroy !!!
Destroy !!!
Destroy !!!
Destroy everything !!!!

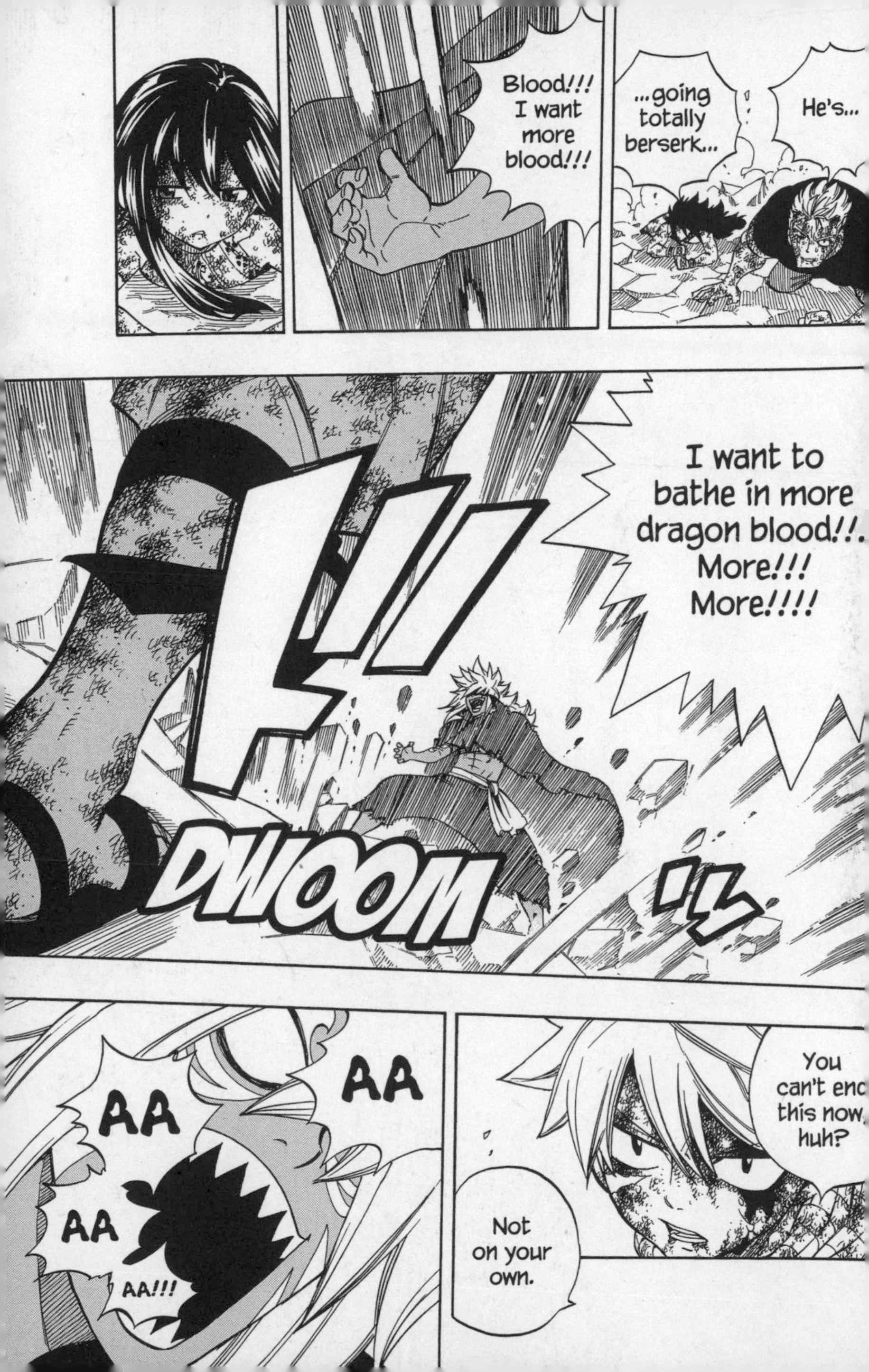
He's...
...going totally berserk...
Blood!!! I want more blood!!!
I want to bathe in more dragon blood!!. More!!! More!!!!
DWOOM
You can't end this now, huh?
Not on your own.
AA
AA
AA
AA!!!

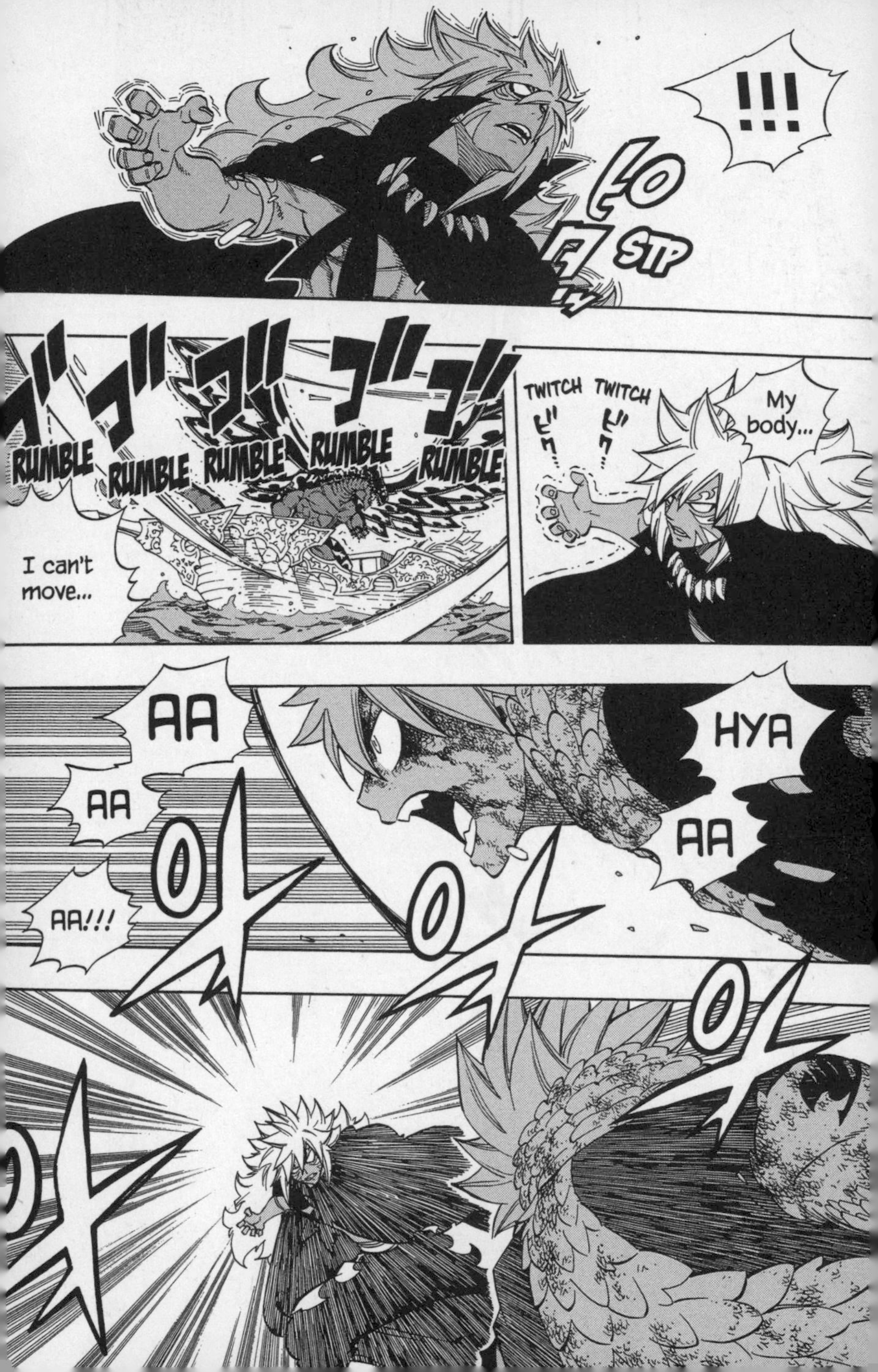
!!!
STP
RUMBLE
RUMBLE
RUMBLE
RUMBLE
RUMBLE
TWITCH TWITCH
My body...
I can't move...
HYA
AA
AA
AA
AA!!!

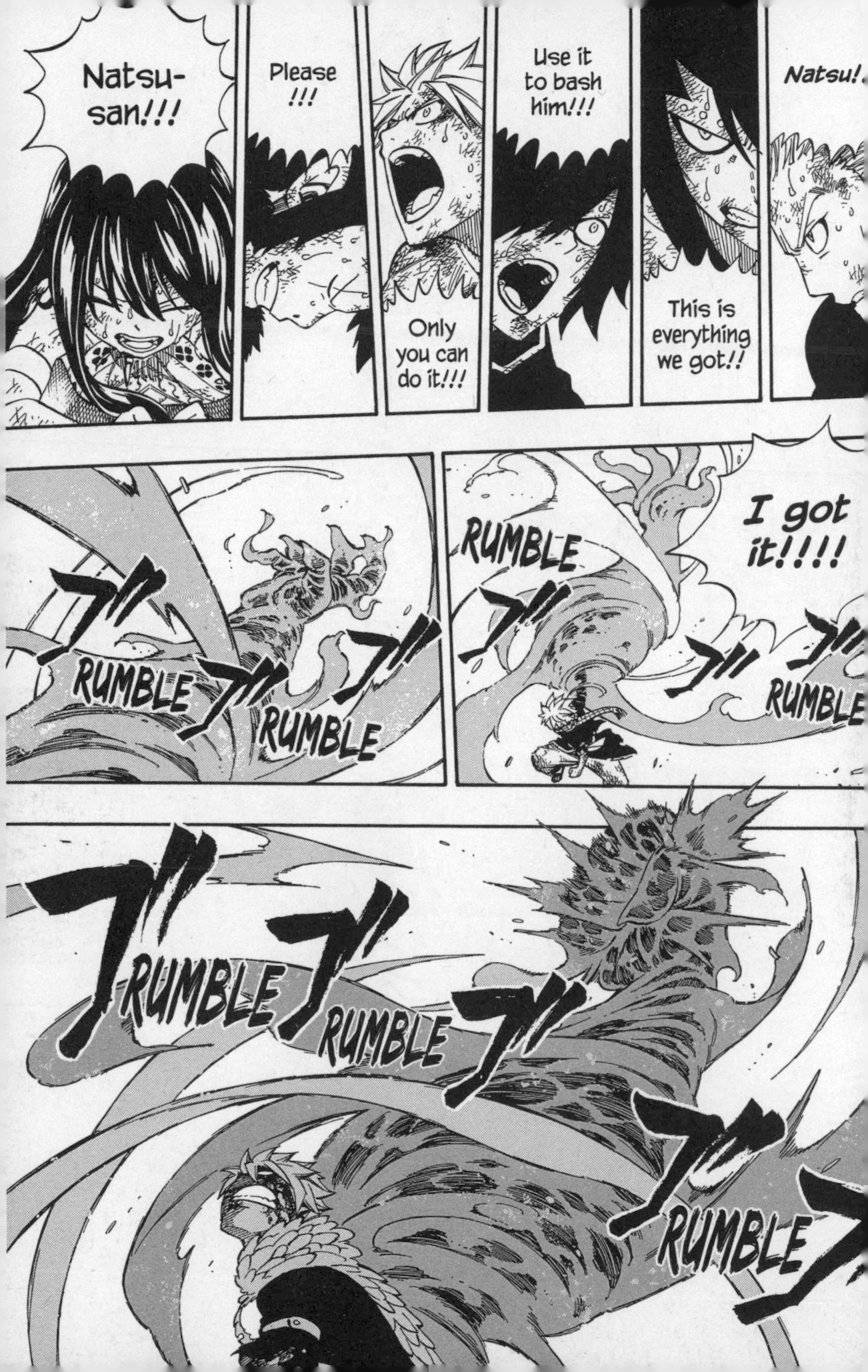
Natsu!!
This is everything we got!!
Use it to bash him!!!
Only you can do it!!!
Please!!!
Natsu-san!!!
I got it!!!!
RUMBLE
RUMBLE
RUMBLE
RUMBLE
RUMBLE
RUMBLE
RUMBLE

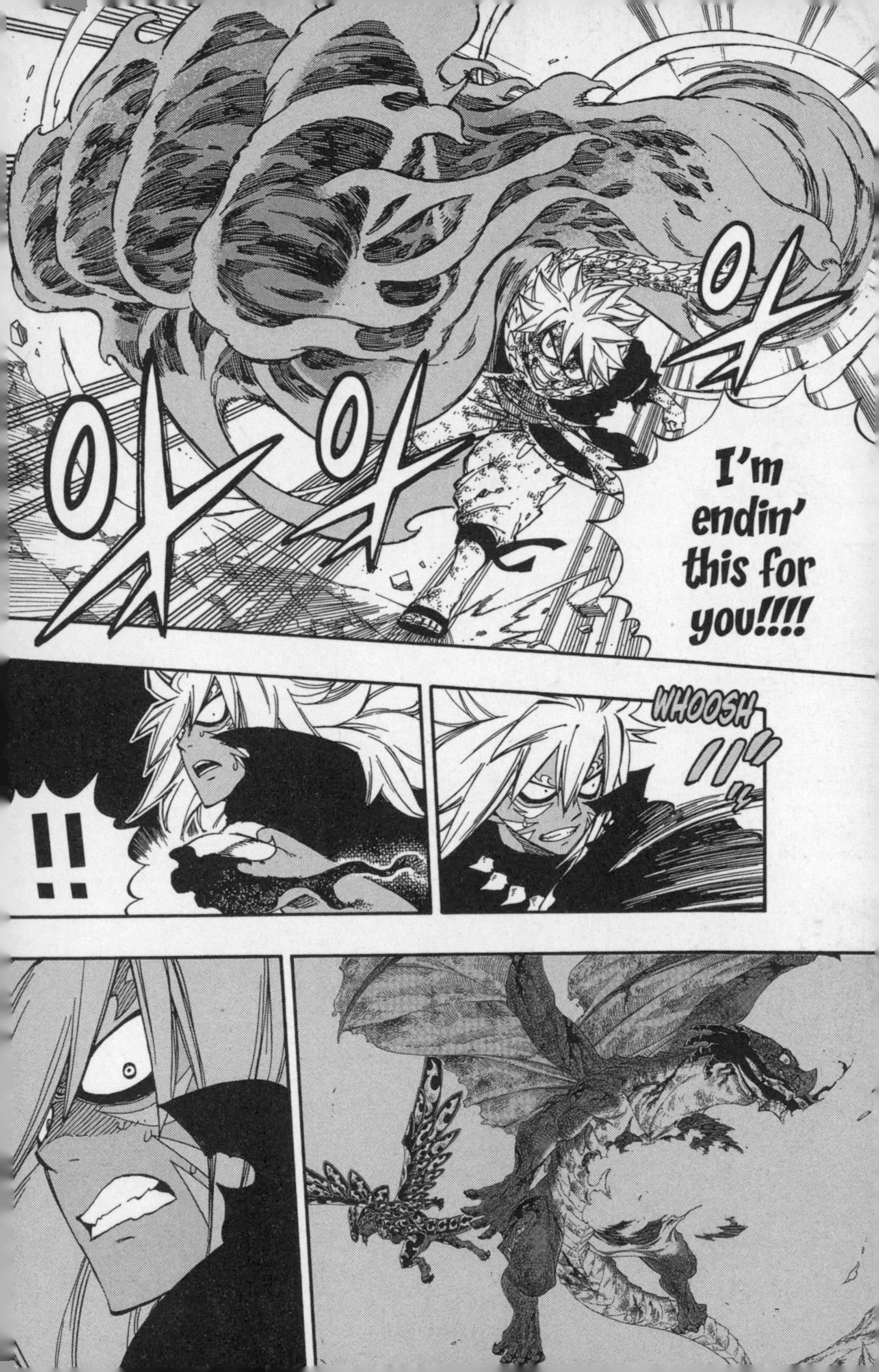
I'm endin' this for you!!!!
WHOOSH
!!

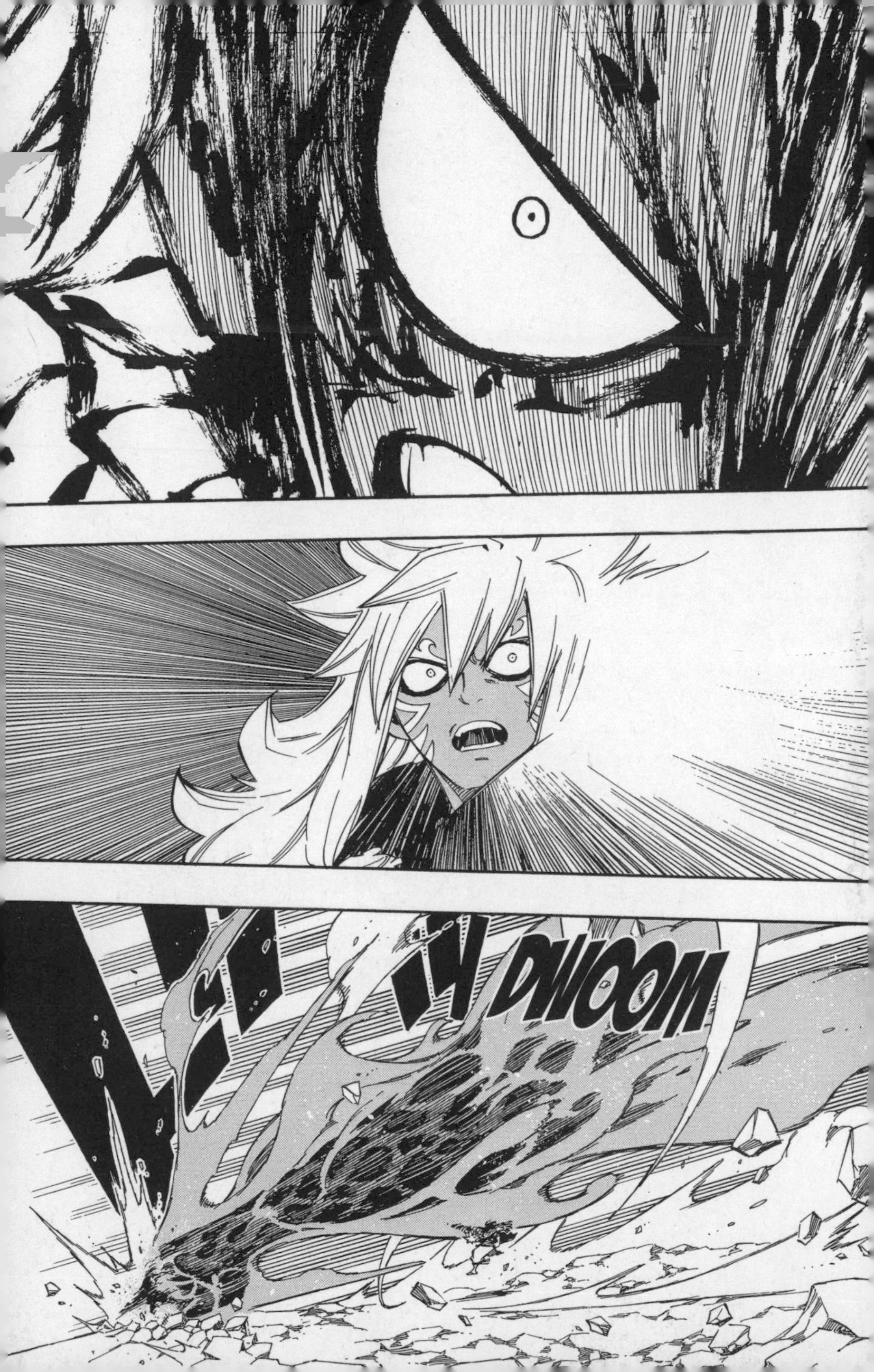
DWOOM

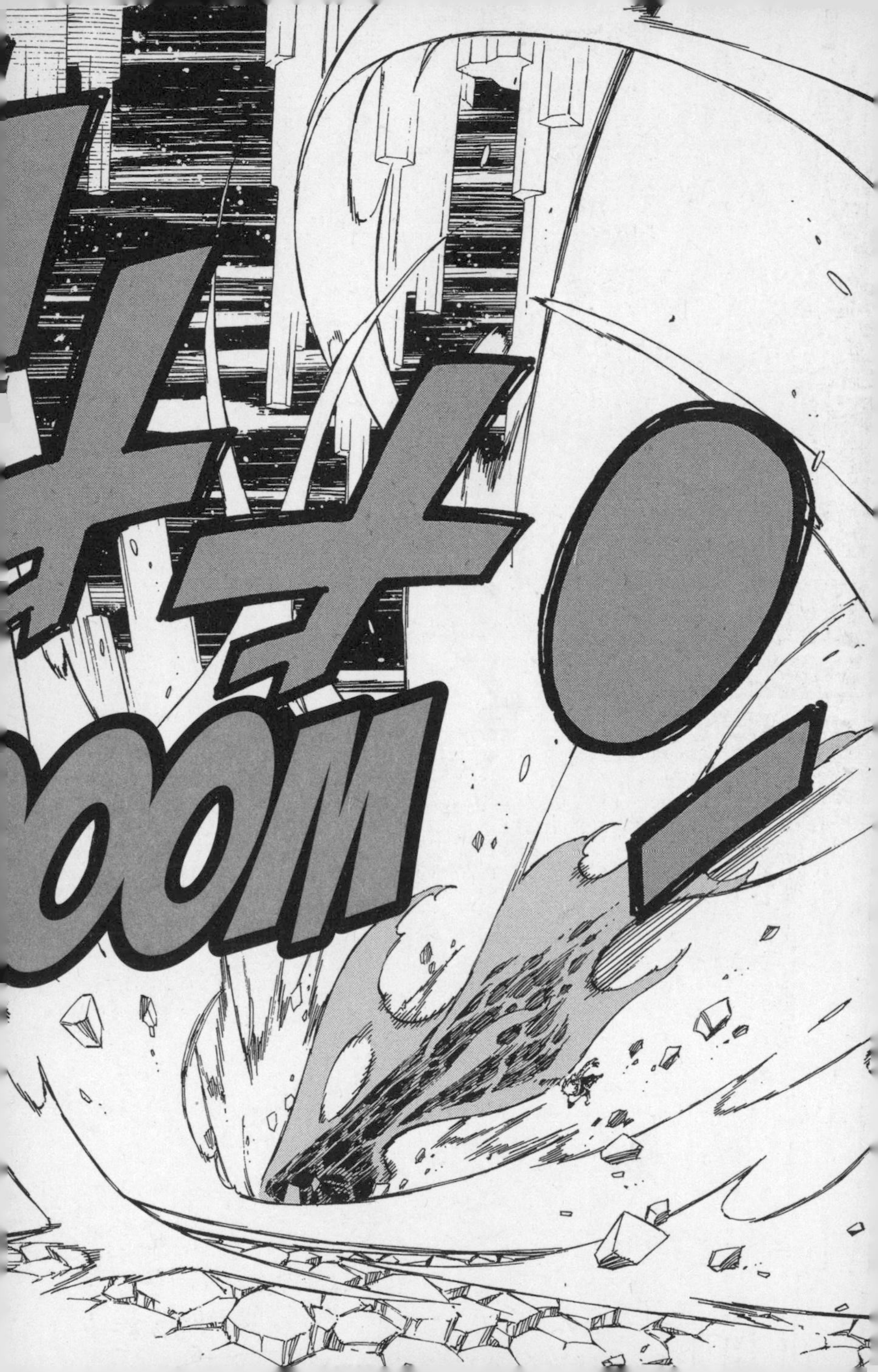

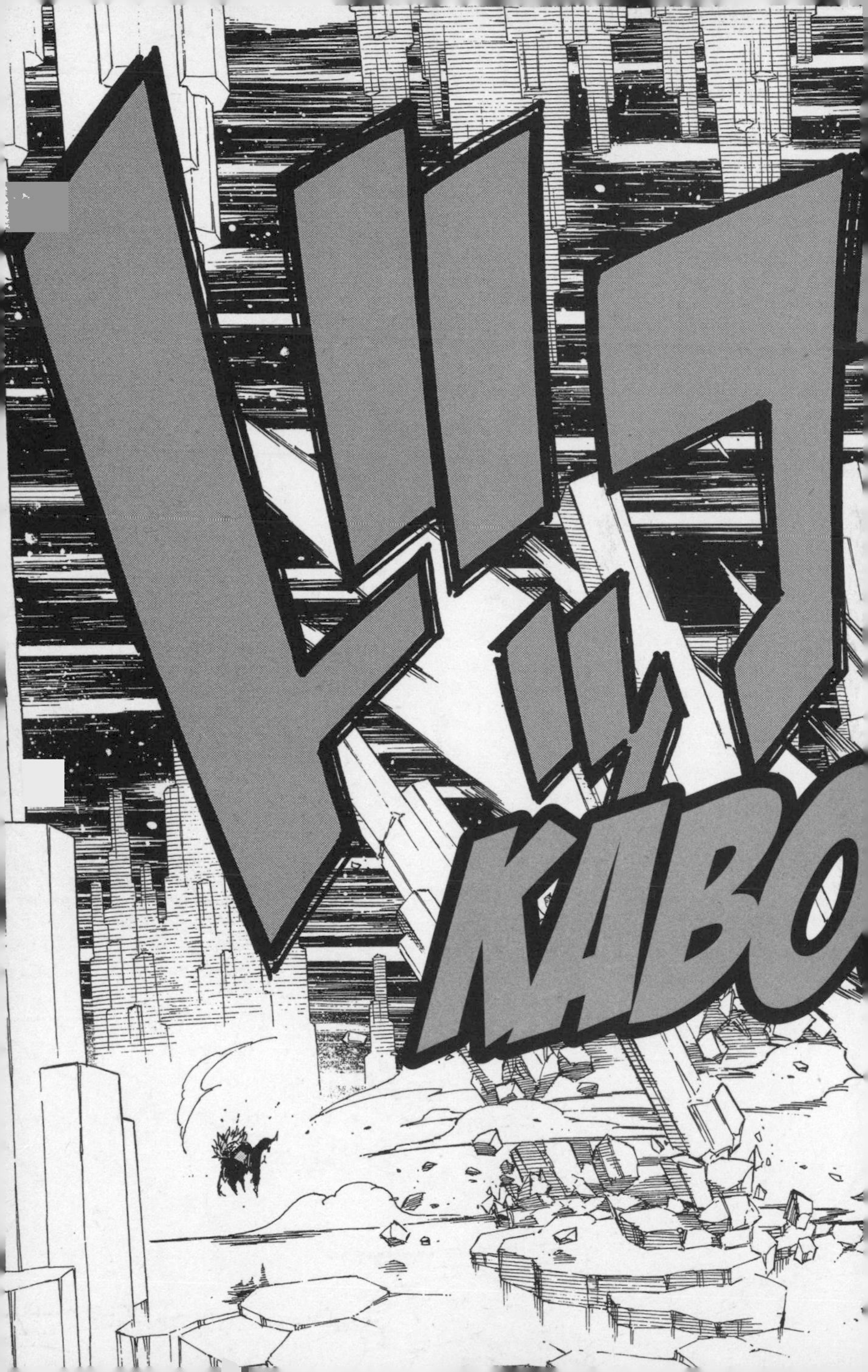
KABO

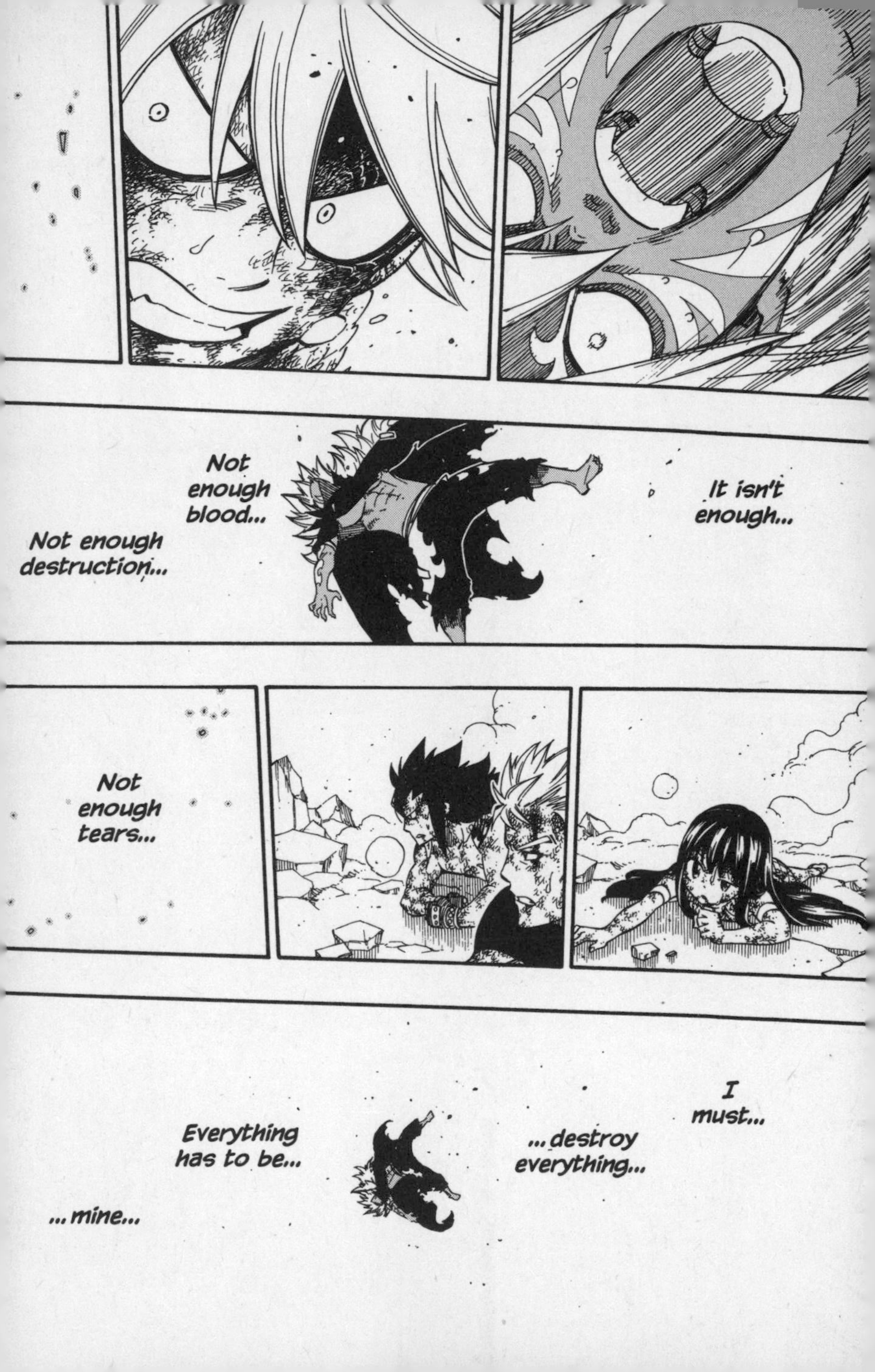
It isn't enough...
Not enough blood...
Not enough destruction...
Not enough tears...
I must...
...destroy everything...
Everything has to be...
...mine...

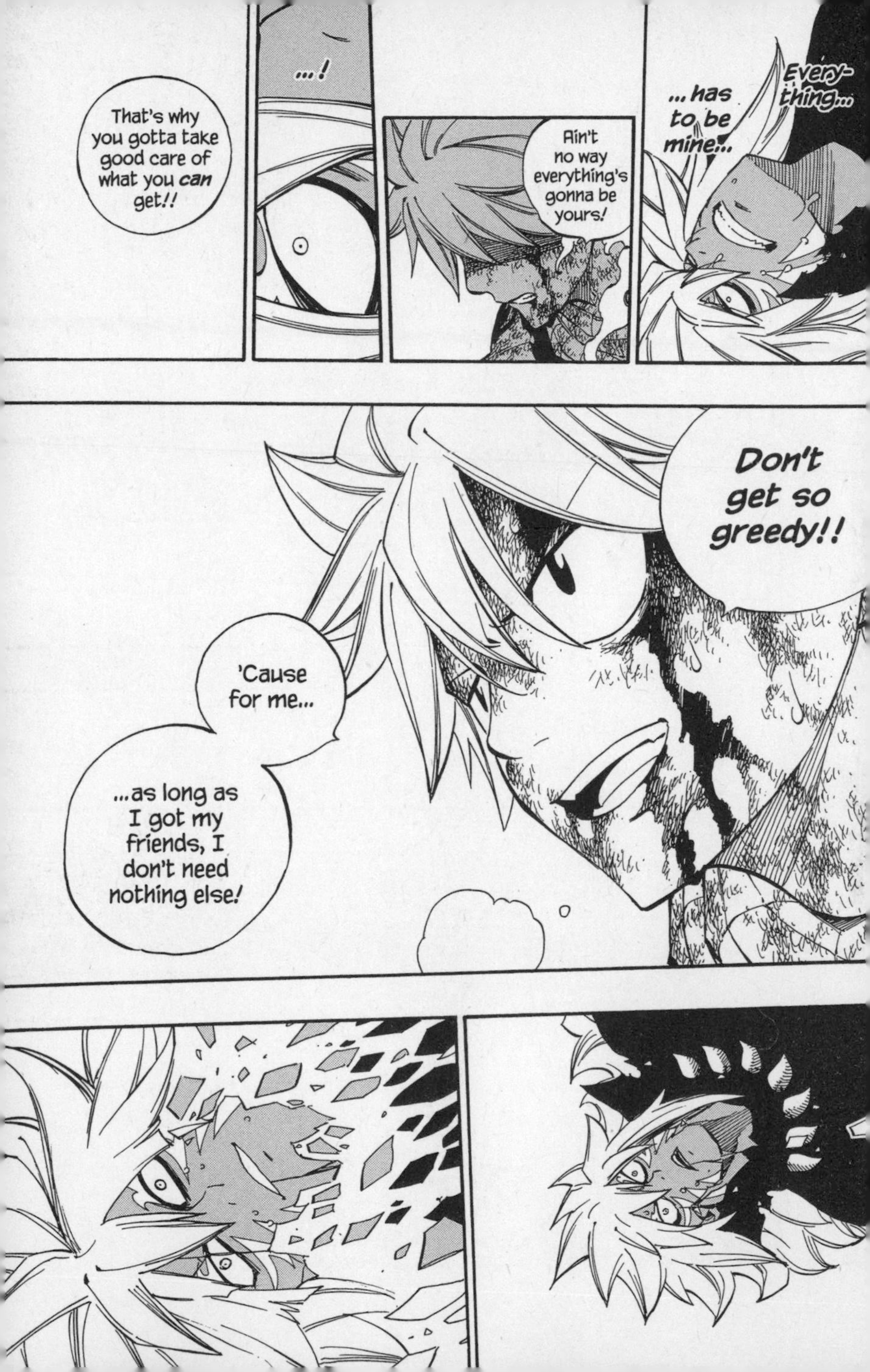
Every-thing...
...has to be mine...
Ain't no way everything's gonna be yours!
...!
That's why you gotta take good care of what you *can* get!!
Don't get so greedy!!
'Cause for me...
...as long as I got my friends, I don't need nothing else!

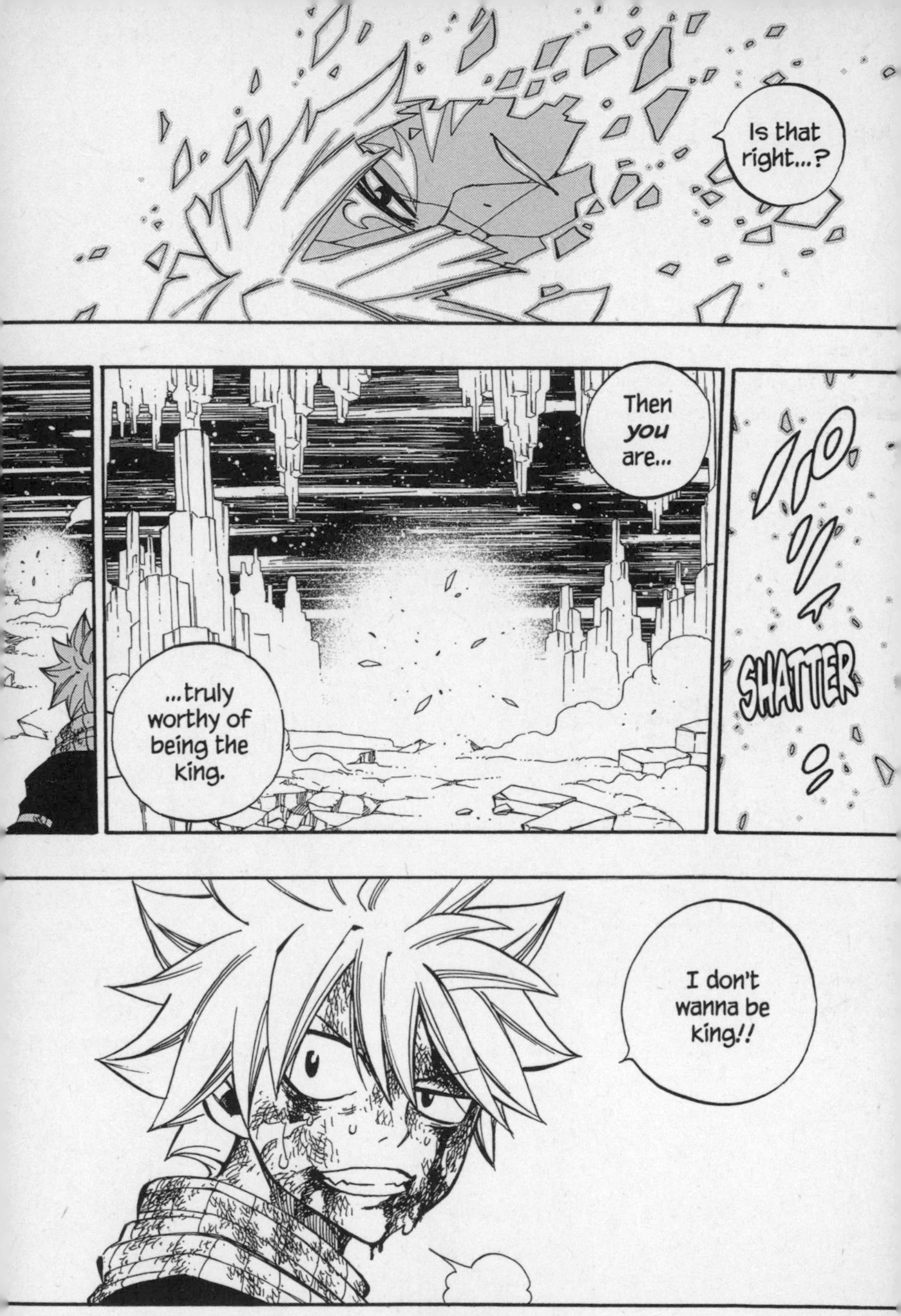
Is that right...?
SHATTER
Then *you* are...
...truly worthy of being the king.
I don't wanna be king!!

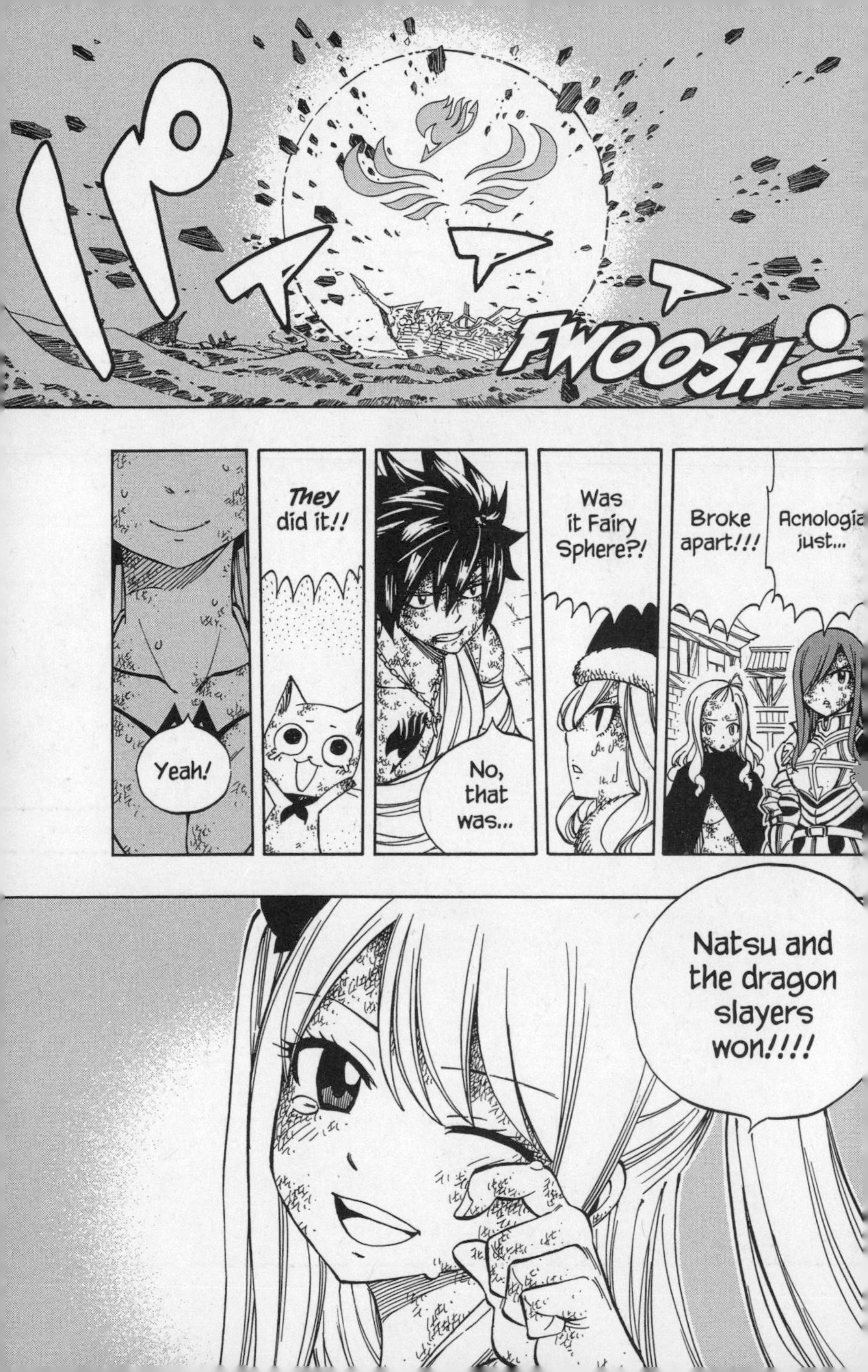
FWOOSH
Acnologia just...
Broke apart!!!
Was it Fairy Sphere?!
No, that was...
They did it!!
Yeah!
Natsu and the dragon slayers won!!!!

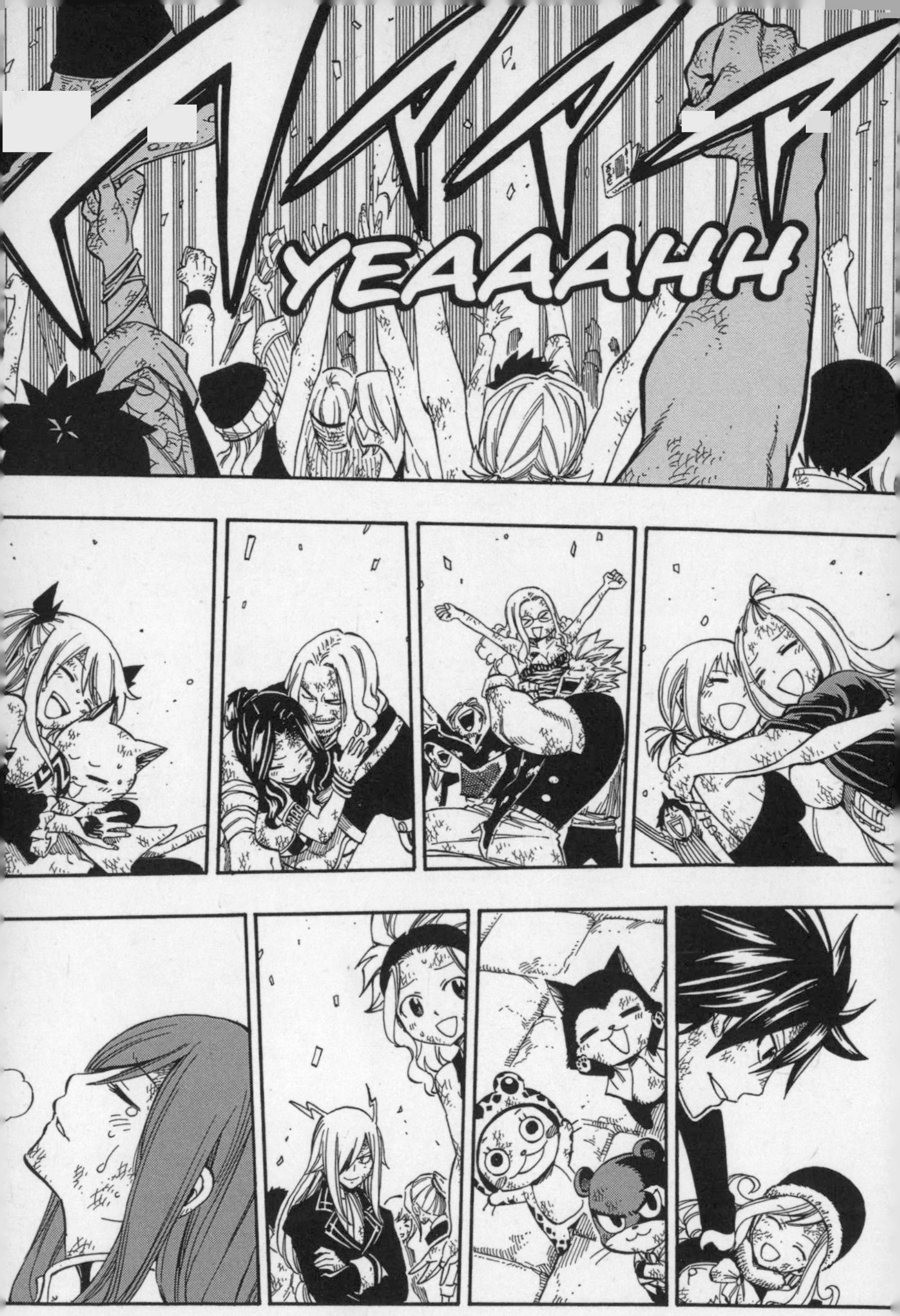
YEAAAHH

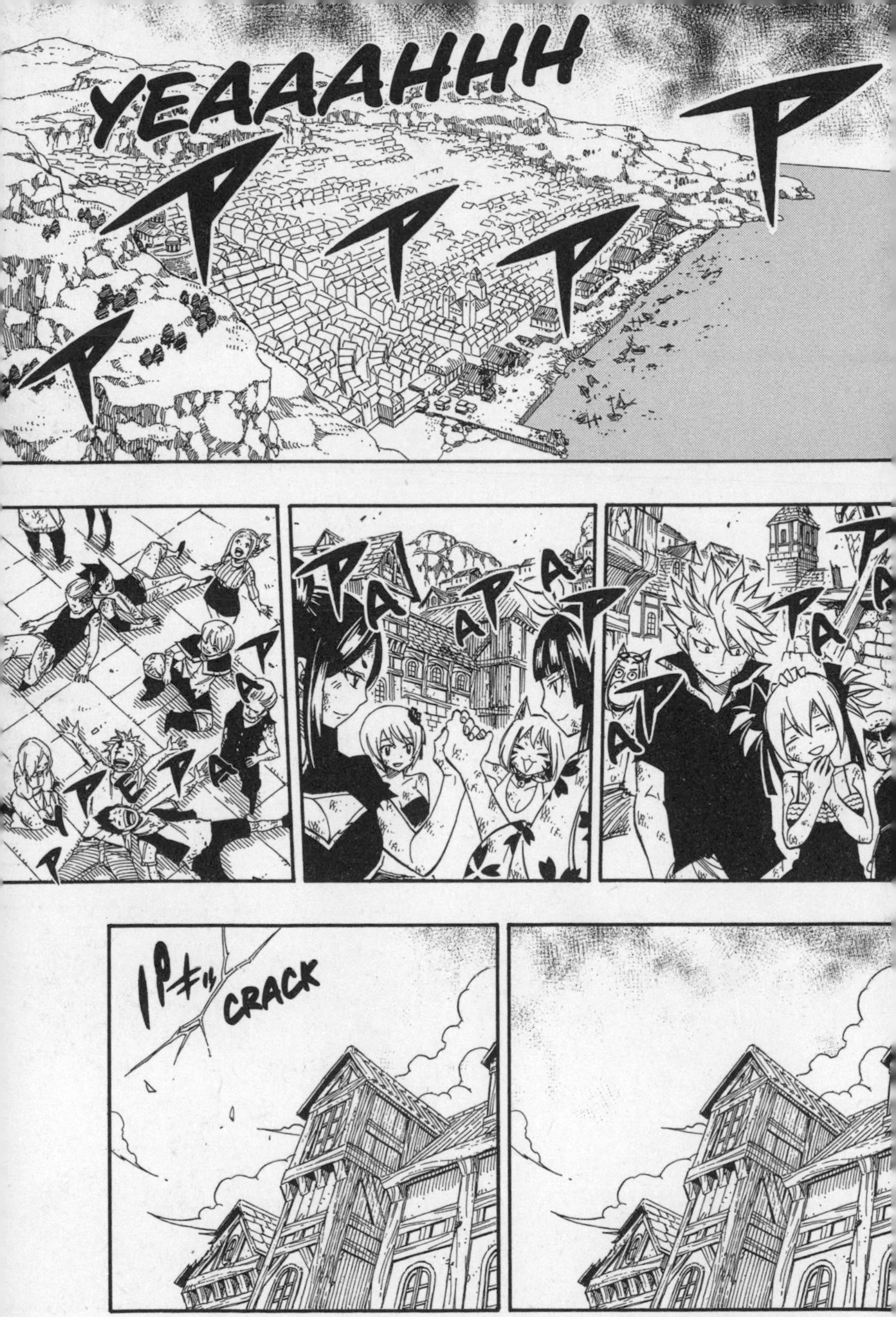
YEAAAHHH
CRACK

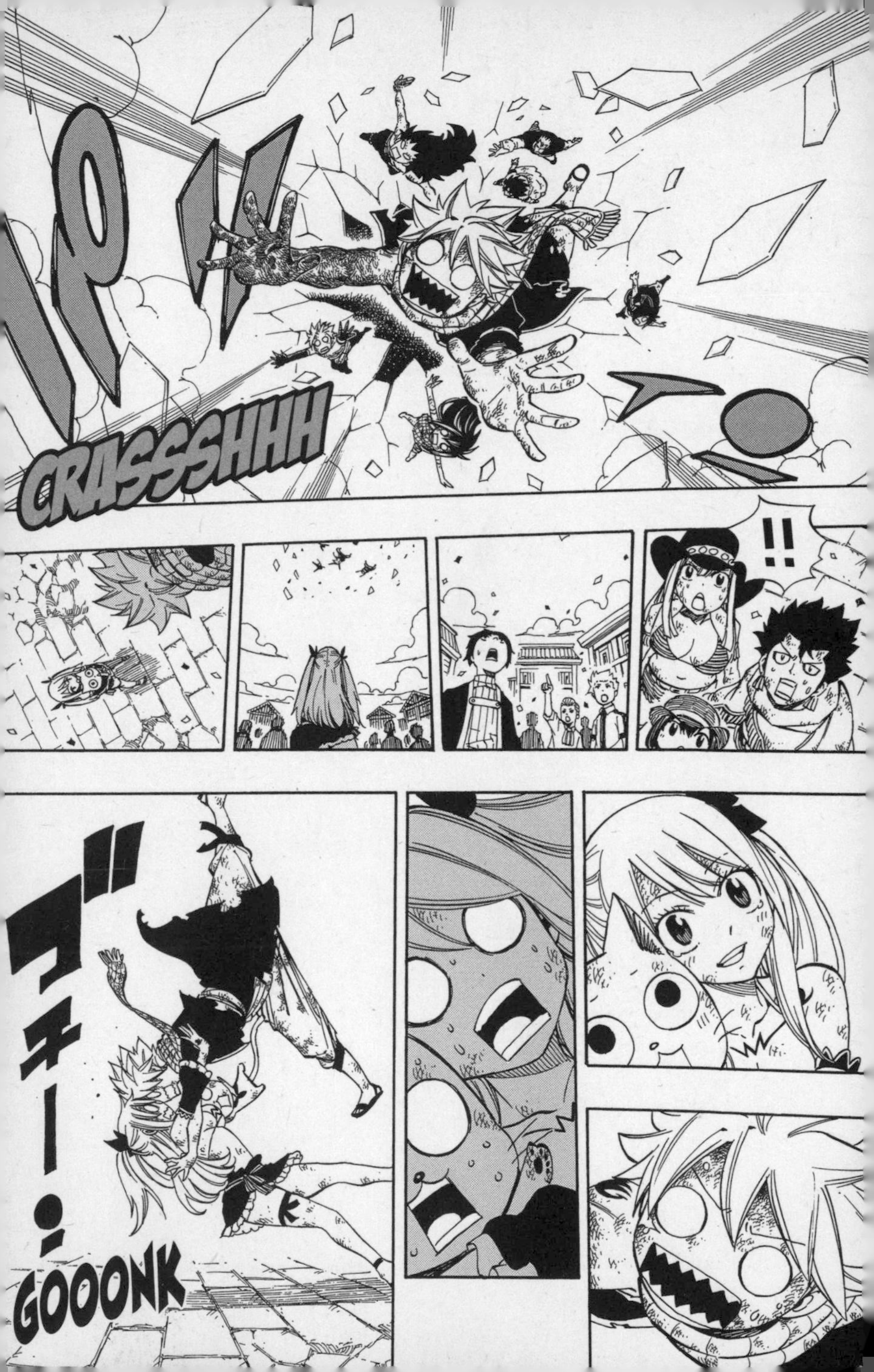
CRASSSHHH
!!
GOOONK

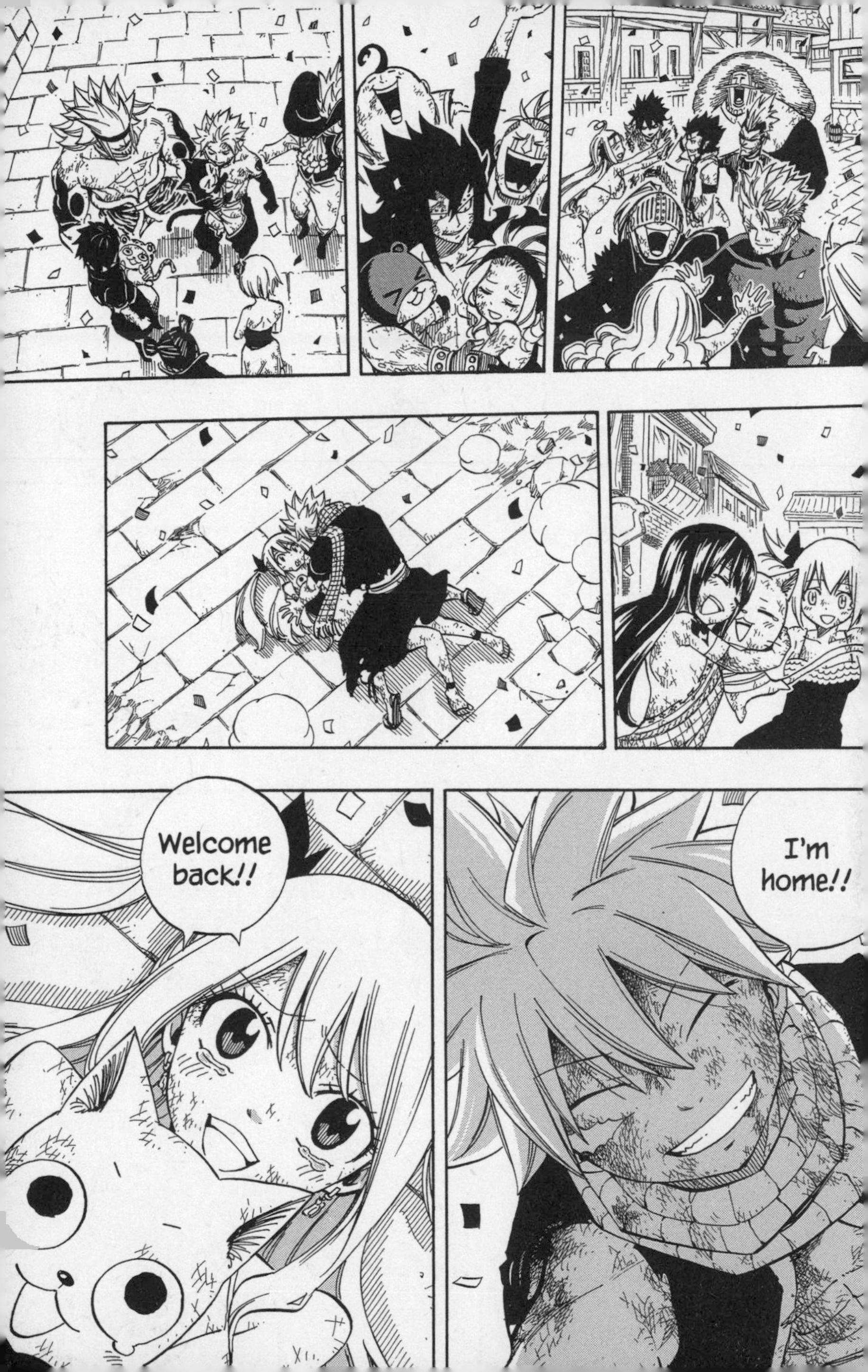
I'm home!!
Welcome back!!

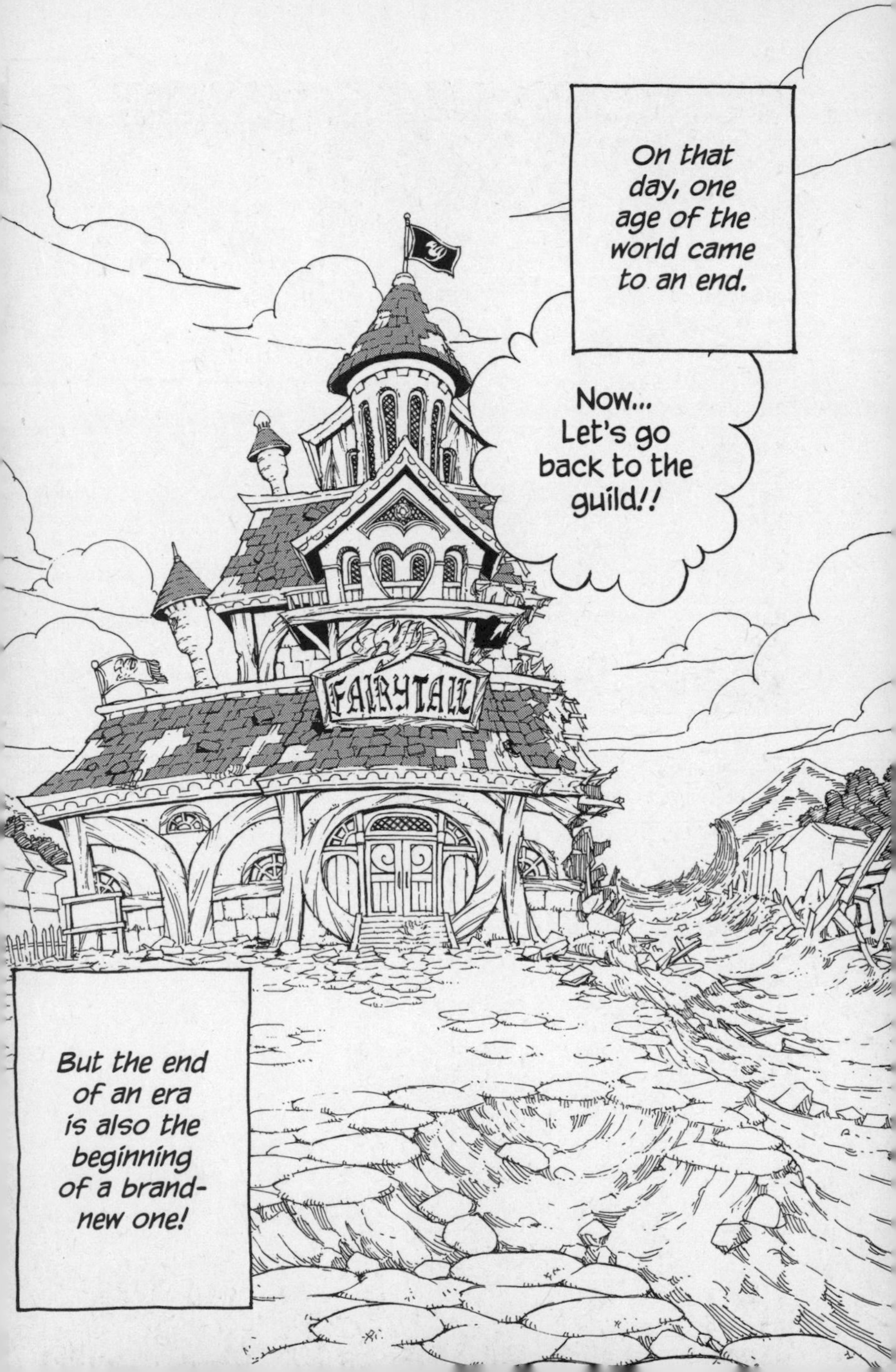
On that day, one age of the world came to an end.
Now... Let's go back to the guild!!
FAIRY TAIL
But the end of an era is also the beginning of a brand-new one!

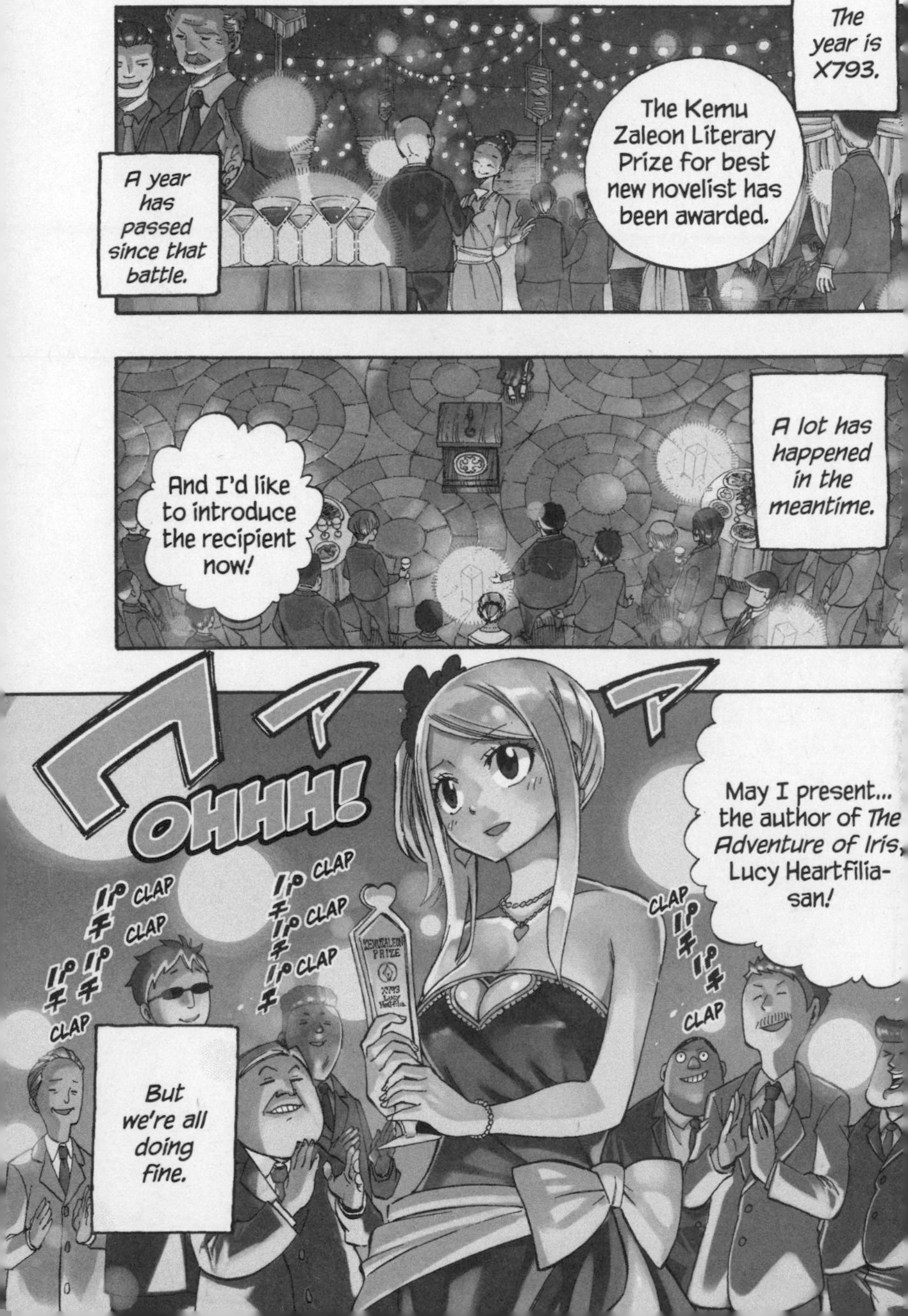
The year is X793.
The Kemu Zaleon Literary Prize for best new novelist has been awarded.
A year has passed since that battle.
A lot has happened in the meantime.
And I'd like to introduce the recipient now!
May I present... the author of *The Adventure of Iris*, Lucy Heartfilia-san!
ワァア
OHHH!
パチ CLAP
パチ CLAP
パチ CLAP
CLAP
KEMUZALEON PRIZE
But we're all doing fine.

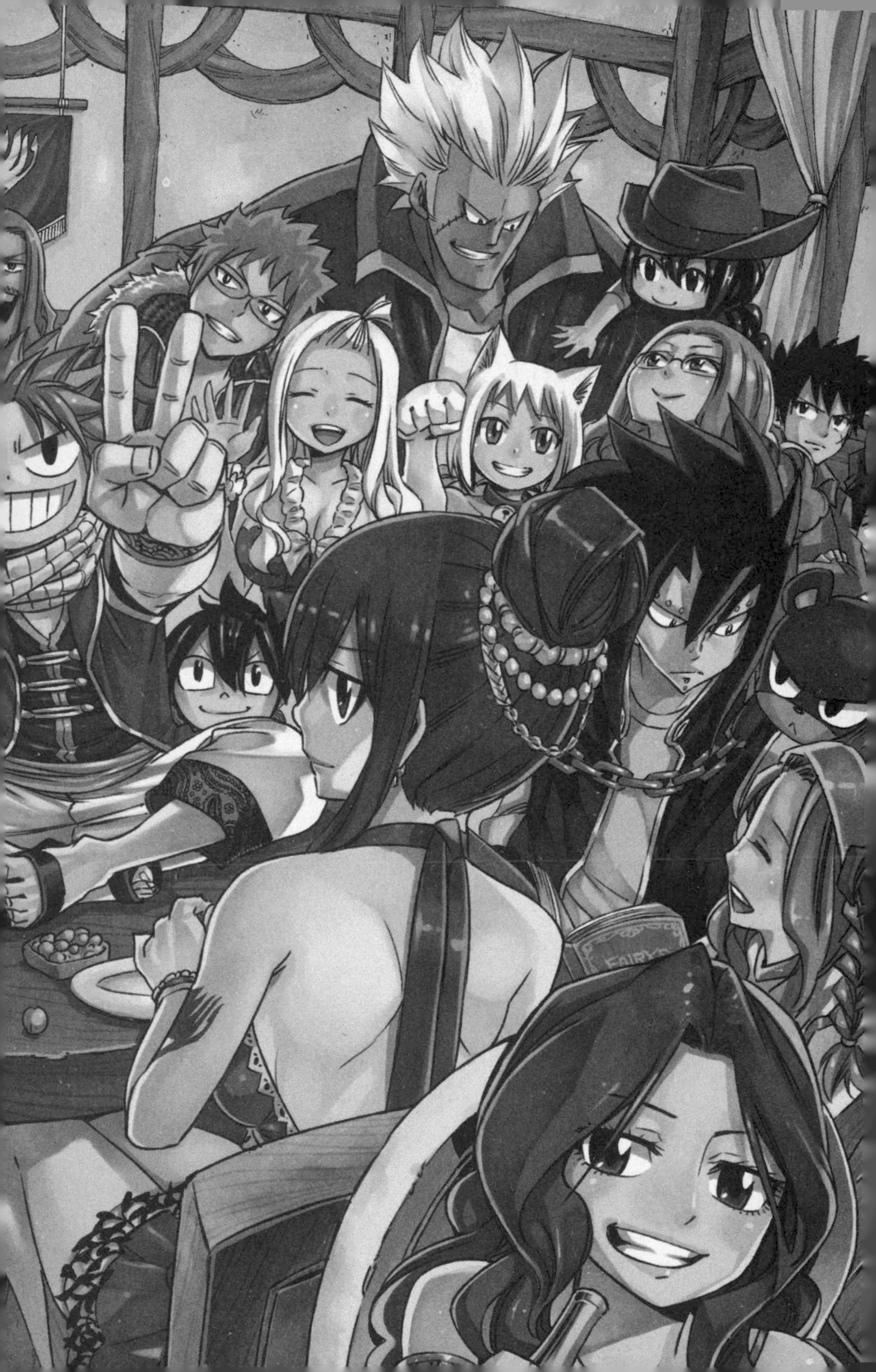

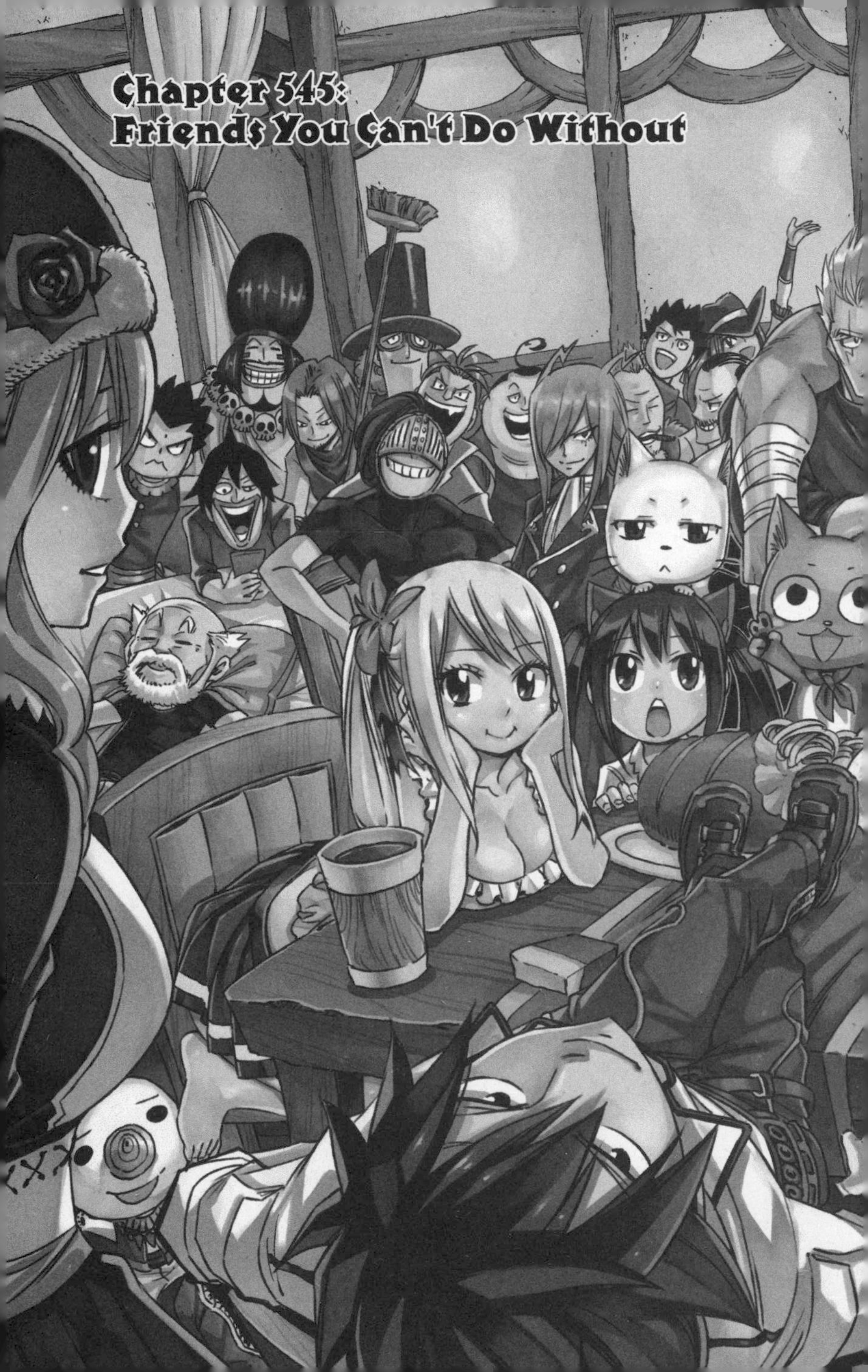
Chapter 545:
Friends You Can't Do Without

FAIRY TAIL
フェアリーテイル

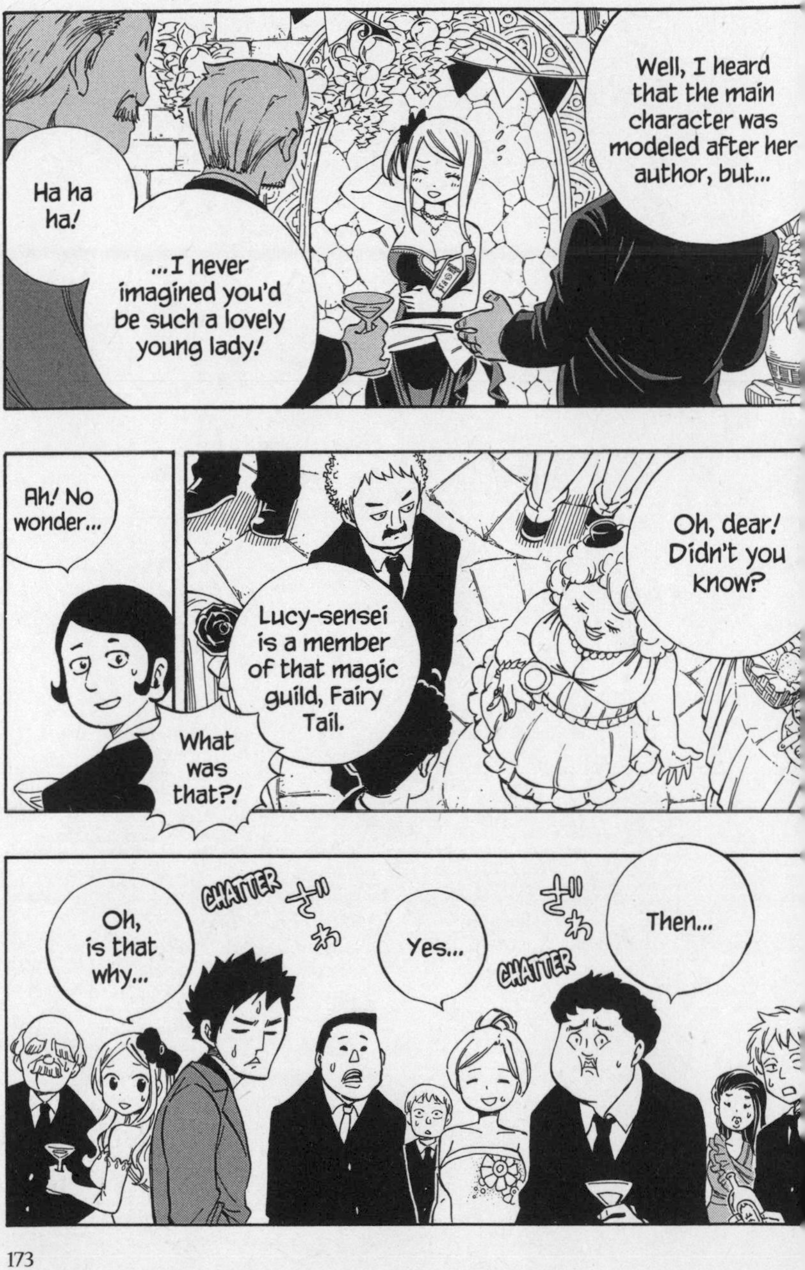
Well, I heard that the main character was modeled after her author, but...
...I never imagined you'd be such a lovely young lady!
Ha ha ha!
Oh, dear! Didn't you know?
Lucy-sensei is a member of that magic guild, Fairy Tail.
What was that?!
Ah! No wonder...
Then...
CHATTER
ざわ
Yes...
ざわ
CHATTER
Oh, is that why...

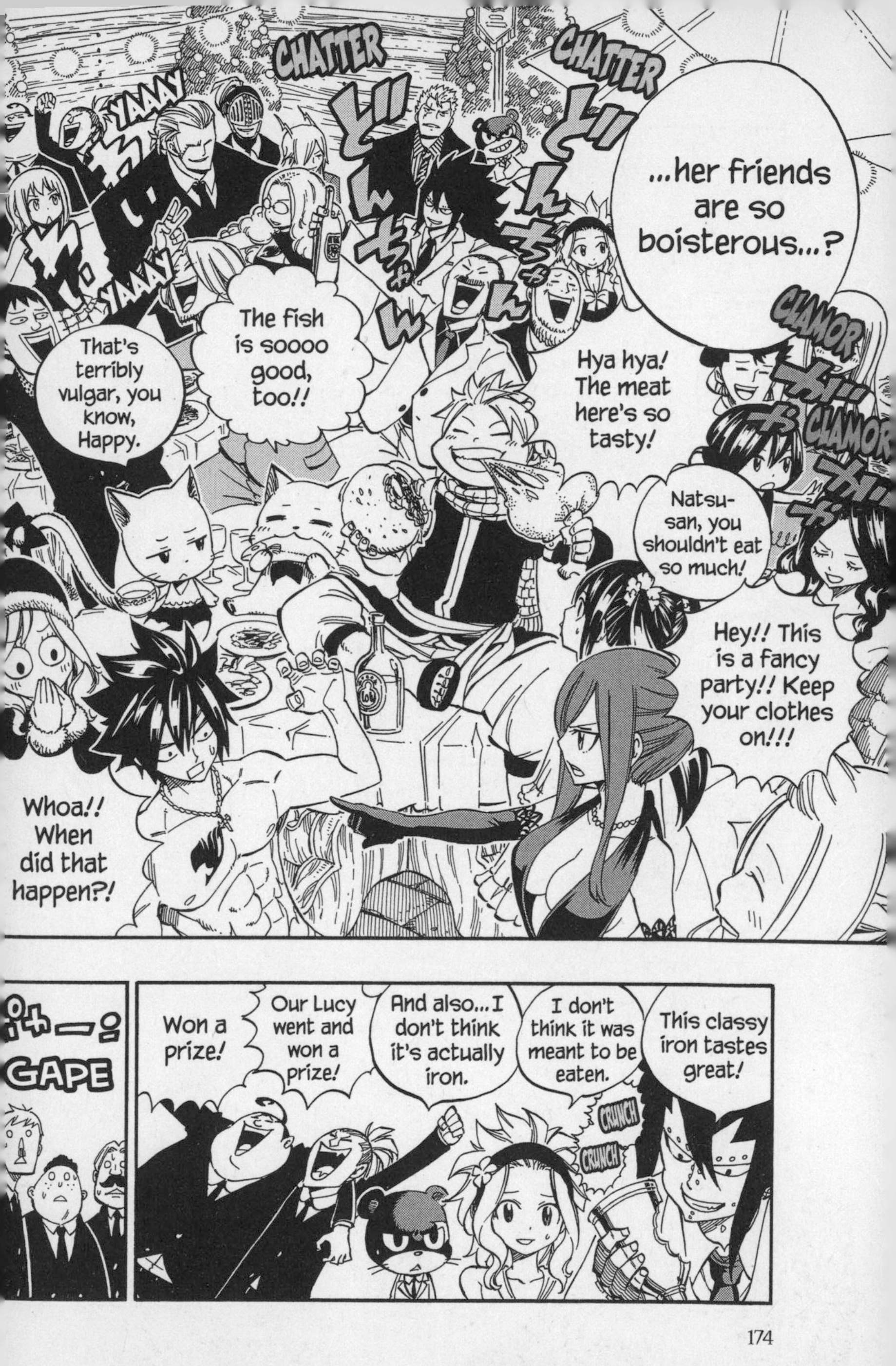
...her friends are so boisterous...?
CHATTER
CHATTER
YAAAY
YAAAY
CLAMOR
CLAMOR
Hya hya! The meat here's so tasty!
Natsu-san, you shouldn't eat so much!
The fish is soooo good, too!!
That's terribly vulgar, you know, Happy.
Hey!! This is a fancy party!! Keep your clothes on!!!
Whoa!! When did that happen?!
This classy iron tastes great!
I don't think it was meant to be eaten.
CRUNCH
CRUNCH
And also...I don't think it's actually iron.
Our Lucy went and won a prize!
Won a prize!
GAPE

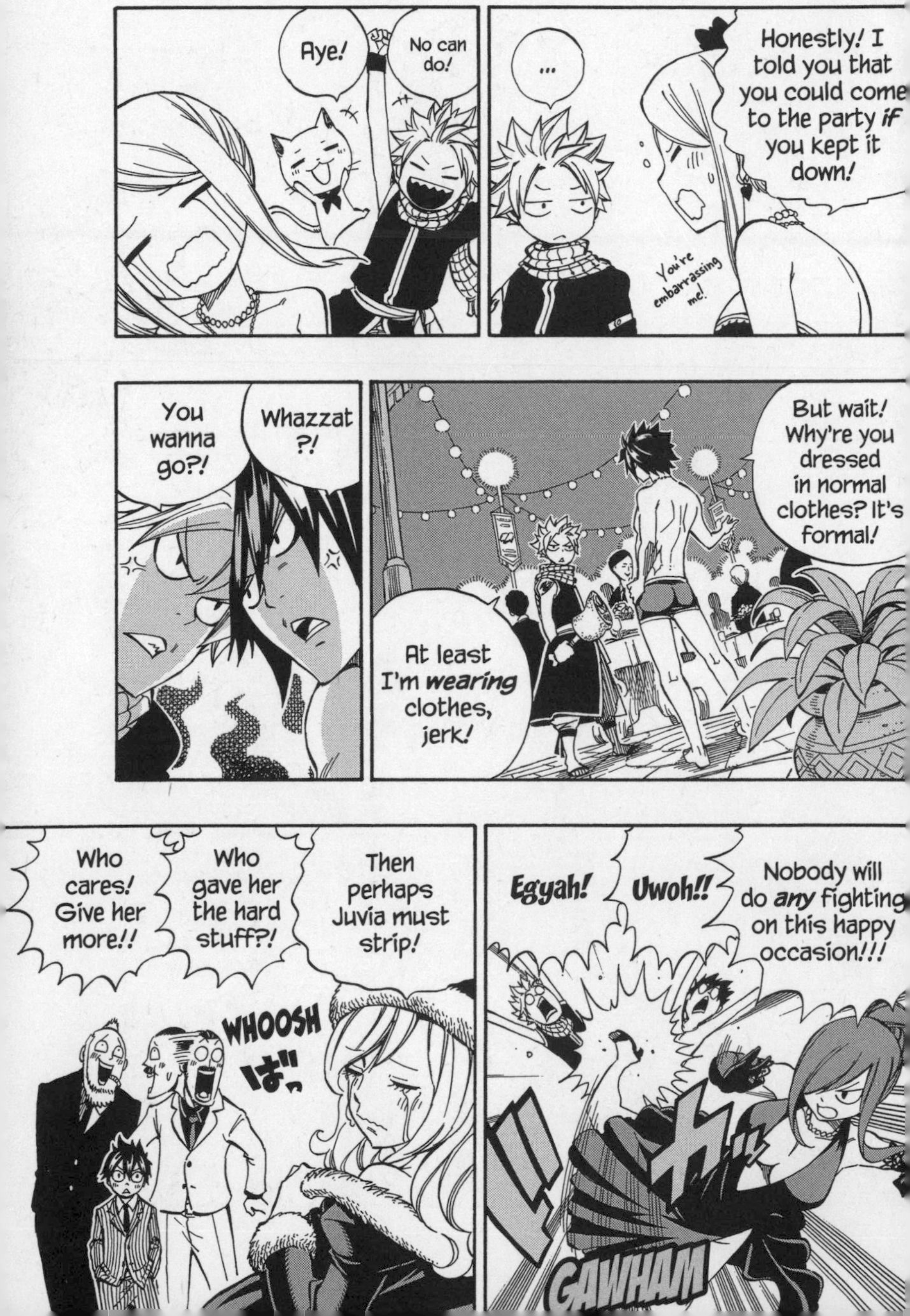
Honestly! I told you that you could come to the party *if* you kept it down!
You're embarrassing me!
...
No can do!
Aye!
But wait! Why're you dressed in normal clothes? It's formal!
At least I'm *wearing* clothes, jerk!
Whazzat?!
You wanna go?!
Nobody will do *any* fighting on this happy occasion!!!
Uwoh!!
Egyah!
GAWHAM
Then perhaps Juvia must strip!
Who gave her the hard stuff?!
Who cares! Give her more!!
WHOOSH
ばっ

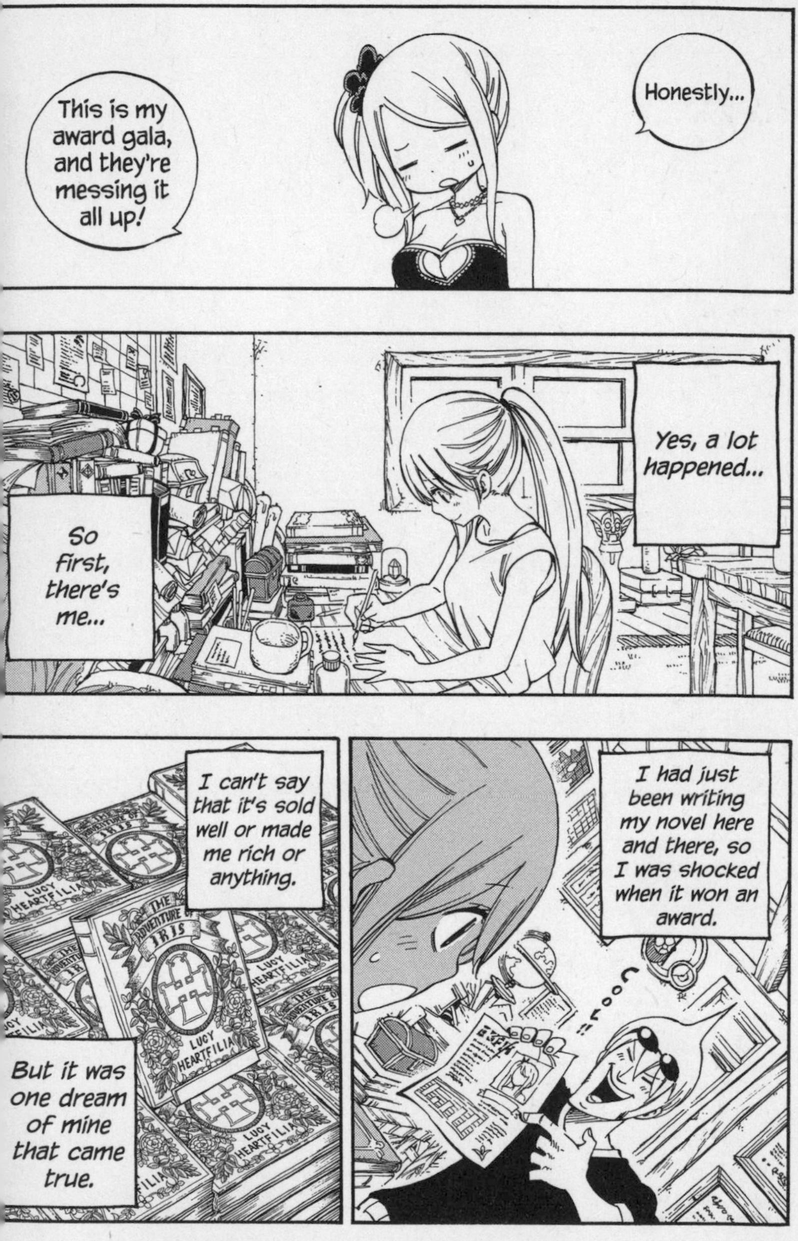
Honestly...
This is my award gala, and they're messing it all up!
Yes, a lot happened...
So first, there's me...
I had just been writing my novel here and there, so I was shocked when it won an award.
Cool!!
I can't say that it's sold well or made me rich or anything.
But it was one dream of mine that came true.
THE ADVENTURE OF IRIS
LUCY HEARTFILIA

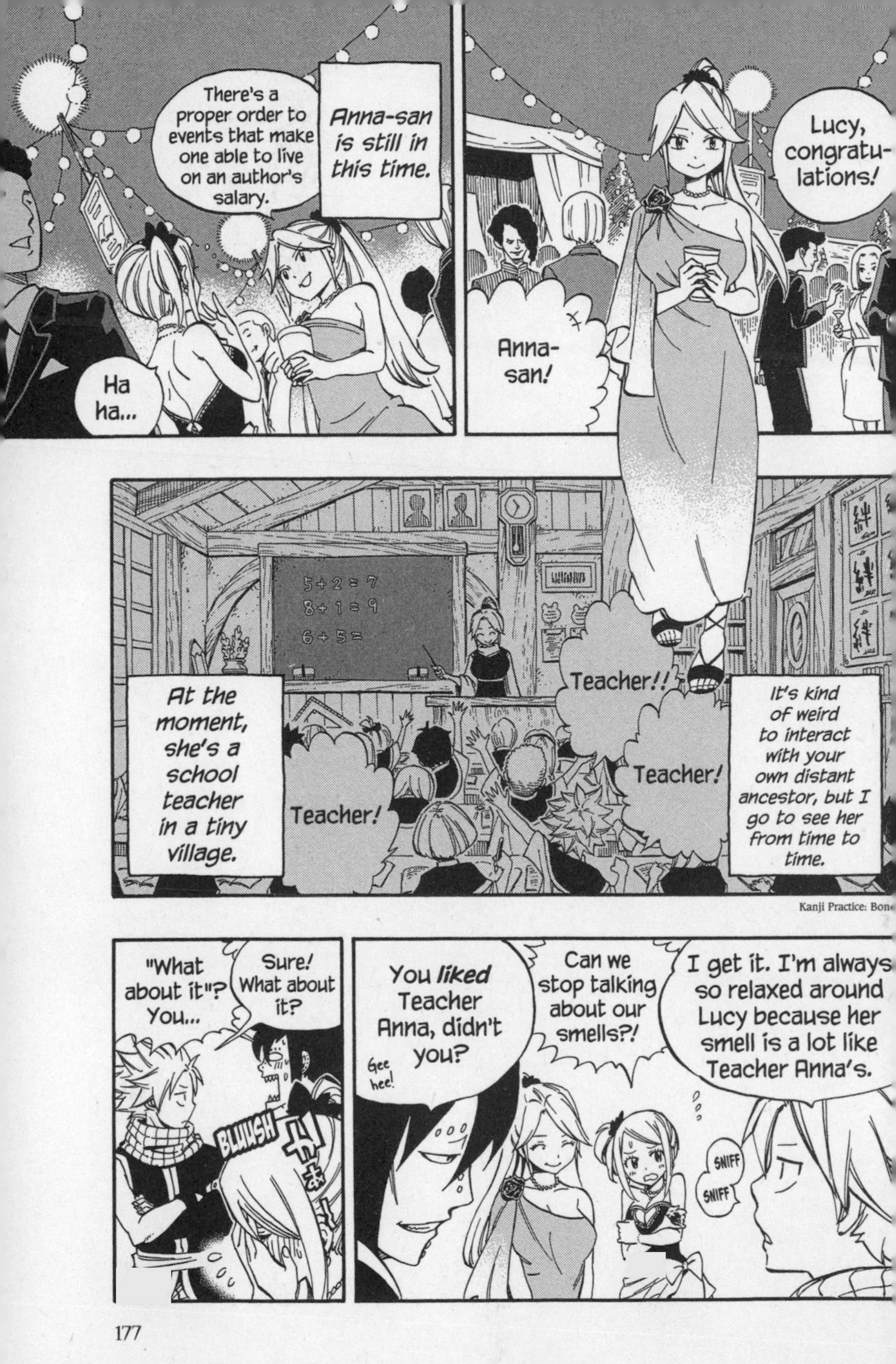

Lucy, congratulations!
Anna-san!
Anna-san is still in this time.
There's a proper order to events that make one able to live on an author's salary.
Ha ha...
It's kind of weird to interact with your own distant ancestor, but I go to see her from time to time.
Teacher!!
Teacher!
Teacher!
At the moment, she's a school teacher in a tiny village.
I get it. I'm always so relaxed around Lucy because her smell is a lot like Teacher Anna's.
SNIFF
SNIFF
Can we stop talking about our smells?!
You *liked* Teacher Anna, didn't you?
Gee hee!
Sure! What about it?
"What about it"? You...
BLUUSH

Kanji Practice: Bon

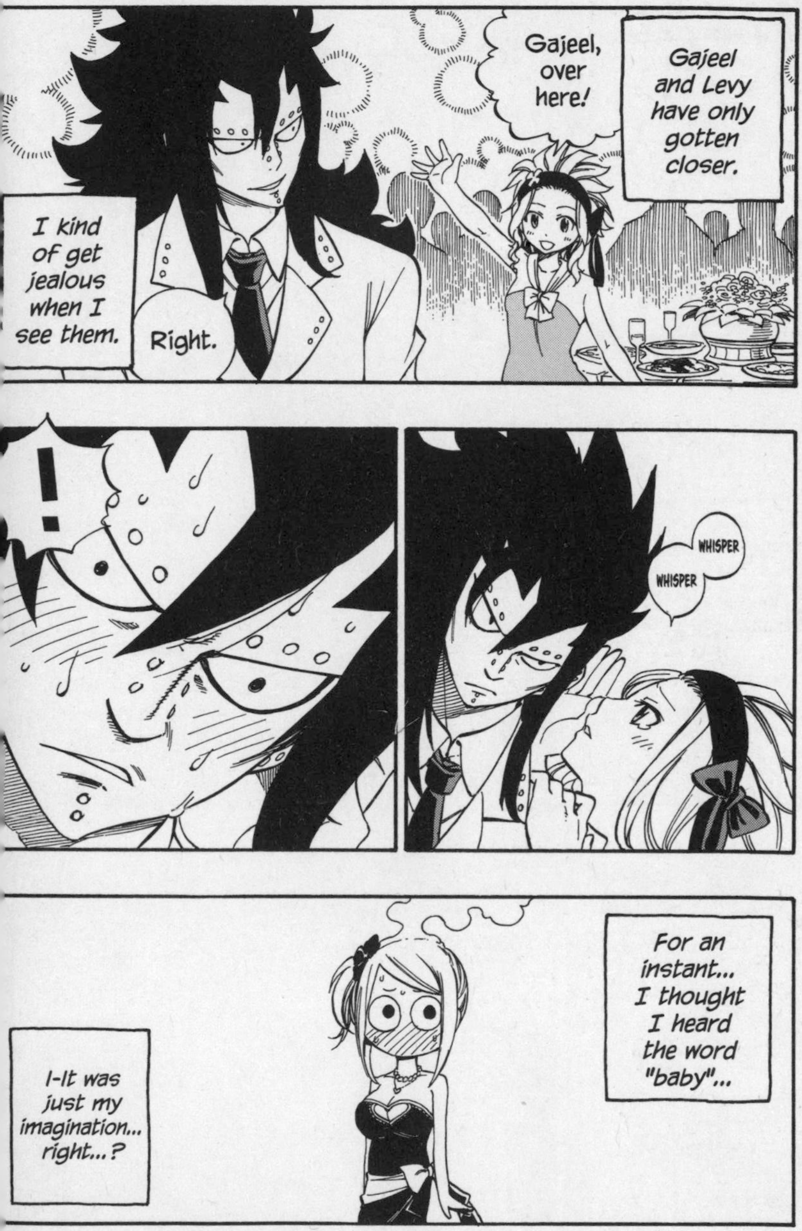
Gajeel and Levy have only gotten closer.
Gajeel, over here!
Right.
I kind of get jealous when I see them.
WHISPER
WHISPER
!
For an instant... I thought I heard the word "baby"...
I-It was just my imagination... right...?

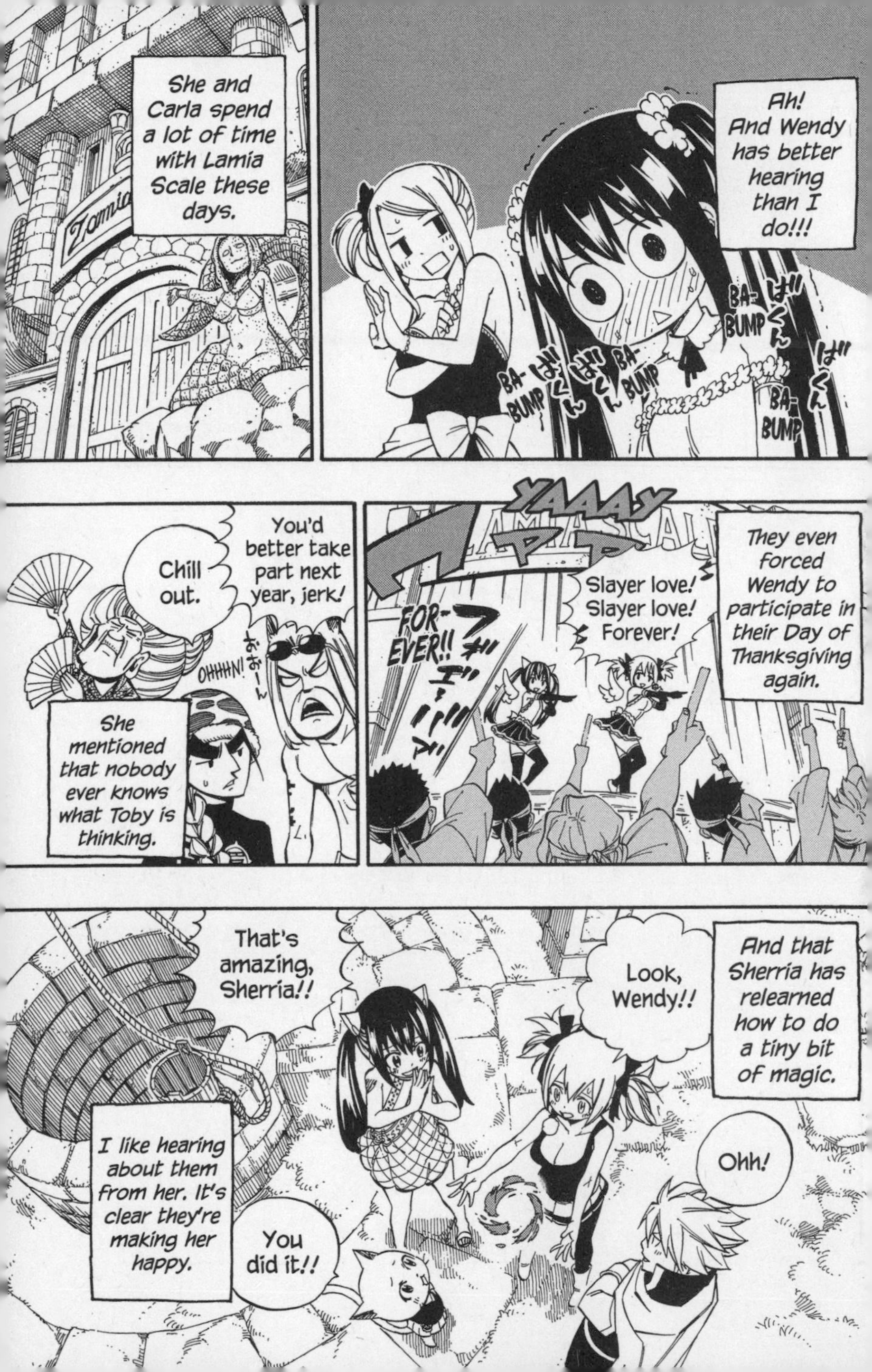

Ah! And Wendy has better hearing than I do!!!
BA-BUMP
ばくん
BA-BUMP
ばくん
BA-BUMP
ばくん
BA-BUMP
ばくん
She and Carla spend a lot of time with Lamia Scale these days.
YAAAY
They even forced Wendy to participate in their Day of Thanksgiving again.
Slayer love! Slayer love! Forever!
FOR-EVER!!
You'd better take part next year, jerk!
Chill out.
OHHHN!
おおーん
She mentioned that nobody ever knows what Toby is thinking.
And that Sherria has relearned how to do a tiny bit of magic.
Look, Wendy!!
That's amazing, Sherria!!
Ohh!
I like hearing about them from her. It's clear they're making her happy.
You did it!!

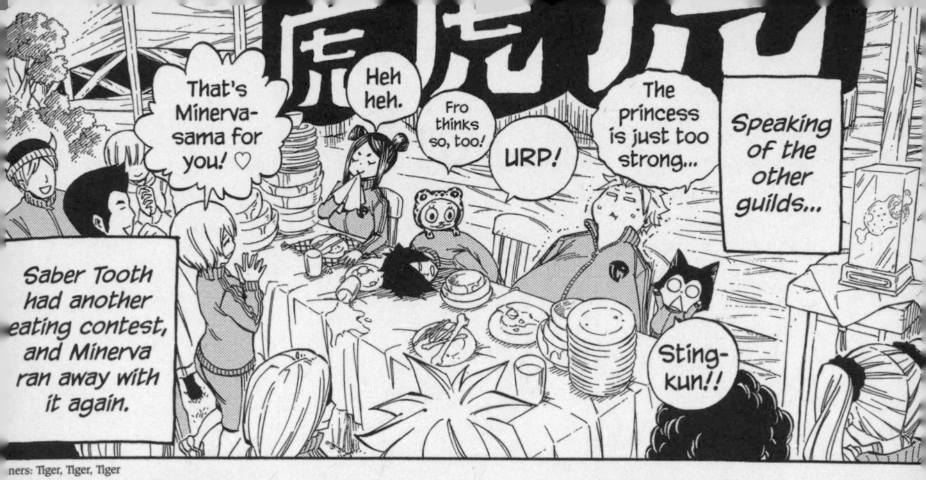
Speaking of the other guilds...
The princess is just too strong...
URP!
Fro thinks so, too!
Heh heh.
That's Minerva-sama for you! ♡
Sting-kun!!
Saber Tooth had another eating contest, and Minerva ran away with it again.

ners: Tiger, Tiger, Tiger

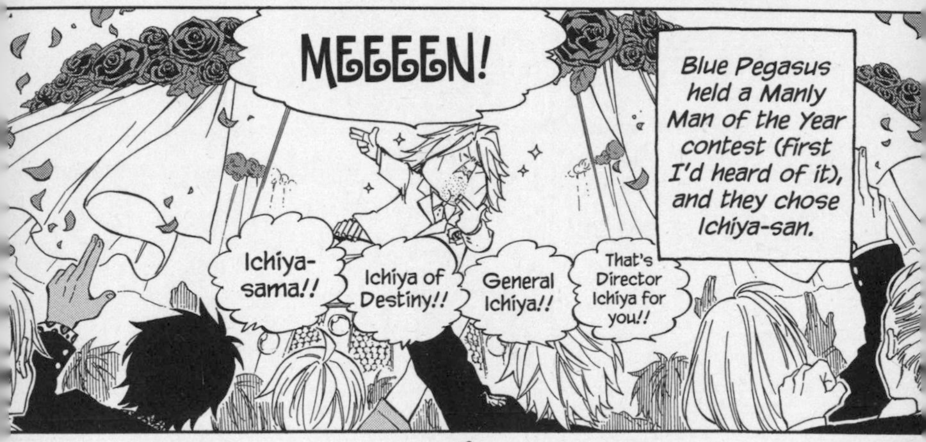
Blue Pegasus held a Manly Man of the Year contest (first I'd heard of it), and they chose Ichiya-san.
MEEEEN!
That's Director Ichiya for you!!
General Ichiya!!
Ichiya of Destiny!!
Ichiya-sama!!

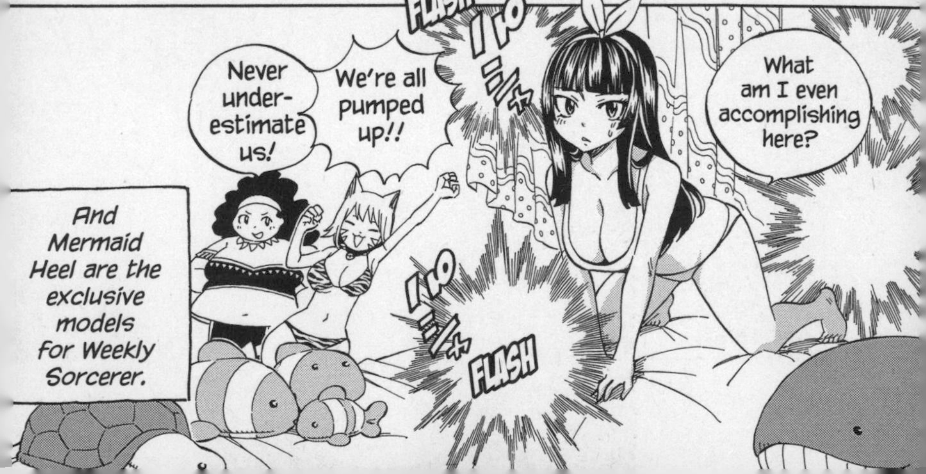
What am I even accomplishing here?
FLASH
We're all pumped up!!
Never under-estimate us!
FLASH
And Mermaid Heel are the exclusive models for Weekly Sorcerer.

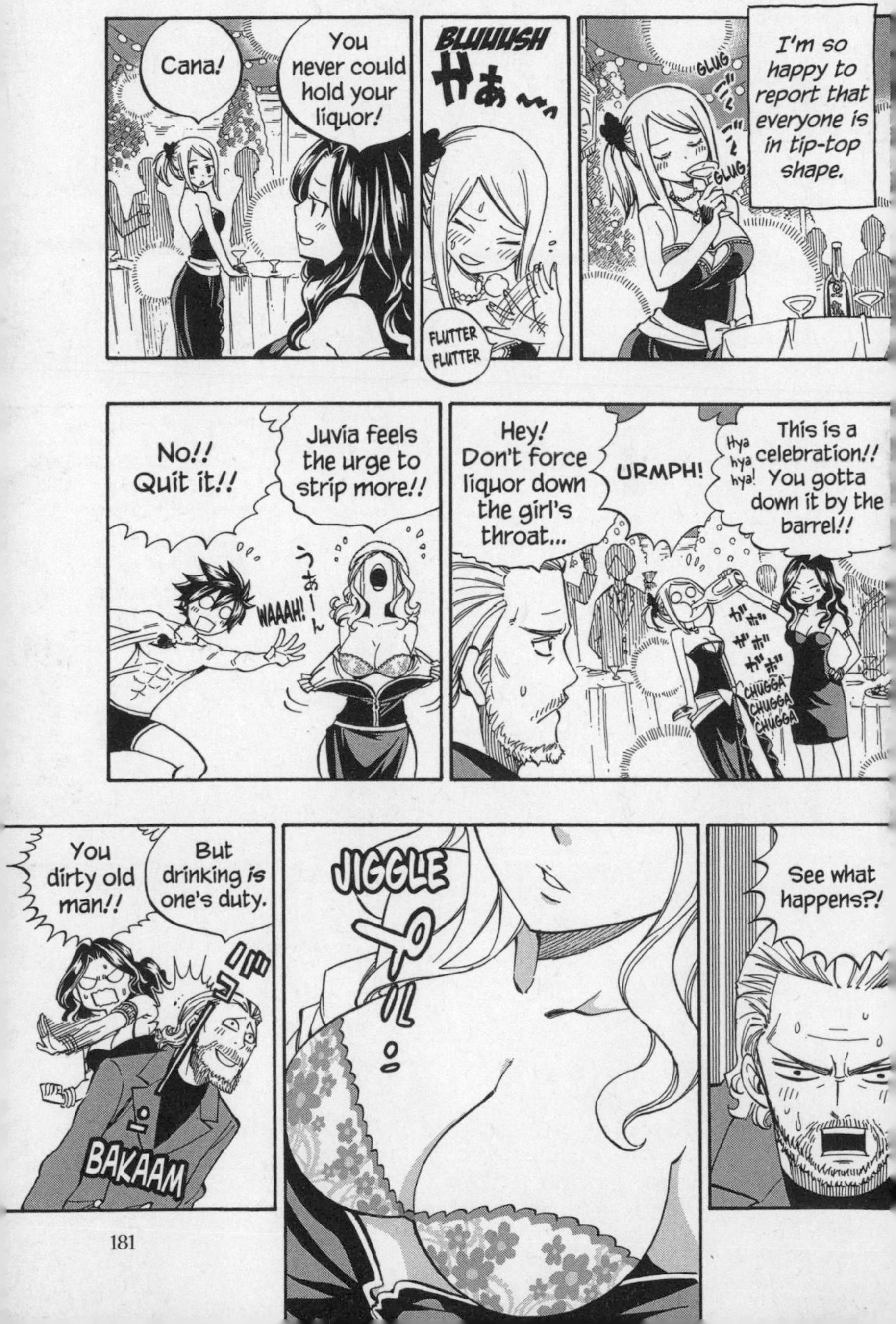

I'm so happy to report that everyone is in tip-top shape.
GLUG
GLUG
BLUUUSH
FLUTTER FLUTTER
You never could hold your liquor!
Cana!
This is a celebration!! You gotta down it by the barrel!!
Hya hya hya!
URMPH!
Hey! Don't force liquor down the girl's throat...
CHUGGA CHUGGA CHUGGA
Juvia feels the urge to strip more!!
No!! Quit it!!
WAAAH!
See what happens?!
JIGGLE
But drinking *is* one's duty.
You dirty old man!!
BAKAAM

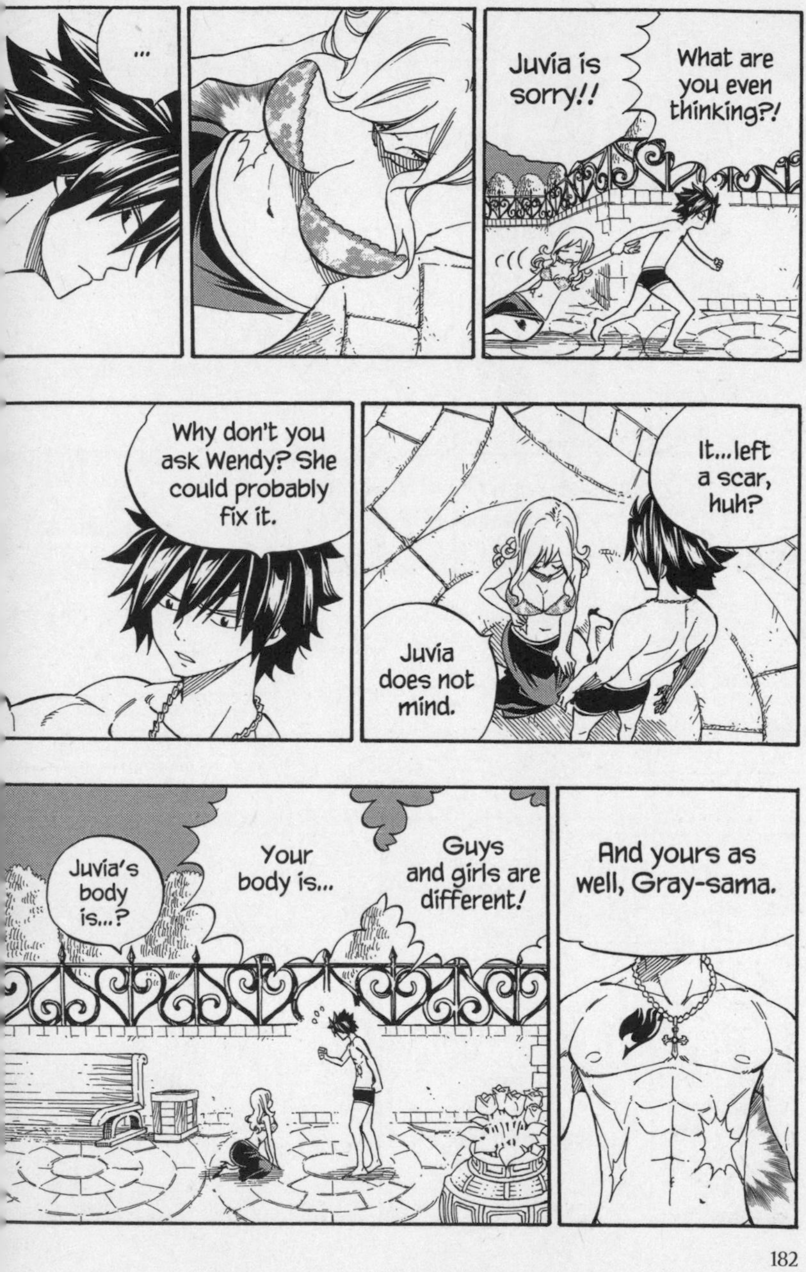
What are you even thinking?!
Juvia is sorry!!
...
It...left a scar, huh?
Juvia does not mind.
Why don't you ask Wendy? She could probably fix it.
And yours as well, Gray-sama.
Guys and girls are different!
Your body is...
Juvia's body is...?

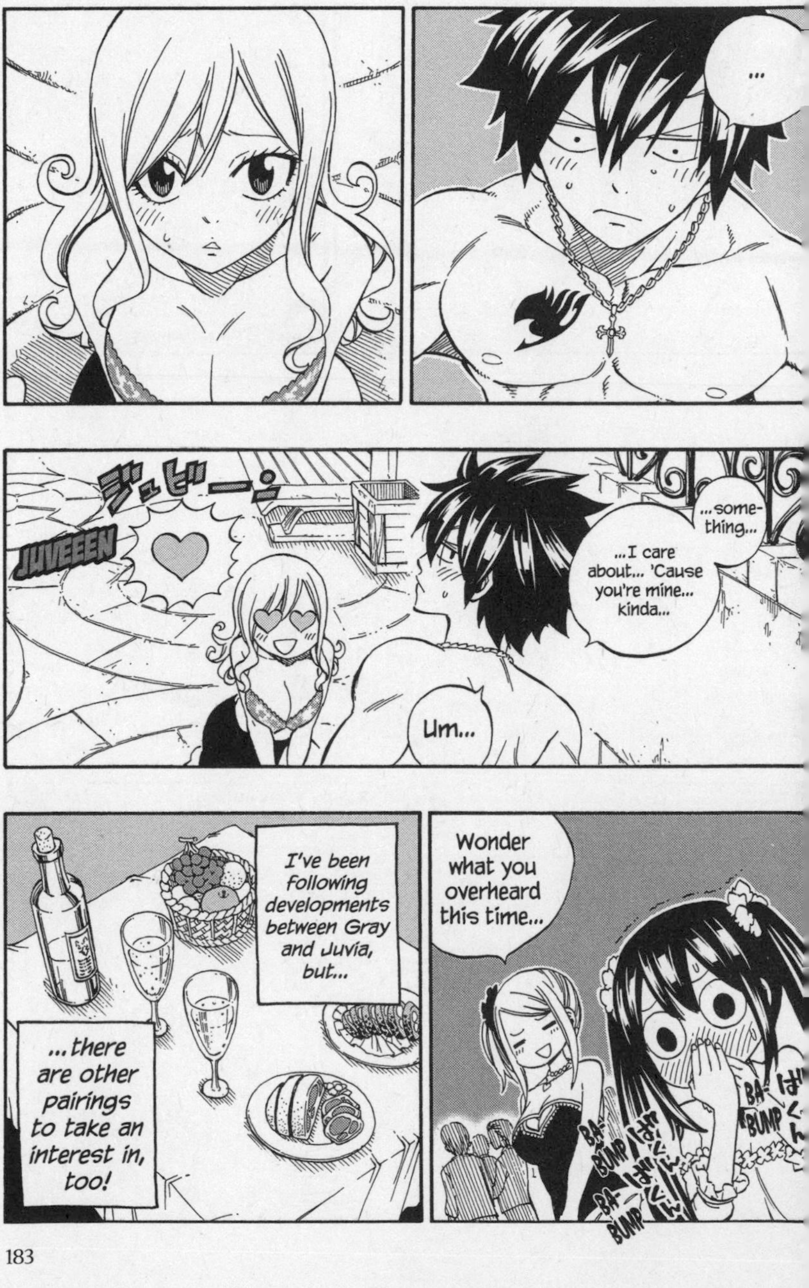
...
...some-thing...
...I care about... 'Cause you're mine... kinda...
ジュビーン
JUVEEEN
Um...
Wonder what you overheard this time...
BA-BUMP
ばくん
BA-BUMP
ばくん
BA-BUMP
ばくん
I've been following developments between Gray and Juvia, but...
...there are other pairings to take an interest in, too!

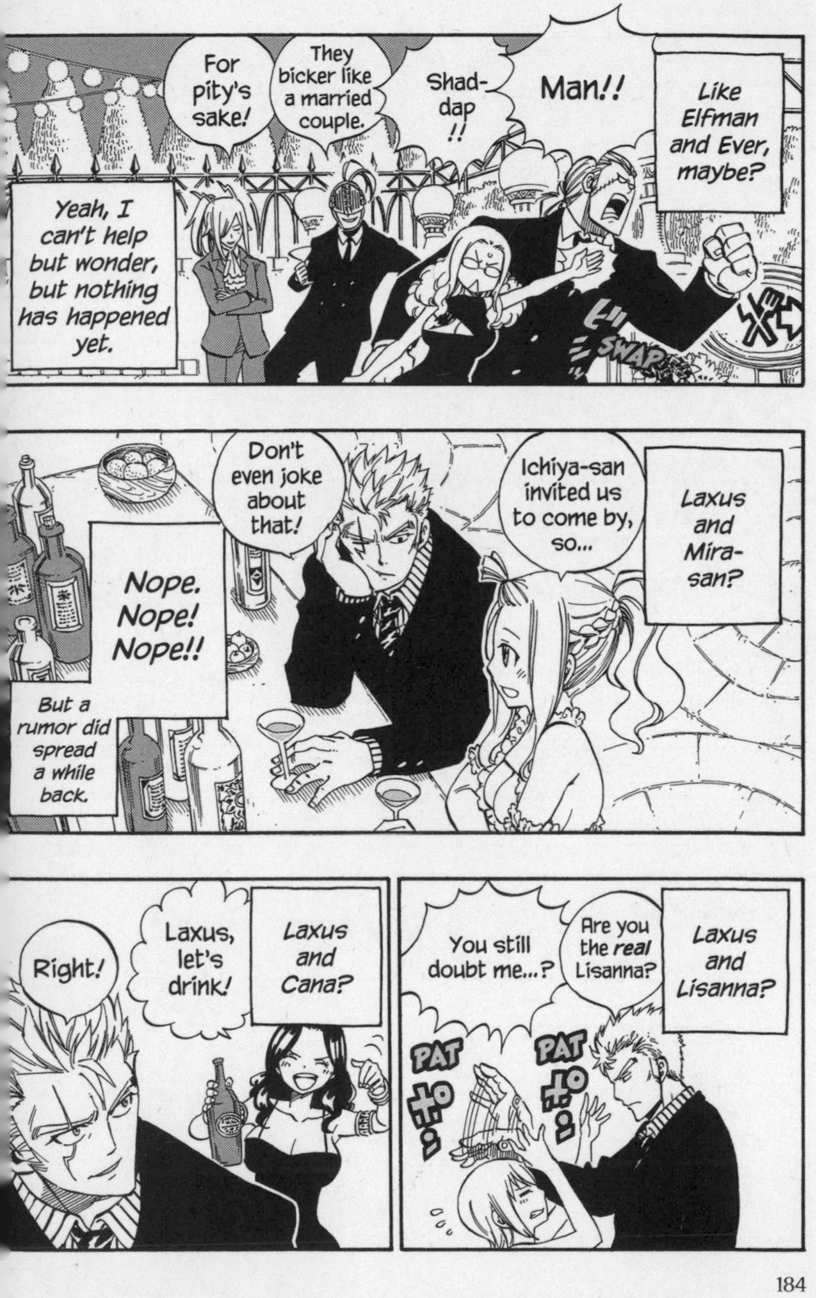

Like Elfman and Ever, maybe?
Man!!
Shad-dap!!
They bicker like a married couple.
For pity's sake!
Yeah, I can't help but wonder, but nothing has happened yet.
SWAP
Laxus and Mira-san?
Ichiya-san invited us to come by, so...
Don't even joke about that!
Nope. Nope! Nope!!
But a rumor did spread a while back.
Laxus and Lisanna?
Are you the *real* Lisanna?
You still doubt me...?
PAT
PAT
Laxus and Cana?
Laxus, let's drink!
Right!

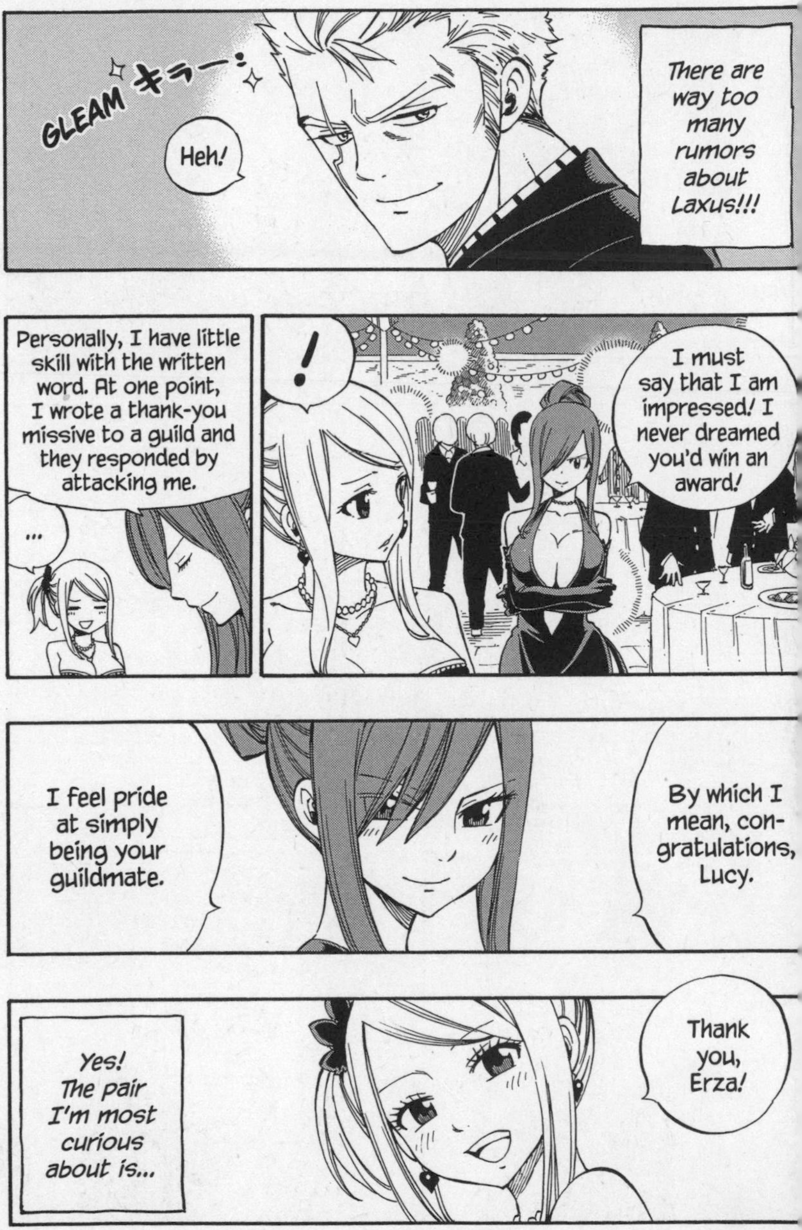
There are way too many rumors about Laxus!!!
GLEAM キラー
Heh!
I must say that I am impressed! I never dreamed you'd win an award!
!
Personally, I have little skill with the written word. At one point, I wrote a thank-you missive to a guild and they responded by attacking me.
...
By which I mean, congratulations, Lucy.
I feel pride at simply being your guildmate.
Thank you, Erza!
Yes! The pair I'm most curious about is...

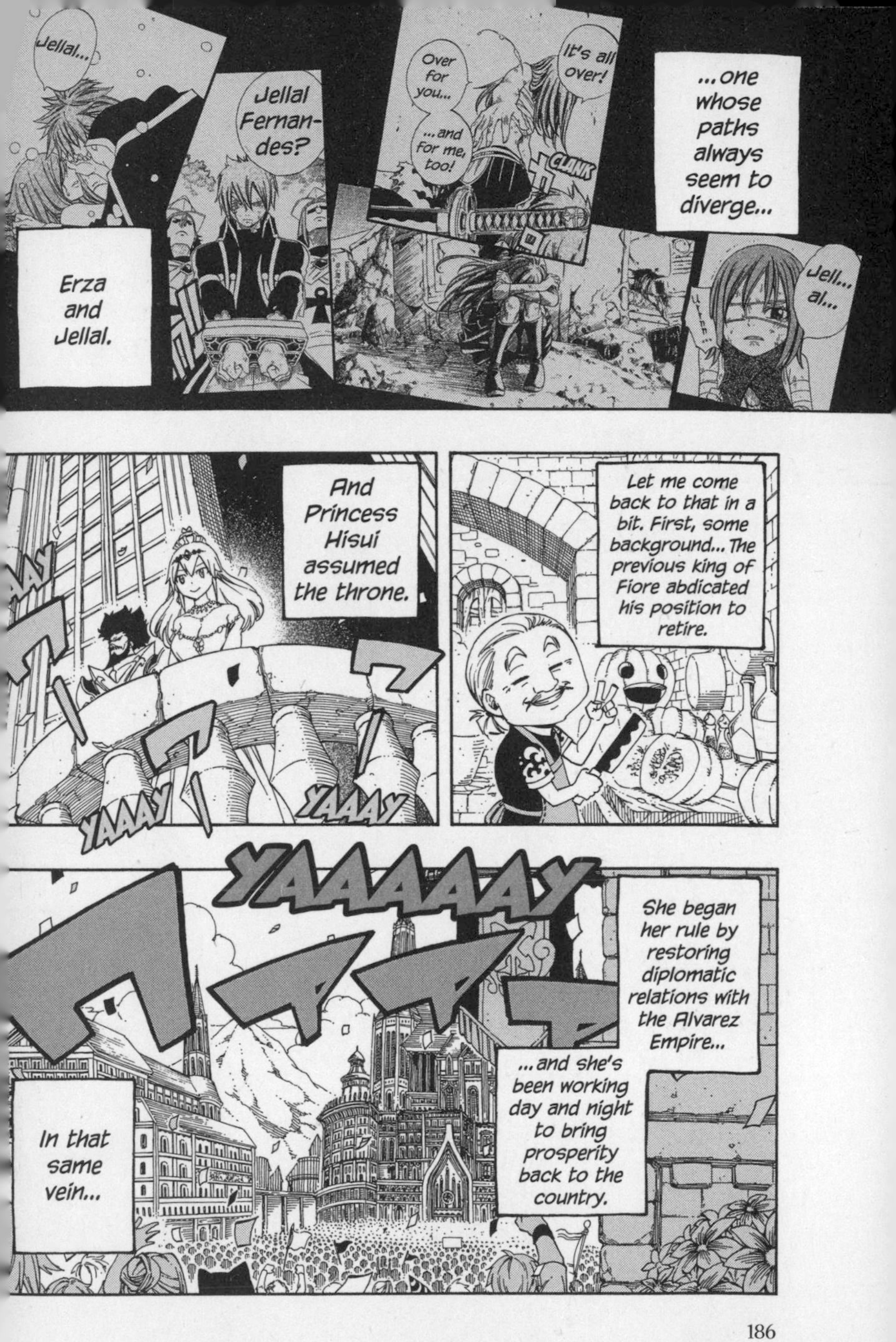

...one whose paths always seem to diverge...
Jell... al...
It's all over!
Over for you...
...and for me, too!
CLANK
Jellal Fernandes?
Jellal...
Erza and Jellal.
Let me come back to that in a bit. First, some background... The previous king of Fiore abdicated his position to retire.
And Princess Hisui assumed the throne.
YAAAY
YAAAY
YAAAY
YAAAAAY
She began her rule by restoring diplomatic relations with the Alvarez Empire...
...and she's been working day and night to bring prosperity back to the country.
In that same vein...

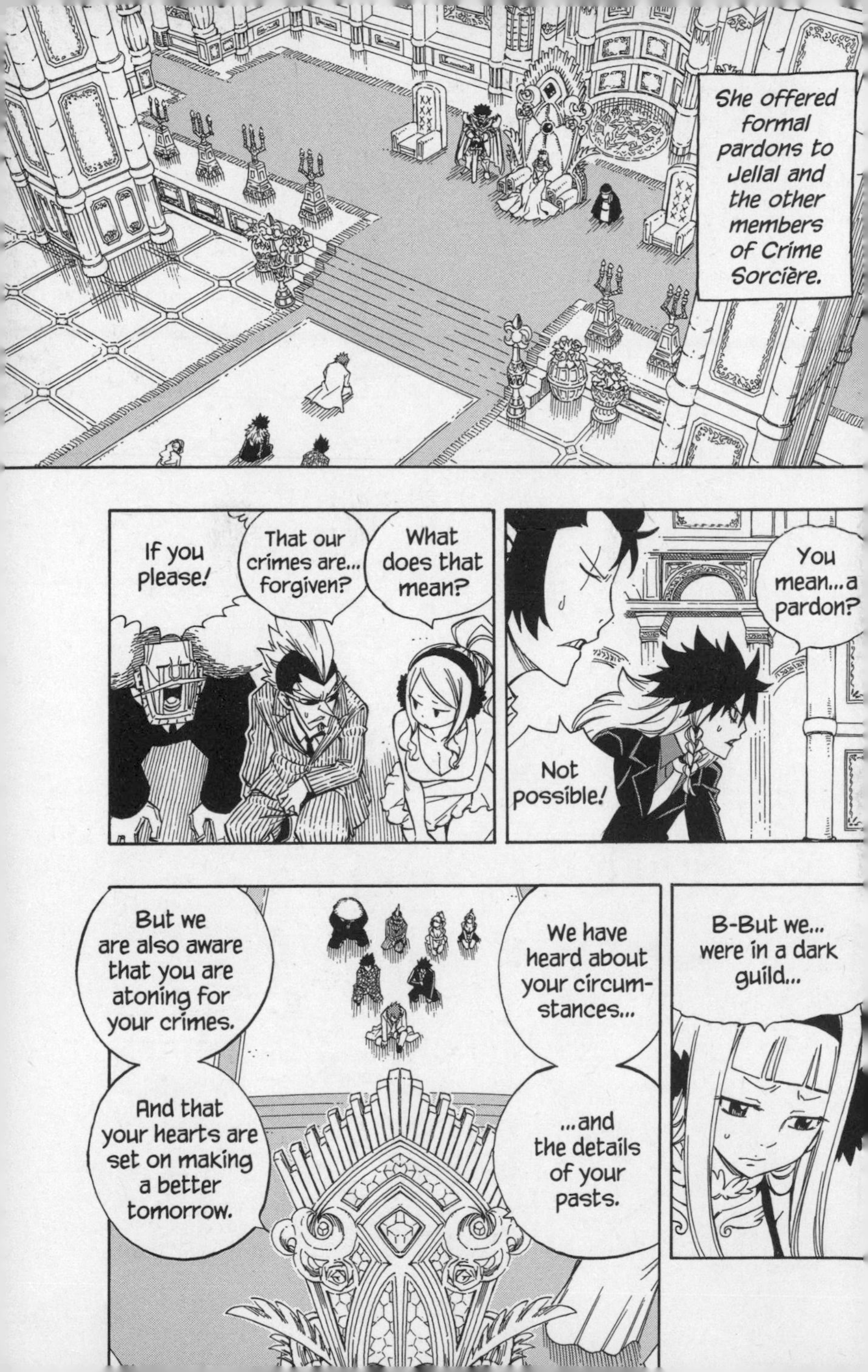
She offered formal pardons to Jellal and the other members of Crime Sorcière.
You mean...a pardon?
Not possible!
What does that mean?
That our crimes are... forgiven?
If you please!
B-But we... were in a dark guild...
We have heard about your circum-stances...
...and the details of your pasts.
But we are also aware that you are atoning for your crimes.
And that your hearts are set on making a better tomorrow.

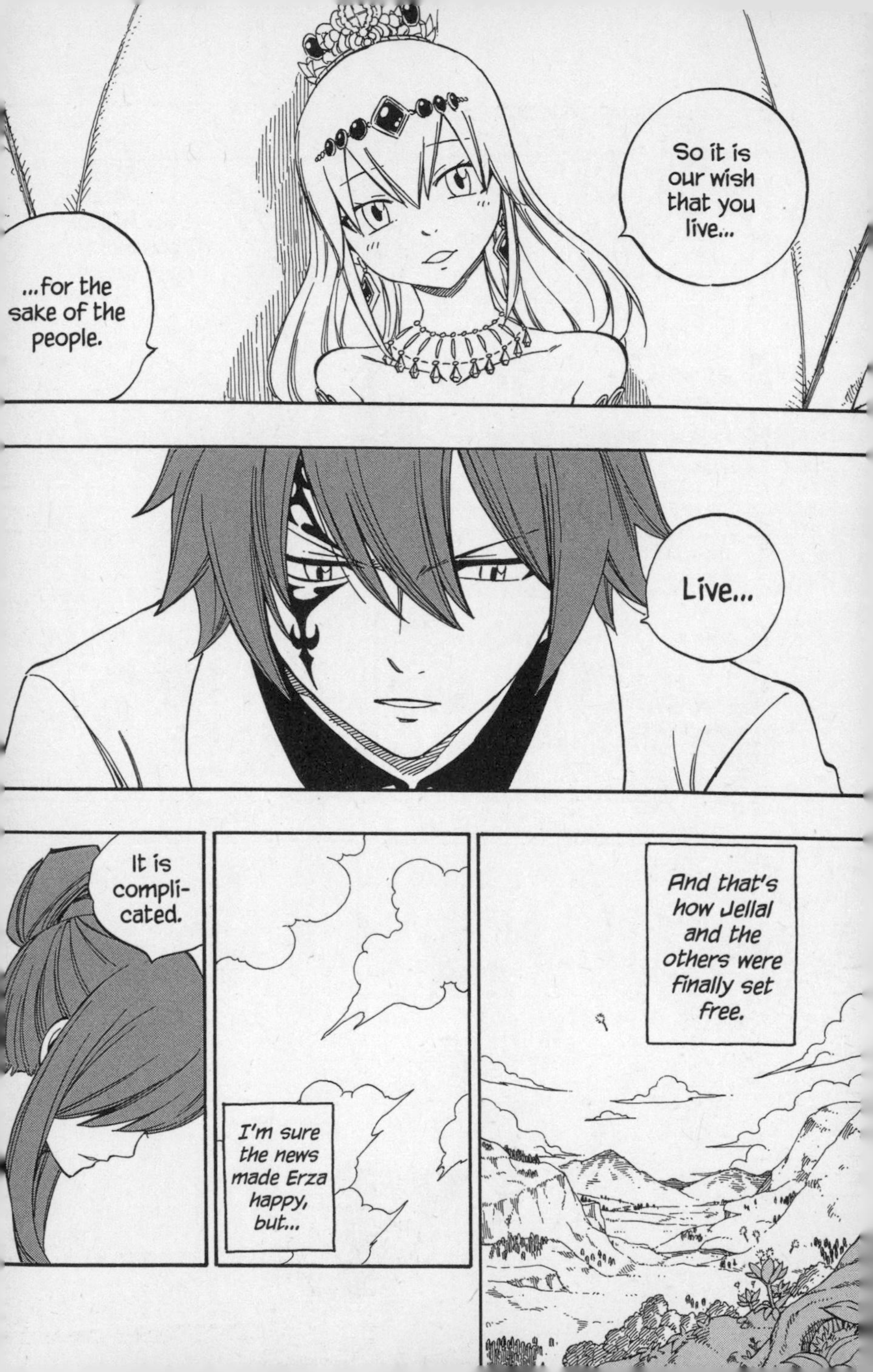
So it is our wish that you live...
...for the sake of the people.
Live...
And that's how Jellal and the others were finally set free.
I'm sure the news made Erza happy, but...
It is compli-cated.

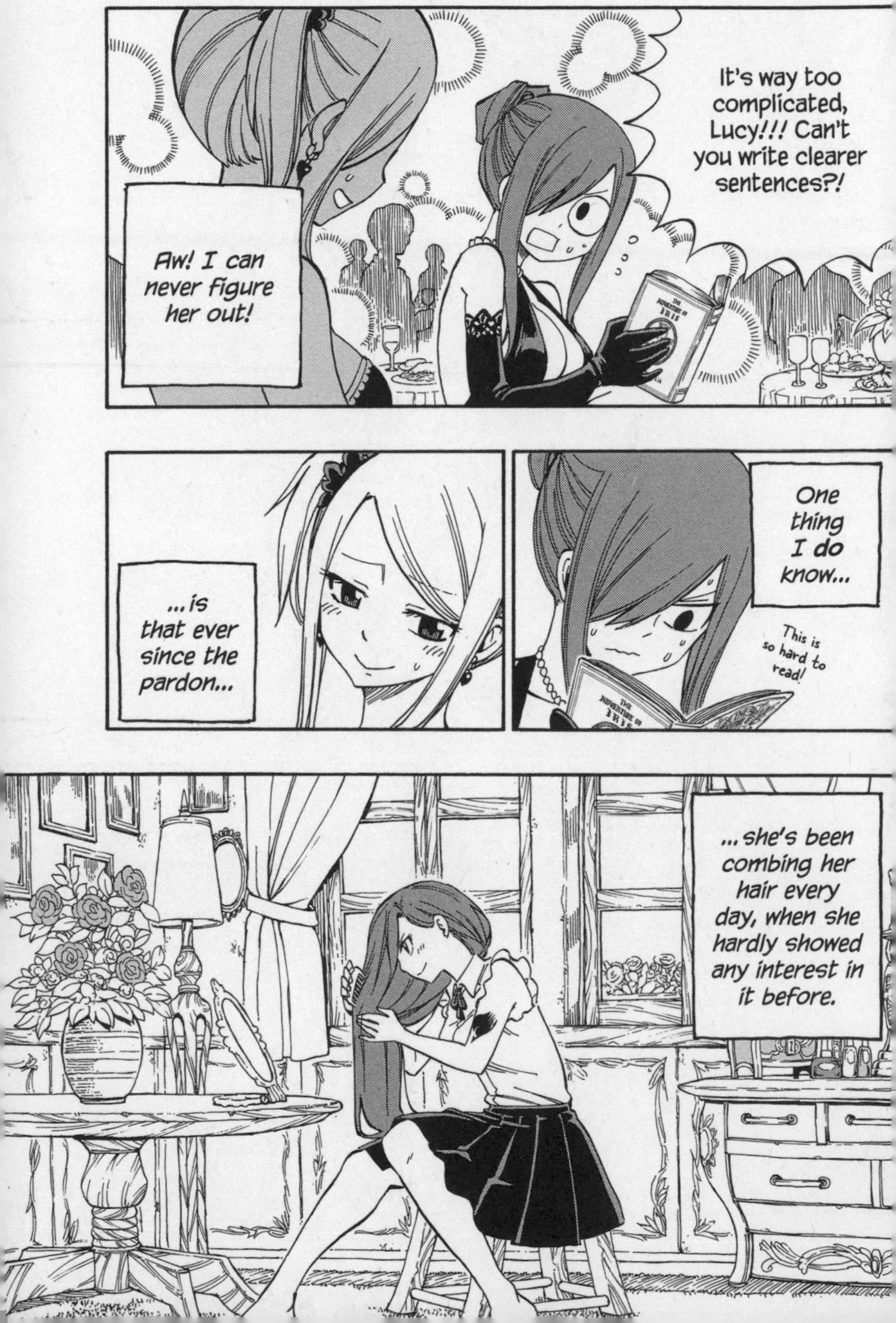
It's way too complicated, Lucy!!! Can't you write clearer sentences?!
Aw! I can never figure her out!
One thing I do know...
This is so hard to read!
...is that ever since the pardon...
...she's been combing her hair every day, when she hardly showed any interest in it before.

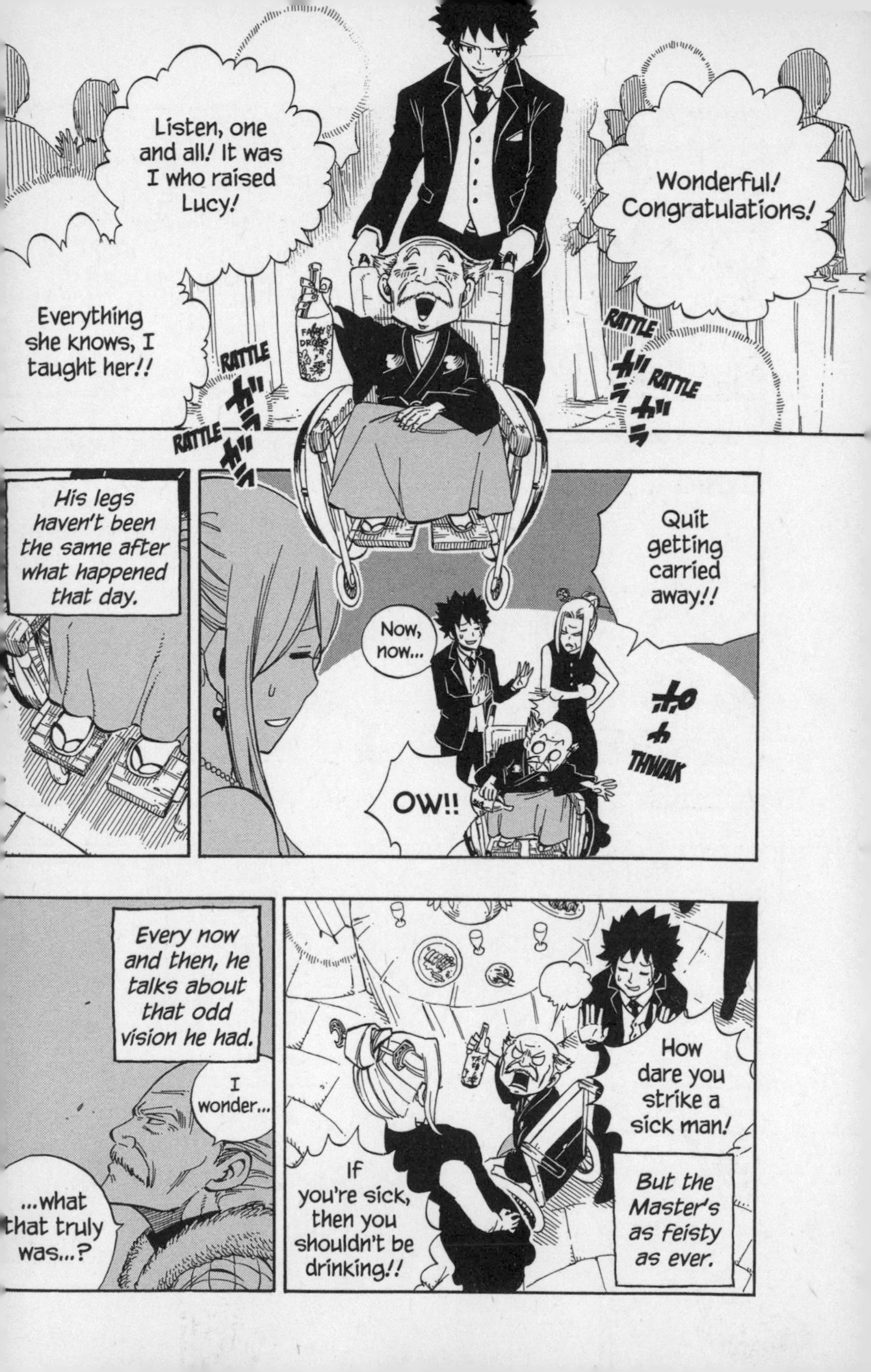
Wonderful! Congratulations!
RATTLE
RATTLE
Listen, one and all! It was I who raised Lucy!
Everything she knows, I taught her!!
RATTLE
RATTLE
Quit getting carried away!!
Now, now...
THWAK
OW!!
His legs haven't been the same after what happened that day.
How dare you strike a sick man!
But the Master's as feisty as ever.
If you're sick, then you shouldn't be drinking!!
Every now and then, he talks about that odd vision he had.
I wonder...
...what that truly was...?

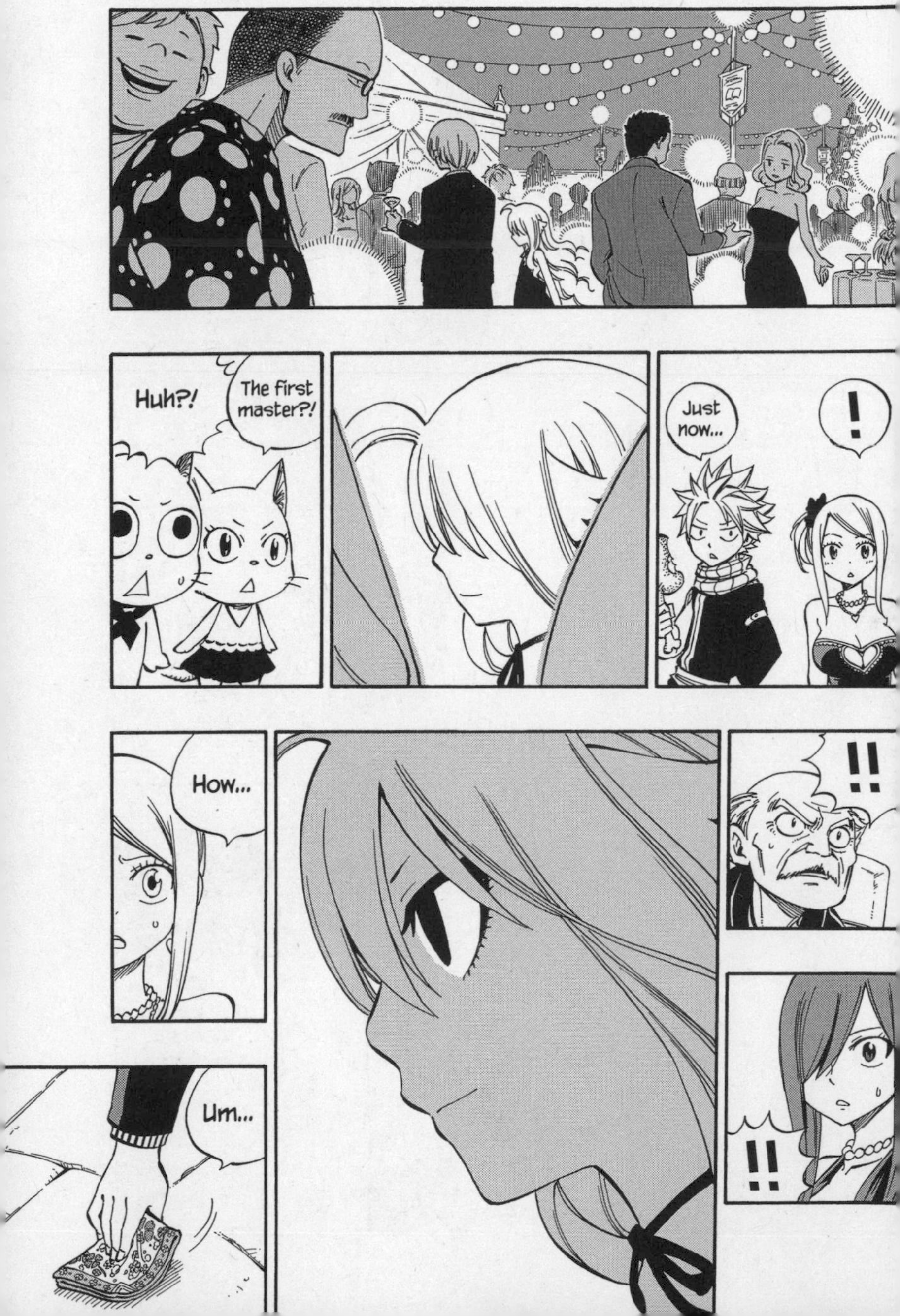
!
Just now...
The first master?!
Huh?!
!!
!!
How...
Um...

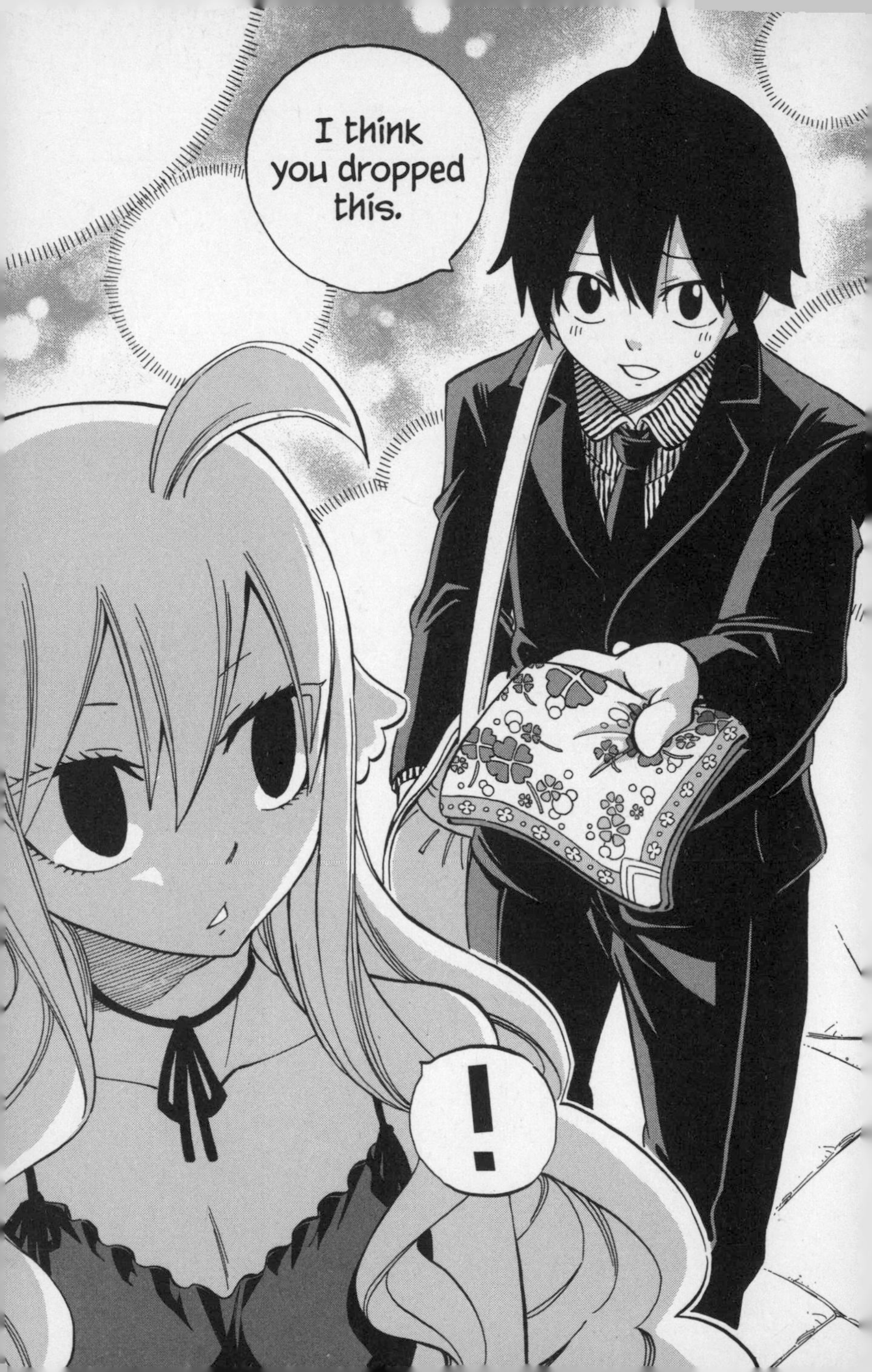
I think you dropped this.
!

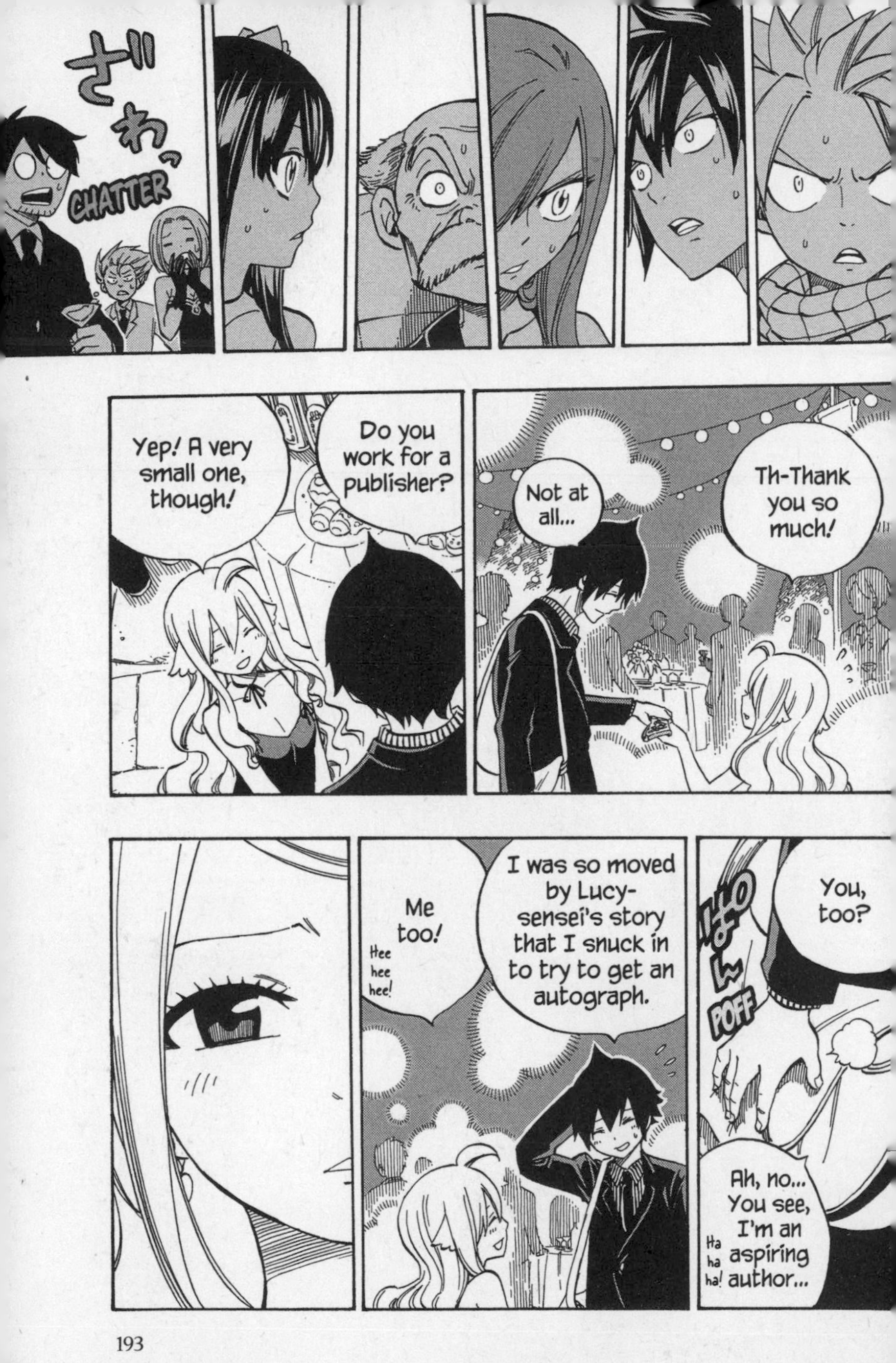
ざわっ
CHATTER
Th-Thank you so much!
Not at all...
Do you work for a publisher?
Yep! A very small one, though!
You, too?
POFF
Ah, no... You see, I'm an aspiring author...
Ha ha ha!
I was so moved by Lucy-sensei's story that I snuck in to try to get an autograph.
Me too!
Hee hee hee!

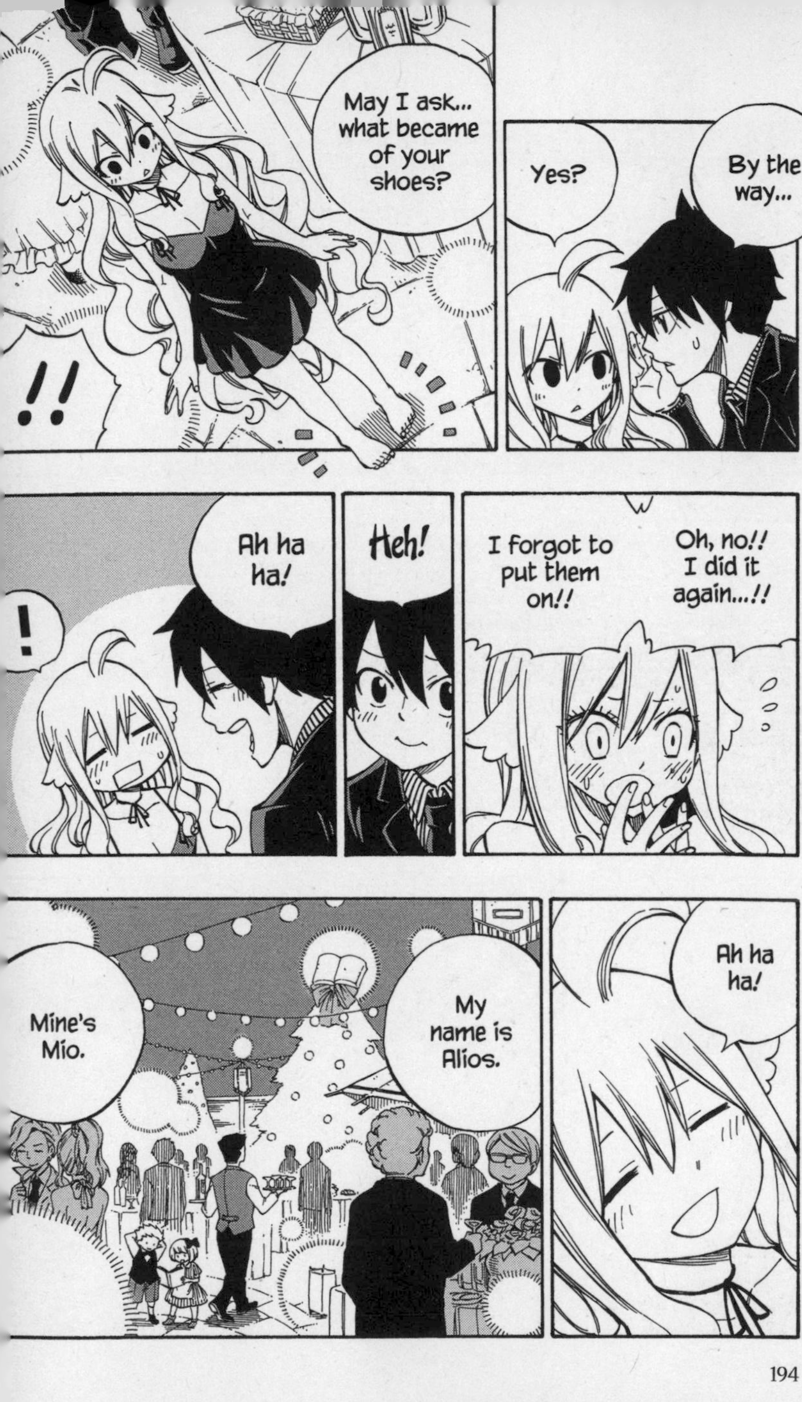
By the way...
Yes?
May I ask... what became of your shoes?
!!
Oh, no!! I did it again...!!
I forgot to put them on!!
Heh!
Ah ha ha!
!
Ah ha ha!
My name is Alios.
Mine's Mio.

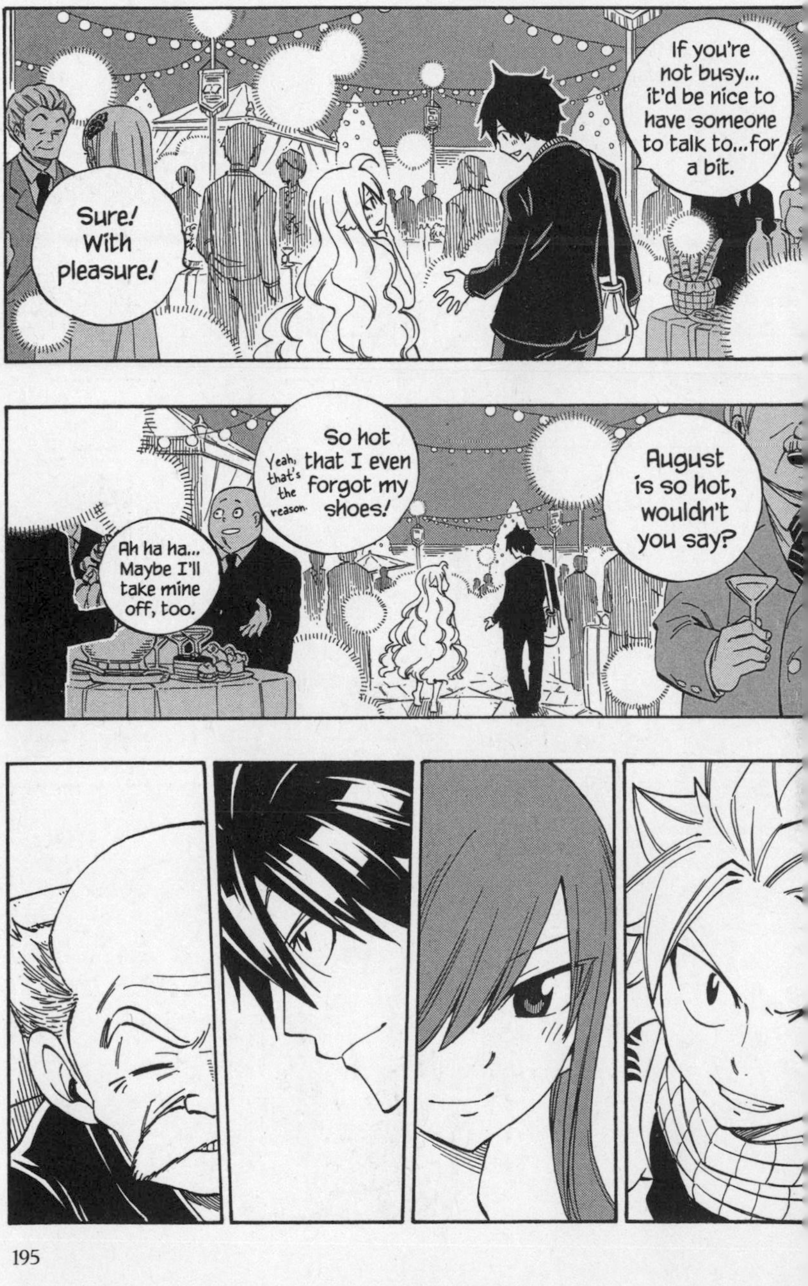
If you're not busy... it'd be nice to have someone to talk to...for a bit.
Sure! With pleasure!
August is so hot, wouldn't you say?
So hot that I even forgot my shoes!
Yeah, that's the reason.
Ah ha ha... Maybe I'll take mine off, too.

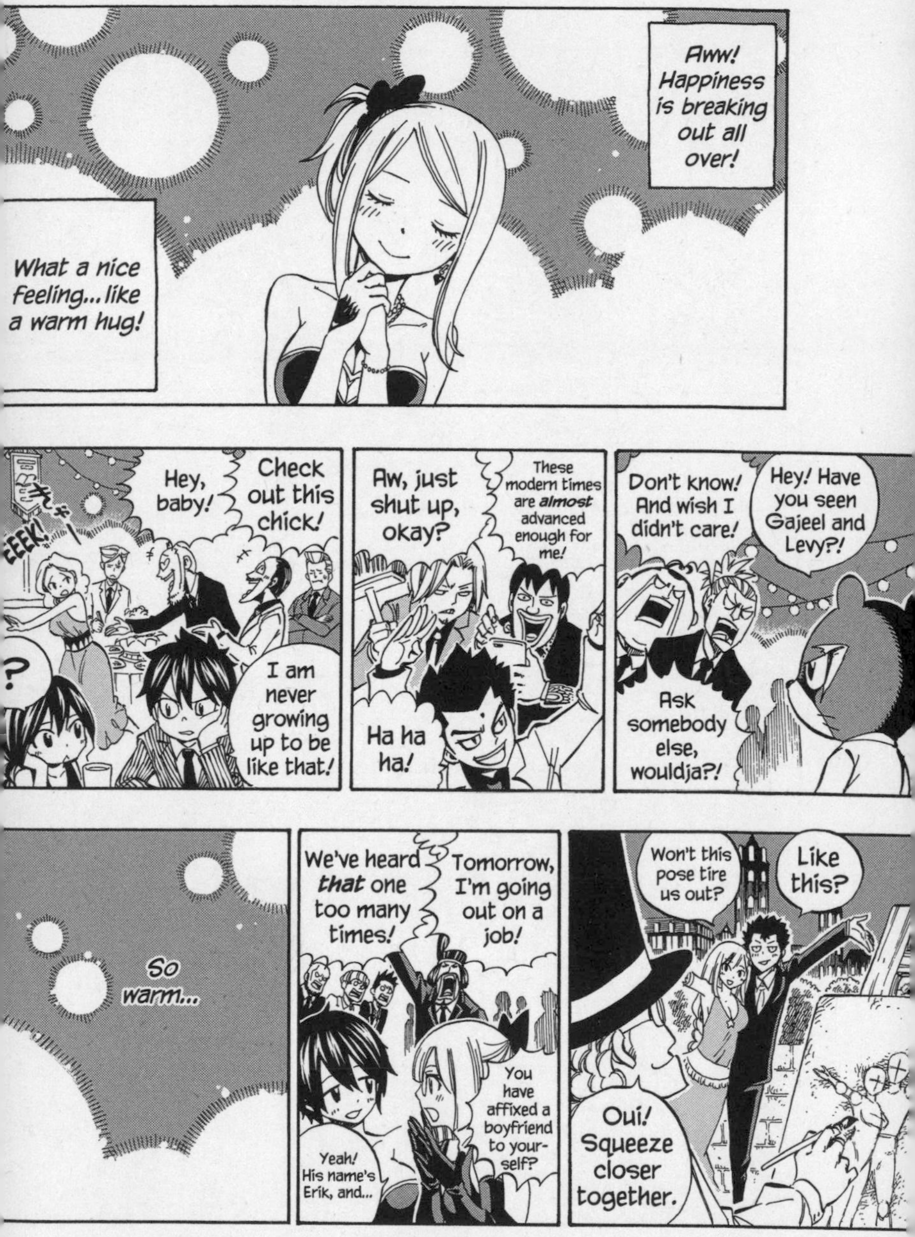
Aww! Happiness is breaking out all over!
What a nice feeling... like a warm hug!
Hey! Have you seen Gajeel and Levy?!
Don't know! And wish I didn't care!
Ask somebody else, wouldja?!
These modern times are *almost* advanced enough for me!
Aw, just shut up, okay?
Ha ha ha!
Check out this chick!
Hey, baby!
EEEK!
?
I am never growing up to be like that!
Like this?
Won't this pose tire us out?
Oui! Squeeze closer together.
Tomorrow, I'm going out on a job!
We've heard *that* one too many times!
You have affixed a boyfriend to your-self?
Yeah! His name's Erik, and...
So warm...

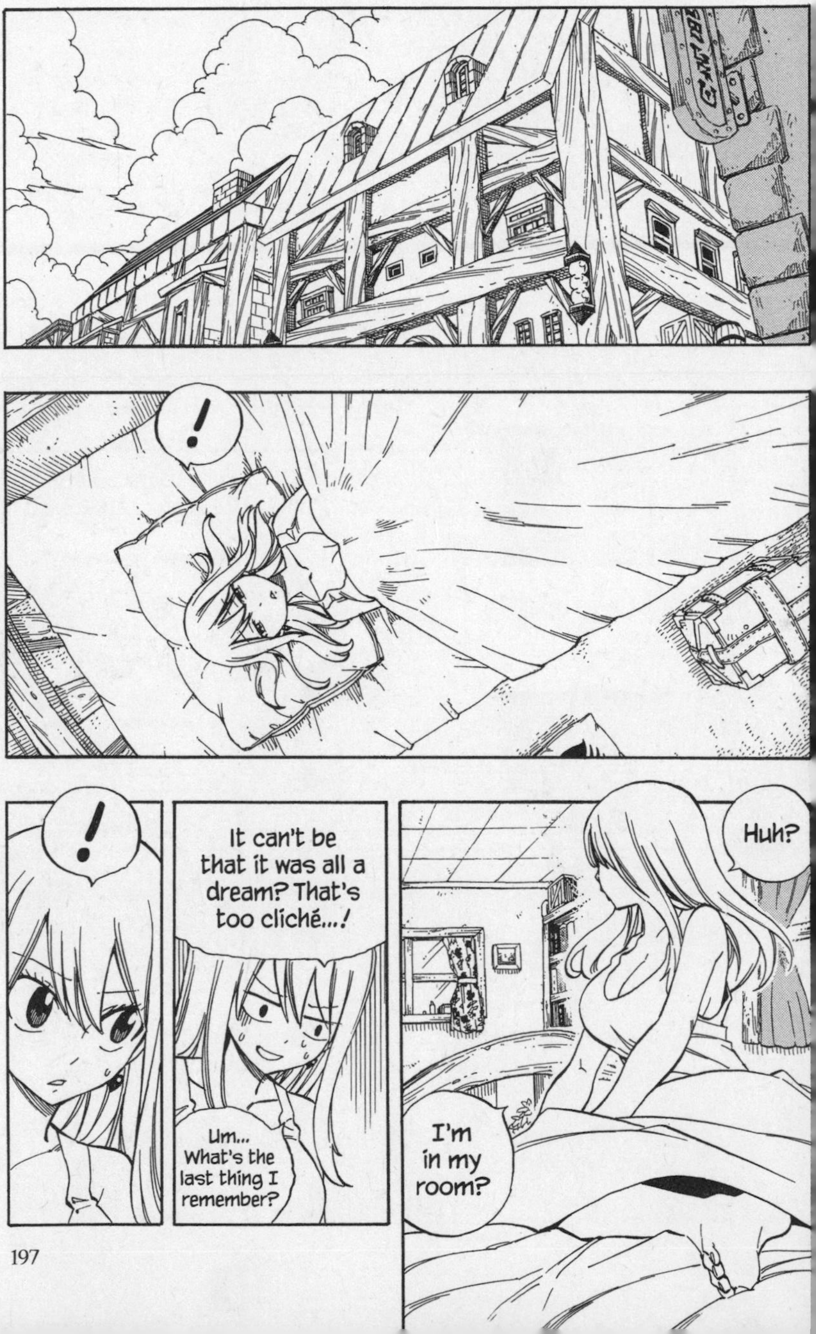
!
Huh?
I'm in my room?
It can't be that it was all a dream? That's too cliché...!
Um... What's the last thing I remember?
!

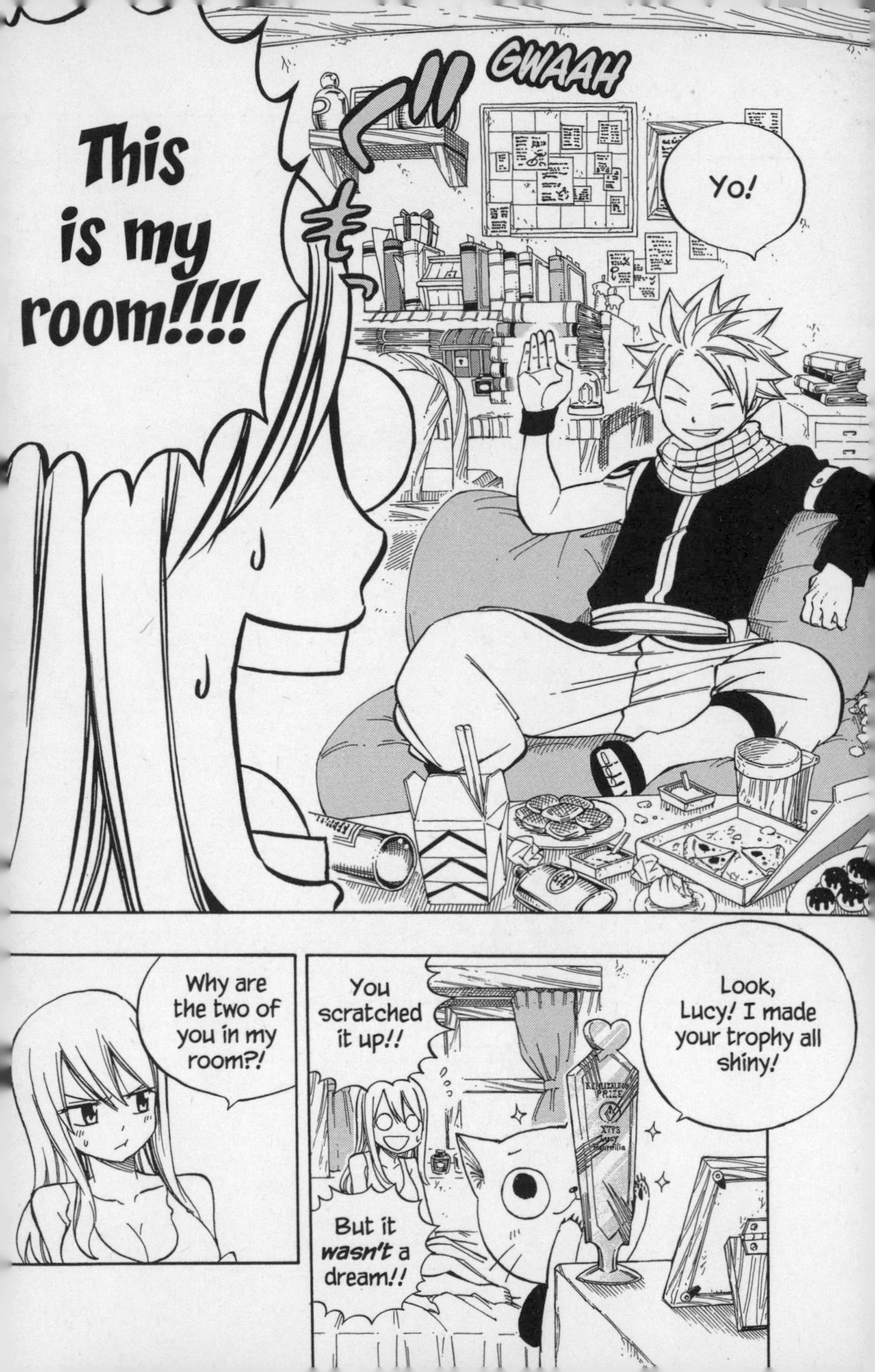

Yo!
GWAAH
This is my room!!!!
Look, Lucy! I made your trophy all shiny!
You scratched it up!!
But it *wasn't* a dream!!
Why are the two of you in my room?!

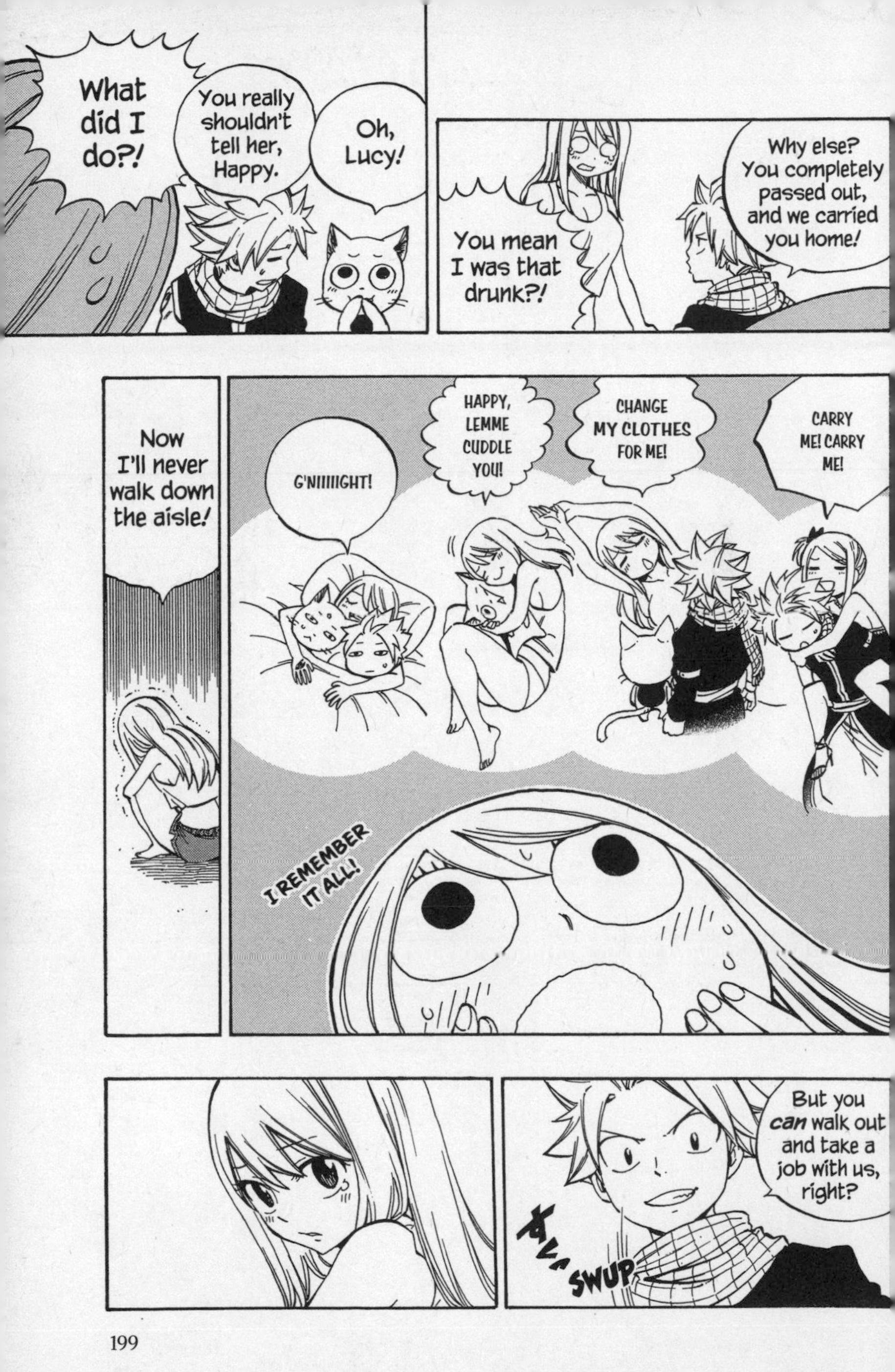
Why else? You completely passed out, and we carried you home!
You mean I was that drunk?!
Oh, Lucy!
You really shouldn't tell her, Happy.
What did I do?!
CARRY ME! CARRY ME!
CHANGE MY CLOTHES FOR ME!
HAPPY, LEMME CUDDLE YOU!
G'NIIIIIGHT!
I REMEMBER IT ALL!
Now I'll never walk down the aisle!
But you *can* walk out and take a job with us, right?
SWUP

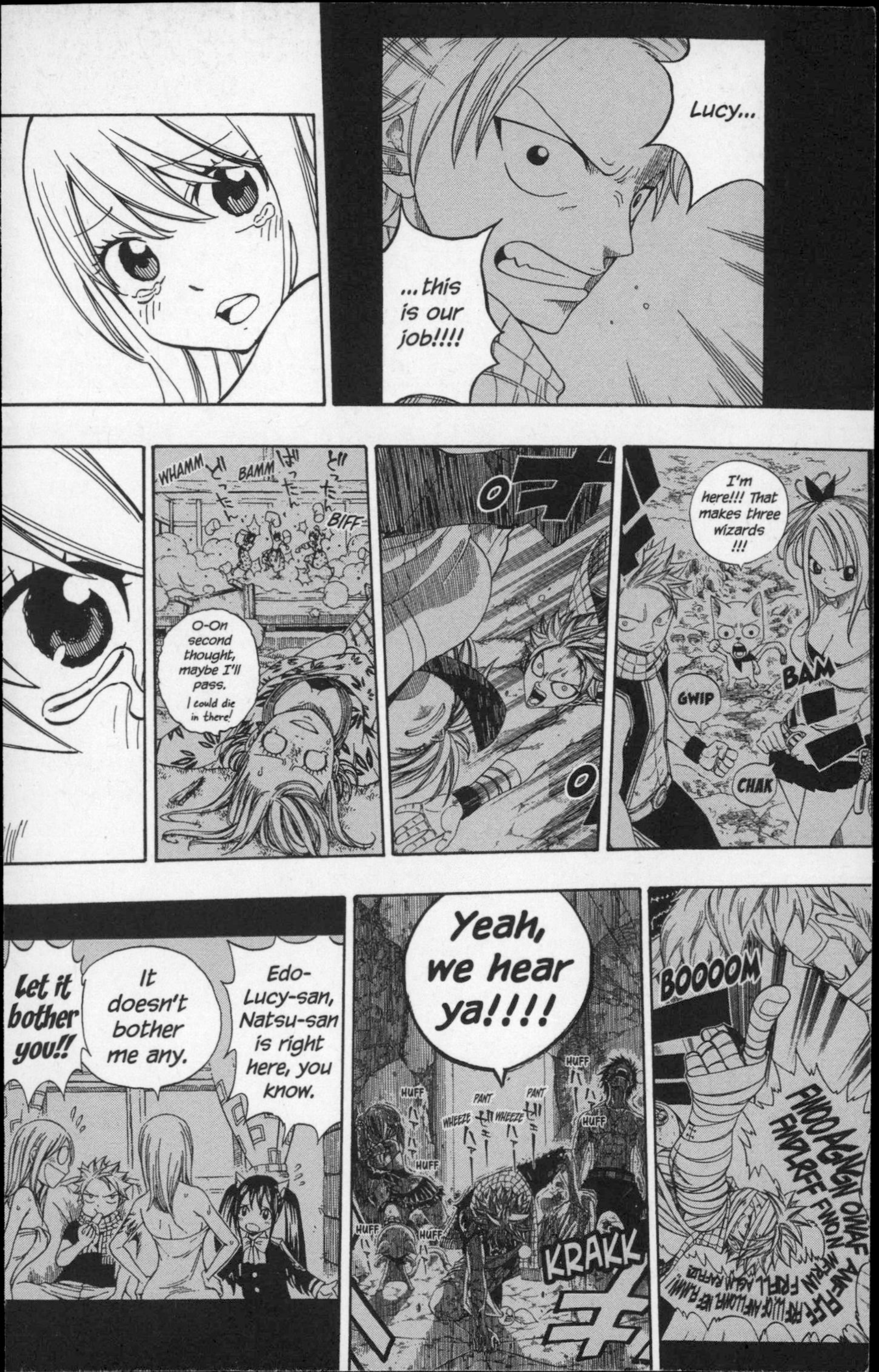
Lucy...
...this is our job!!!!
I'm here!!! That makes three wizards !!!
BAM
GWIP
CHAK
WHAMM
BAMM
BIFF
O-On second thought, maybe I'll pass.
I could die in there!
BOOOOM
Yeah, we hear ya!!!!
HUFF
PANT
WHEEZE
KRAKK
Edo-Lucy-san, Natsu-san is right here, you know.
It doesn't bother me any.
Let it bother you!!

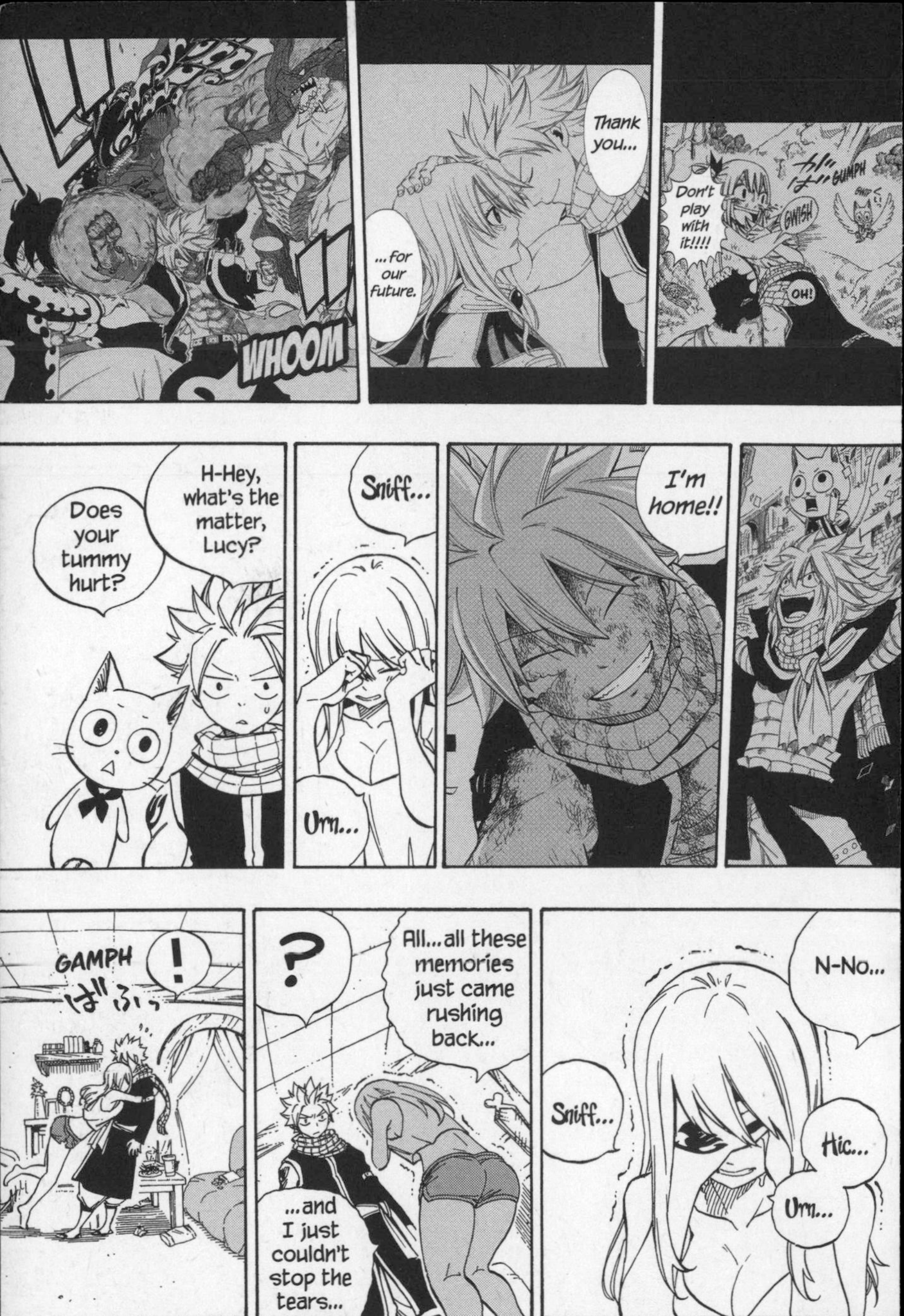
Don't play with it!!!!
GUMPH
GWISH
OH!
Thank you...
...for our future.
WHOOM
I'm home!!
Sniff...
Urn...
H-Hey, what's the matter, Lucy?
Does your tummy hurt?
N-No...
Sniff...
Hic...
Urn...
All...all these memories just came rushing back...
?
...and I just couldn't stop the tears...
!
GAMPH
ばふっ

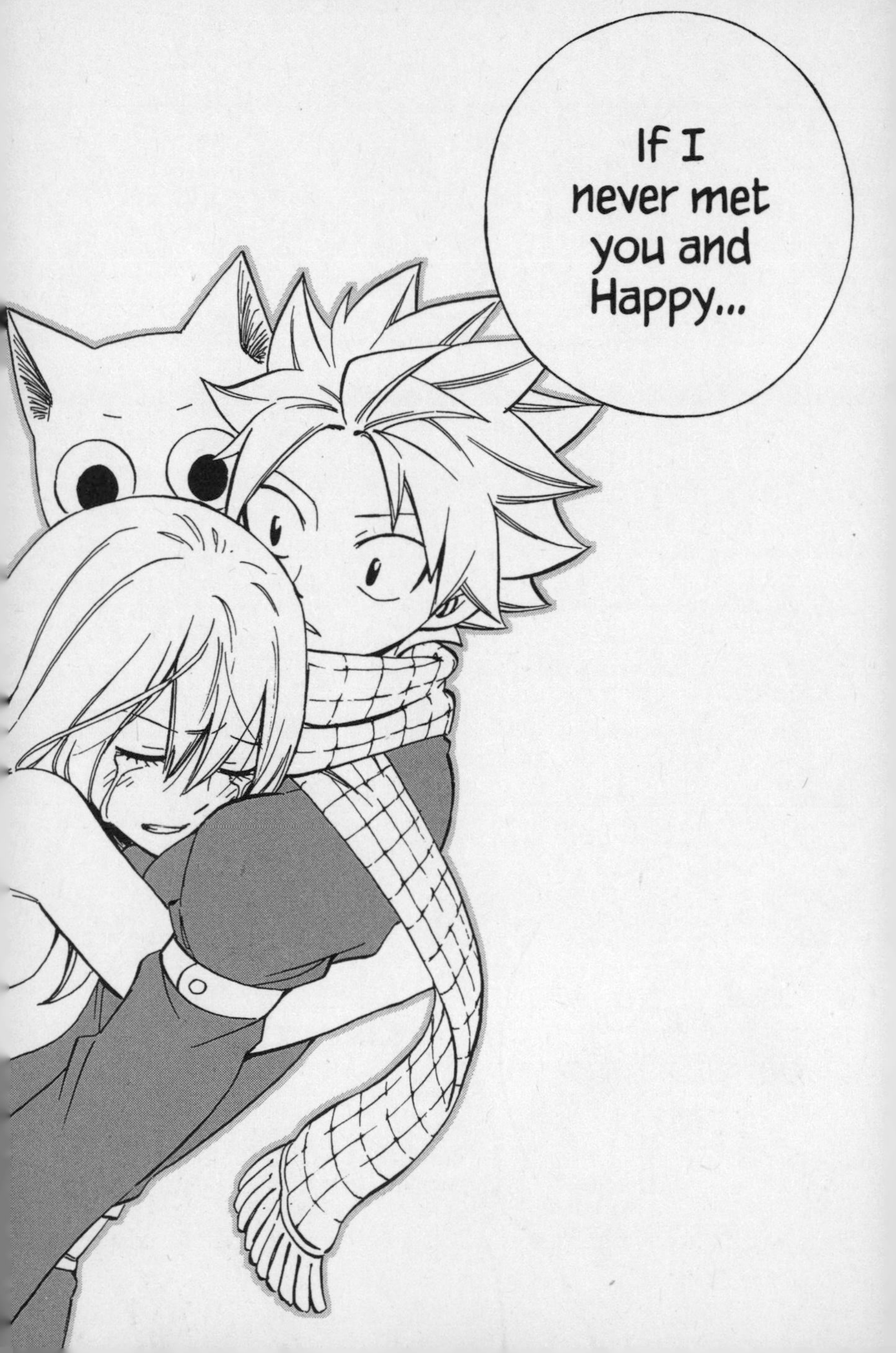
If I never met you and Happy...

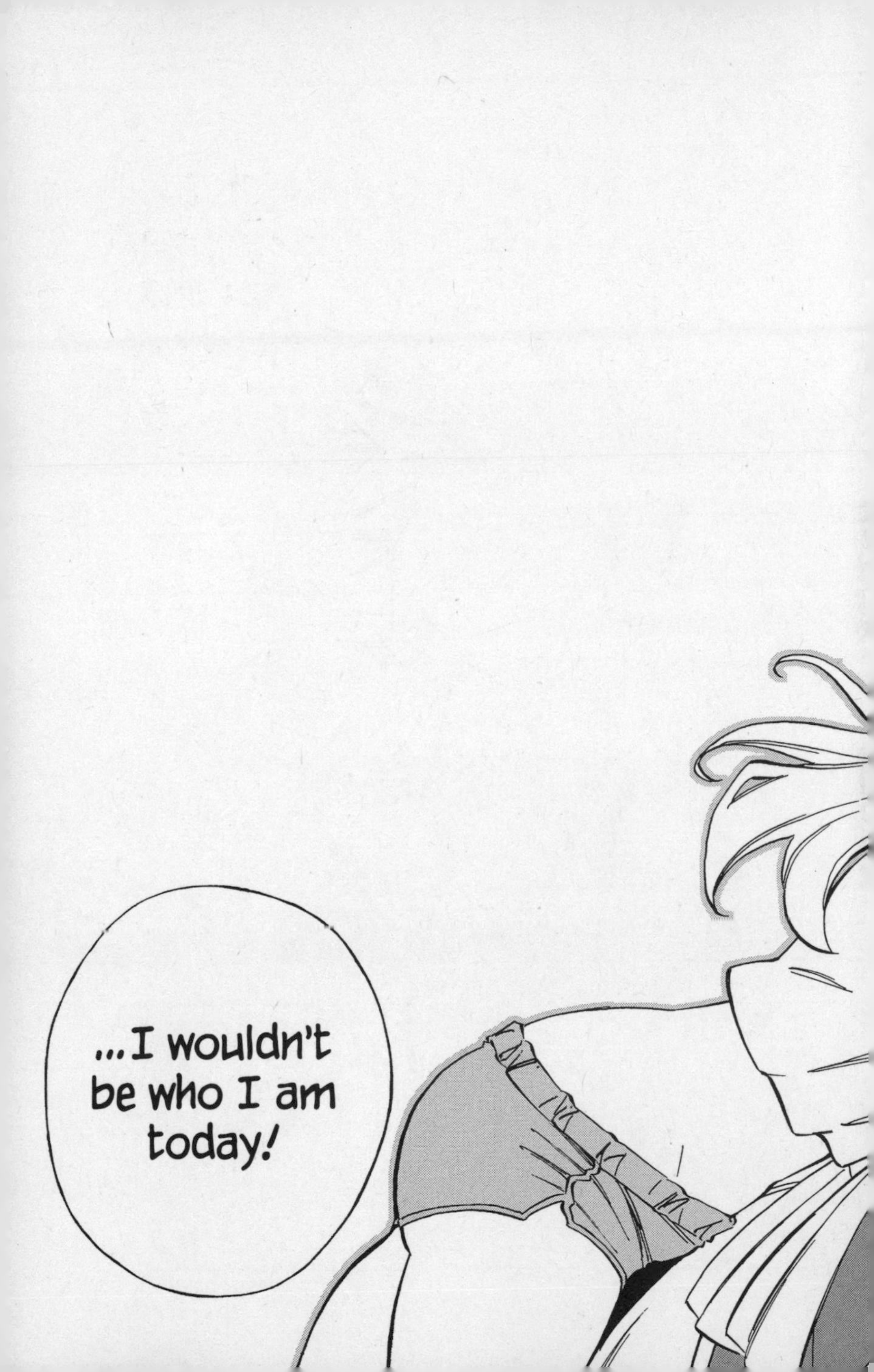
...I wouldn't be who I am today!

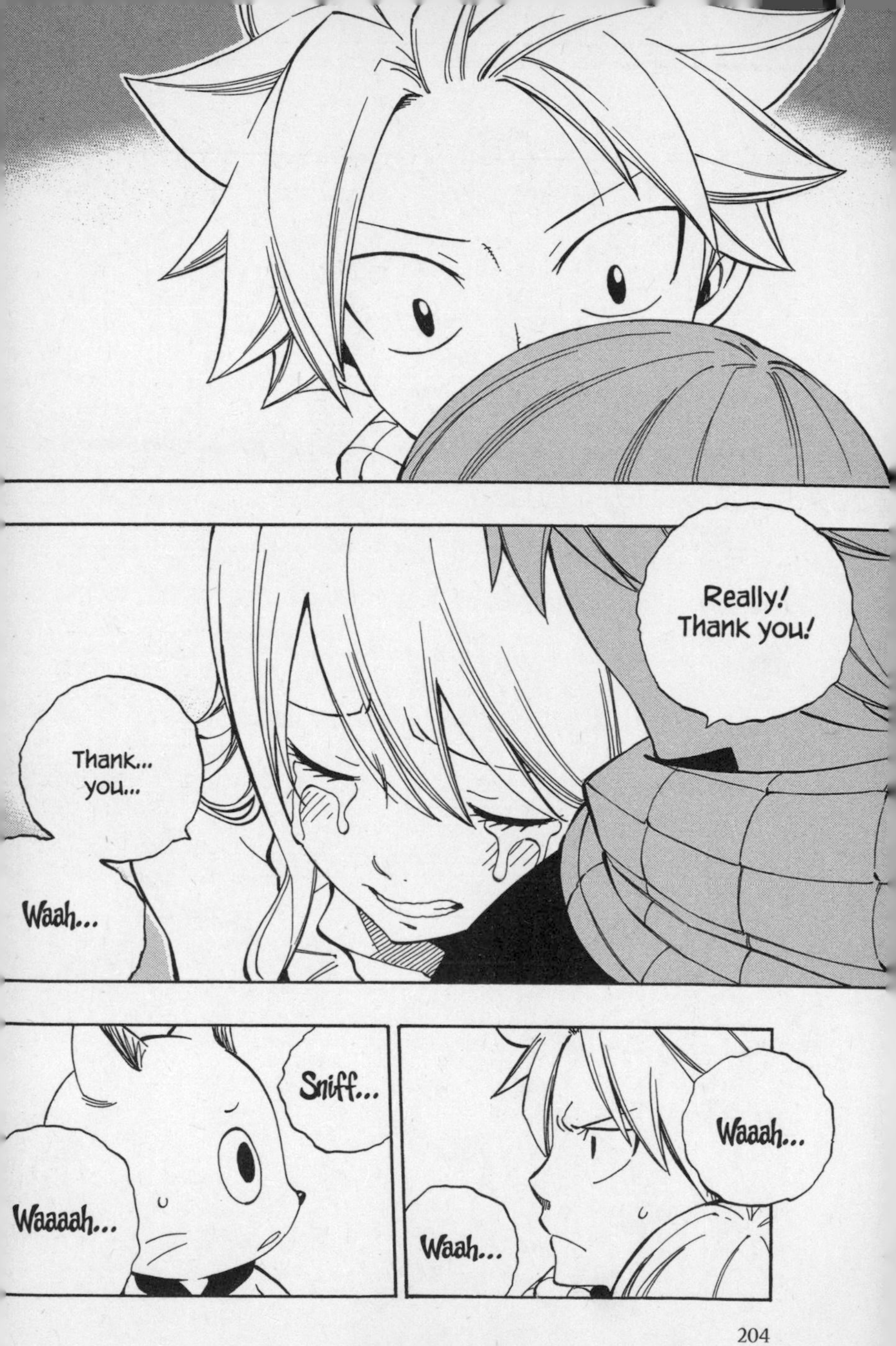
Really! Thank you!
Thank... you...
Waah...
Waaah...
Waah...
Sniff...
Waaaah...

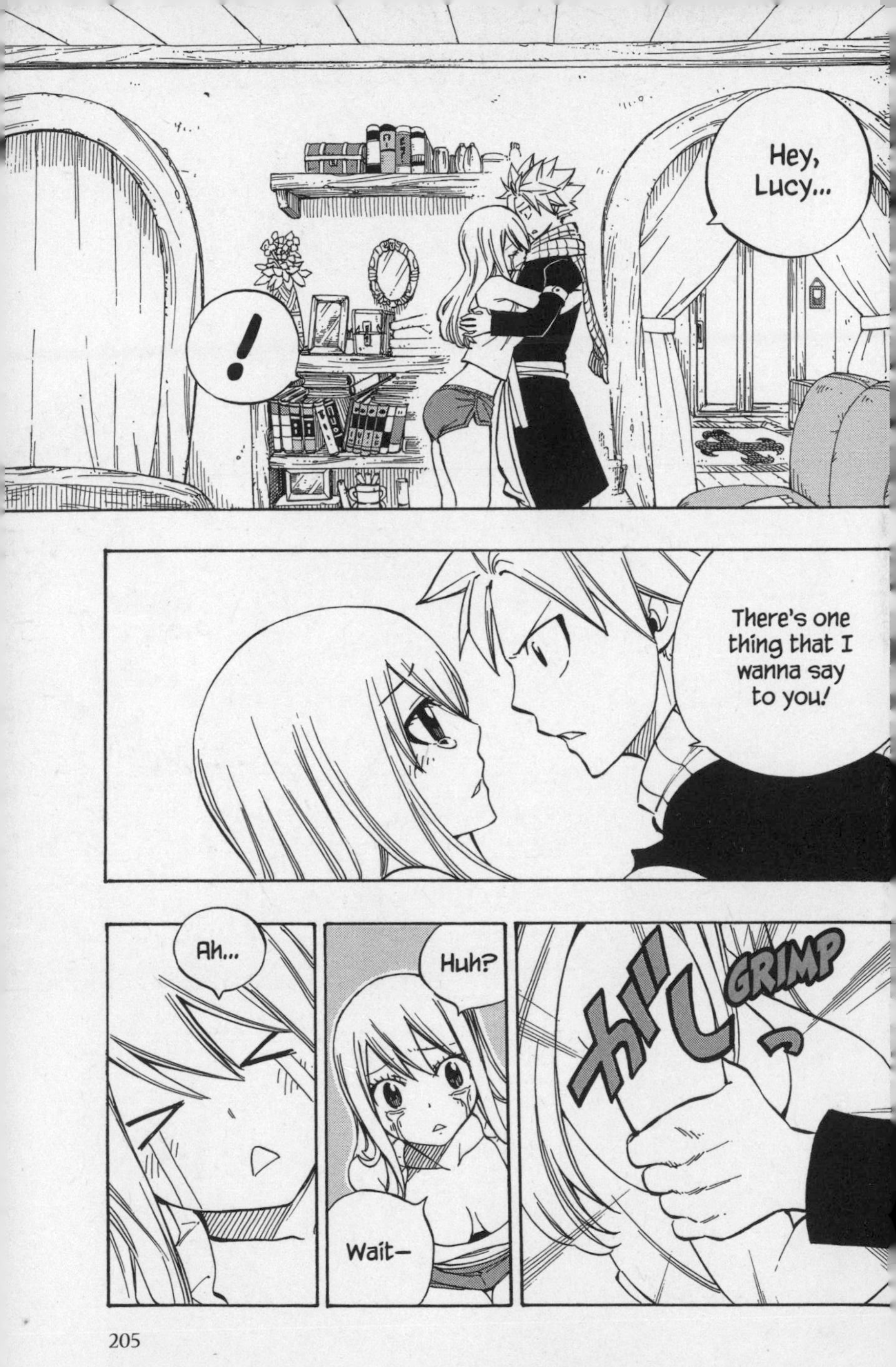
Hey, Lucy...
!
There's one thing that I wanna say to you!
がしっ
GRIMP
Huh?
Wait–
Ah...

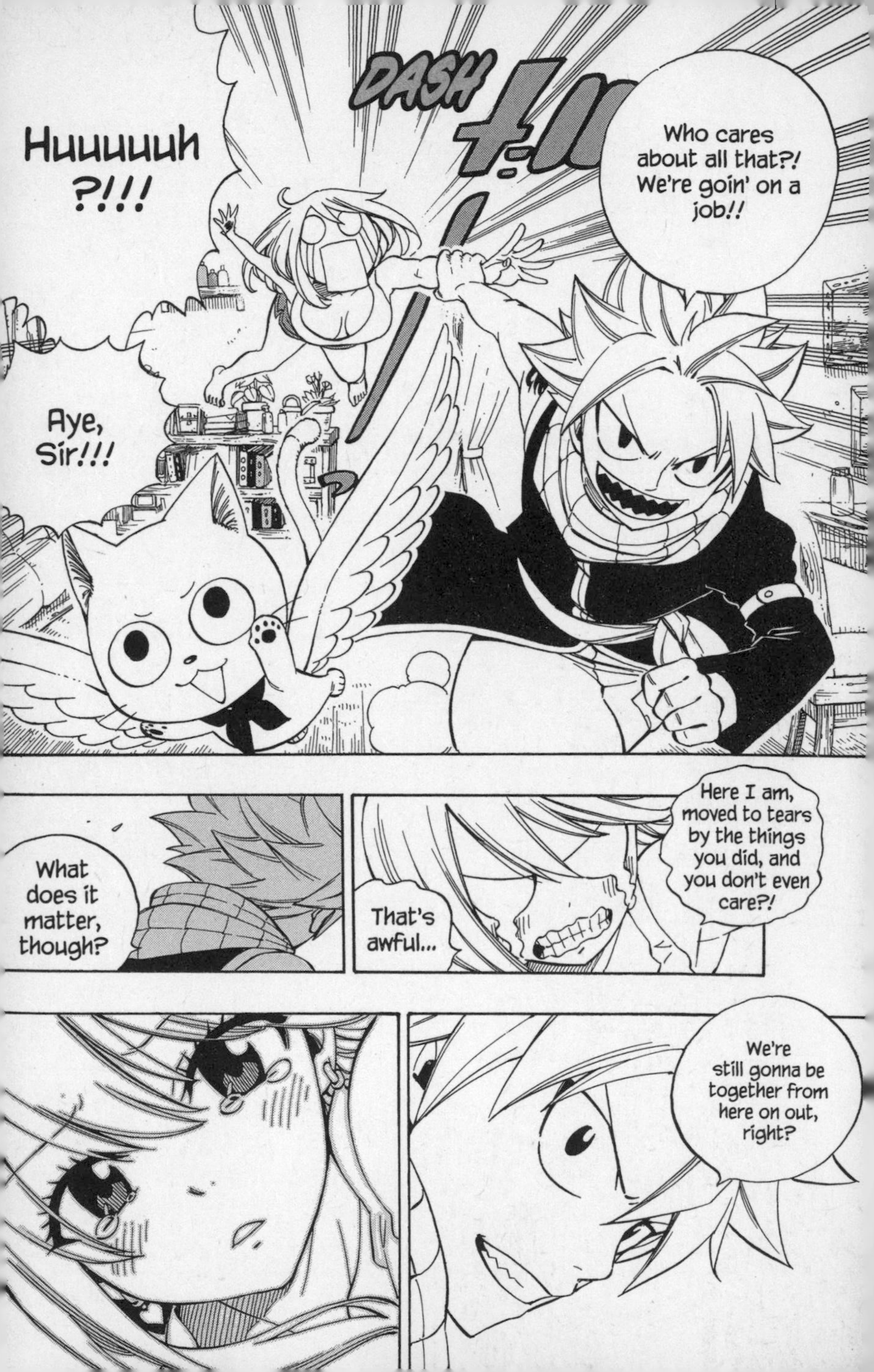
Who cares about all that?! We're goin' on a job!!
DASH
Huuuuuh ?!!!
Aye, Sir!!!
Here I am, moved to tears by the things you did, and you don't even care?!
That's awful...
What does it matter, though?
We're still gonna be together from here on out, right?

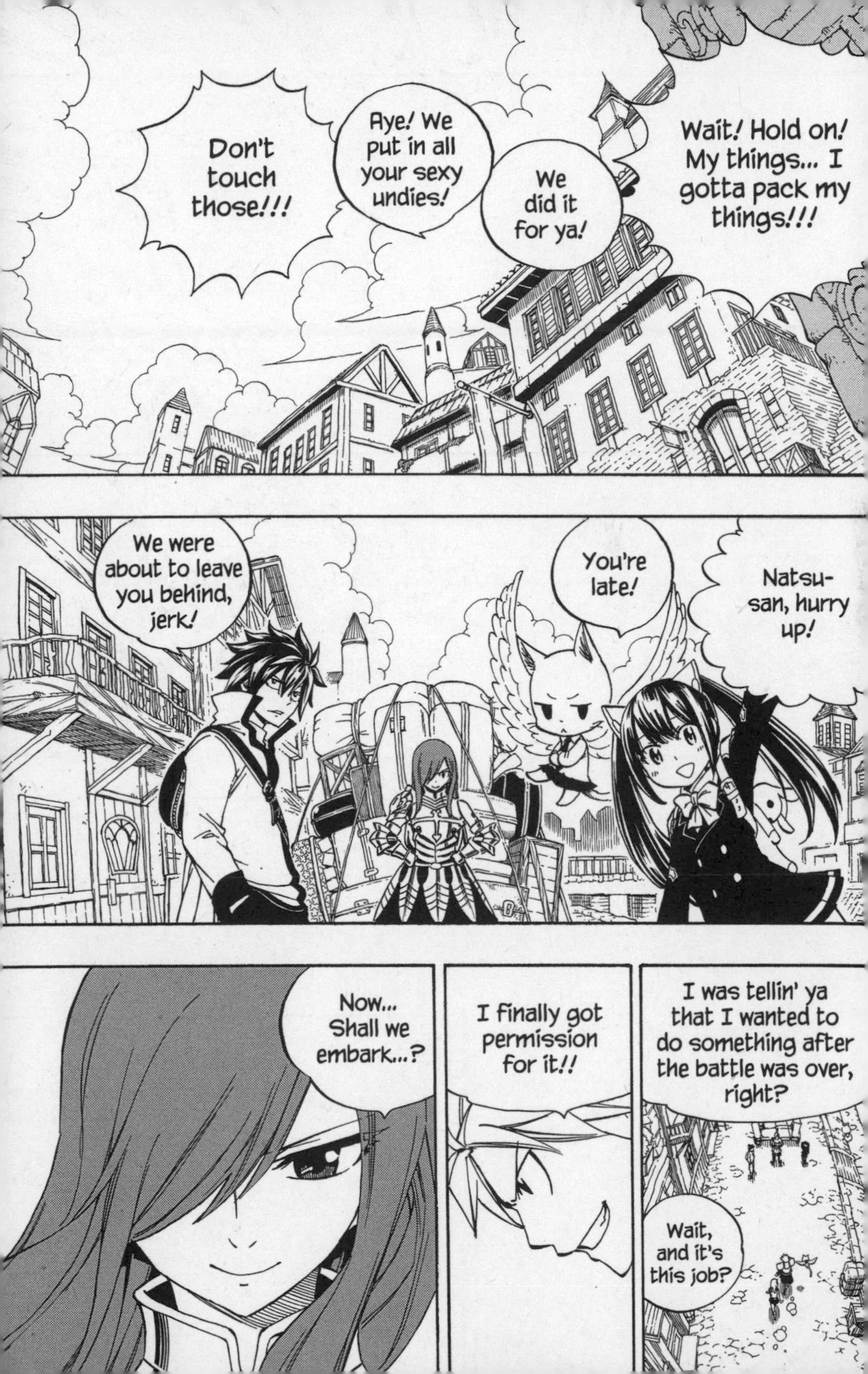
Wait! Hold on! My things... I gotta pack my things!!!
We did it for ya!
Aye! We put in all your sexy undies!
Don't touch those!!!
Natsu-san, hurry up!
You're late!
We were about to leave you behind, jerk!
I was tellin' ya that I wanted to do something after the battle was over, right?
Wait, and it's this job?
I finally got permission for it!!
Now... Shall we embark...?

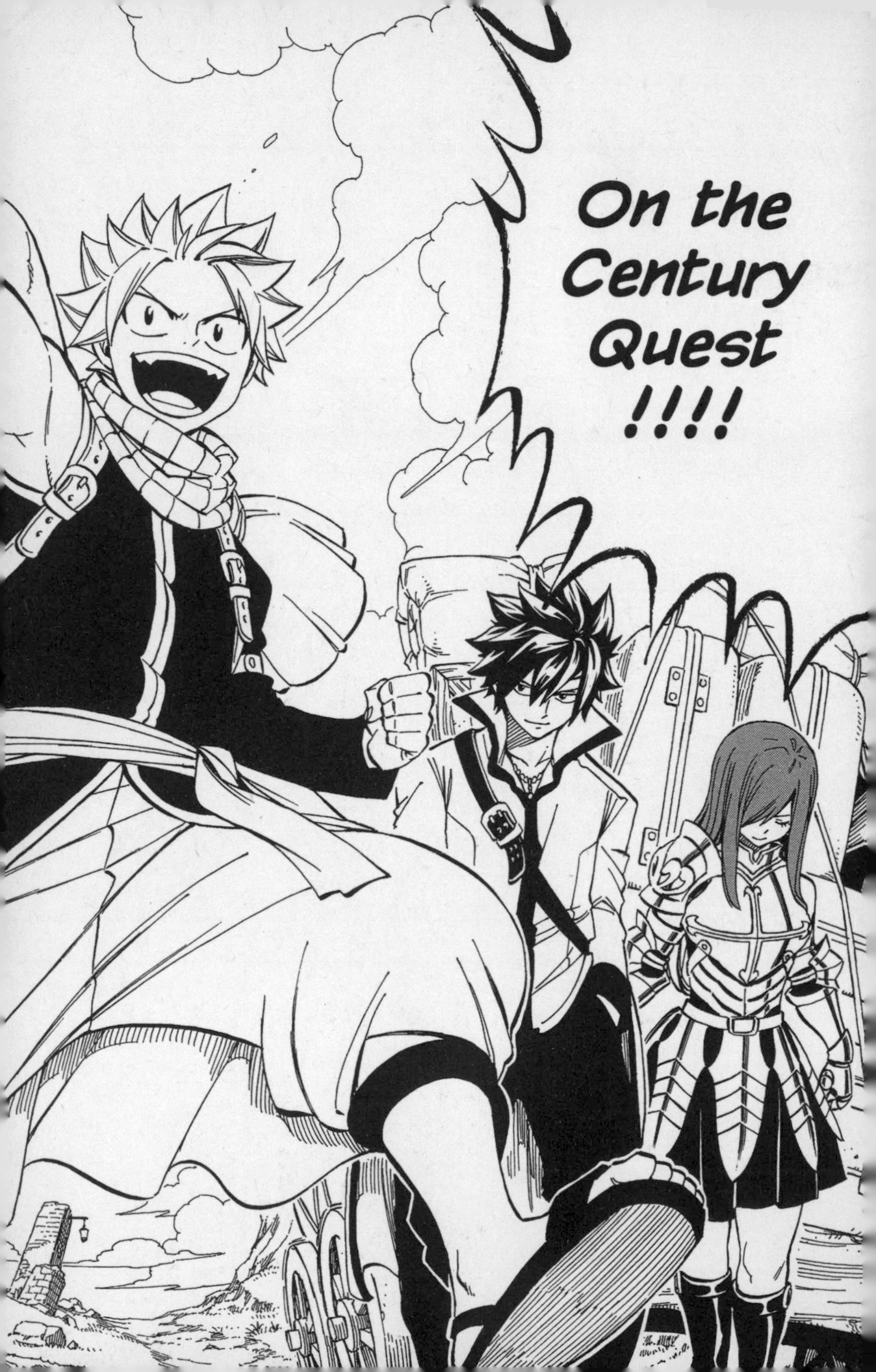
On the Century Quest !!!!

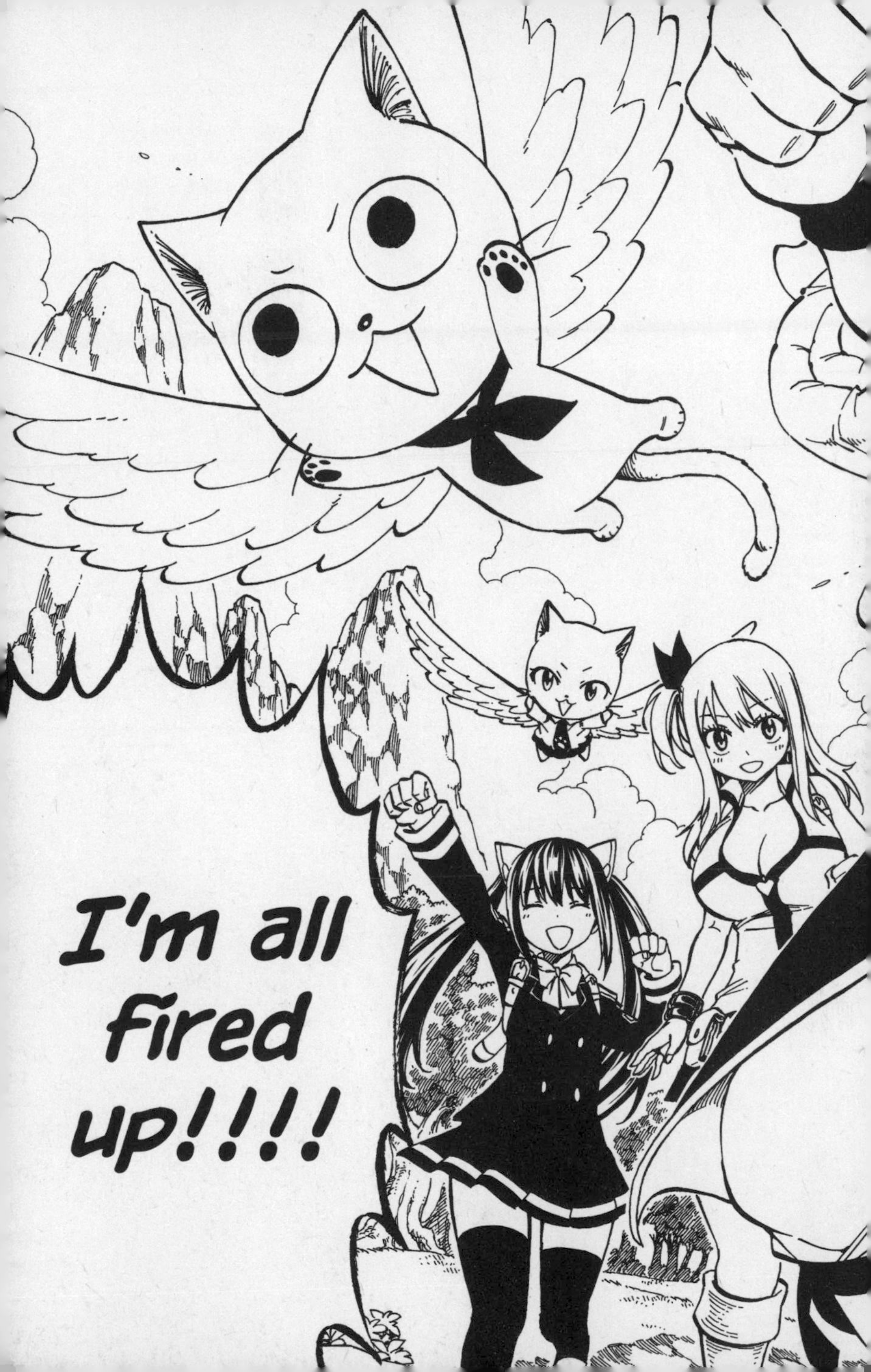
I'm all fired up!!!!

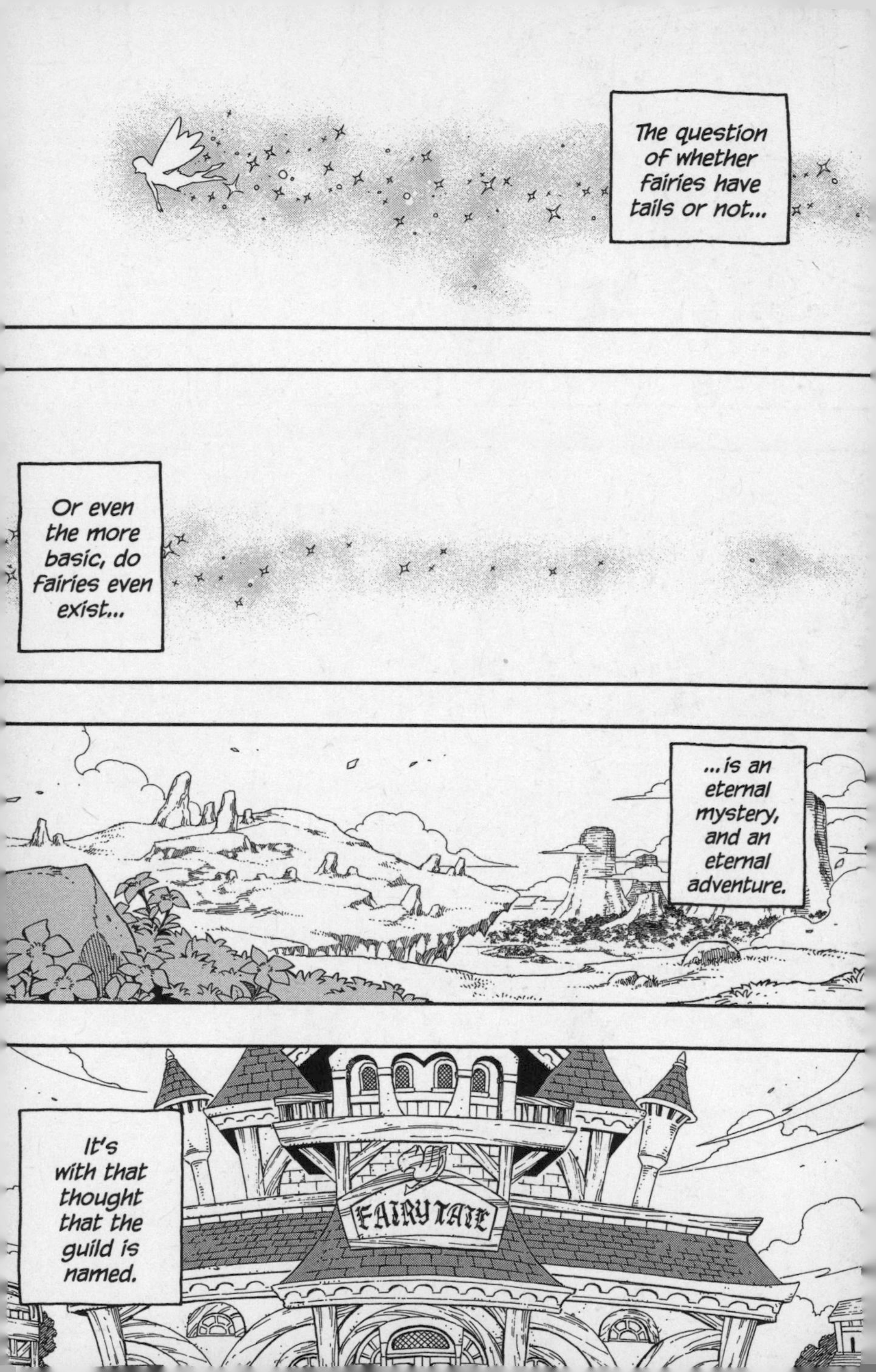
The question of whether fairies have tails or not...
Or even the more basic, do fairies even exist...
...is an eternal mystery, and an eternal adventure.
It's with that thought that the guild is named.
FAIRY TAIL

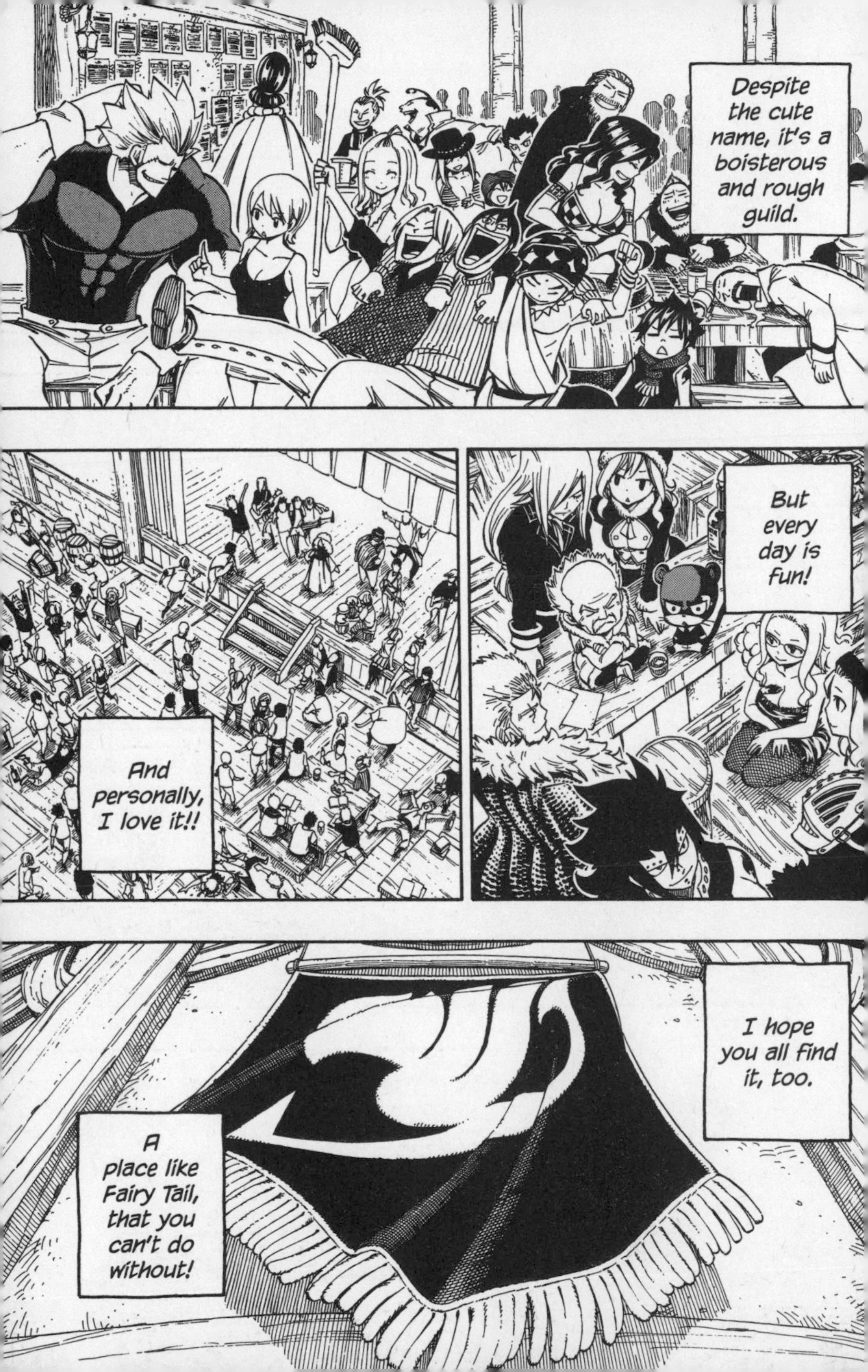
Despite the cute name, it's a boisterous and rough guild.
But every day is fun!
And personally, I love it!!
I hope you all find it, too.
A place like Fairy Tail, that you can't do without!

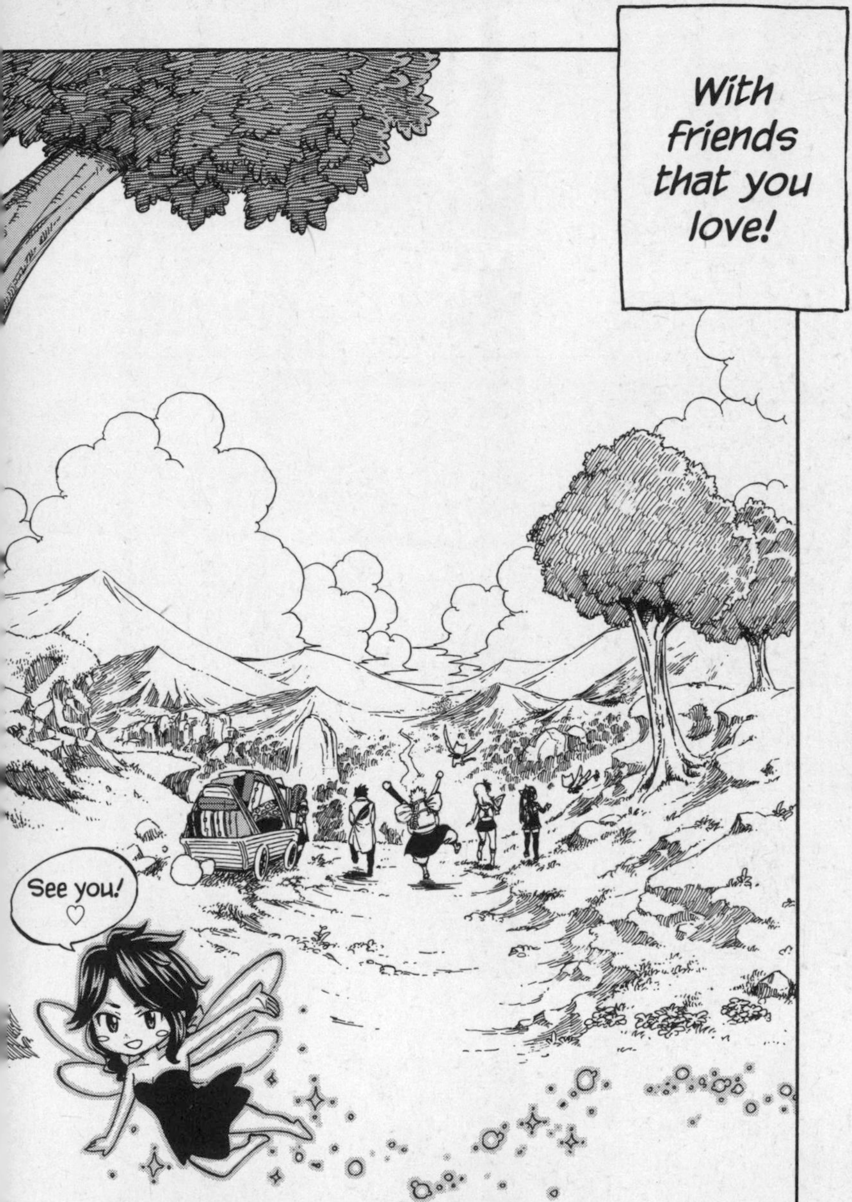
With friends that you love!
See you! ♡

THE•END

Thank you to all the fans

FAIRY TAIL

フェアリーテイル

Hiro Mashima

— STAFF —

Bobby Ohsawa
Shin Mikuni
Yui Ueda
Harami
Kina Kobayashi
Chiko
Marimo Enda
Kenji Okada
Cain

— SPECIAL THANKS —

Koji Nakamura
Miki Yoshikawa
Kondo

AND MORE!!

— EDITOR —

Noriaki Matsuki
Hiroshi Takikawa
Tomohiro Uchida

Takeharu Yoshida
Shu Hashimoto
Takeshi Ozawa

Yuiko Toriumi (COMICS)
Hideki Morooka (COMICS)
Eriko Nozawa (COMICS)

I wanted to infuse the final chapter of this series with many meanings, but in the end, it sort of came out to be a very *Fairy Tail*-ish ending. I'm sure each reader has their own thoughts on what is "*Fairy Tail*-ish," but when drawing the ending, I prioritized what I felt was *Fairy Tail*-ish. It's the end, so it's okay, right? I really love happy endings. I know that there are characters who often get caught in miserable situations, and there are a lot of characters who look like they're heading toward sad endings, but still I love happy endings. So barring any unforeseen crises, my stories are going to end happily (haha).

As for what I'm doing after this, I'd like to explain my current situation. At the time I'm writing this, it's been four months since I finished serialization, but I still can't seem to find spare time. I know some might say, "Well, since you're not drawing *Fairy Tail*, what can you be doing?!" and I can only answer that I've been working. I can't announce it yet, but I've been drawing a lot. I've also been doing preparatory work for the new series such as watching movies, playing games, and reading books. Although doing those things are my hobbies, the part that makes this not my hobby is that I'm not limiting myself to works that I know I will like. And I am getting ideas and new sketches from this endeavor.

Aside from that, I've taken foreign business trips and had meetings regarding the anime, games, and goods, so much so that I feel busier than when I was drawing the series. And because of that, it looks like I will have to put off my long-held plan of taking it easy for a while right after I finished drawing the series.

So, with my internal drive to hurry up and get back to drawing manga colliding with my impulse to take it easy for a while (including staying healthy), I haven't figured things out myself yet. But I have to say that everyday has turned out pretty fun.

And so, with the support of all you readers, we come to the denouement of *Fairy Tail*. I want to ask, what did you think? I imagine your opinions are wide and varied. Maybe you've talked it over with your family or friends, and that's cool. So is talking it over on internet message boards, or just coming up with your own *Fairy Tail* ideas that you alone enjoy. That's good, too.

You can send me letters or try to send me your thoughts directly on Twitter. All of your opinions and impressions will come to resonate with the new work I'm coming up with.

I truly want to thank you for supporting me for such a long time! I want to assure you that the next series will be even more interesting than this one, so please look forward to it! So for a short while, see you later!

Afterword

With this volume, *Fairy Tail* comes to a close. I want to thank you all for supporting it this whole long time.

The first thing I want to do is deeply apologize on behalf of myself and the *Fairy Tail* editorial team for giving away portions of the plot in the Afterword section of the last volume (in the first printing of the Japanese-language edition only). I'm sure it was a great shock to many fans who were waiting patiently to read the story for themselves, and I'm very sorry.

Now, this story has gone on a very long time. At first, I had planned for it to only last around ten volumes, but between the fan's reactions and my own desire to draw more of it, 11 years and 63 volumes passed before I knew it. I think the only way it could have gone on so long was thanks to all you fans.

To tell the truth, there were periods when I thought I could draw *Fairy Tail* for the rest of my life, but at some point I thought, "Can't you come up with something even more interesting?" and that was the trigger that led to *Fairy Tail*'s conclusion. I hadn't thought up even one character for this new world, nor had I written even a word of it. It was the challenge of starting from zero that brought out the great feelings of anticipation that still haven't settled down yet.

It was about two years ago, at the beginning of the Alvarez arc, that I had a discussion with the staff and editor-in-chief and let them know that this would be the final story arc of the series. They were sad, but they came around when it became apparent that I was passionate about doing something new.

Well, it's true that after drawing the series for so long, I would feel a little sad at its end, too, but even after the magazine serialization finished, what with one thing and another, I found myself still drawing Natsu and Lucy quite a lot. And because they're still working on the final season of the anime, it still doesn't feel like *Fairy Tail* is "over."

Come to think of it, there are many people asking me to write a sequel series to *Fairy Tail*, but as of now, there are absolutely no plans for it at all. It's possible that I might consider it after a number of years have passed, but right after the series has finally come to an end is no time to start thinking about continuations.

Although I won't be drawing more *Fairy Tail* myself, it's certainly possible for a different artist to draw it. If that does happen, I'll be doing everything I can to help out with it, so if such a book comes about, I'd like you to consider picking it up.

Thank you so much for
being enthusiastic readers
all the way to the end!

FAIRY TAIL 63

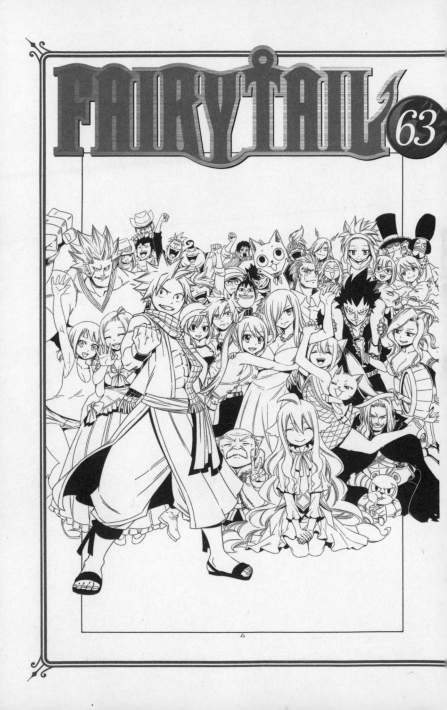

FROM HIRO MASHIMA

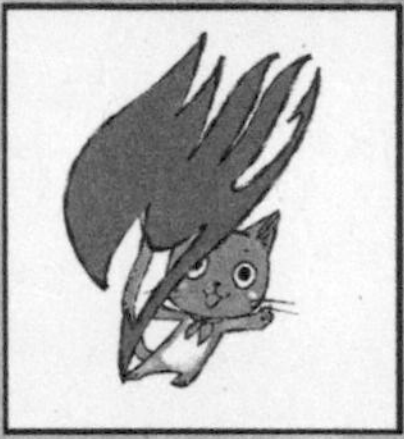

"It's over!" "The drawing's all done!" — These feelings of accomplishment haven't quite hit me yet. This volume represents the end of the original *Fairy Tail* story, but from now on the *Fairy Tail* world will continue with other things like anime, games, goods, events, and maybe even new spinoff manga...? Natsu and Lucy will still be in our hearts. With that in mind, I wonder how the fairies' long journey will ultimately conclude? I hope you'll look forward to it!

Original Jacket Design: Hisao Ogawa

FAIRY TAIL
フェアリーテイル

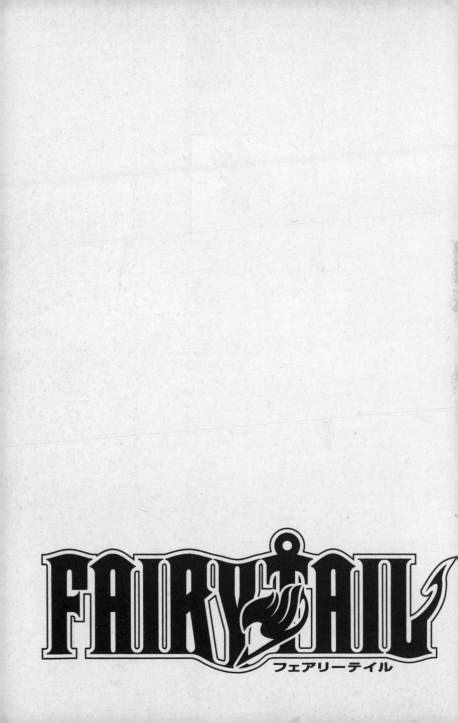

FAIRY TAIL S

r the members of Fairy
l, a guild member's work
never done. While they
y not always be away on
ssions, that doesn't mean
r magic-wielding heroes
n rest easy at home. What
ppens when a copycat
ef begins to soil the good
me of Fairy Tail, or when
eemingly unstoppable
us threatens the citizens
Magnolia? And when a
t after the Grand Magic
mes goes sour, can Natsu,
cy, Gray, and Erza turn the
bles in their favor? Come
e what a "day in the life"
he strongest guild in Fiore
ike in nine brand new
ort stories!

KC
KODANSHA
COMICS

A collection of *Fairy Tail* short stories drawn by original creator Hiro Mashima!

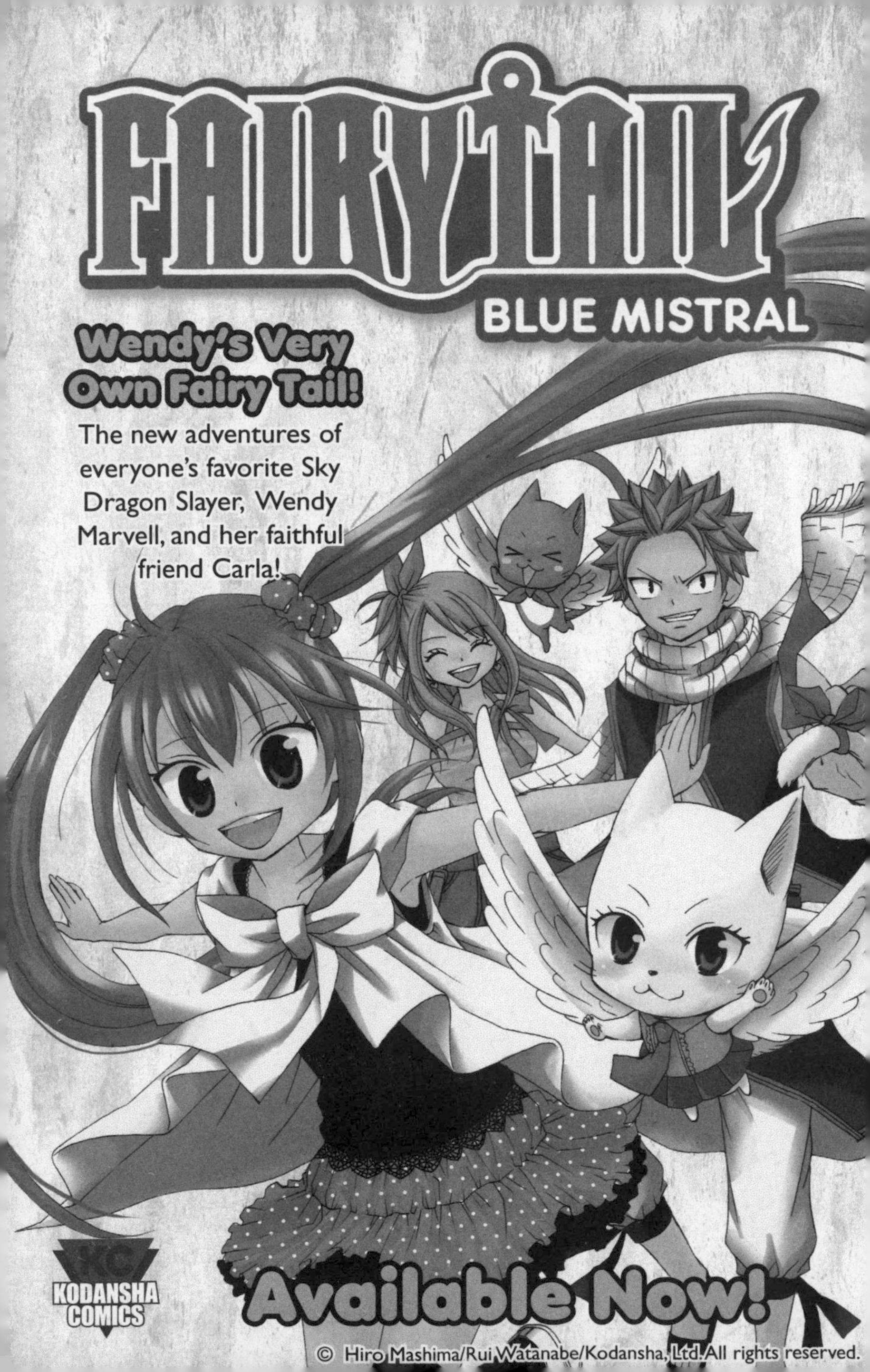
FAIRY TAIL
BLUE MISTRAL
Wendy's Very Own Fairy Tail!
The new adventures of everyone's favorite Sky Dragon Slayer, Wendy Marvell, and her faithful friend Carla!
KODANSHA COMICS
Available Now!
© Hiro Mashima/Rui Watanabe/Kodansha, Ltd. All rights reserved.

"A fun adventure that fantasy readers will relate to and enjoy." –
Adventures in Poor Taste

Mikami's middle age hasn't gone as he planned: He never found a girlfriend, he got stuck in a dead-end job, and he was abruptly stabbed to death in the street at 37. So when he wakes up in a new world straight out of a fantasy RPG, he's disappointed, but not exactly surprised to find that he's facing down a dragon, not as a knight or a wizard, but as a blind slime monster. But there are chances for even a slime to become a hero...

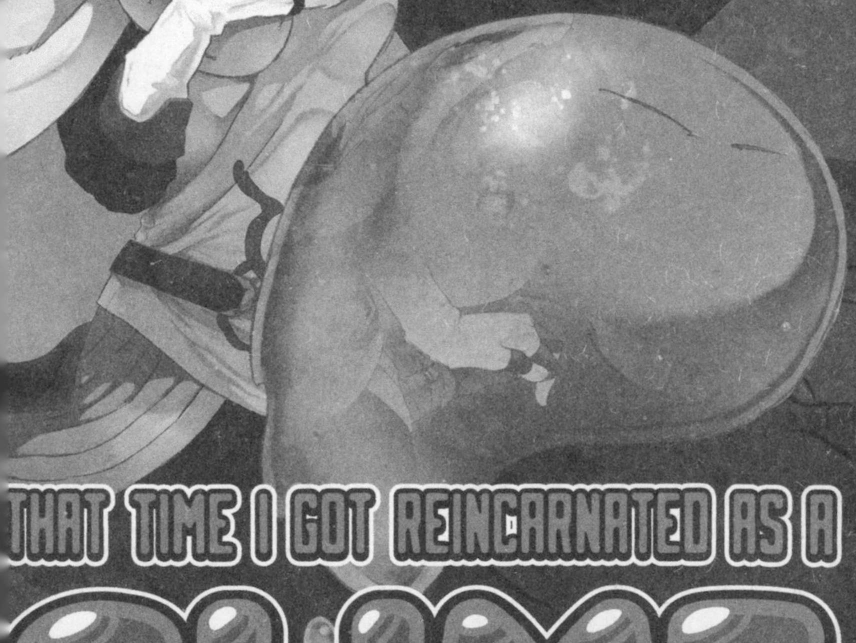

THAT TIME I GOT REINCARNATED AS A SLIME

A Kodansha Comics Trade Paperback Original.

Published in the United States by Kodansha Comics, an imprint of Kodansha USA Publishing, LLC, New York.

Publication rights for this English edition arranged through Kodansha Ltd., Tokyo.

First published in Japan in 2017 by Kodansha Ltd., Tokyo
ISBN 978-1-63236-476-0

Printed in the United States of America.

www.kodanshacomics.com

9 8 7 6 5 4 3 2 1

Translation: William Flanagan
Lettering: AndWorld Design
Editing: Lauren Scanlan and Haruko Hashimoto
Kodansha Comics edition cover design by Phil Balsman

TOMARE!

止まれ

[STOP!]

You're going the wrong way!

Manga is a completely different type of reading experience.

To start at the *beginning*, go to the *end*!

That's right! Authentic manga is read the traditional Japanese way—from right to left, exactly the *opposite* of how American books are read. It's easy to follow: Just go to the other end of the book and read each page—and each panel—from right side to left side, starting at the top right. Now you're experiencing manga as it was meant to be!